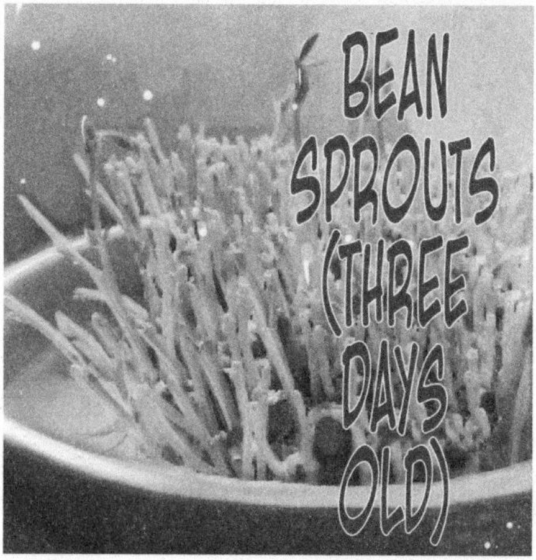
BEAN SPROUTS (THREE DAYS OLD)

I was thinking about getting a cute pet (like a finch perhaps), but when I mentioned it to my family, they all said, "You won't make a good pet owner. It'll die in your hands!" Actually, they're probably right, so I decided to raise bean sprouts for now.

—Kyousuke Motomi

Author Bio

Born on August 1, **Kyousuke Motomi** debuted in *Deluxe Betsucomi* with *Hetakuso Kyupiddo* (No Good Cupid) in 2002. She is the creator of *Dengeki Daisy*, *Beast Master* and *QQ Sweeper*, all available in North America from VIZ Media. Motomi enjoys sleeping, tea ceremonies and reading Haruki Murakami.

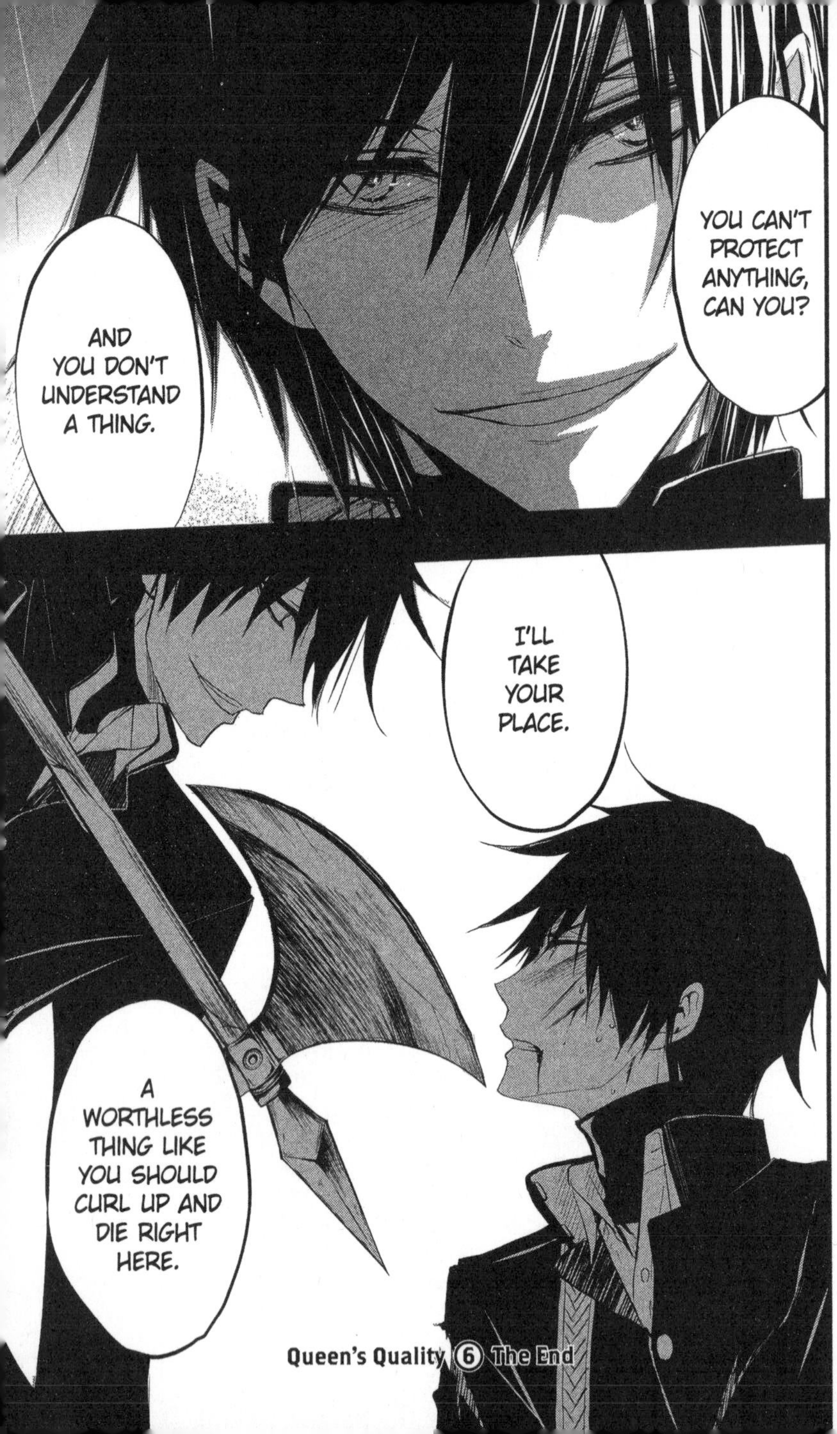
YOU CAN'T PROTECT ANYTHING, CAN YOU?
AND YOU DON'T UNDERSTAND A THING.
I'LL TAKE YOUR PLACE.
A WORTHLESS THING LIKE YOU SHOULD CURL UP AND DIE RIGHT HERE.
Queen's Quality 6 The End

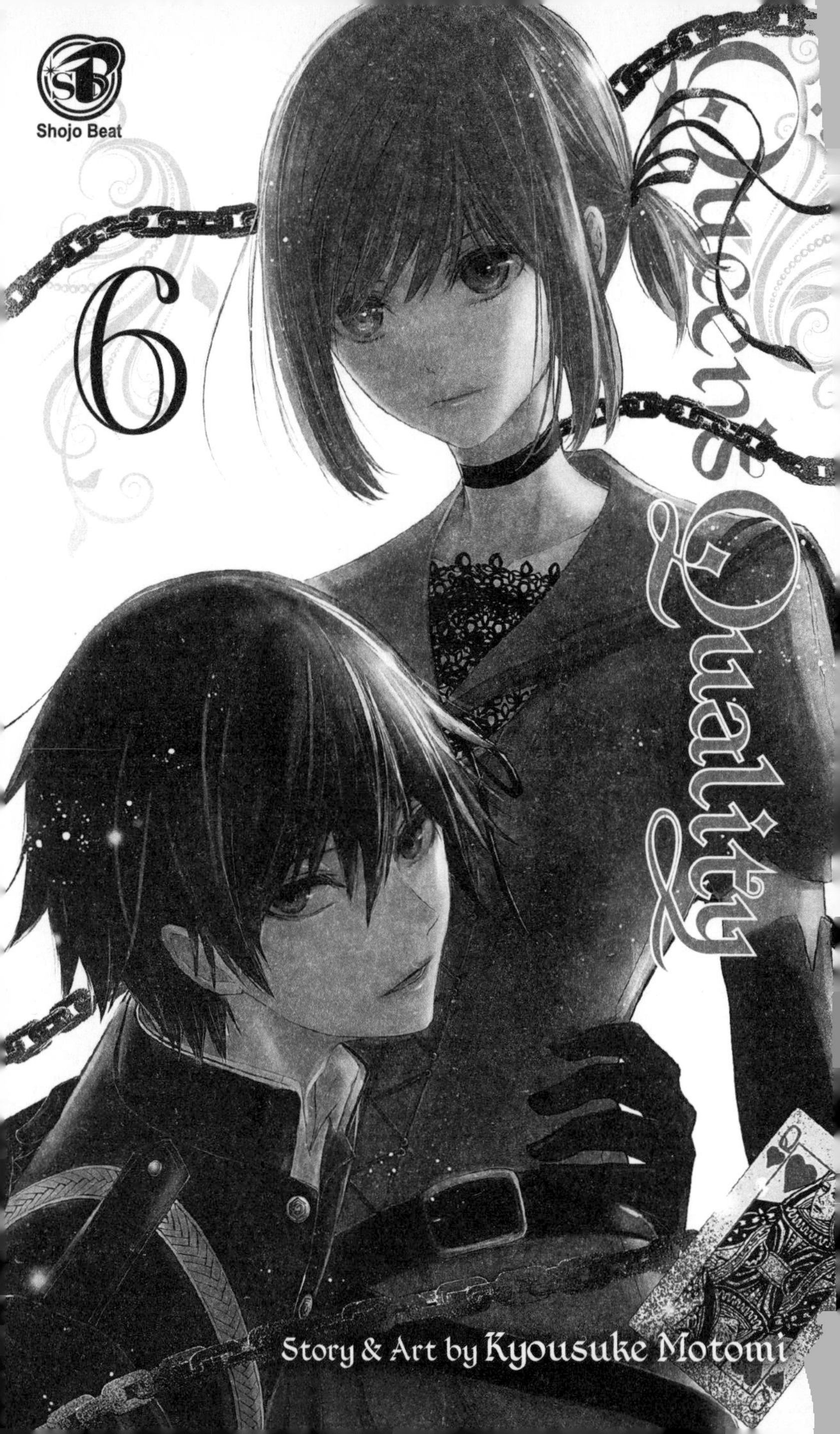
Shojo Beat
6
Queen's Quality
Story & Art by Kyousuke Motomi

Queen's Quality

CONTENTS

6

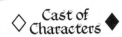

Cast of Characters

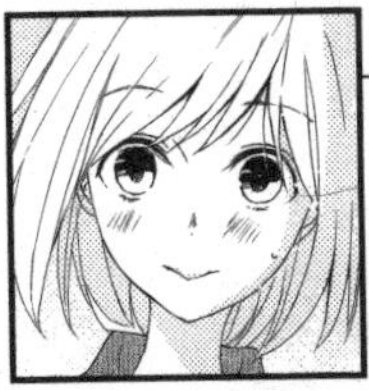

Fumi Nishioka

An apprentice Sweeper with the powers of a Queen, this second-year high school student dreams of finding her very own Prince Charming.

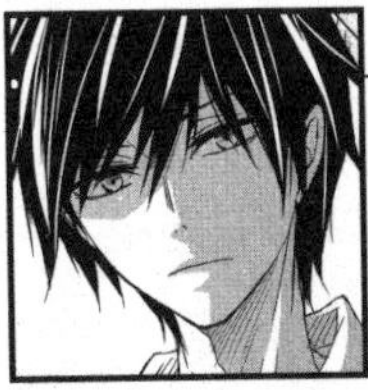

Kyutaro Horikita

A mind Sweeper who cleanses people's minds of dangerous impurities. He's incredibly awkward with people, but he has feelings for Fumi.

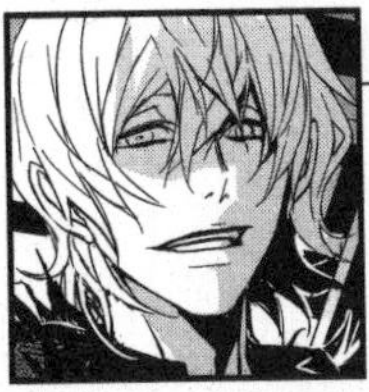

Ataru Shikata

A former bug handler who uses bugs to manipulate people. Saved by Fumi and Kyutaro, he has joined the Genbu Clan.

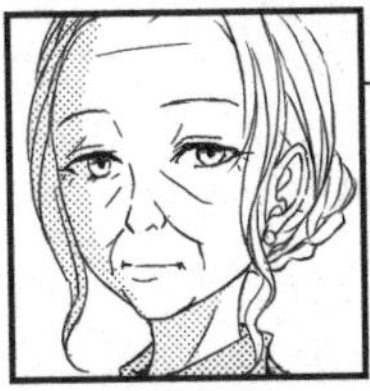

Miyako Horikita

The prior head of the Genbu Gate Sweepers. She can be both strict and kind, and she watches over and advises Fumi.

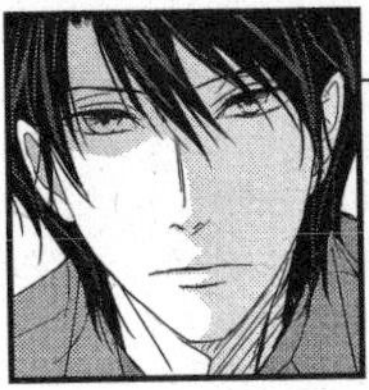

Koichi Kitagawa

The chairman of the school Fumi and Kyutaro attend. He's a Sweeper as well as being Kyutaro's brother-in-law.

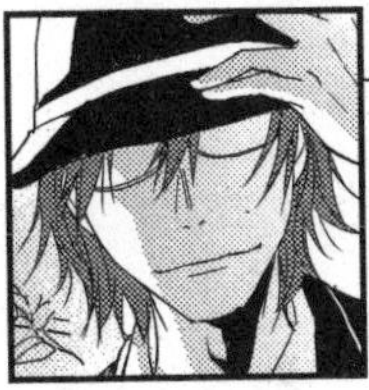

Takaya Kitahara

A psychiatrist who's related to the Genbu Gate Sweepers. He's an expert with suggestive therapy, and he counsels Fumi.

Story Thus Far

The Horikitas are a family of Sweepers—people who cleanse impurities from human hearts. After seeing Fumi's potential, they take her on as an assistant and trainee. However, Fumi has the untapped, immense power of a Queen, and she's awakened both the White Queen and the Black Queen inside of her.

While in bug handler Ataru's mind vault, Fumi realizes the truth about the Black Queen. She awakens the Dark-Gray Queen within her and saves Ataru with Kyutaro's assistance. Meanwhile, the Black Queen quietly fades away...

MONTHLY BETSUCOMI SALE DATE NOTICE ON TWITTER

CHAPTER 26

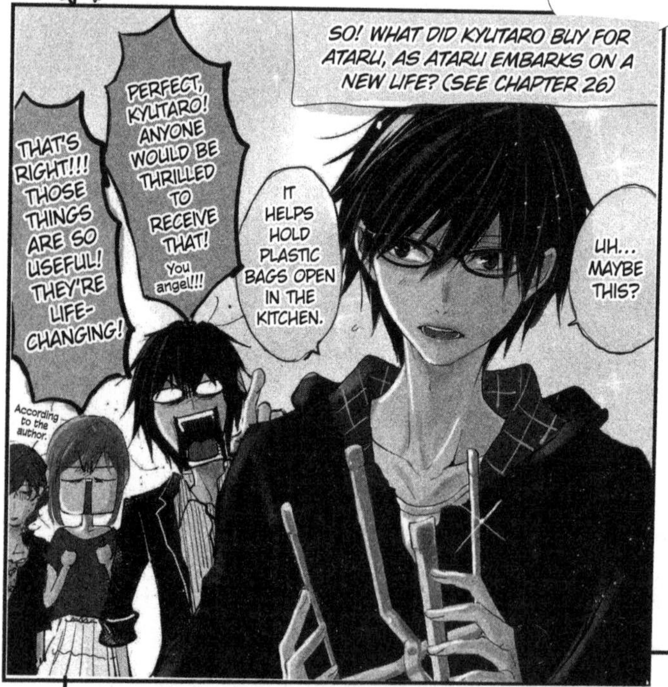
SO! WHAT DID KYUTARO BUY FOR ATARU, AS ATARU EMBARKS ON A NEW LIFE? (SEE CHAPTER 26)
UH... MAYBE THIS?
IT HELPS HOLD PLASTIC BAGS OPEN IN THE KITCHEN.
PERFECT, KYUTARO! ANYONE WOULD BE THRILLED TO RECEIVE THAT!
You angel!!!
THAT'S RIGHT!!! THOSE THINGS ARE SO USEFUL! THEY'RE LIFE-CHANGING!
According to the author.

LET'S SEE... WHAT'S UP IN *QUEEN'S QUALITY* THIS MONTH?
(1) KYUTARO GETS ENSNARED AGAIN.
(2) IT'S MIDSUMMER, SO REALLY, NISHIOKA SHOULD'VE BEEN ON GUARD FROM THE MOMENT SHE SAW THAT OVERCOAT AND THOSE FINGERLESS GLOVES.
(3) WHAT HAPPENED TO THE TENMUSU*?
WE'RE EMBARKING ON A NEW ACT OF THE STORY, FEATURING THE INTRODUCTION OF A NEW CHARACTER! MY EDITOR TOLD ME TO MAKE HIM HANDSOME, BUT I DIDN'T!

**shrimp tempura rice ball*

I POST TWEETS LIKE THIS EVERY MONTH. YOU'LL FIND ME MUTTERING ABOUT OTHER SILLY STUFF TOO.

@motomikyosuke

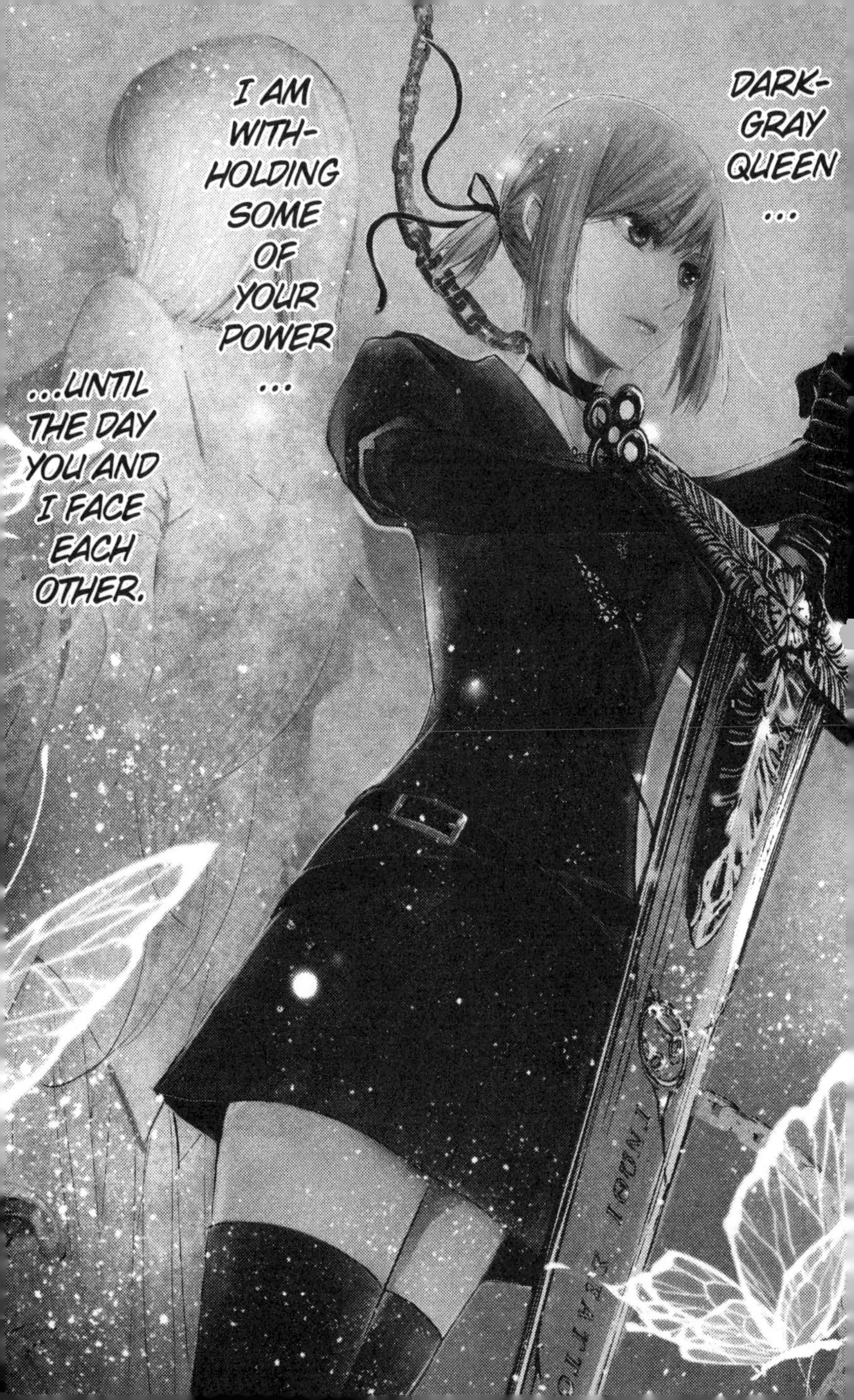
DARK-GRAY QUEEN...
I AM WITH-HOLDING SOME OF YOUR POWER...
...UNTIL THE DAY YOU AND I FACE EACH OTHER.

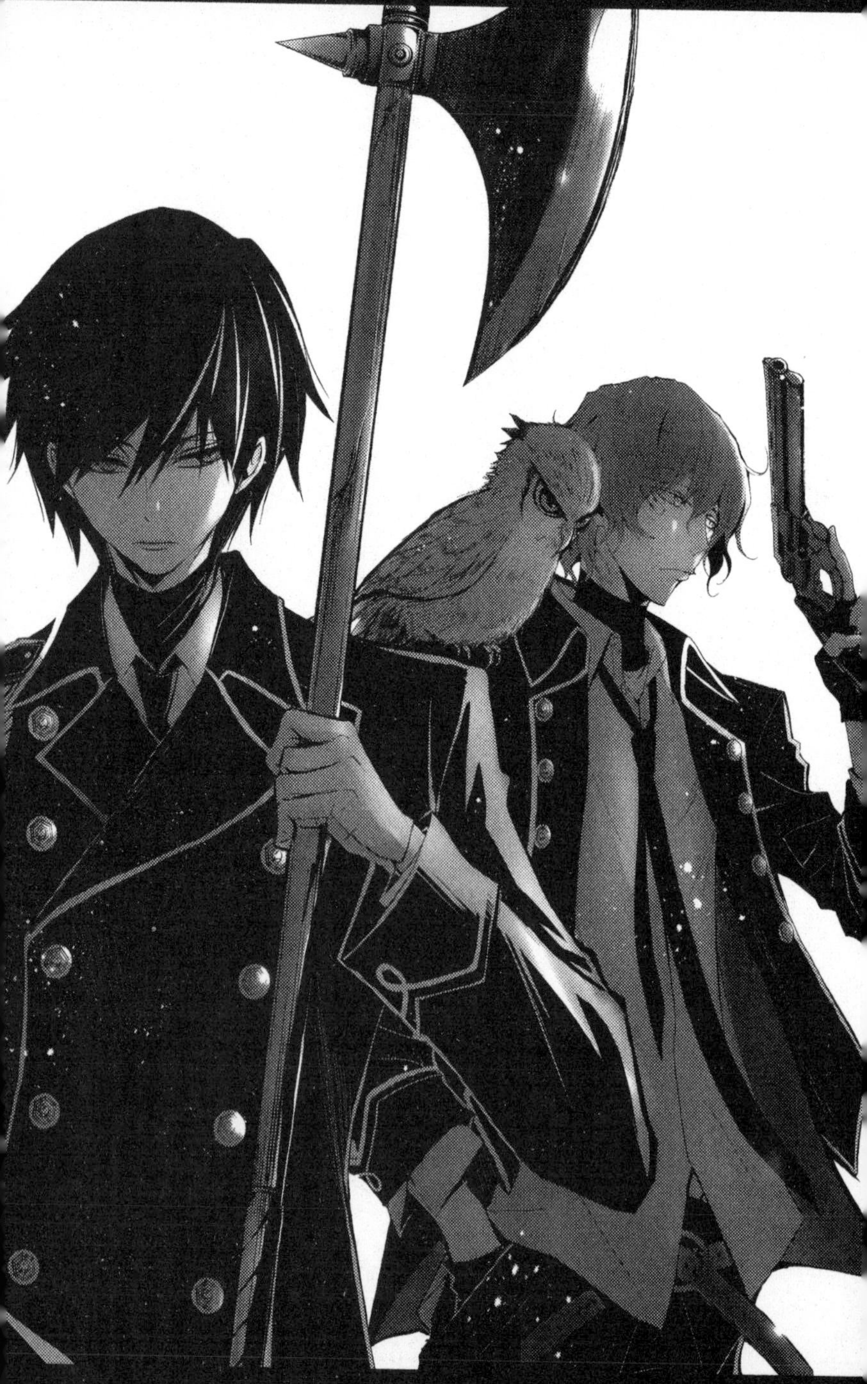

Chapter 26

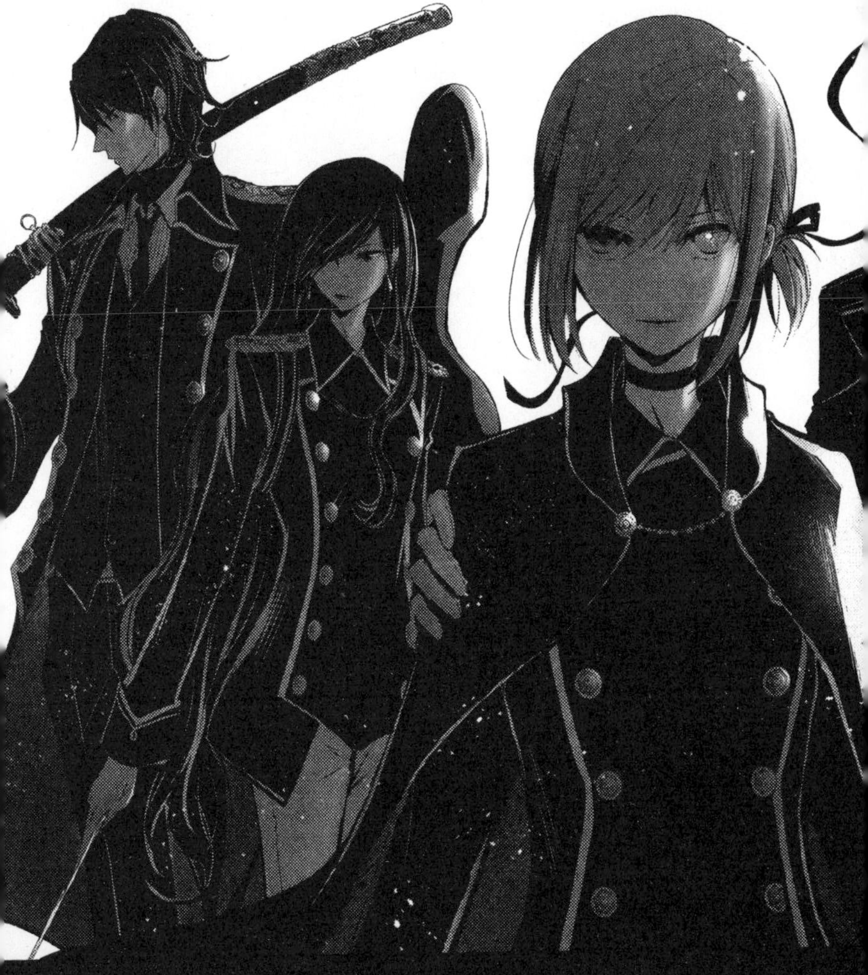

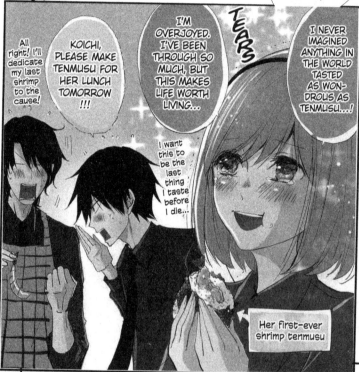

CHAPTER 27

MONTHLY BETSUCOMI SALE DATE NOTICE ON TWITTER

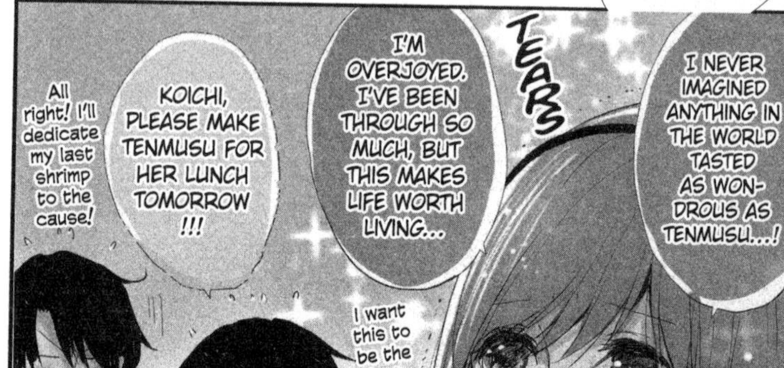

I NEVER IMAGINED ANYTHING IN THE WORLD TASTED AS WON-DROUS AS TENMUSU...!
TEARS
I'M OVERJOYED. I'VE BEEN THROUGH SO MUCH, BUT THIS MAKES LIFE WORTH LIVING...
KOICHI, PLEASE MAKE TENMUSU FOR HER LUNCH TOMORROW!!!
All right! I'll dedicate my last shrimp to the cause!
I want this to be the last thing I taste before I die...
Her first-ever shrimp tenmusu

LET'S SEE... WHAT'S UP IN QUEEN'S QUALITY THIS MONTH?
(1) HOW DOES AKIYAMA (WHO'S MASKED) DRINK HIS TEA?
(2) BUT HE LEAVES TWO OF THE FIVE.
(3) TENMUSU REALLY IS DELICIOUS, ISN'T IT? IT DESERVES A NOBEL PRIZE.
THE CAPABLE ADULTS OF THE GENBU CLAN FIND THEMSELVES IN STICKY SITUATIONS. EVEN KYUTARO IS IN DANGER IN CHAPTER 27!

REALISTICALLY, IF THERE WERE SEVERAL PEOPLE AND JUST A SINGLE TENMUSU, IT'D BE A MIRACLE IF THEY AVOIDED BLOODSHED. YOU CAN TELL HOW MUCH KYUTARO LOVES HER!

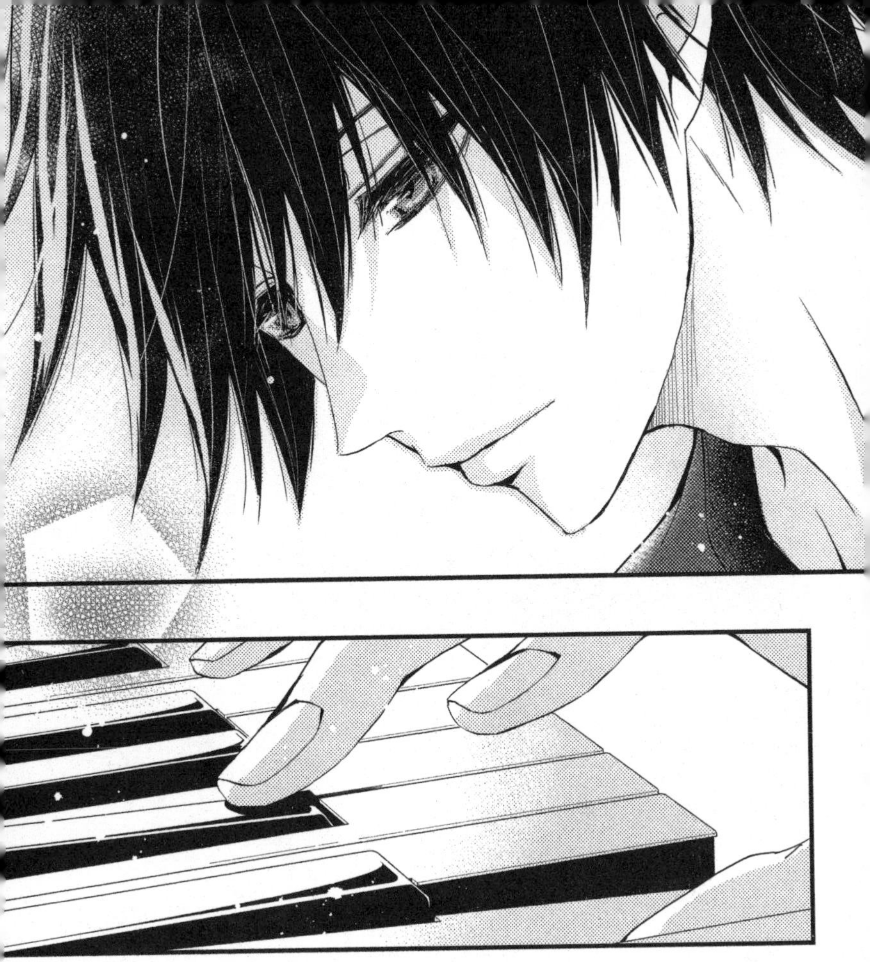

Hello, everyone! Kyousuke Motomi here! Thanks to you, we've reached volume 6 of *Queen's Quality*. This feels like the beginning of a new act. I hope you'll continue enjoying the story.

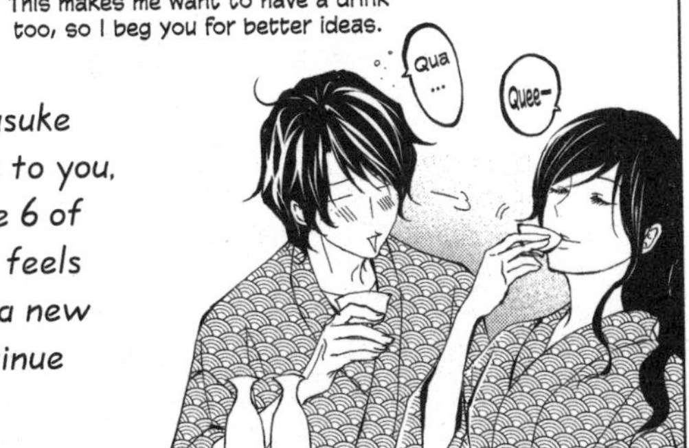
This makes me want to have a drink too, so I beg you for better ideas.
Qua ...
Quee-

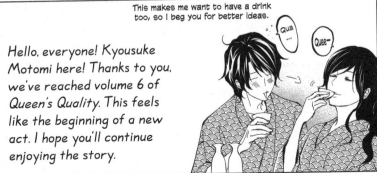

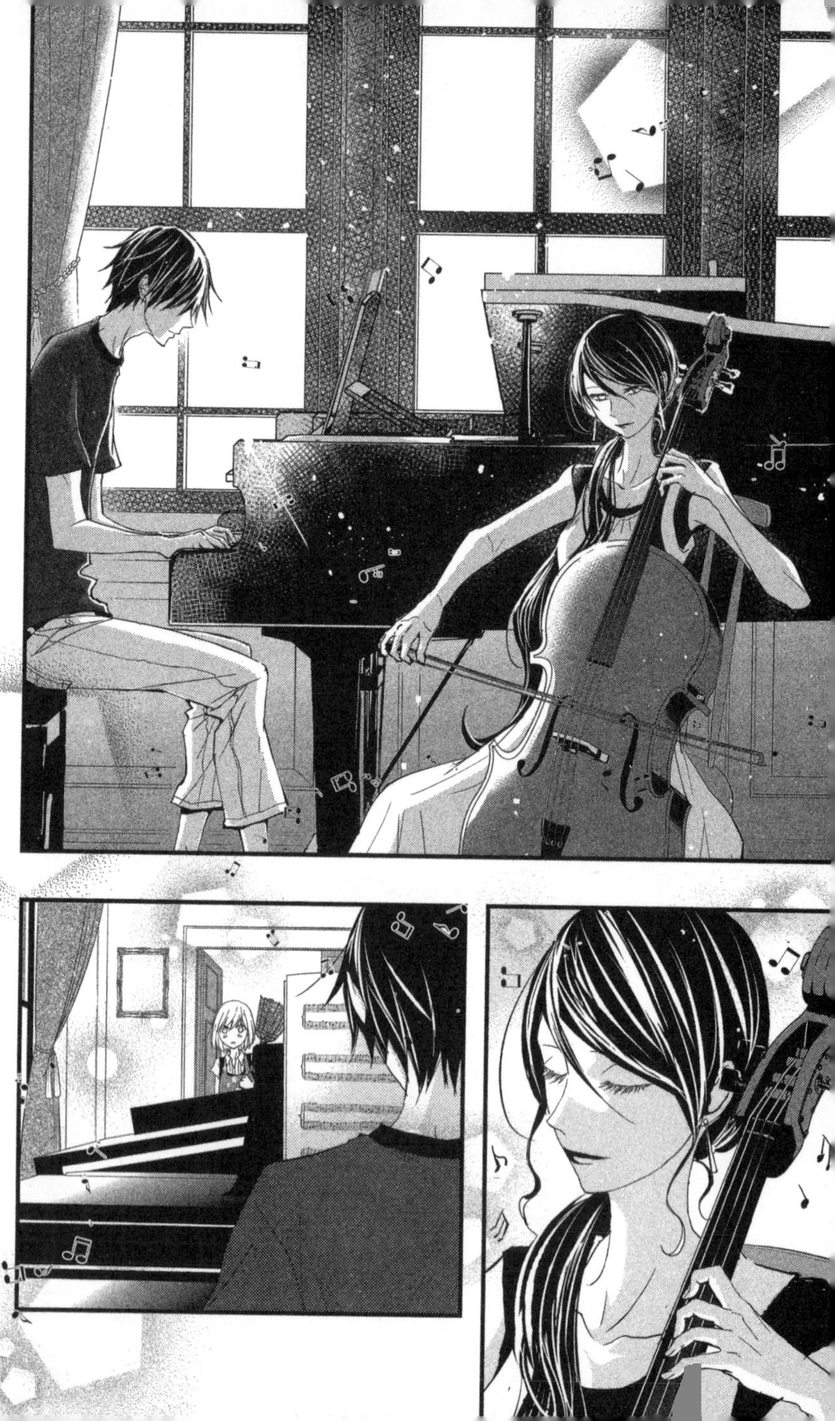

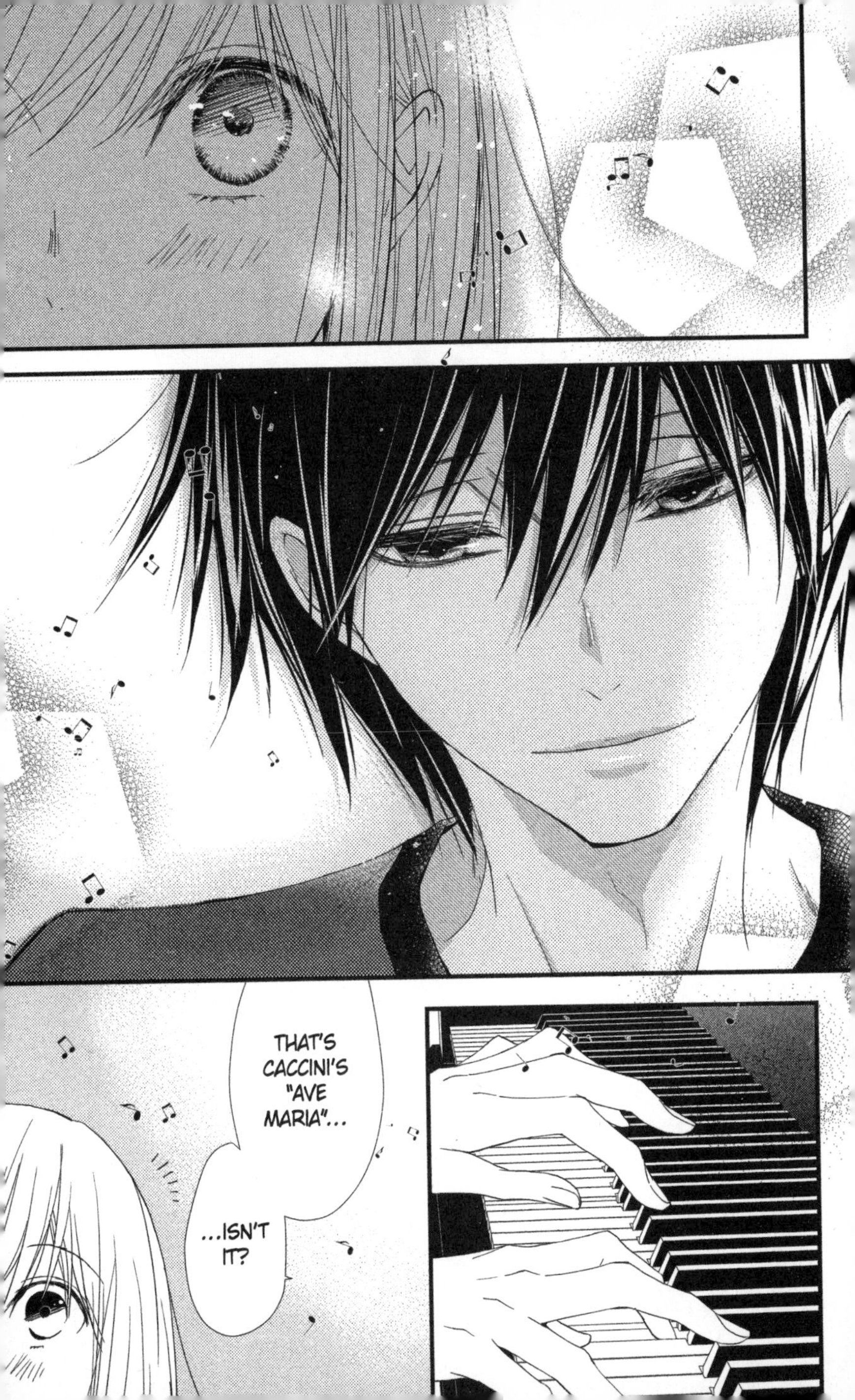
THAT'S CACCINI'S "AVE MARIA"...
...ISN'T IT?

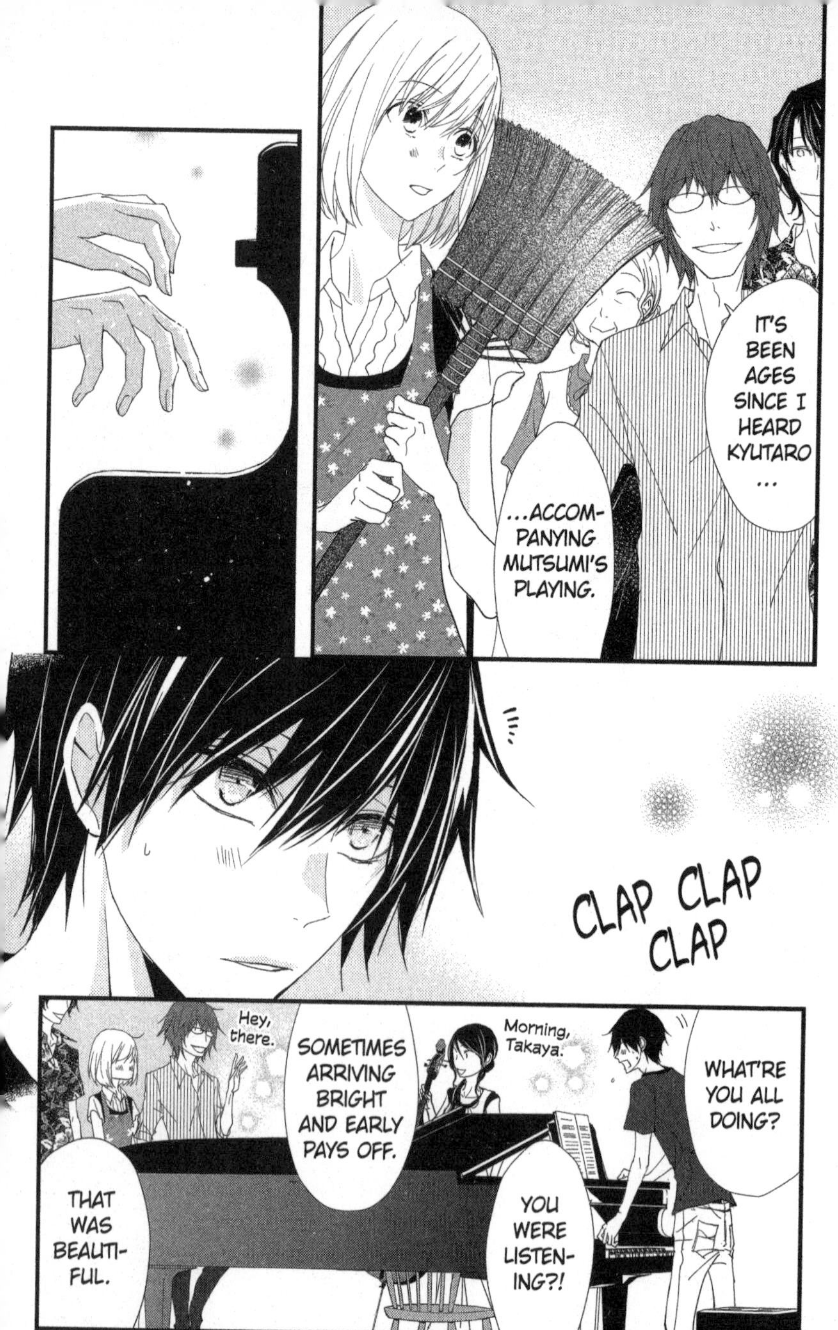
IT'S BEEN AGES SINCE I HEARD KYUTARO...
...ACCOM-PANYING MUTSUMI'S PLAYING.
CLAP CLAP CLAP
WHAT'RE YOU ALL DOING?
Morning, Takaya.
YOU WERE LISTEN-ING?!
SOMETIMES ARRIVING BRIGHT AND EARLY PAYS OFF.
Hey, there.
THAT WAS BEAUTI-FUL.

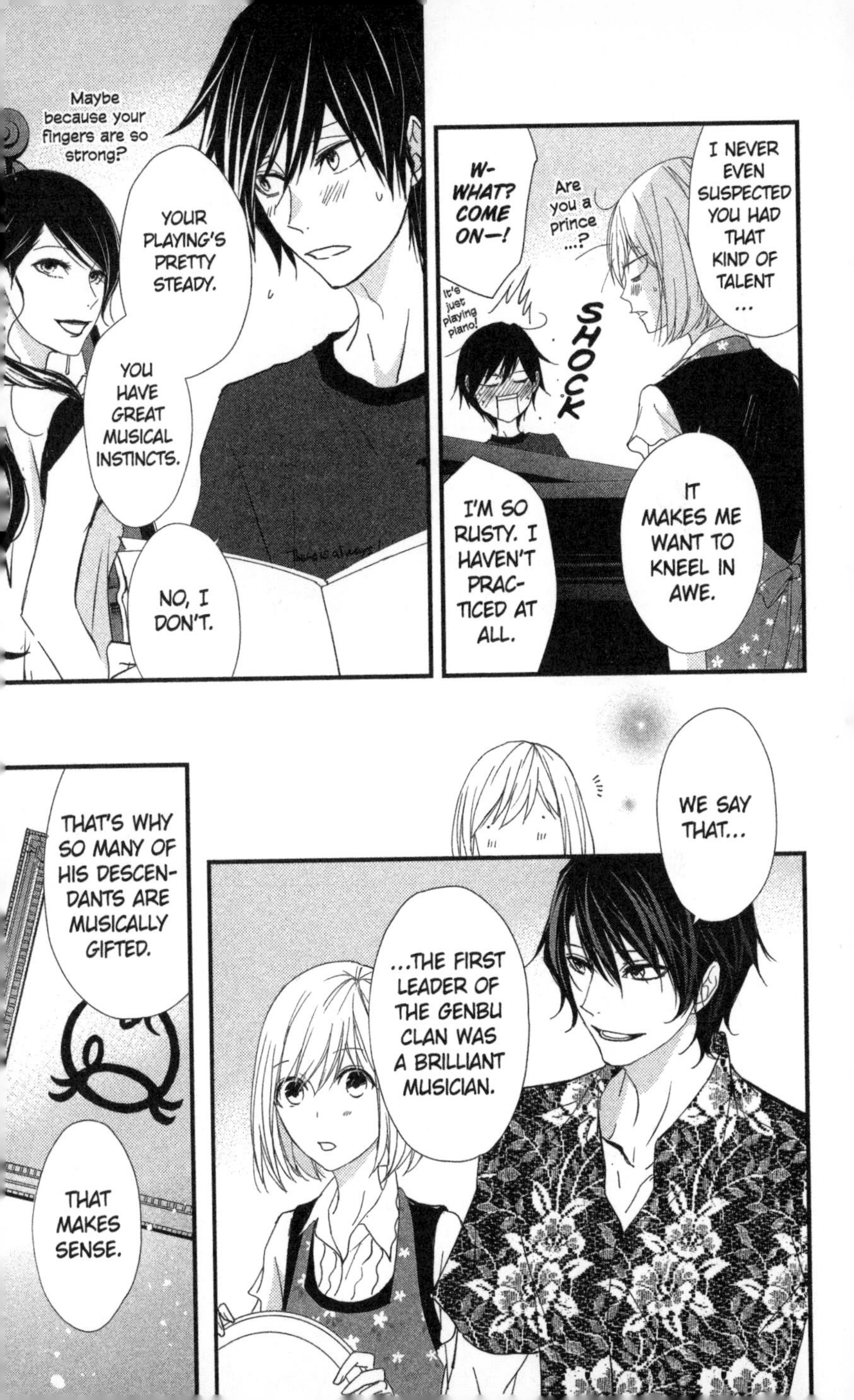
I NEVER EVEN SUSPECTED YOU HAD THAT KIND OF TALENT...
Are you a prince ...?
W-WHAT? COME ON—!
SHOCK
It's just playing piano!
IT MAKES ME WANT TO KNEEL IN AWE.
I'M SO RUSTY. I HAVEN'T PRAC-TICED AT ALL.
YOUR PLAYING'S PRETTY STEADY.
YOU HAVE GREAT MUSICAL INSTINCTS.
NO, I DON'T.
Maybe because your fingers are so strong?
WE SAY THAT...
...THE FIRST LEADER OF THE GENBU CLAN WAS A BRILLIANT MUSICIAN.
THAT'S WHY SO MANY OF HIS DESCEN-DANTS ARE MUSICALLY GIFTED.
THAT MAKES SENSE.

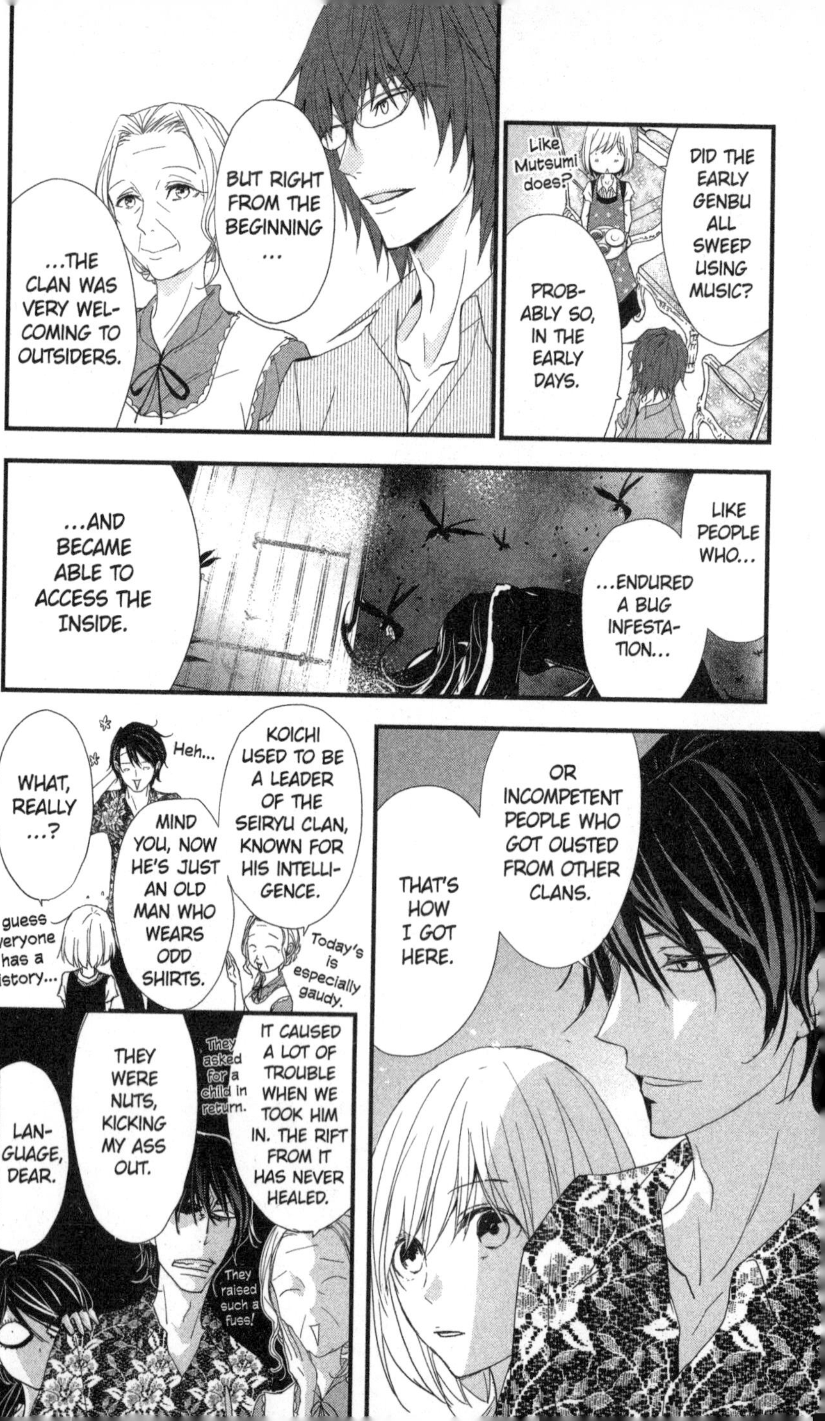
DID THE EARLY GENBU ALL SWEEP USING MUSIC?
Like Mutsumi does?
PROBABLY SO, IN THE EARLY DAYS.
BUT RIGHT FROM THE BEGINNING...
...THE CLAN WAS VERY WELCOMING TO OUTSIDERS.
LIKE PEOPLE WHO...
...ENDURED A BUG INFESTATION...
...AND BECAME ABLE TO ACCESS THE INSIDE.
OR INCOMPETENT PEOPLE WHO GOT OUSTED FROM OTHER CLANS.
THAT'S HOW I GOT HERE.
KOICHI USED TO BE A LEADER OF THE SEIRYU CLAN, KNOWN FOR HIS INTELLIGENCE.
Heh...
MIND YOU, NOW HE'S JUST AN OLD MAN WHO WEARS ODD SHIRTS.
Today's is especially gaudy.
WHAT, REALLY...?
I guess everyone has a history...
IT CAUSED A LOT OF TROUBLE WHEN WE TOOK HIM IN. THE RIFT FROM IT HAS NEVER HEALED.
They asked for a child in return.
THEY WERE NUTS, KICKING MY ASS OUT.
They raised such a fuss!
LANGUAGE, DEAR.

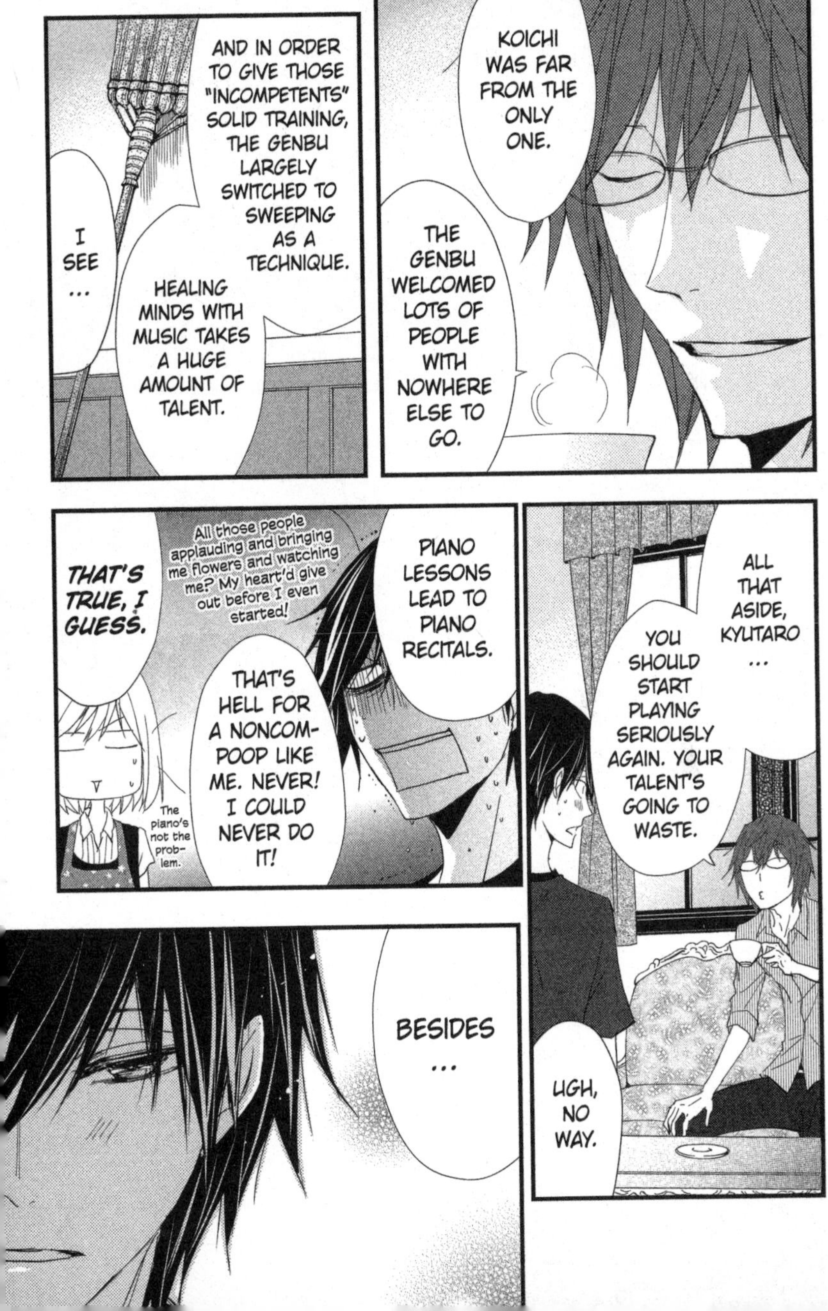
KOICHI WAS FAR FROM THE ONLY ONE.
THE GENBU WELCOMED LOTS OF PEOPLE WITH NOWHERE ELSE TO GO.
AND IN ORDER TO GIVE THOSE "INCOMPETENTS" SOLID TRAINING, THE GENBU LARGELY SWITCHED TO SWEEPING AS A TECHNIQUE.
HEALING MINDS WITH MUSIC TAKES A HUGE AMOUNT OF TALENT.
I SEE...
ALL THAT ASIDE, KYUTARO...
YOU SHOULD START PLAYING SERIOUSLY AGAIN. YOUR TALENT'S GOING TO WASTE.
UGH, NO WAY.
PIANO LESSONS LEAD TO PIANO RECITALS.
THAT'S HELL FOR A NONCOM-POOP LIKE ME. NEVER! I COULD NEVER DO IT!
All those people applauding and bringing me flowers and watching me? My heart'd give out before I even started!
THAT'S TRUE, I GUESS.
The piano's not the prob-lem.
BESIDES...

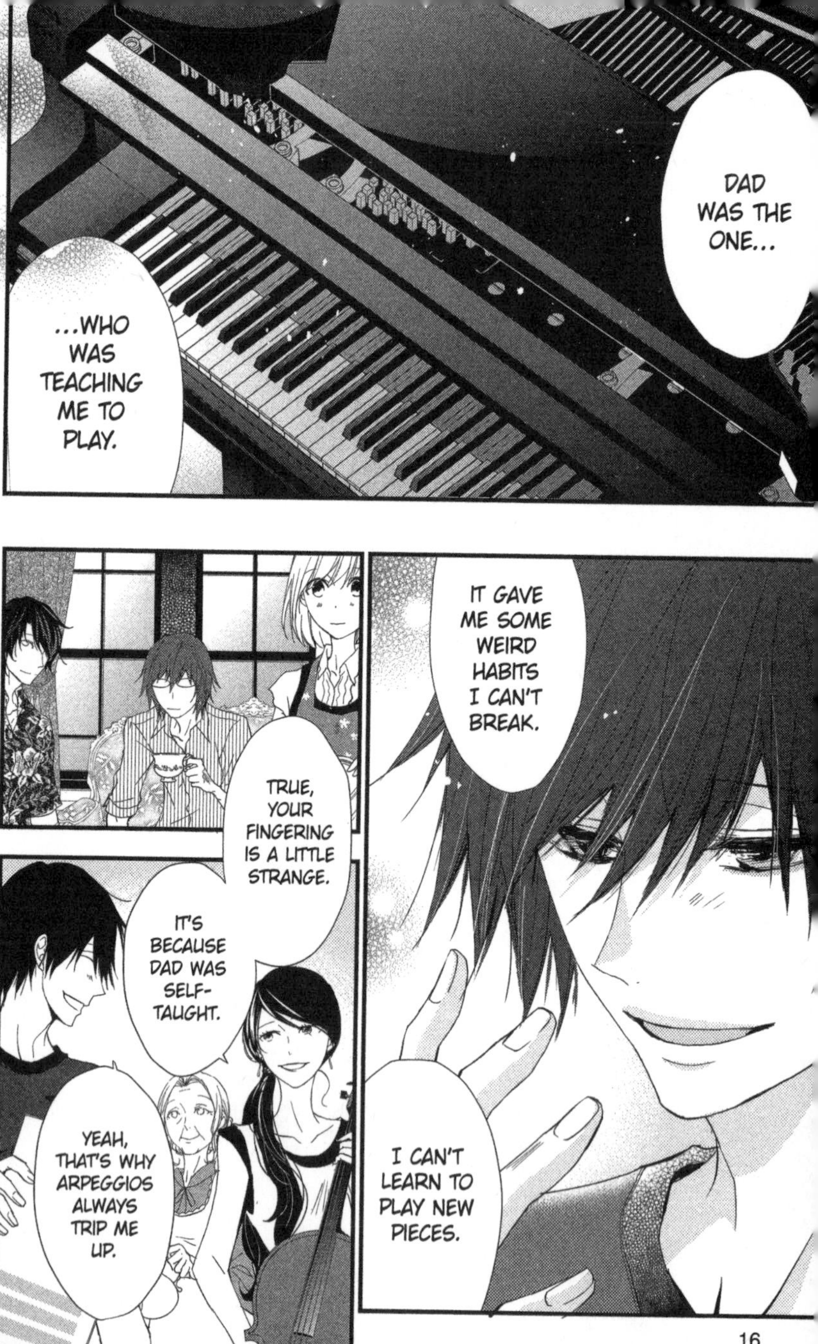
DAD WAS THE ONE...
...WHO WAS TEACHING ME TO PLAY.
IT GAVE ME SOME WEIRD HABITS I CAN'T BREAK.
I CAN'T LEARN TO PLAY NEW PIECES.
TRUE, YOUR FINGERING IS A LITTLE STRANGE.
IT'S BECAUSE DAD WAS SELF-TAUGHT.
YEAH, THAT'S WHY ARPEGGIOS ALWAYS TRIP ME UP.

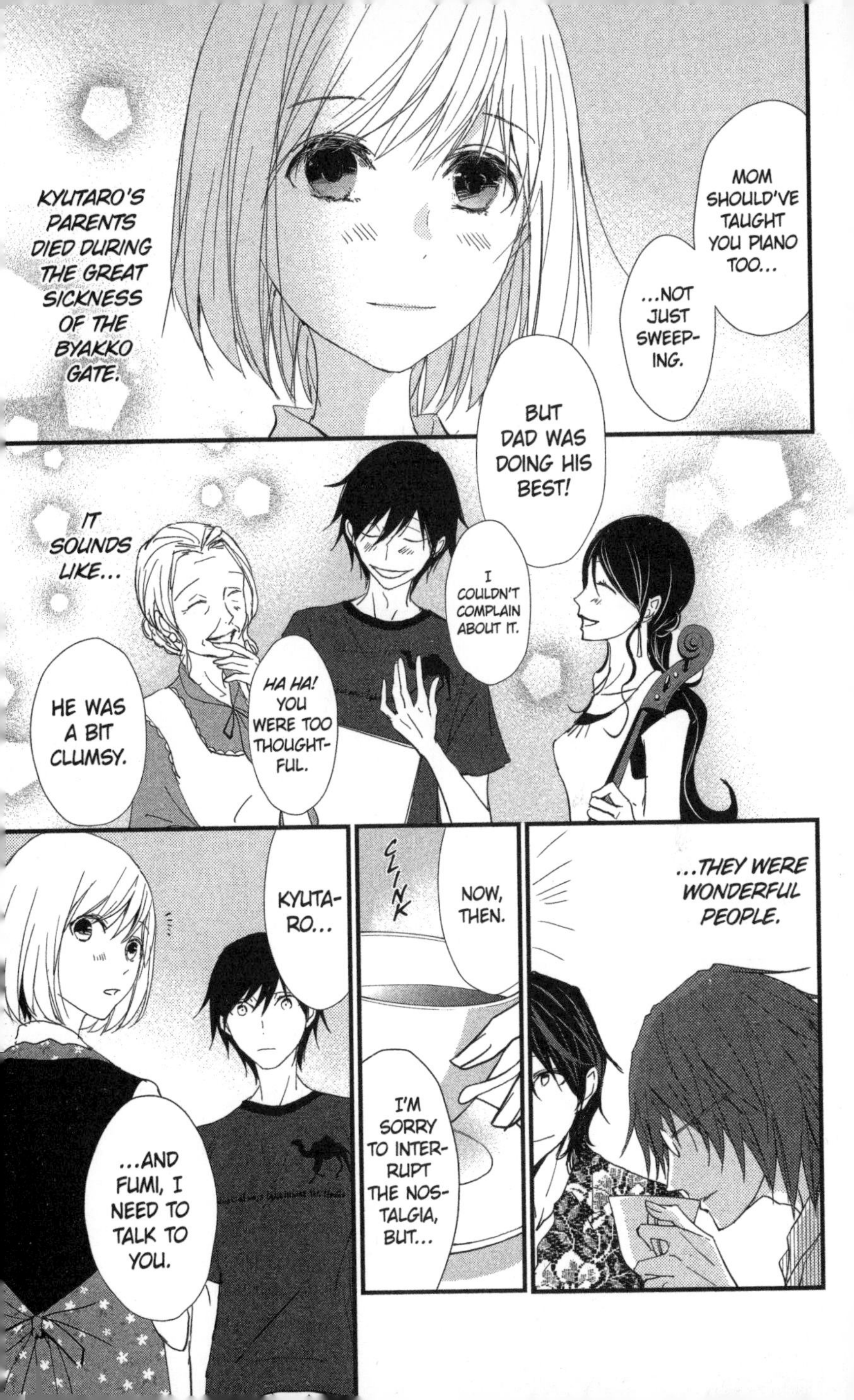
MOM SHOULD'VE TAUGHT YOU PIANO TOO...
...NOT JUST SWEEP-ING.
KYUTARO'S PARENTS DIED DURING THE GREAT SICKNESS OF THE BYAKKO GATE.
BUT DAD WAS DOING HIS BEST!
I COULDN'T COMPLAIN ABOUT IT.
IT SOUNDS LIKE...
HA HA! YOU WERE TOO THOUGHT-FUL.
HE WAS A BIT CLUMSY.
...THEY WERE WONDERFUL PEOPLE.
CLINK
NOW, THEN.
I'M SORRY TO INTER-RUPT THE NOS-TALGIA, BUT...
KYUTA-RO...
...AND FUMI, I NEED TO TALK TO YOU.

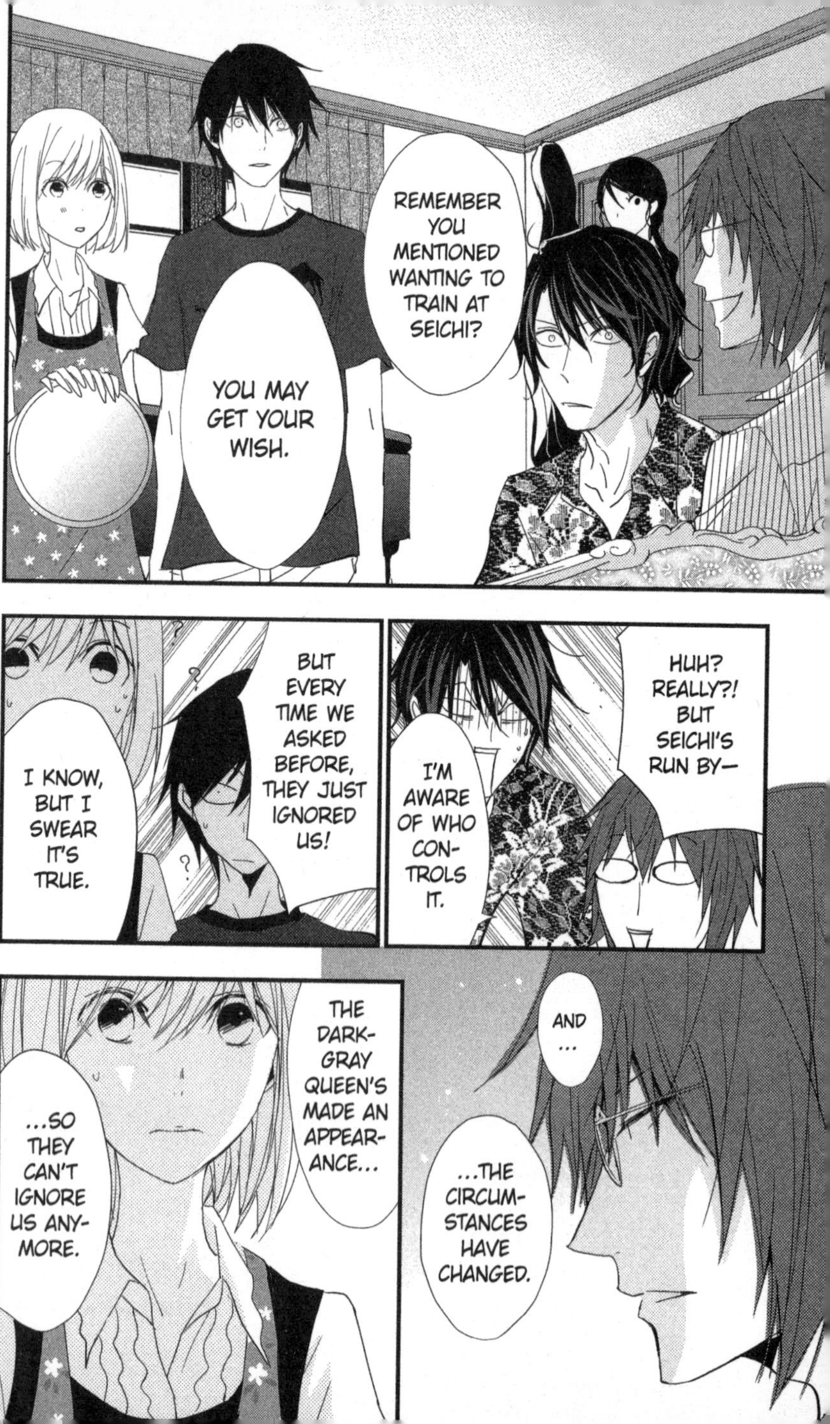
REMEMBER YOU MENTIONED WANTING TO TRAIN AT SEICHI?
YOU MAY GET YOUR WISH.
HUH? REALLY?! BUT SEICHI'S RUN BY—
I'M AWARE OF WHO CON-TROLS IT.
BUT EVERY TIME WE ASKED BEFORE, THEY JUST IGNORED US!
I KNOW, BUT I SWEAR IT'S TRUE.
AND ...
...THE CIRCUM-STANCES HAVE CHANGED.
THE DARK-GRAY QUEEN'S MADE AN APPEAR-ANCE...
...SO THEY CAN'T IGNORE US ANY-MORE.

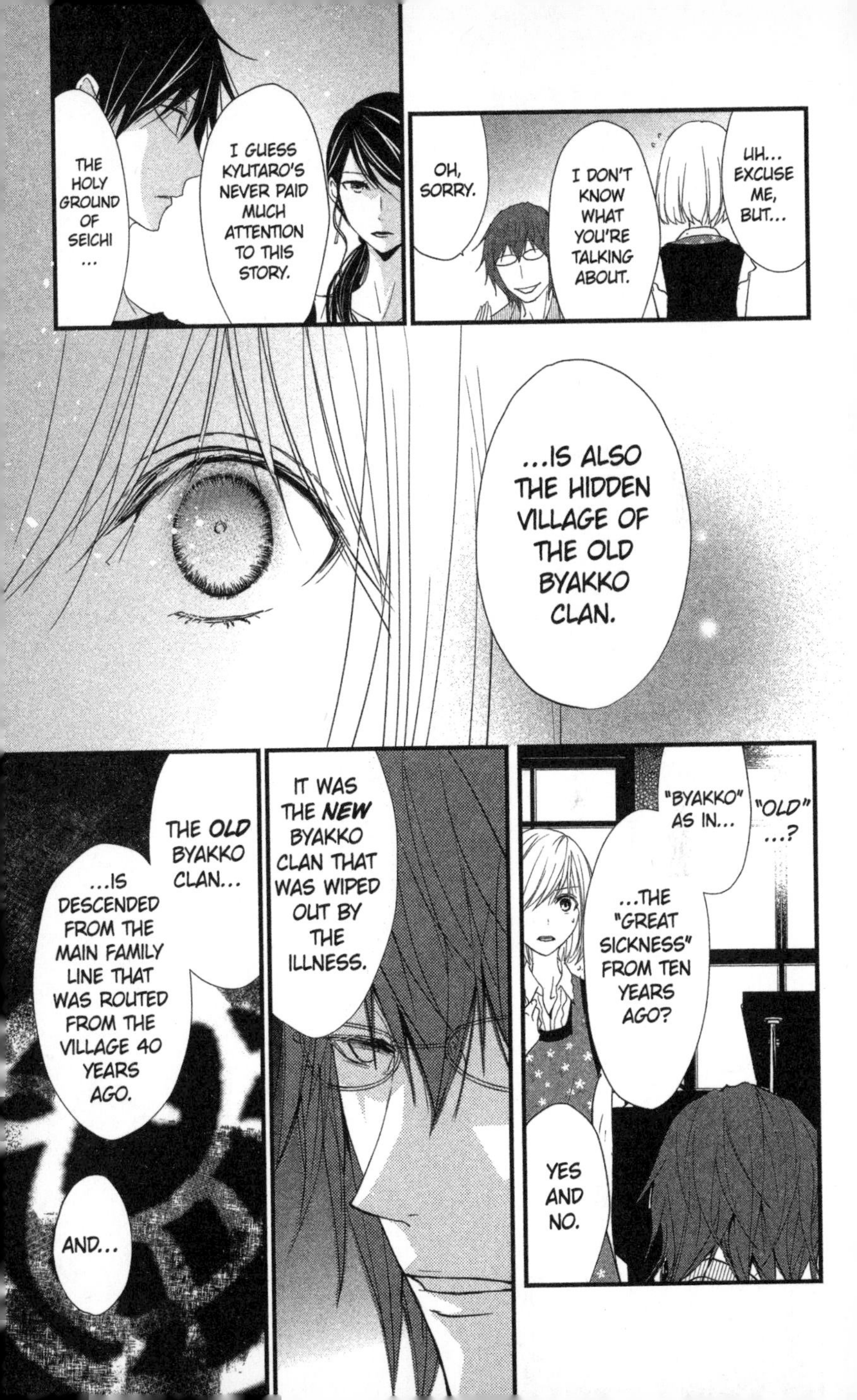
UH... EXCUSE ME, BUT...
I DON'T KNOW WHAT YOU'RE TALKING ABOUT.
OH, SORRY.
I GUESS KYUTARO'S NEVER PAID MUCH ATTENTION TO THIS STORY.
THE HOLY GROUND OF SEICHI...
...IS ALSO THE HIDDEN VILLAGE OF THE OLD BYAKKO CLAN.
"OLD"...?
"BYAKKO" AS IN...
...THE "GREAT SICKNESS" FROM TEN YEARS AGO?
YES AND NO.
IT WAS THE NEW BYAKKO CLAN THAT WAS WIPED OUT BY THE ILLNESS.
THE OLD BYAKKO CLAN...
...IS DESCENDED FROM THE MAIN FAMILY LINE THAT WAS ROUTED FROM THE VILLAGE 40 YEARS AGO.
AND...

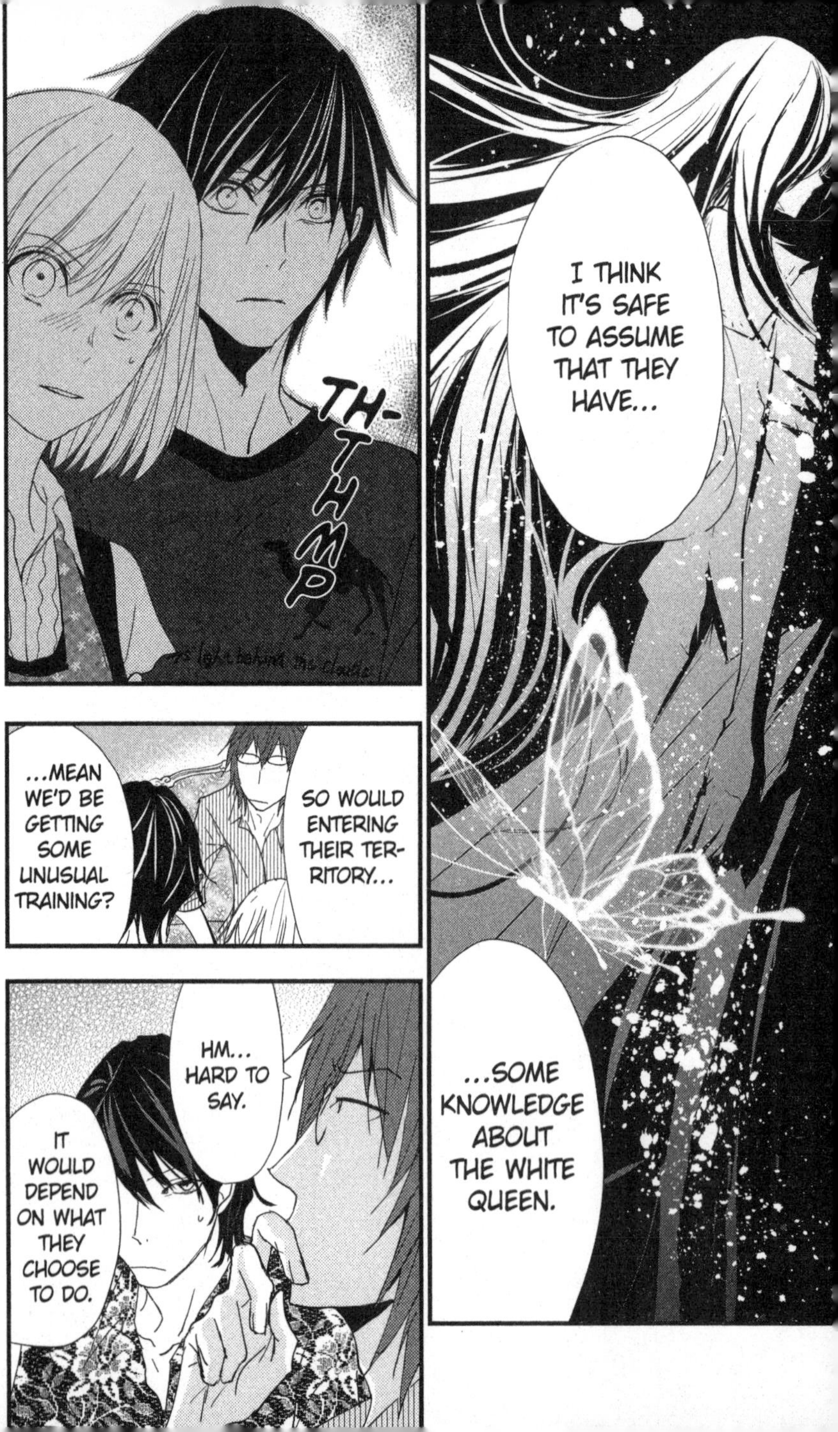
I THINK IT'S SAFE TO ASSUME THAT THEY HAVE...
...SOME KNOWLEDGE ABOUT THE WHITE QUEEN.
TH-THMP
SO WOULD ENTERING THEIR TER-RITORY...
...MEAN WE'D BE GETTING SOME UNUSUAL TRAINING?
HM... HARD TO SAY.
IT WOULD DEPEND ON WHAT THEY CHOOSE TO DO.

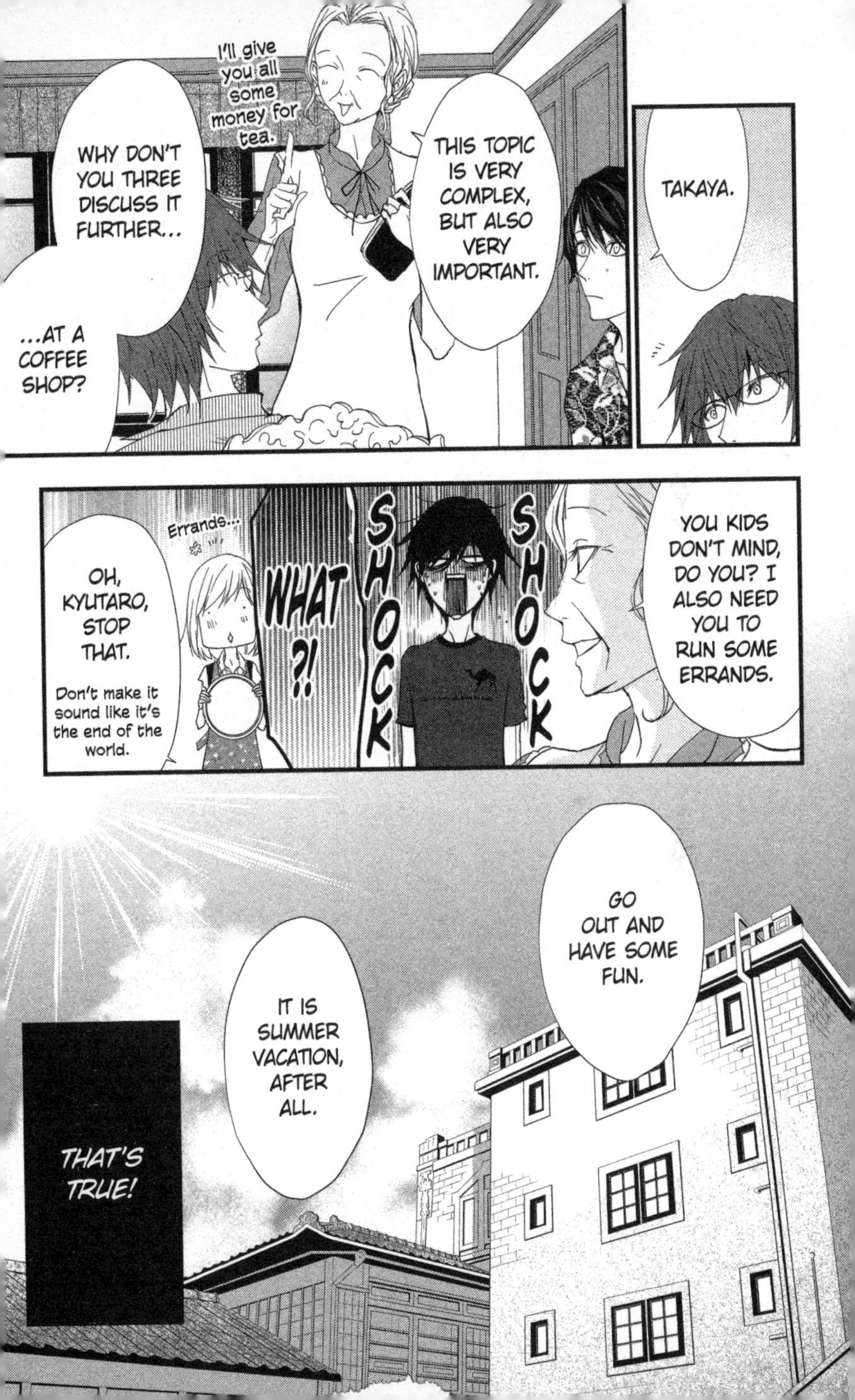
TAKAYA.
THIS TOPIC IS VERY COMPLEX, BUT ALSO VERY IMPORTANT.
I'll give you all some money for tea.
WHY DON'T YOU THREE DISCUSS IT FURTHER...
...AT A COFFEE SHOP?
YOU KIDS DON'T MIND, DO YOU? I ALSO NEED YOU TO RUN SOME ERRANDS.
SHOCK
WHAT?!
SHOCK
Errands...
OH, KYUTARO, STOP THAT.
Don't make it sound like it's the end of the world.
GO OUT AND HAVE SOME FUN.
IT IS SUMMER VACATION, AFTER ALL.
THAT'S TRUE!

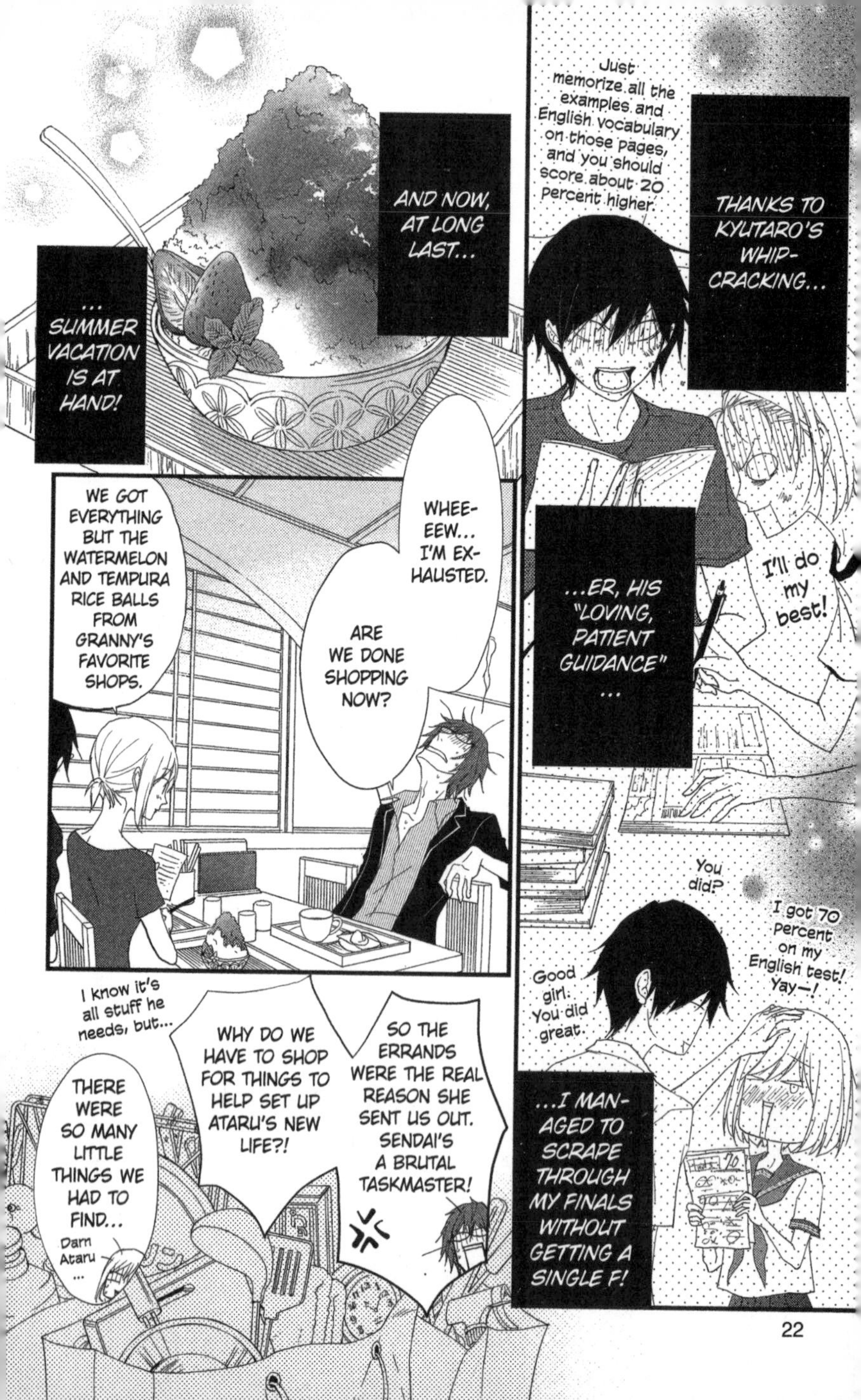
THANKS TO KYUTARO'S WHIP-CRACKING...
Just memorize all the examples and English vocabulary on those pages, and you should score about 20 percent higher.
...ER, HIS "LOVING, PATIENT GUIDANCE"...
I'll do my best!
I got 70 percent on my English test! Yay—!
You did?
Good girl. You did great.
...I MANAGED TO SCRAPE THROUGH MY FINALS WITHOUT GETTING A SINGLE F!
AND NOW, AT LONG LAST...
...SUMMER VACATION IS AT HAND!
WHEEEEW... I'M EXHAUSTED.
ARE WE DONE SHOPPING NOW?
WE GOT EVERYTHING BUT THE WATERMELON AND TEMPURA RICE BALLS FROM GRANNY'S FAVORITE SHOPS.
SO THE ERRANDS WERE THE REAL REASON SHE SENT US OUT. SENDAI'S A BRUTAL TASKMASTER!
WHY DO WE HAVE TO SHOP FOR THINGS TO HELP SET UP ATARU'S NEW LIFE?!
I know it's all stuff he needs, but...
THERE WERE SO MANY LITTLE THINGS WE HAD TO FIND...
Darn Ataru...

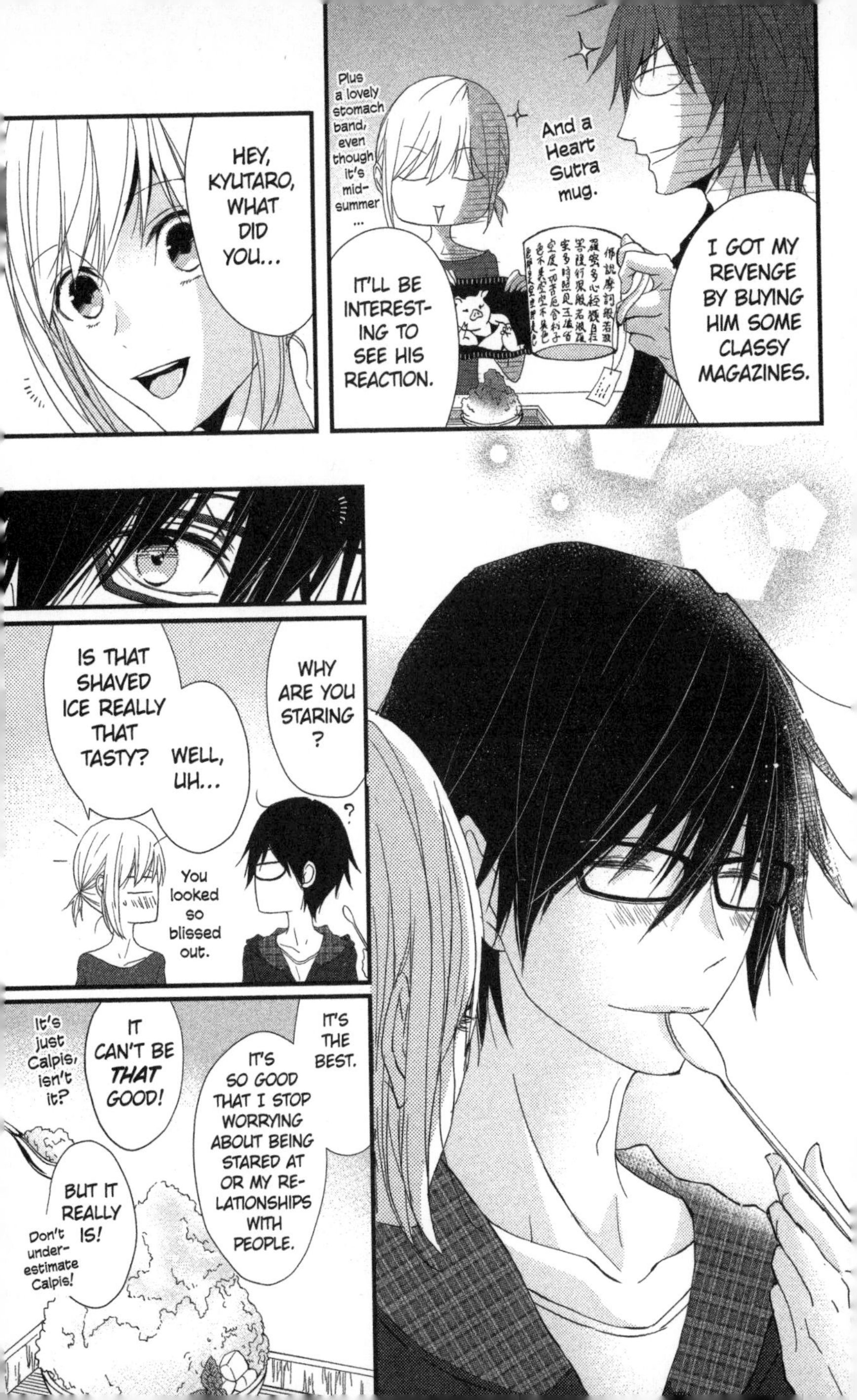
I GOT MY REVENGE BY BUYING HIM SOME CLASSY MAGAZINES.
And a Heart Sutra mug.
Plus a lovely stomach band, even though it's mid-summer...
IT'LL BE INTERESTING TO SEE HIS REACTION.
HEY, KYUTARO, WHAT DID YOU...
WHY ARE YOU STARING?
?
IS THAT SHAVED ICE REALLY THAT TASTY?
WELL, UH...
You looked so blissed out.
IT'S THE BEST.
IT'S SO GOOD THAT I STOP WORRYING ABOUT BEING STARED AT OR MY RE-LATIONSHIPS WITH PEOPLE.
IT CAN'T BE *THAT* GOOD!
It's just Calpis, isn't it?
BUT IT REALLY IS!
Don't under-estimate Calpis!

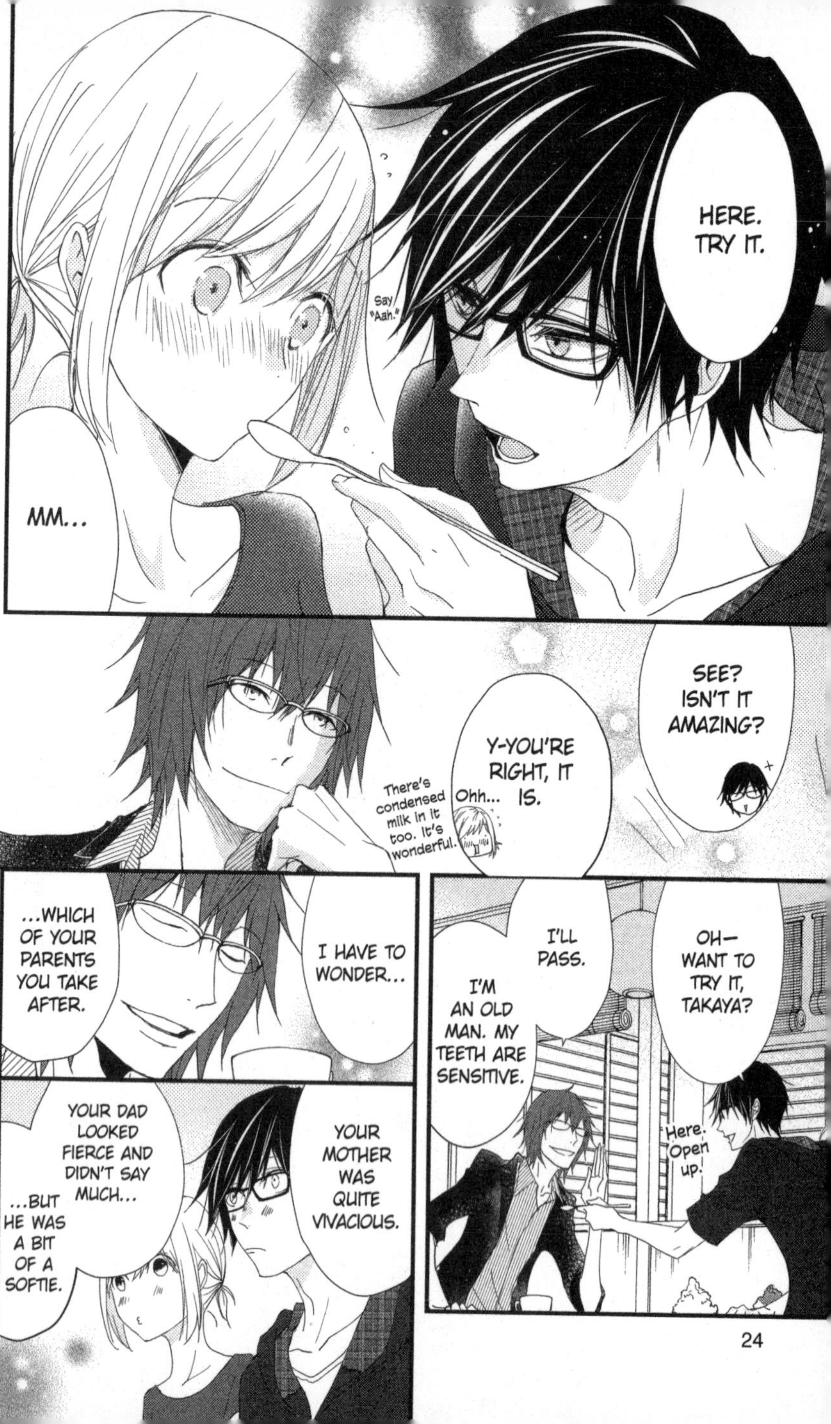
HERE. TRY IT.
Say "Aah."
MM...
SEE? ISN'T IT AMAZING?
Y-YOU'RE RIGHT, IT IS.
Ohh...
There's condensed milk in it too. It's wonderful.
OH— WANT TO TRY IT, TAKAYA?
Here. Open up.
I'LL PASS.
I'M AN OLD MAN. MY TEETH ARE SENSITIVE.
I HAVE TO WONDER...
...WHICH OF YOUR PARENTS YOU TAKE AFTER.
YOUR MOTHER WAS QUITE VIVACIOUS.
YOUR DAD LOOKED FIERCE AND DIDN'T SAY MUCH...
...BUT HE WAS A BIT OF A SOFTIE.

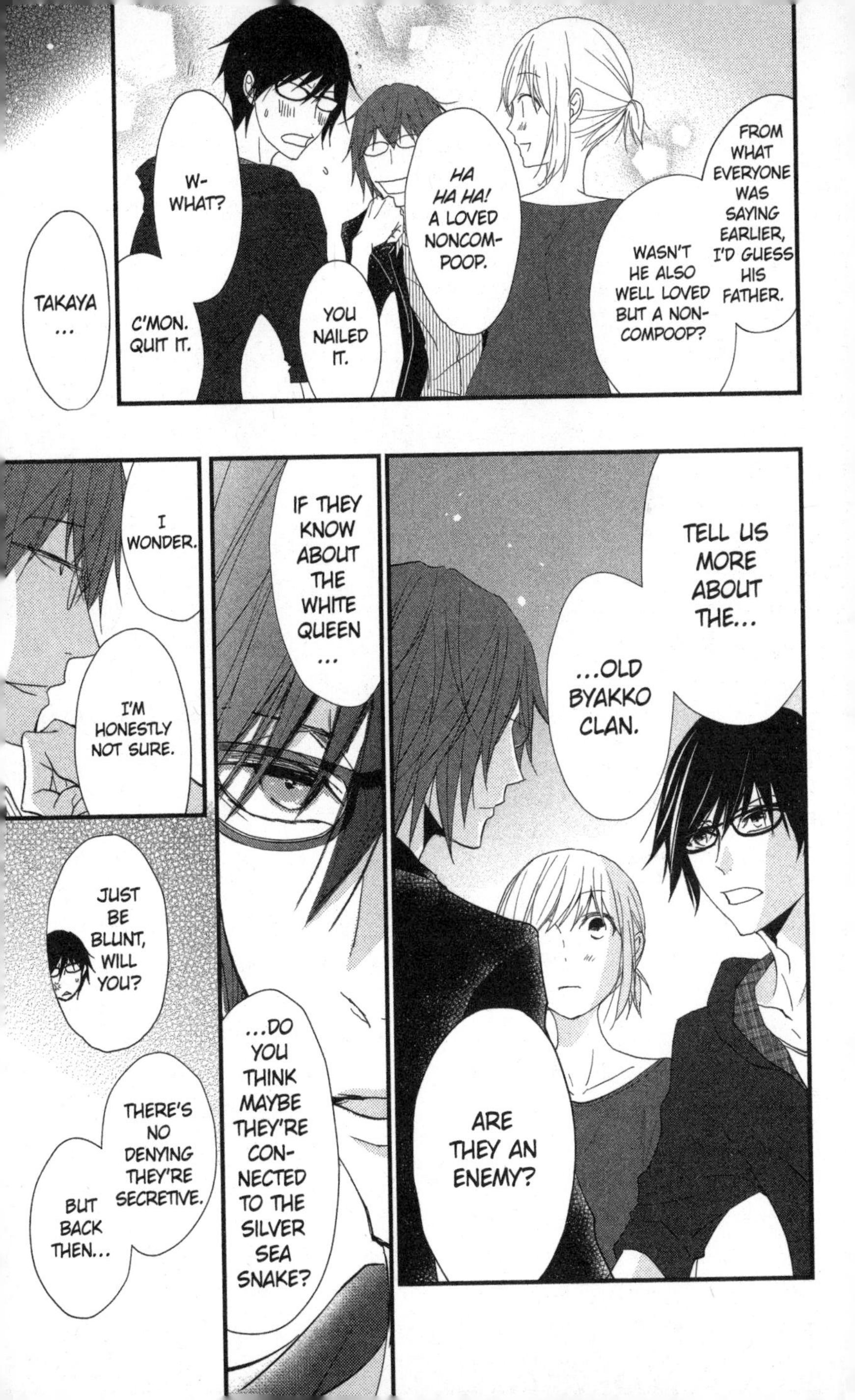
FROM WHAT EVERYONE WAS SAYING EARLIER, I'D GUESS HIS FATHER.
WASN'T HE ALSO WELL LOVED BUT A NONCOMPOOP?
HA HA HA! A LOVED NONCOMPOOP.
YOU NAILED IT.
W-WHAT?
C'MON. QUIT IT.
TAKAYA...
TELL US MORE ABOUT THE...
...OLD BYAKKO CLAN.
ARE THEY AN ENEMY?
IF THEY KNOW ABOUT THE WHITE QUEEN...
...DO YOU THINK MAYBE THEY'RE CONNECTED TO THE SILVER SEA SNAKE?
I WONDER.
I'M HONESTLY NOT SURE.
JUST BE BLUNT, WILL YOU?
THERE'S NO DENYING THEY'RE SECRETIVE.
BUT BACK THEN...

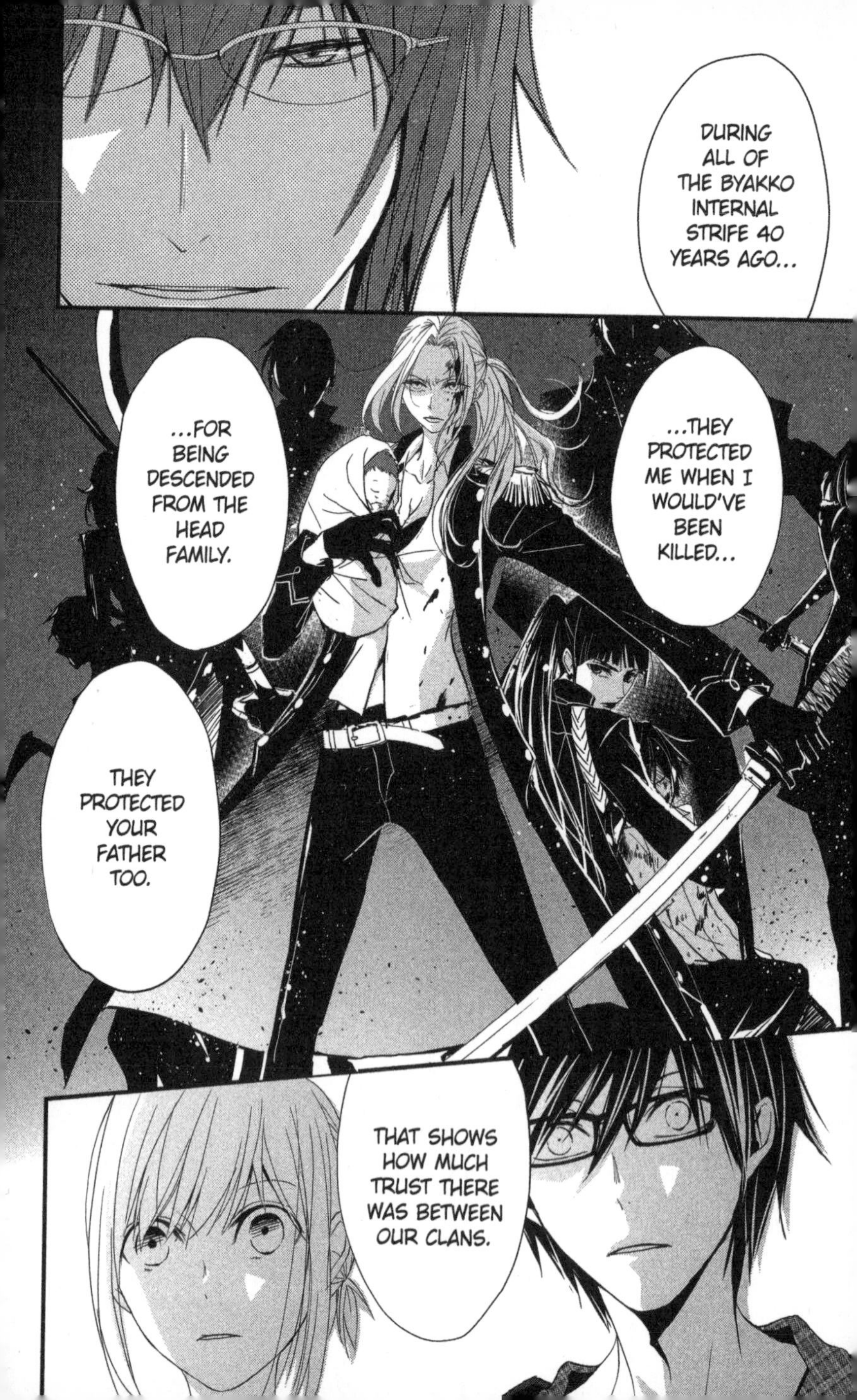
DURING ALL OF THE BYAKKO INTERNAL STRIFE 40 YEARS AGO...
...THEY PROTECTED ME WHEN I WOULD'VE BEEN KILLED...
...FOR BEING DESCENDED FROM THE HEAD FAMILY.
THEY PROTECTED YOUR FATHER TOO.
THAT SHOWS HOW MUCH TRUST THERE WAS BETWEEN OUR CLANS.

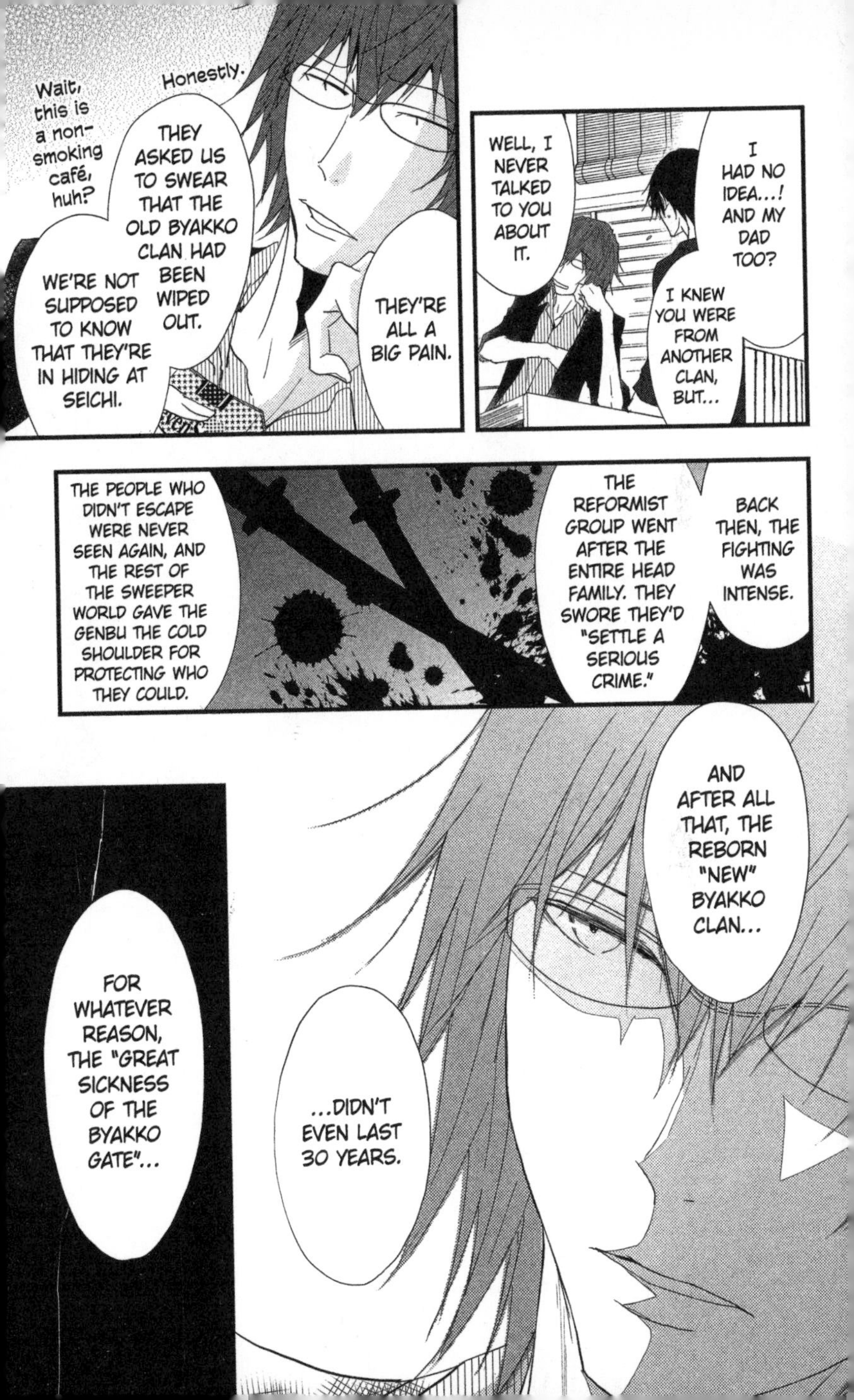
I HAD NO IDEA...! AND MY DAD TOO?
I KNEW YOU WERE FROM ANOTHER CLAN, BUT...
WELL, I NEVER TALKED TO YOU ABOUT IT.
THEY'RE ALL A BIG PAIN.
Honestly.
THEY ASKED US TO SWEAR THAT THE OLD BYAKKO CLAN HAD BEEN WIPED OUT.
Wait, this is a non-smoking café, huh?
WE'RE NOT SUPPOSED TO KNOW THAT THEY'RE IN HIDING AT SEICHI.
BACK THEN, THE FIGHTING WAS INTENSE.
THE REFORMIST GROUP WENT AFTER THE ENTIRE HEAD FAMILY. THEY SWORE THEY'D "SETTLE A SERIOUS CRIME."
THE PEOPLE WHO DIDN'T ESCAPE WERE NEVER SEEN AGAIN, AND THE REST OF THE SWEEPER WORLD GAVE THE GENBU THE COLD SHOULDER FOR PROTECTING WHO THEY COULD.
AND AFTER ALL THAT, THE REBORN "NEW" BYAKKO CLAN...
...DIDN'T EVEN LAST 30 YEARS.
FOR WHATEVER REASON, THE "GREAT SICKNESS OF THE BYAKKO GATE"...

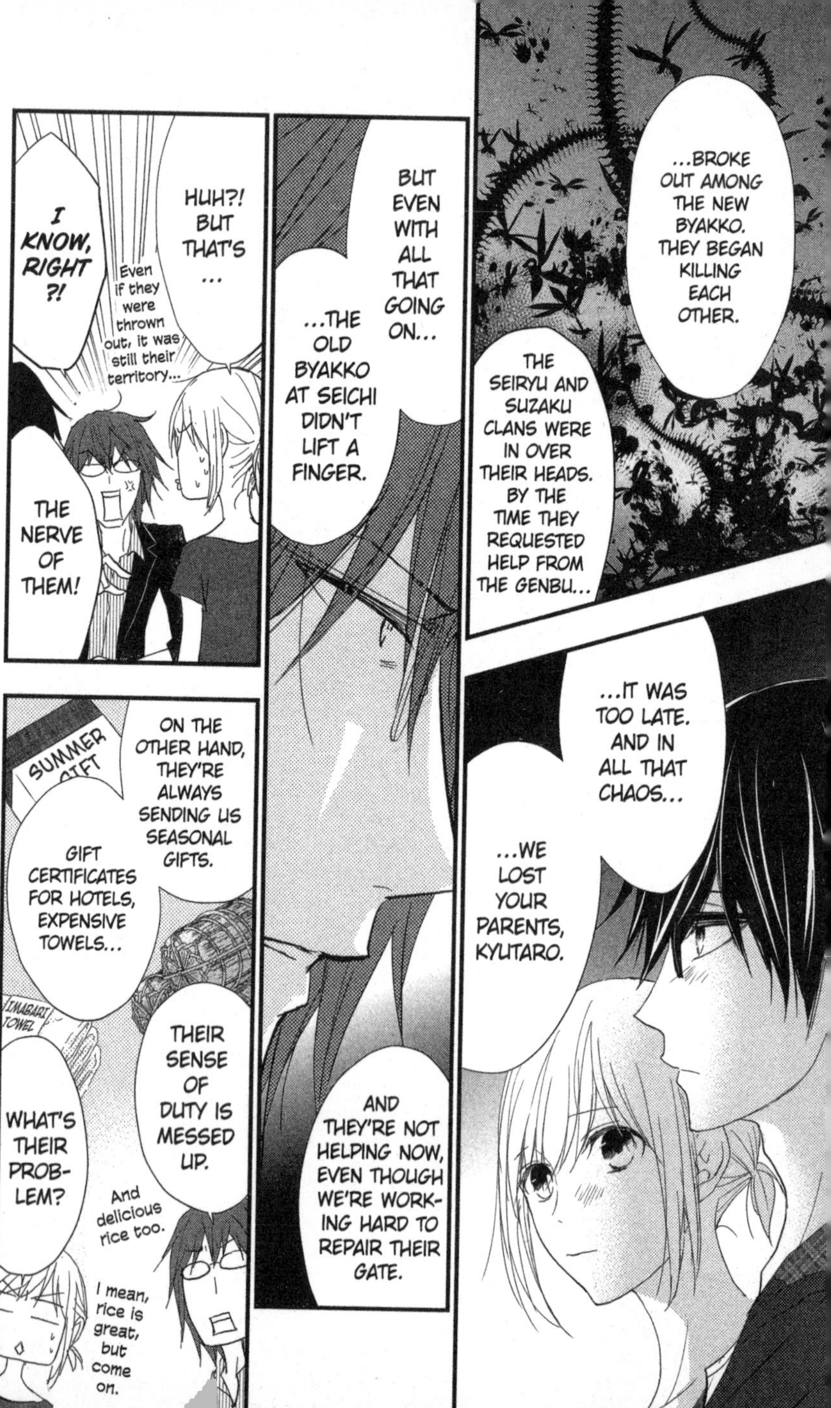
...BROKE OUT AMONG THE NEW BYAKKO. THEY BEGAN KILLING EACH OTHER.
THE SEIRYU AND SUZAKU CLANS WERE IN OVER THEIR HEADS. BY THE TIME THEY REQUESTED HELP FROM THE GENBU...
...IT WAS TOO LATE. AND IN ALL THAT CHAOS...
...WE LOST YOUR PARENTS, KYUTARO.
BUT EVEN WITH ALL THAT GOING ON...
...THE OLD BYAKKO AT SEICHI DIDN'T LIFT A FINGER.
AND THEY'RE NOT HELPING NOW, EVEN THOUGH WE'RE WORKING HARD TO REPAIR THEIR GATE.
HUH?! BUT THAT'S...
I KNOW, RIGHT?!
Even if they were thrown out, it was still their territory...
THE NERVE OF THEM!
SUMMER GIFT
ON THE OTHER HAND, THEY'RE ALWAYS SENDING US SEASONAL GIFTS.
GIFT CERTIFICATES FOR HOTELS, EXPENSIVE TOWELS...
IMABARI TOWEL
THEIR SENSE OF DUTY IS MESSED UP.
WHAT'S THEIR PROBLEM?
And delicious rice too.
I mean, rice is great, but come on.

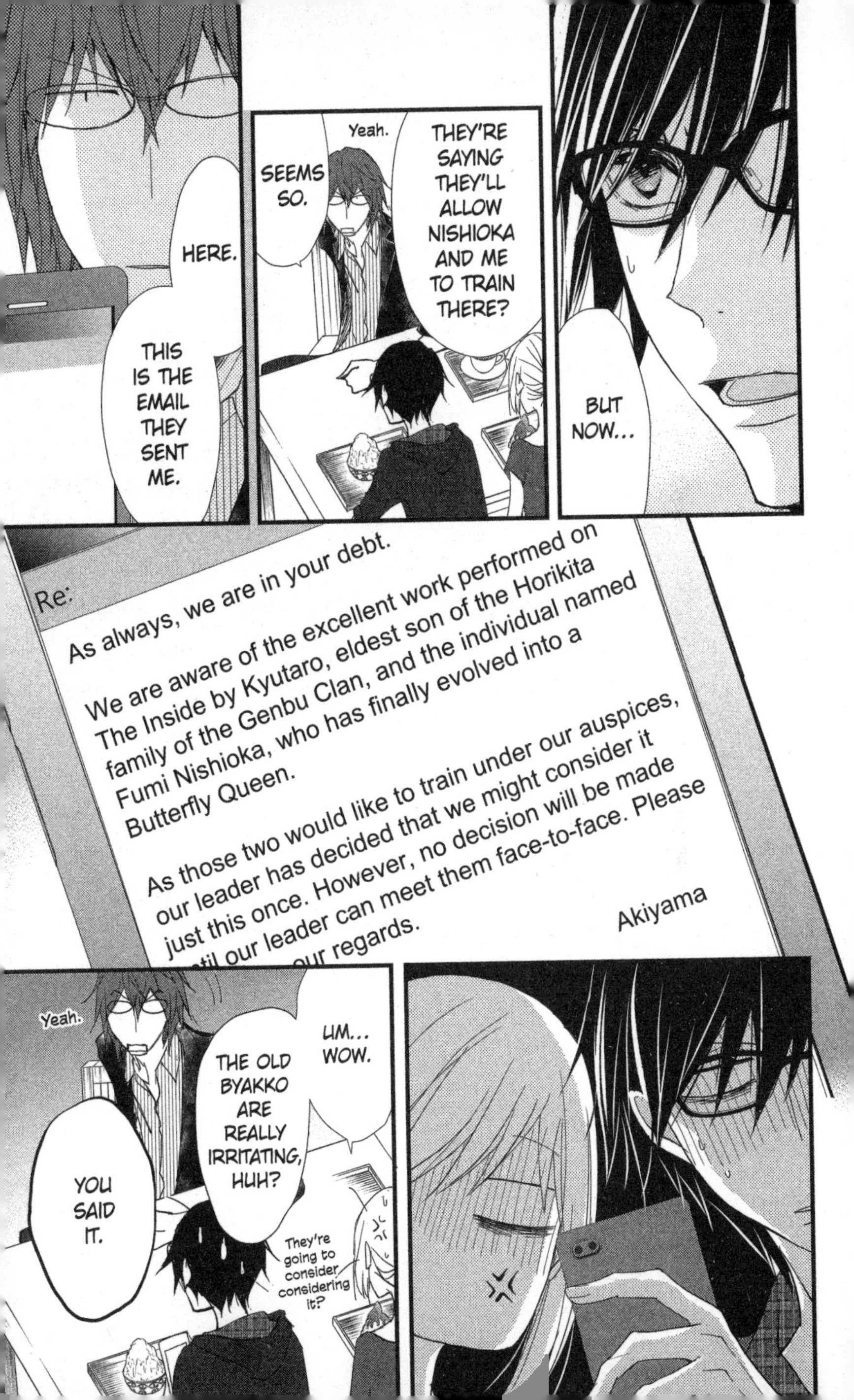
BUT NOW...
THEY'RE SAYING THEY'LL ALLOW NISHIOKA AND ME TO TRAIN THERE?
Yeah.
SEEMS SO.
HERE.
THIS IS THE EMAIL THEY SENT ME.
Re:
As always, we are in your debt.
We are aware of the excellent work performed on The Inside by Kyutaro, eldest son of the Horikita family of the Genbu Clan, and the individual named Fumi Nishioka, who has finally evolved into a Butterfly Queen.
As those two would like to train under our auspices, our leader has decided that we might consider it just this once. However, no decision will be made til our leader can meet them face-to-face. Please
our regards.
Akiyama
UM... WOW.
THE OLD BYAKKO ARE REALLY IRRITATING, HUH?
Yeah.
YOU SAID IT.
They're going to consider considering it?

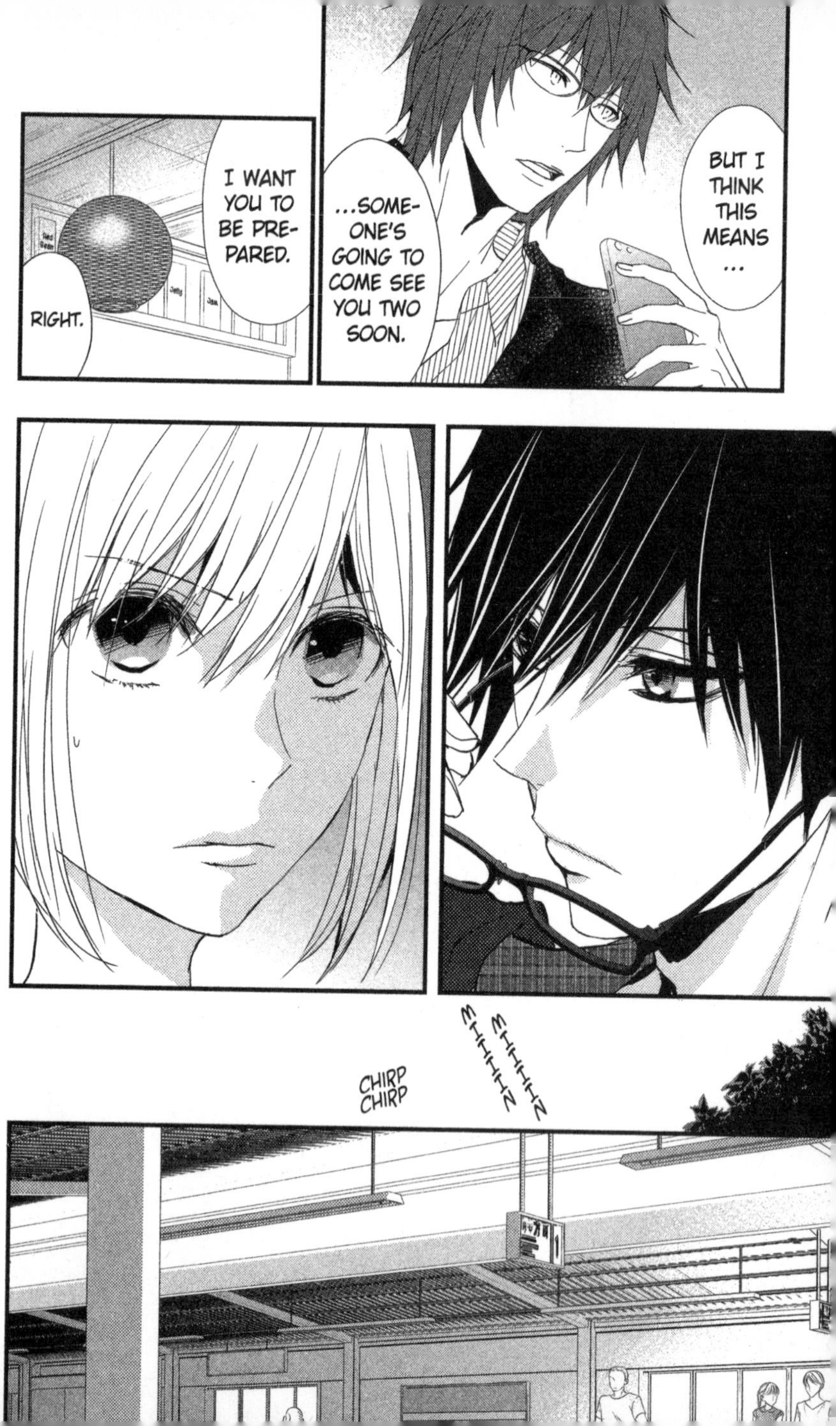
BUT I THINK THIS MEANS...
...SOME-ONE'S GOING TO COME SEE YOU TWO SOON.
I WANT YOU TO BE PRE-PARED.
RIGHT.
MIIIIIIN
MIIIIIIN
CHIRP CHIRP

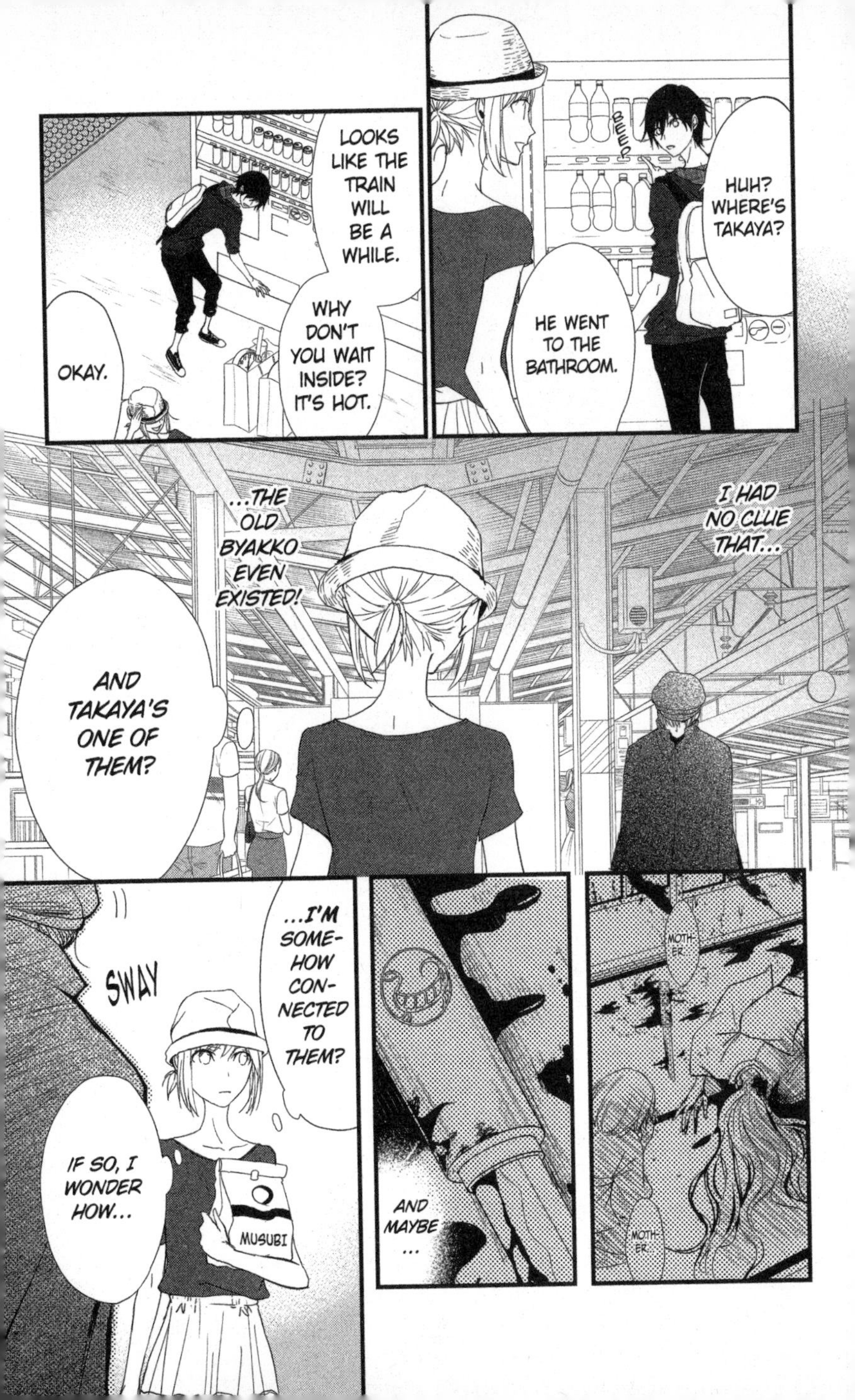
HUH? WHERE'S TAKAYA?
HE WENT TO THE BATHROOM.
LOOKS LIKE THE TRAIN WILL BE A WHILE.
WHY DON'T YOU WAIT INSIDE? IT'S HOT.
OKAY.
I HAD NO CLUE THAT...
...THE OLD BYAKKO EVEN EXISTED!
AND TAKAYA'S ONE OF THEM?
MOTH-ER
MOTH-ER
AND MAYBE ...
...I'M SOME-HOW CON-NECTED TO THEM?
SWAY
IF SO, I WONDER HOW...
MUSUBI

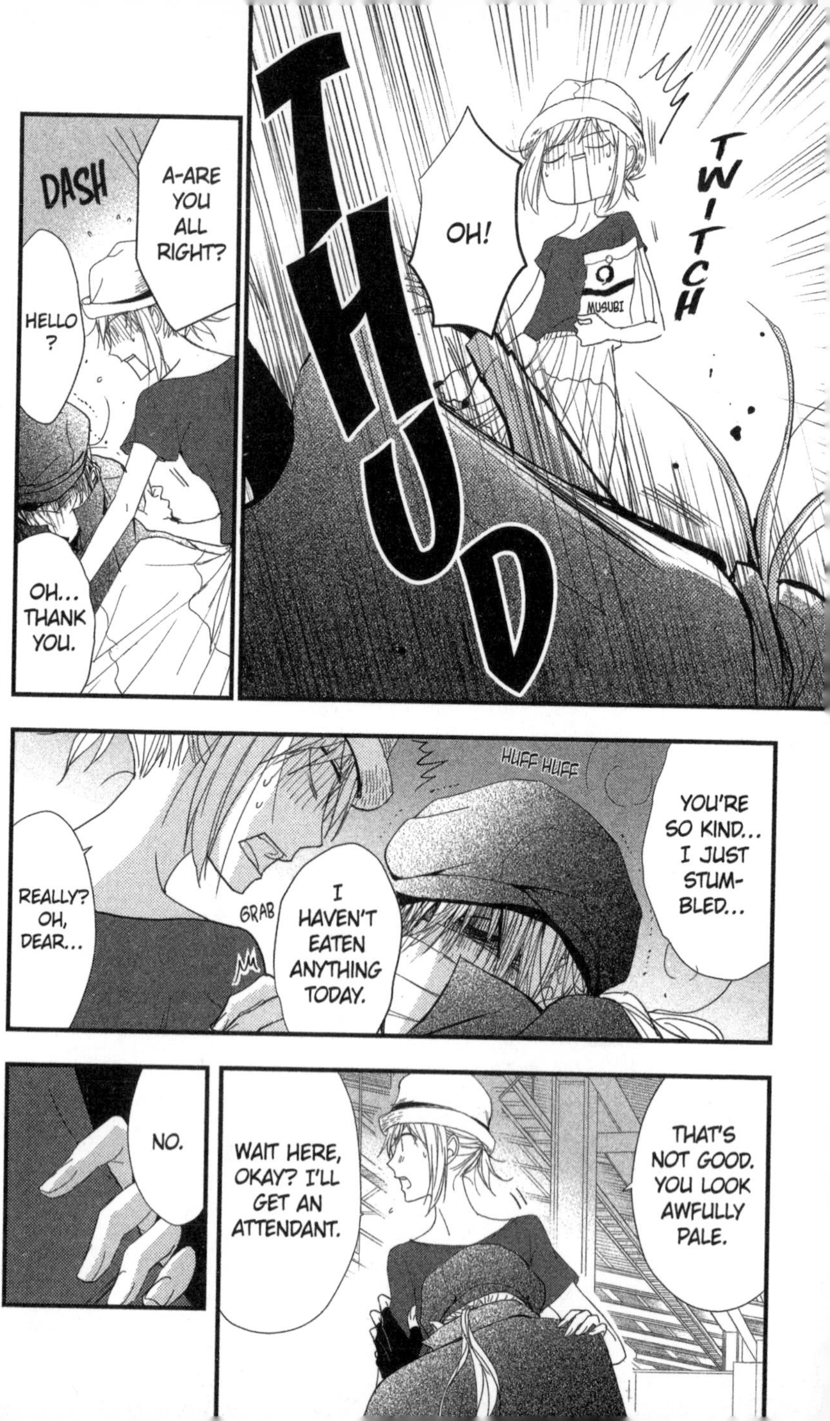
TWITCH
MUSUBI
OH!
THUD
A-ARE YOU ALL RIGHT?
DASH
HELLO?
OH... THANK YOU.
HUFF HUFF
YOU'RE SO KIND... I JUST STUM-BLED...
I HAVEN'T EATEN ANYTHING TODAY.
GRAB
REALLY? OH, DEAR...
THAT'S NOT GOOD. YOU LOOK AWFULLY PALE.
WAIT HERE, OKAY? I'LL GET AN ATTENDANT.
NO.

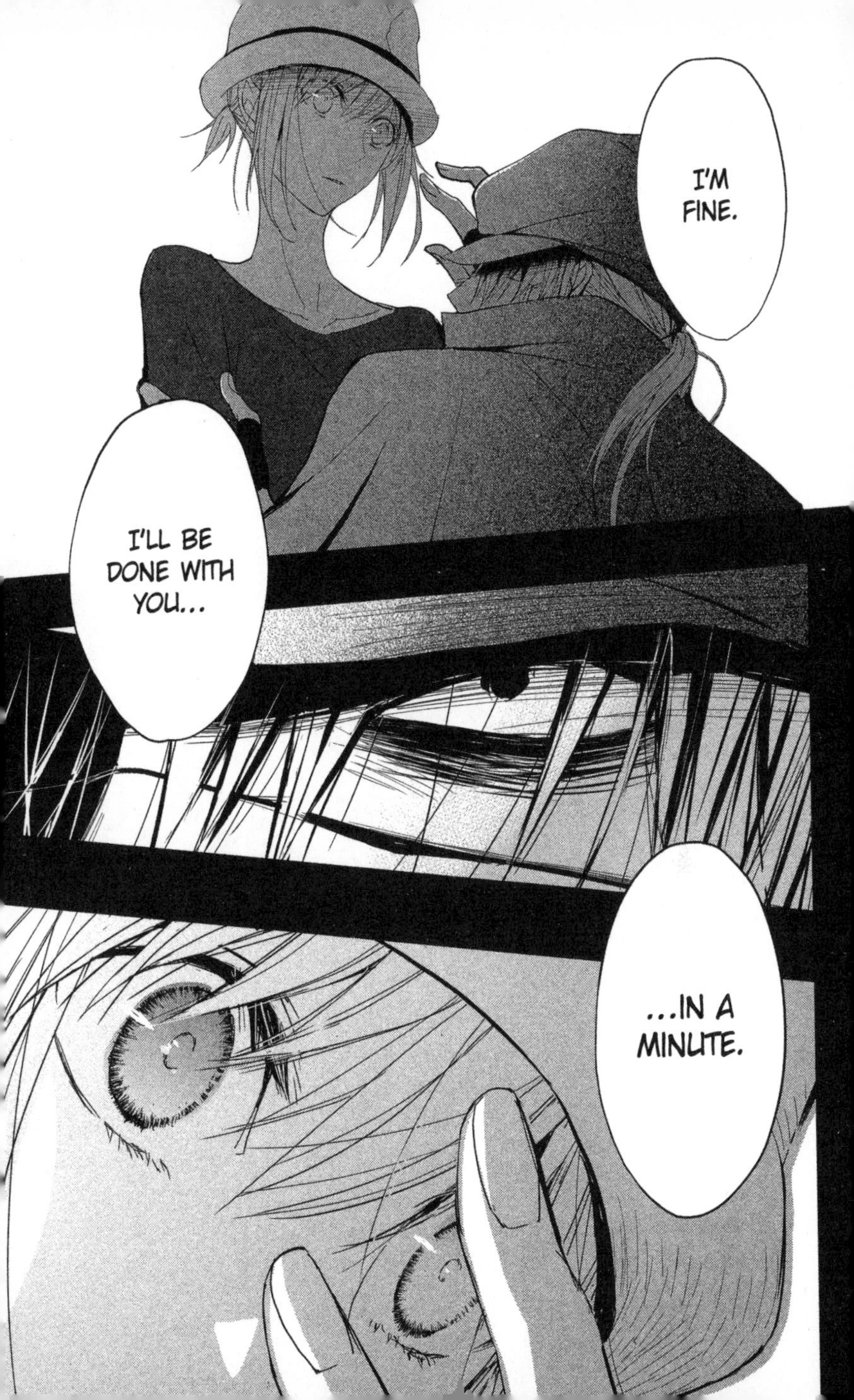
I'M FINE.
I'LL BE DONE WITH YOU...
...IN A MINUTE.

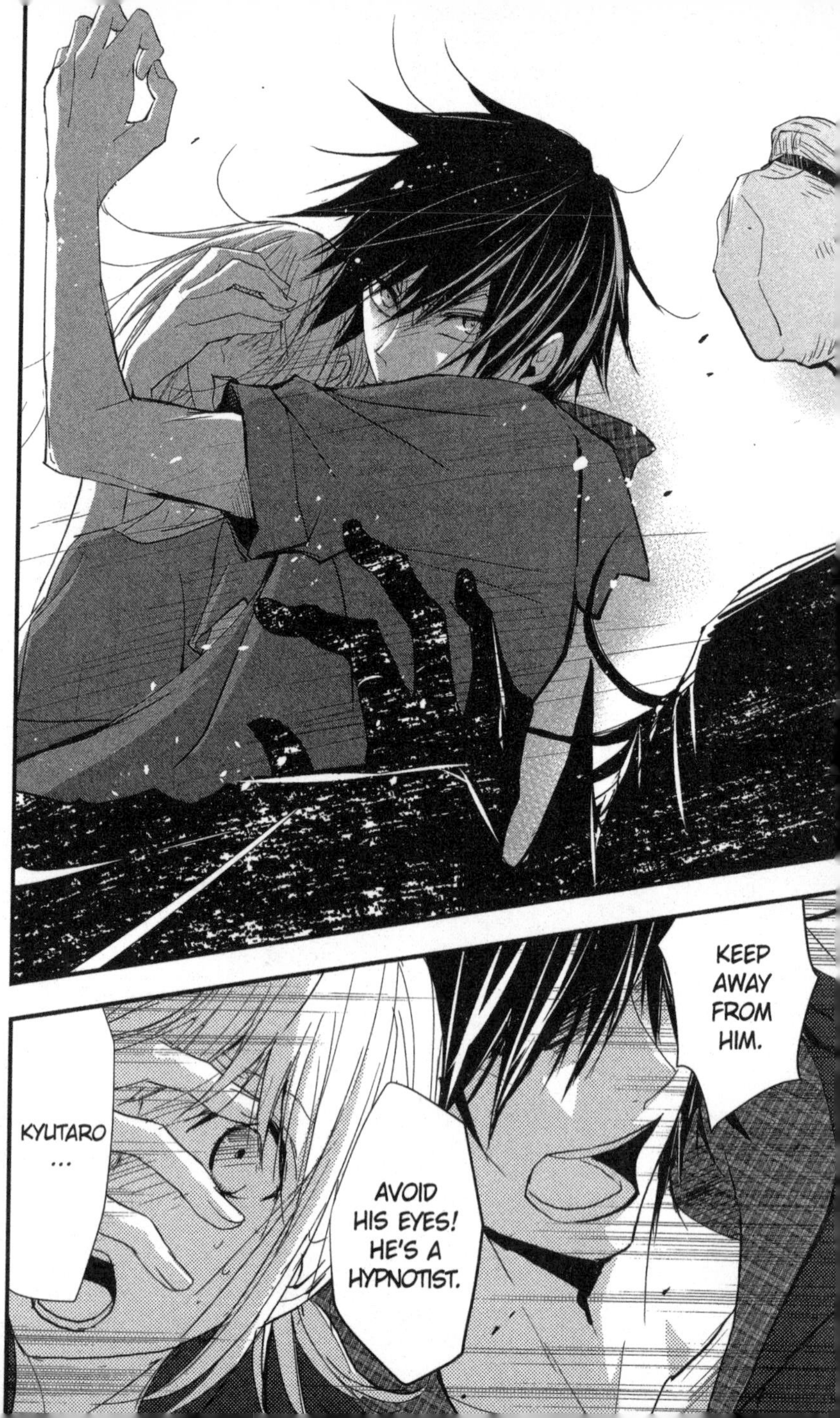
KEEP AWAY FROM HIM.
AVOID HIS EYES! HE'S A HYPNOTIST.
KYUTARO...

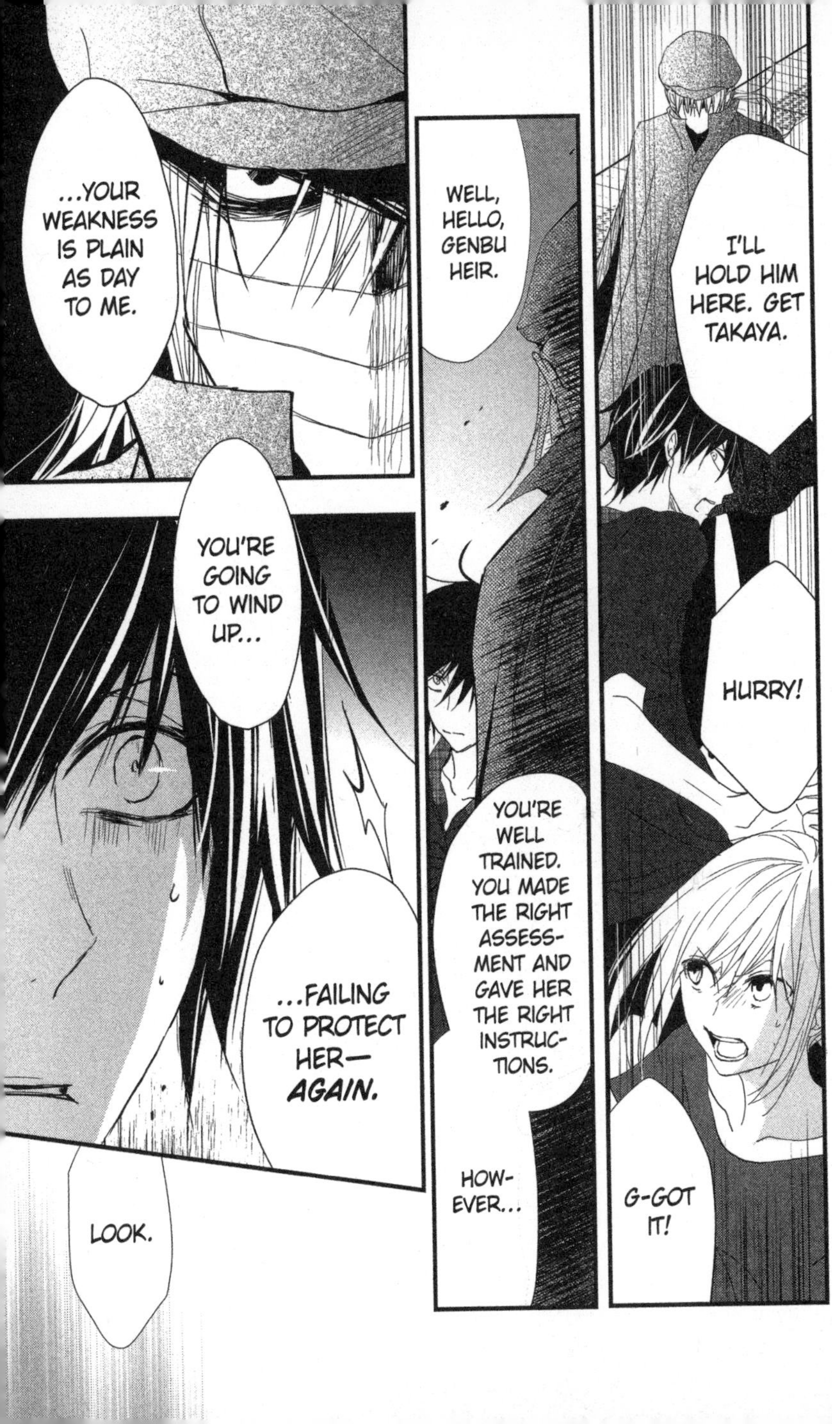
I'LL HOLD HIM HERE. GET TAKAYA.
HURRY!
G-GOT IT!
WELL, HELLO, GENBU HEIR.
YOU'RE WELL TRAINED. YOU MADE THE RIGHT ASSESS-MENT AND GAVE HER THE RIGHT INSTRUC-TIONS.
HOW-EVER...
...YOUR WEAKNESS IS PLAIN AS DAY TO ME.
YOU'RE GOING TO WIND UP...
...FAILING TO PROTECT HER—AGAIN.
LOOK.

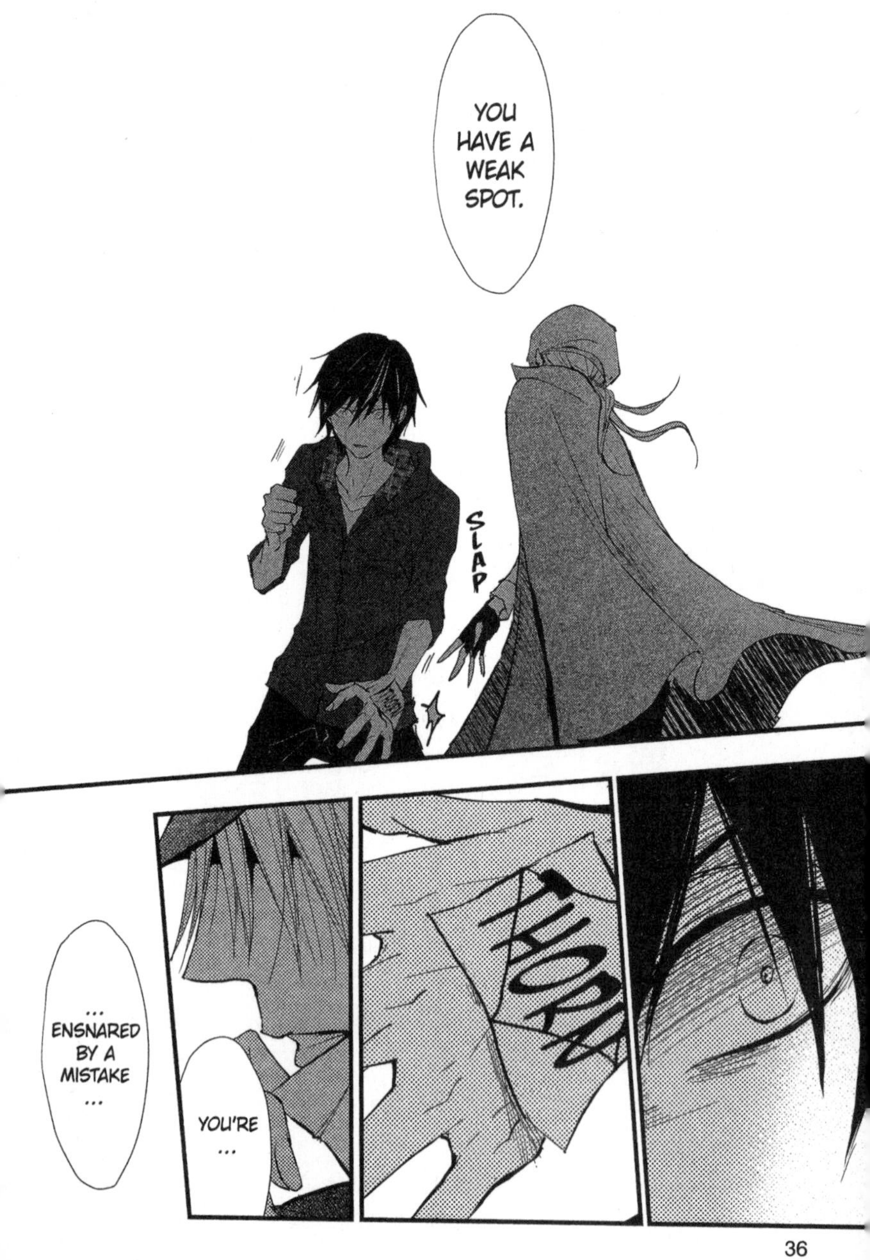
YOU HAVE A WEAK SPOT.
SLAP
THORN
YOU'RE ...
... ENSNARED BY A MISTAKE ...

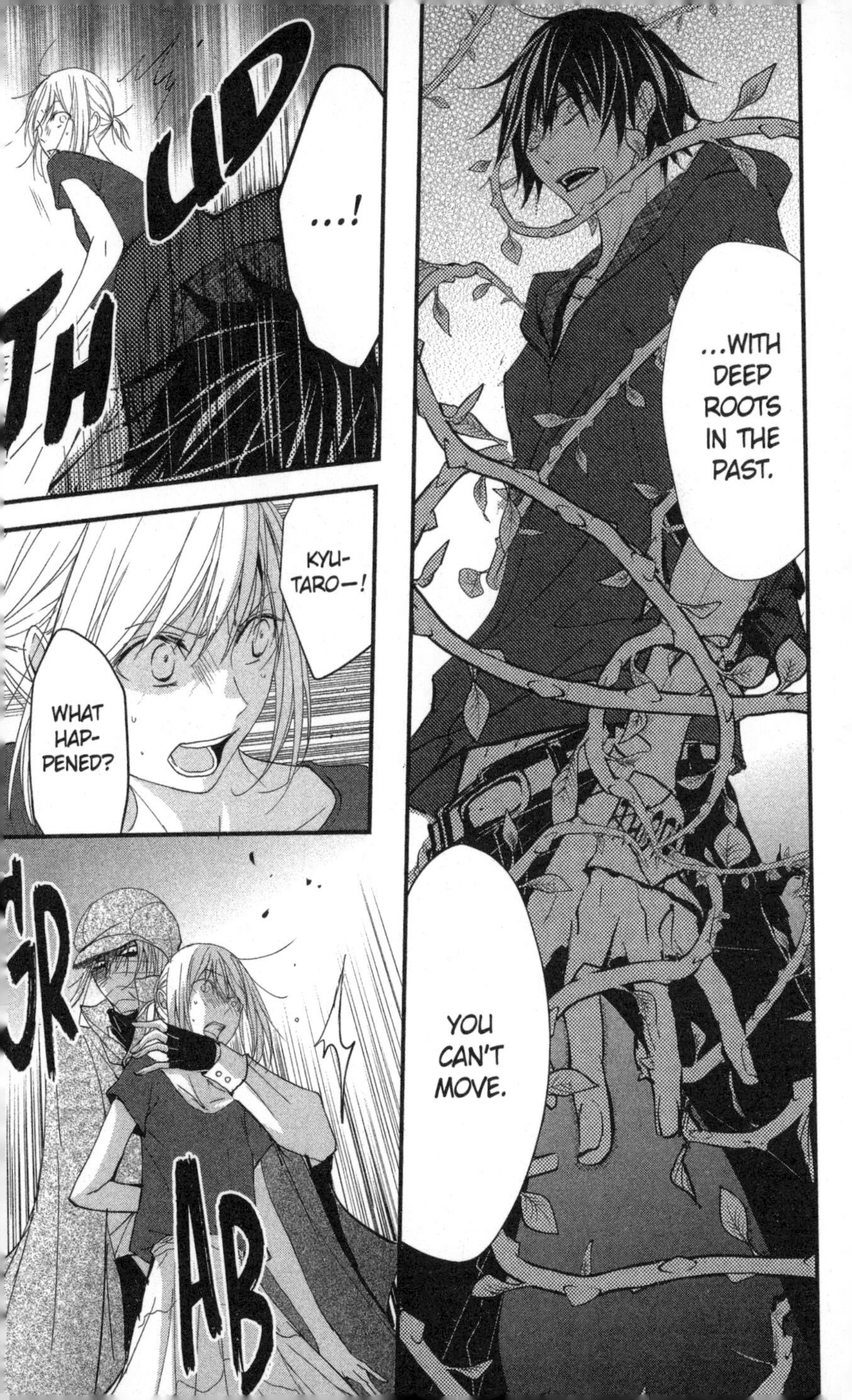
...WITH DEEP ROOTS IN THE PAST.
YOU CAN'T MOVE.
THUD
...!
KYU-TARO—!
WHAT HAP-PENED?
GRAB

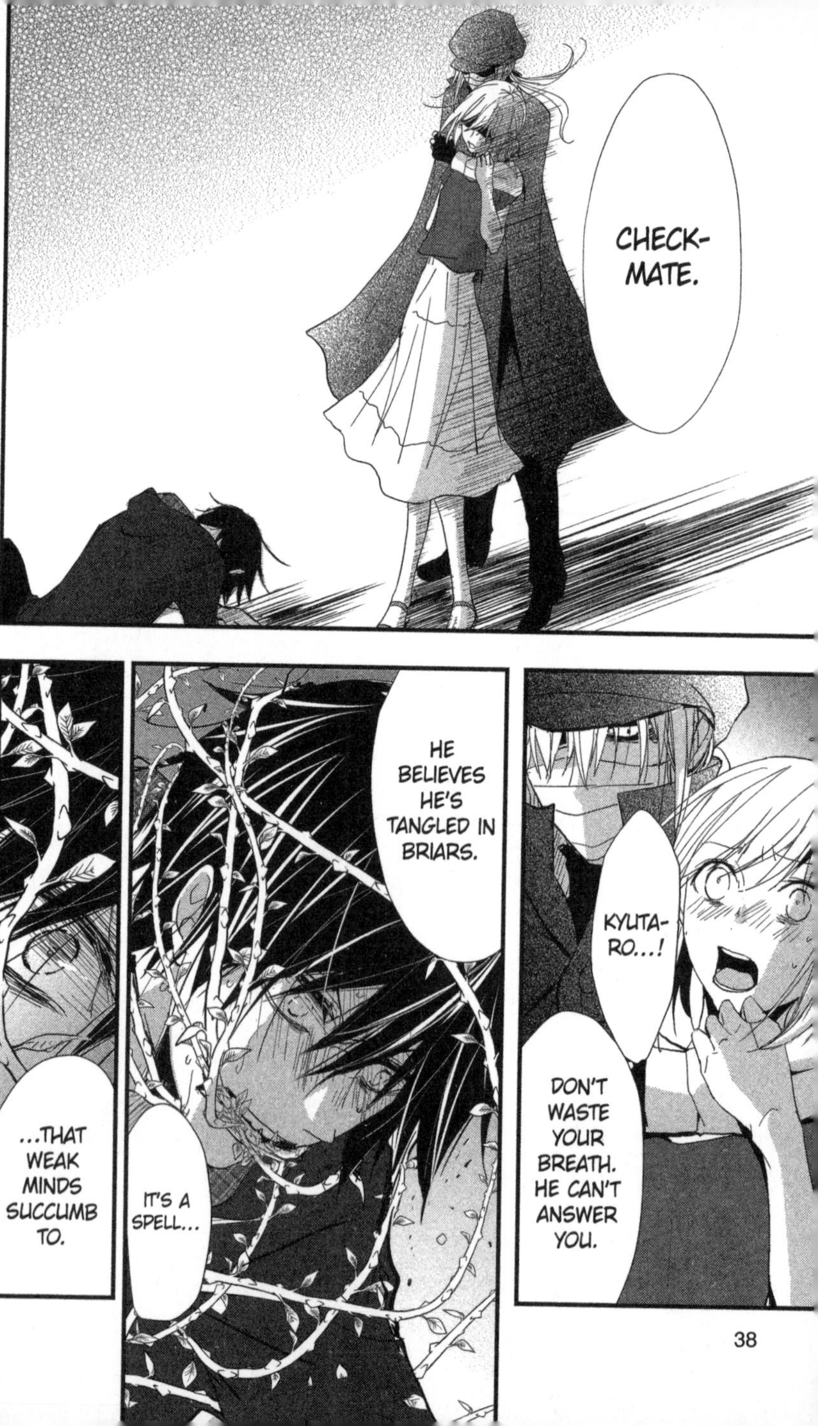
CHECK-MATE.
KYUTA-RO...!
DON'T WASTE YOUR BREATH. HE CAN'T ANSWER YOU.
HE BELIEVES HE'S TANGLED IN BRIARS.
IT'S A SPELL...
...THAT WEAK MINDS SUCCUMB TO.

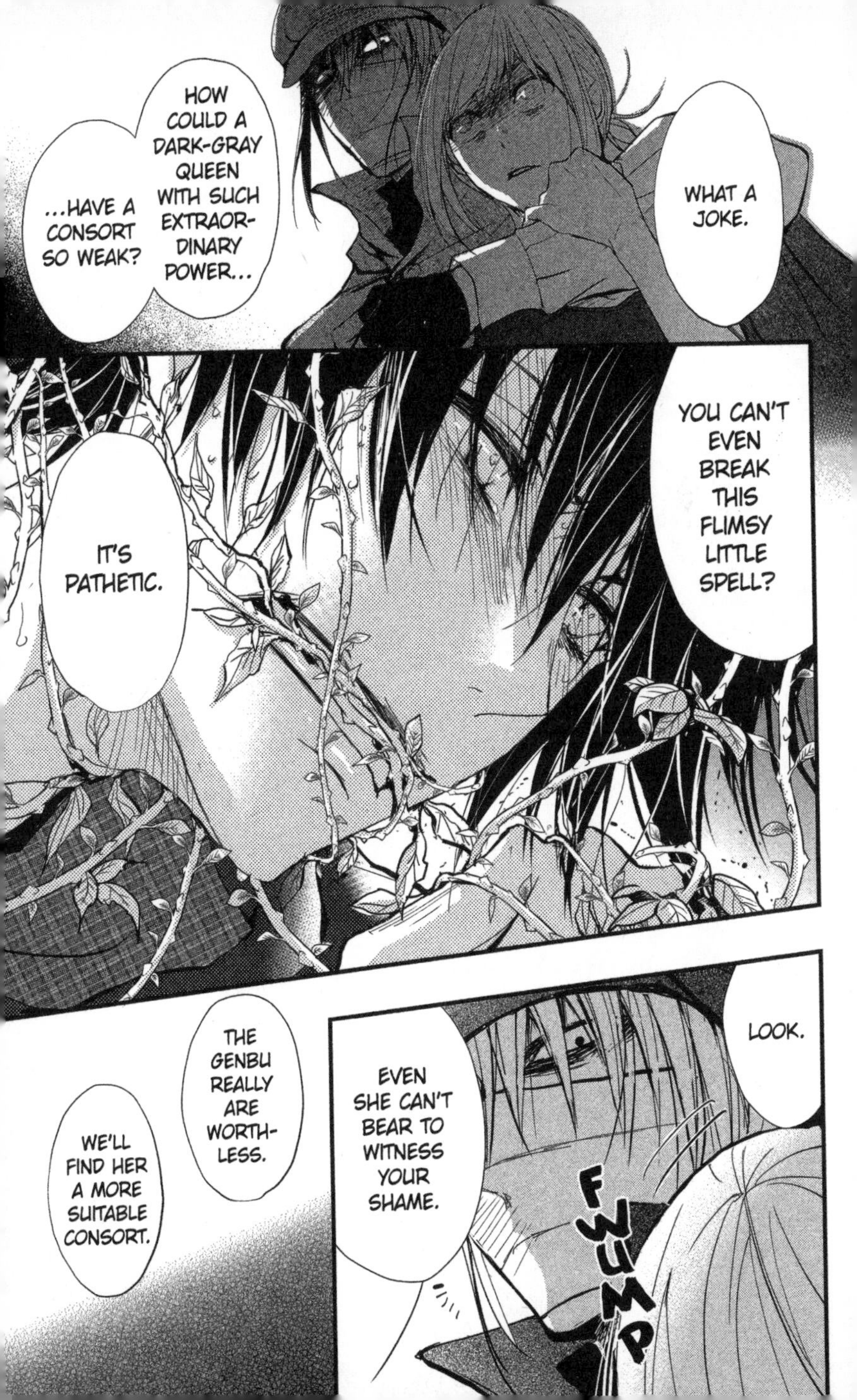
WHAT A JOKE.
HOW COULD A DARK-GRAY QUEEN WITH SUCH EXTRAOR-DINARY POWER...
...HAVE A CONSORT SO WEAK?
YOU CAN'T EVEN BREAK THIS FLIMSY LITTLE SPELL?
IT'S PATHETIC.
LOOK.
EVEN SHE CAN'T BEAR TO WITNESS YOUR SHAME.
FWUMP
THE GENBU REALLY ARE WORTH-LESS.
WE'LL FIND HER A MORE SUITABLE CONSORT.

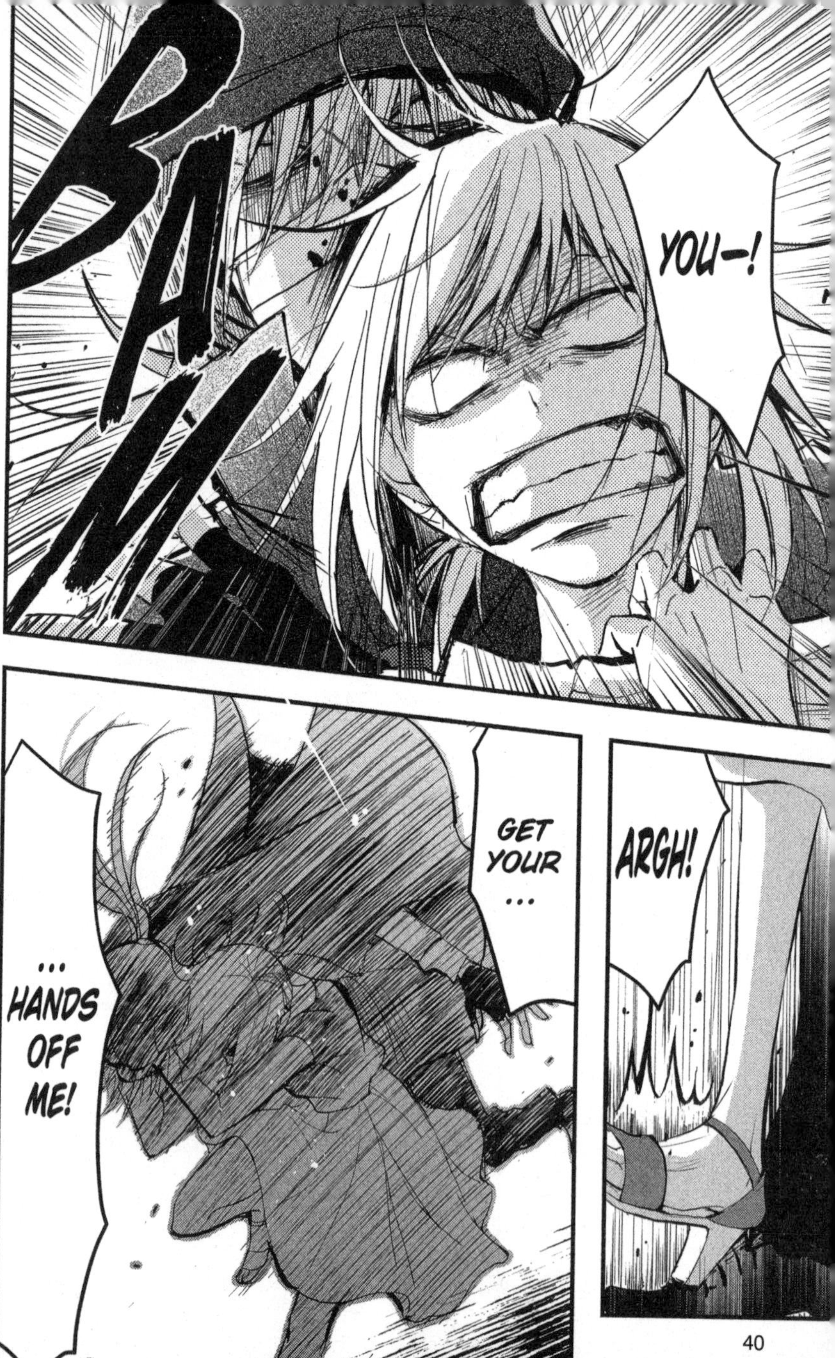
YOU—!
BAM
ARGH!
GET YOUR ...
... HANDS OFF ME!

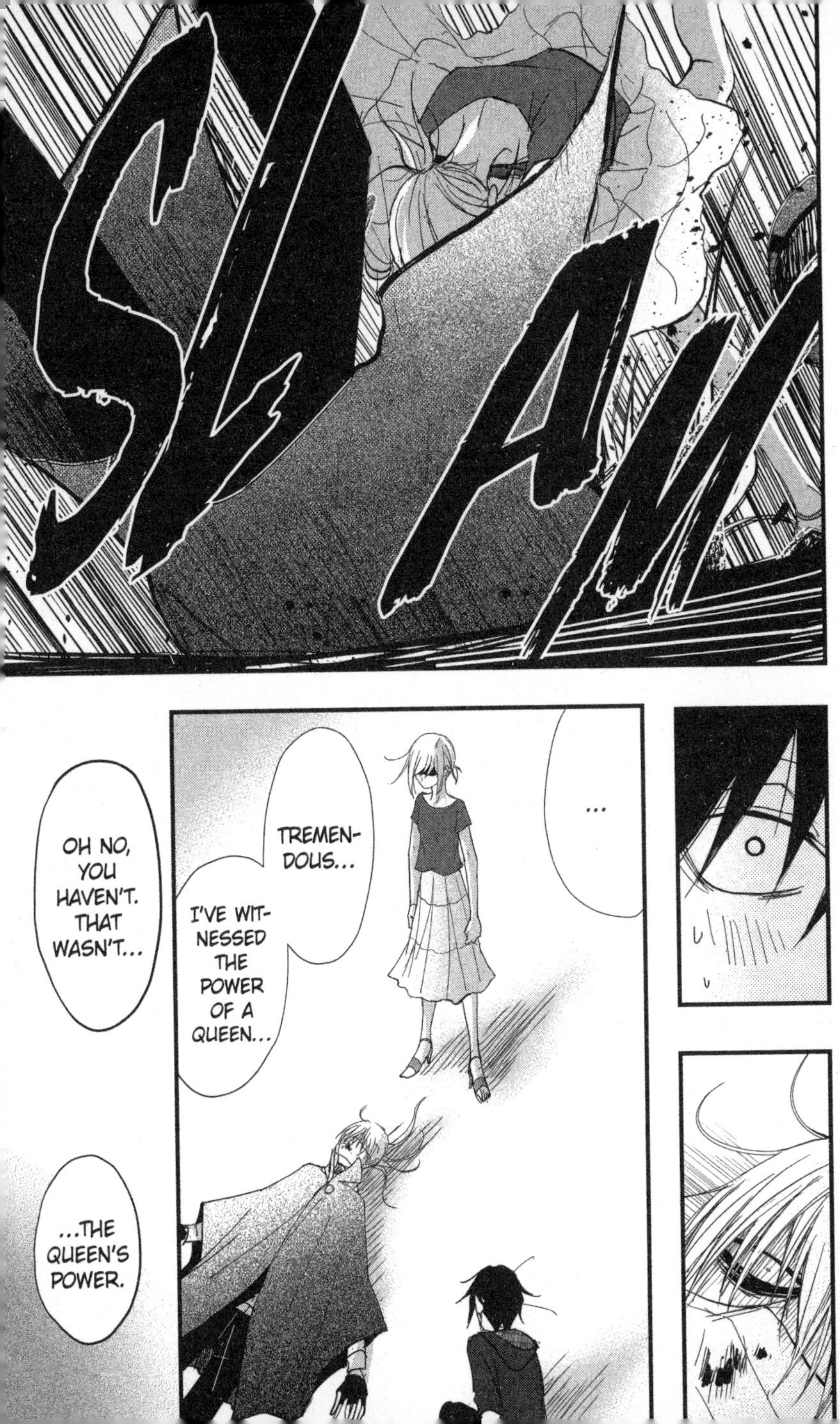
SLAM
...
TREMEN-DOUS...
I'VE WIT-NESSED THE POWER OF A QUEEN...
OH NO, YOU HAVEN'T. THAT WASN'T...
...THE QUEEN'S POWER.

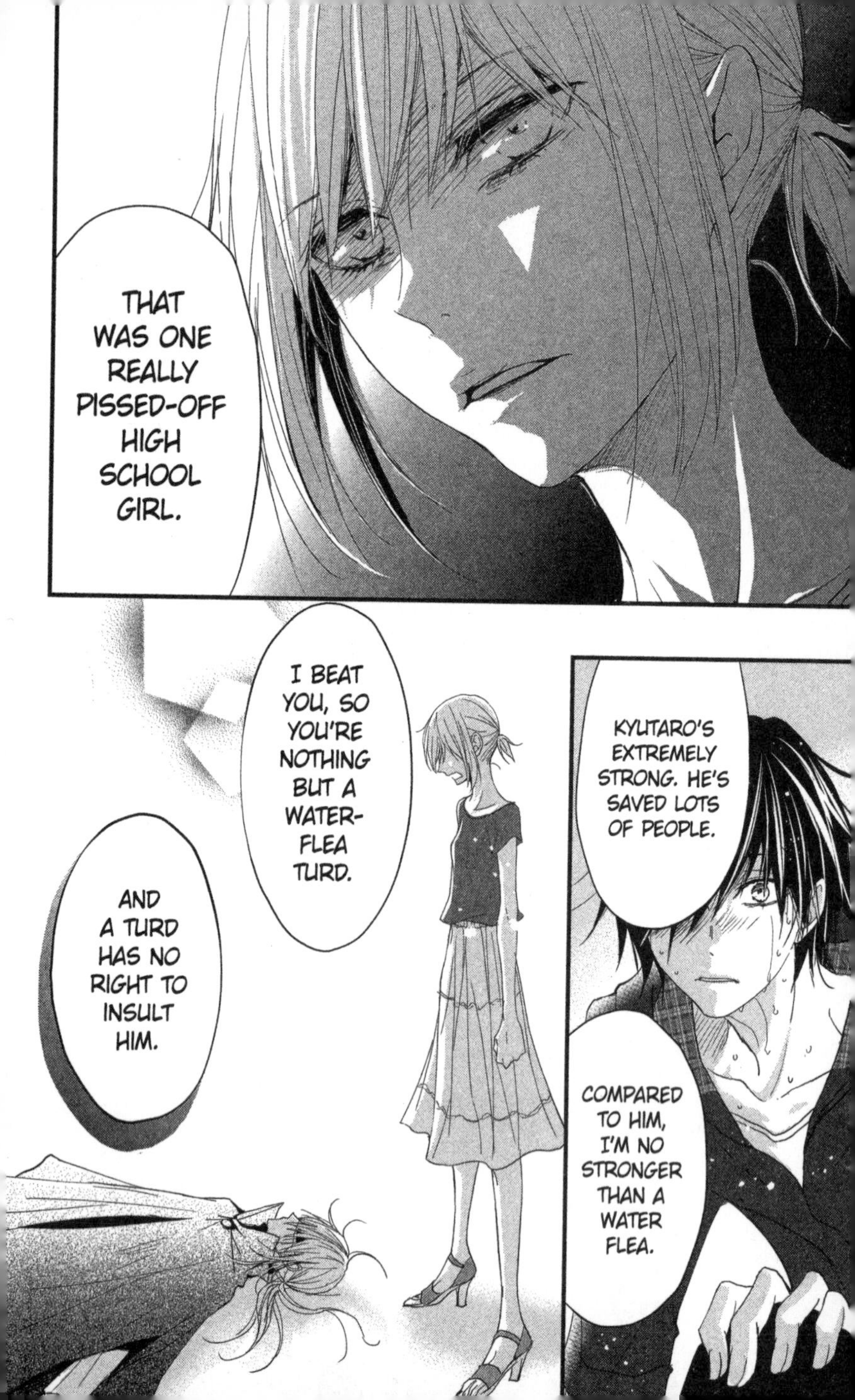
THAT WAS ONE REALLY PISSED-OFF HIGH SCHOOL GIRL.
KYUTARO'S EXTREMELY STRONG. HE'S SAVED LOTS OF PEOPLE.
COMPARED TO HIM, I'M NO STRONGER THAN A WATER FLEA.
I BEAT YOU, SO YOU'RE NOTHING BUT A WATER-FLEA TURD.
AND A TURD HAS NO RIGHT TO INSULT HIM.

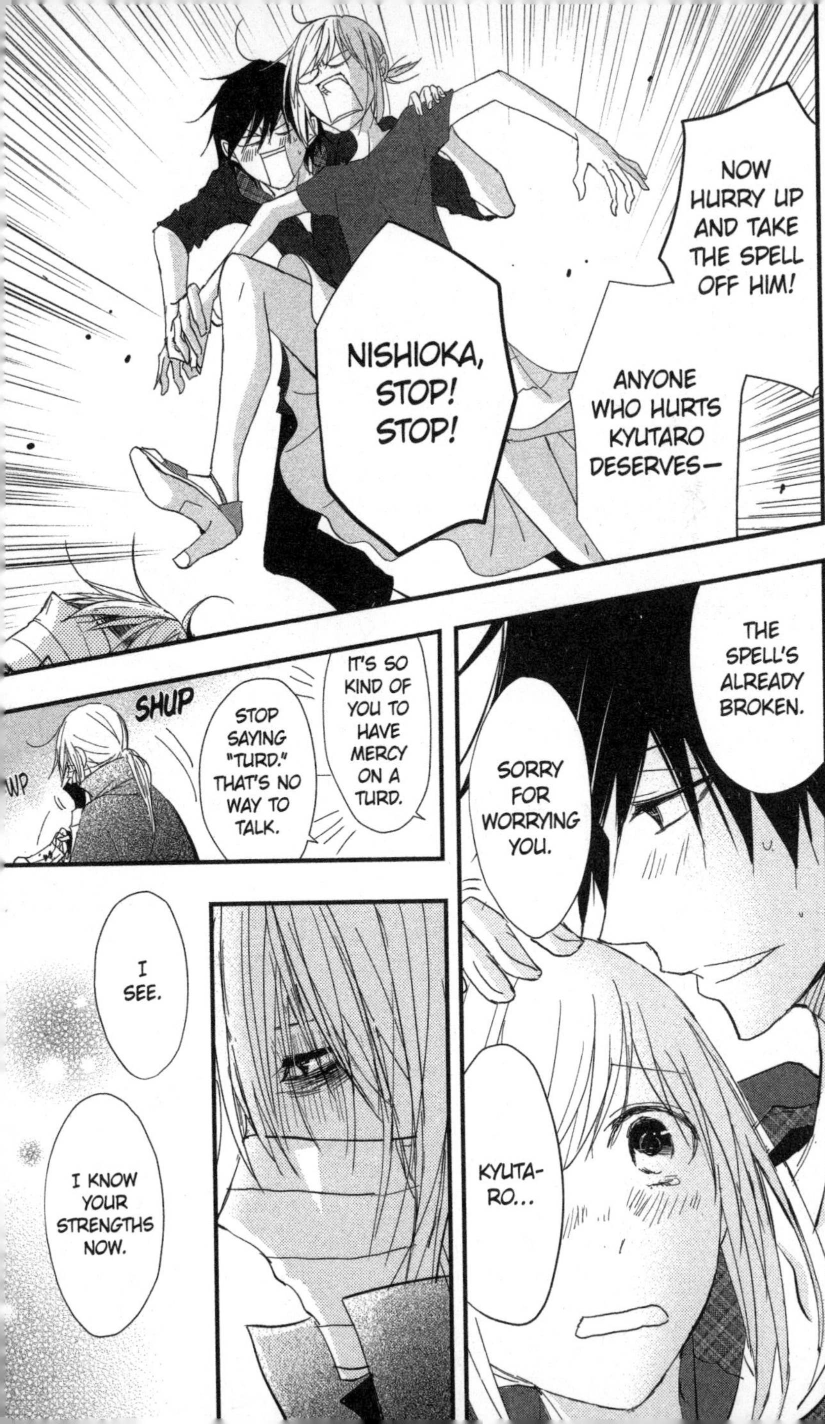
NOW HURRY UP AND TAKE THE SPELL OFF HIM!
ANYONE WHO HURTS KYUTARO DESERVES—
NISHIOKA, STOP! STOP!
THE SPELL'S ALREADY BROKEN.
SORRY FOR WORRYING YOU.
KYUTA-RO...
IT'S SO KIND OF YOU TO HAVE MERCY ON A TURD.
STOP SAYING "TURD." THAT'S NO WAY TO TALK.
SHUP
WP
I SEE.
I KNOW YOUR STRENGTHS NOW.

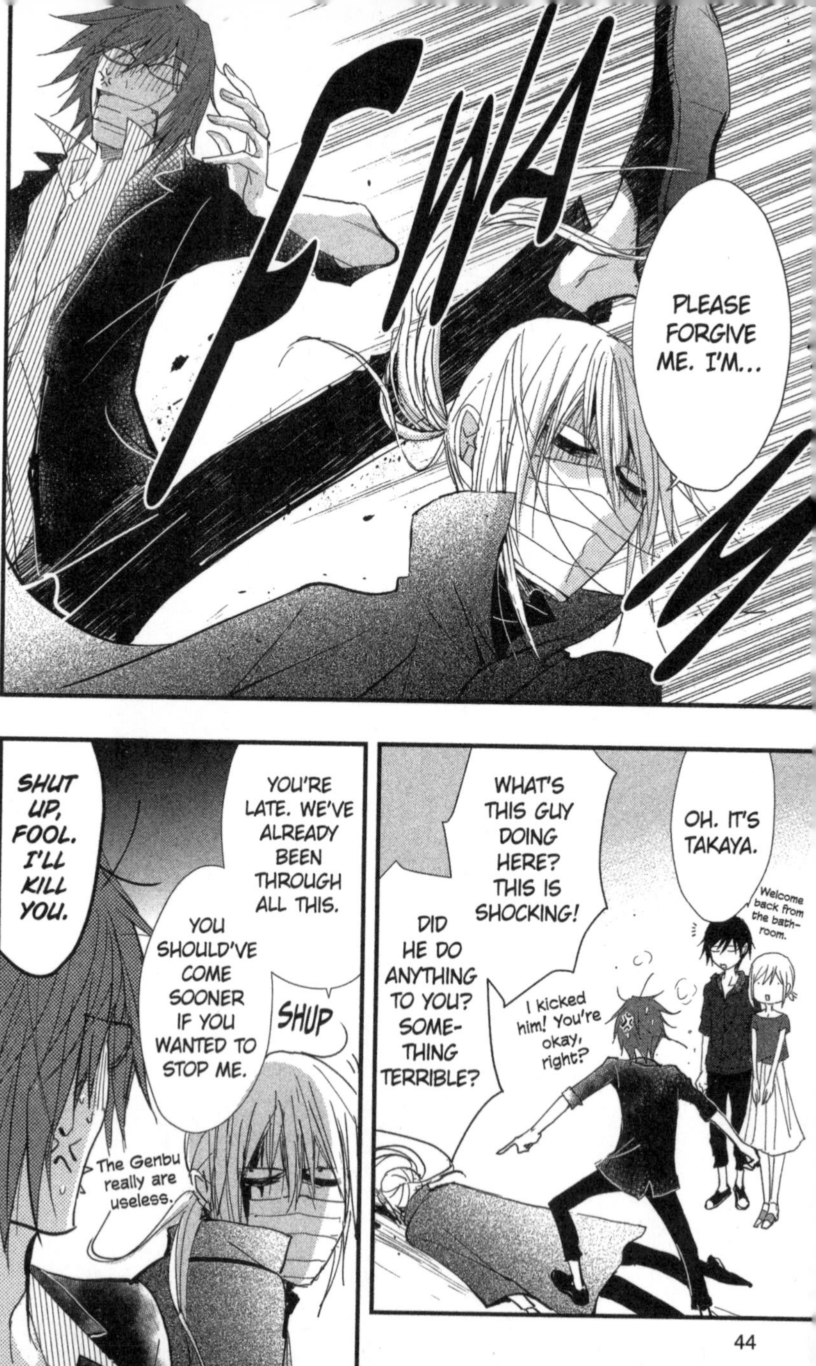
CWAM
PLEASE FORGIVE ME. I'M...
OH. IT'S TAKAYA.
Welcome back from the bathroom.
WHAT'S THIS GUY DOING HERE? THIS IS SHOCKING!
DID HE DO ANYTHING TO YOU? SOME-THING TERRIBLE?
I kicked him! You're okay, right?
YOU'RE LATE. WE'VE ALREADY BEEN THROUGH ALL THIS.
SHUT UP, FOOL. I'LL KILL YOU.
YOU SHOULD'VE COME SOONER IF YOU WANTED TO STOP ME.
SHUP
The Genbu really are useless.

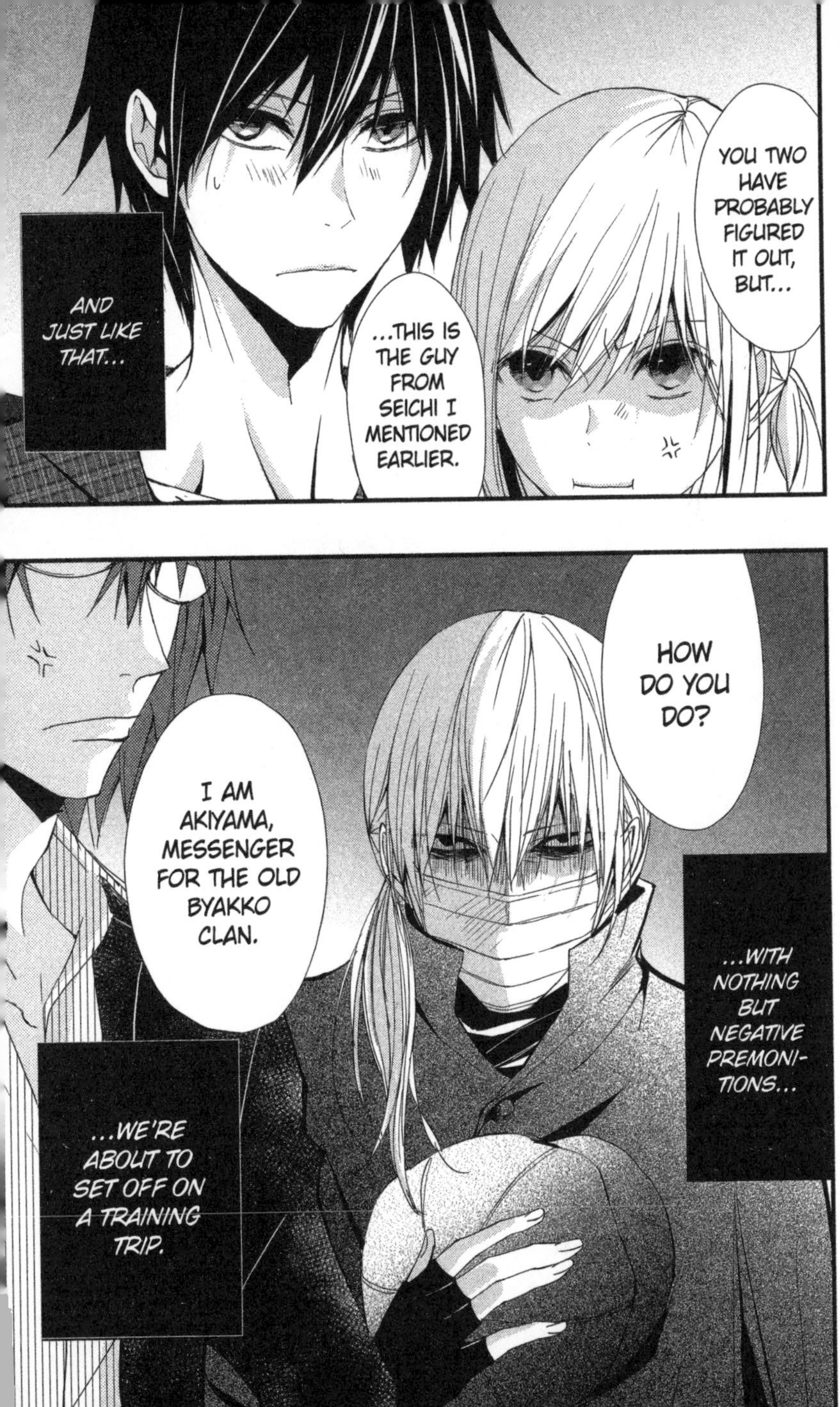
YOU TWO HAVE PROBABLY FIGURED IT OUT, BUT...
...THIS IS THE GUY FROM SEICHI I MENTIONED EARLIER.
AND JUST LIKE THAT...
HOW DO YOU DO?
I AM AKIYAMA, MESSENGER FOR THE OLD BYAKKO CLAN.
...WITH NOTHING BUT NEGATIVE PREMONI-TIONS...
...WE'RE ABOUT TO SET OFF ON A TRAINING TRIP.

MONTHLY BETSUCOMI SALE DATE NOTICE ON TWITTER

CHAPTER 28

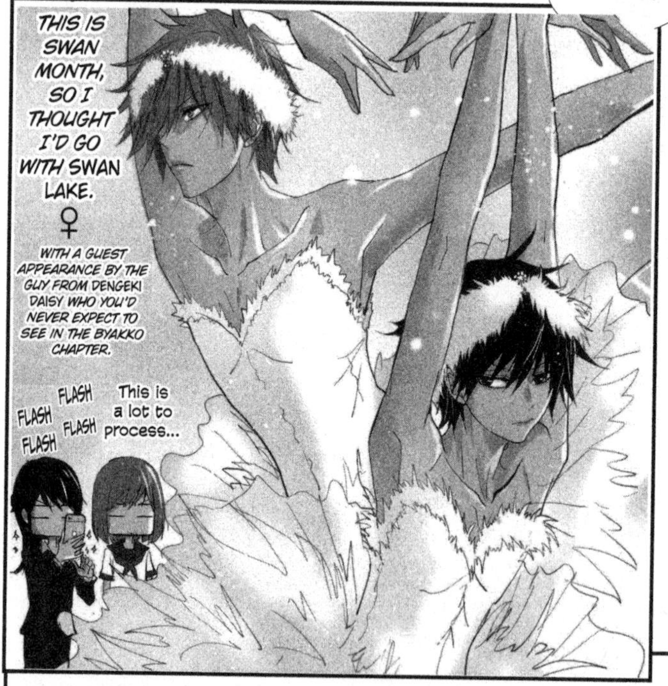
THIS IS SWAN MONTH, SO I THOUGHT I'D GO WITH SWAN LAKE. ♀
WITH A GUEST APPEARANCE BY THE GUY FROM DENGEKI DAISY WHO YOU'D NEVER EXPECT TO SEE IN THE BYAKKO CHAPTER.
FLASH
FLASH
FLASH
FLASH
This is a lot to process...

LET'S SEE... WHAT'S UP IN *QUEEN'S QUALITY* THIS MONTH?
(1) I WONDER IF CHAMELEON PLANT TEA GOES WELL WITH EGGS?
(2) CAN'T HELP BUT SAY YES WHEN ASKED, "IS THIS PERSON OF NOBLE BIRTH?"
(3) BYAKKO MEANS "WHITE TIGER," AND YET THERE'S A BLACK CAT?

THERE ARE SOME NICE HOMEY SCENES, BUT RIGHT AT THE END, CHAPTER 28 TURNS OUT TO BE LIKE A SWAN STORY.

THE GUY DRESSED AS A SWAN WITH KYUTARO AND THE GIRL IN THE BACKGROUND TAKING PICTURES ARE KUROSAKI AND TERU FROM THE SERIES *DENGEKI DAISY*. NO, THEY AREN'T IN THE BYAKKO STORY, BUT I SOMETIMES DRAW THEM FOR MY TWITTER POSTS. HOPE YOU LIKE IT!

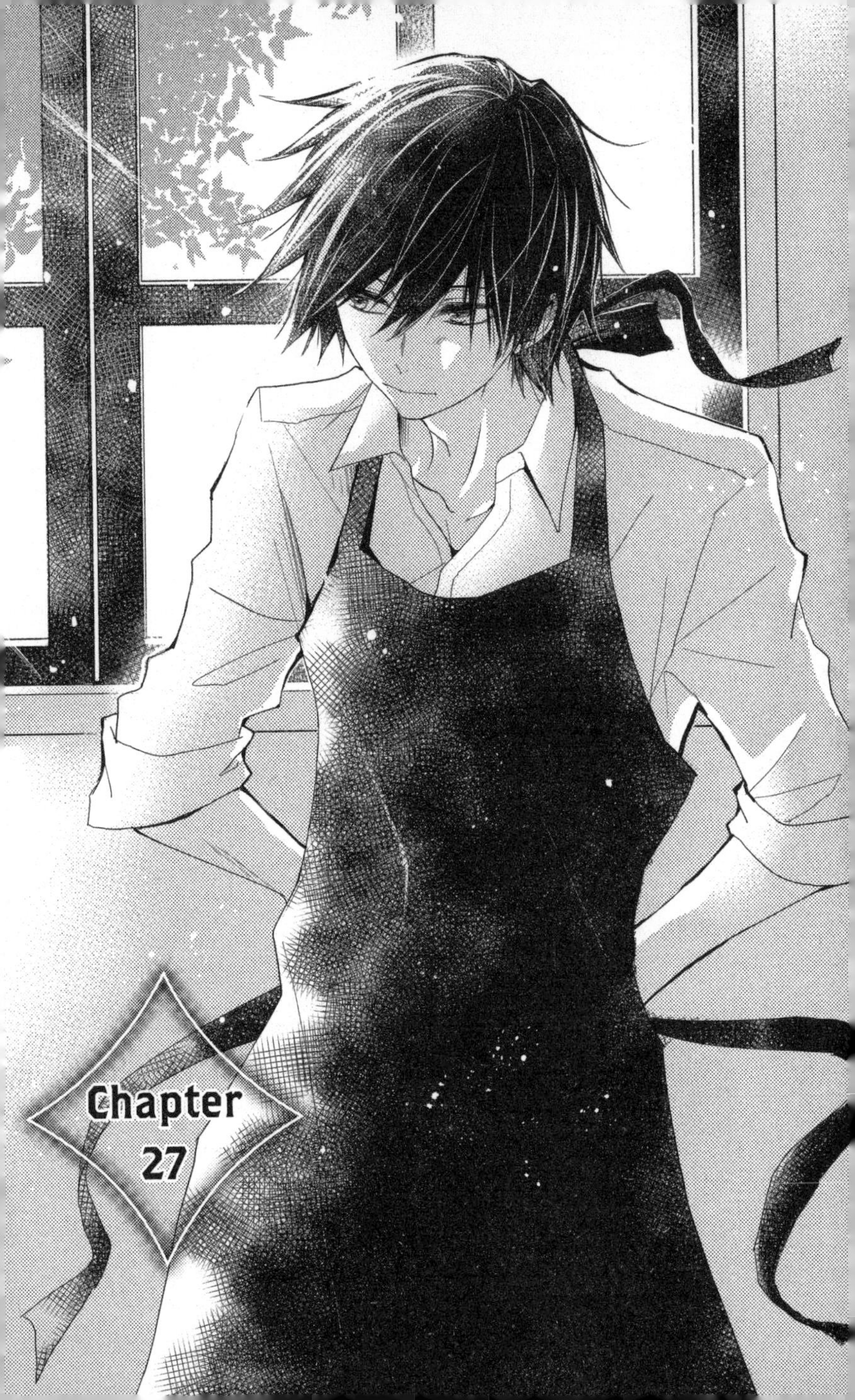
Chapter 27

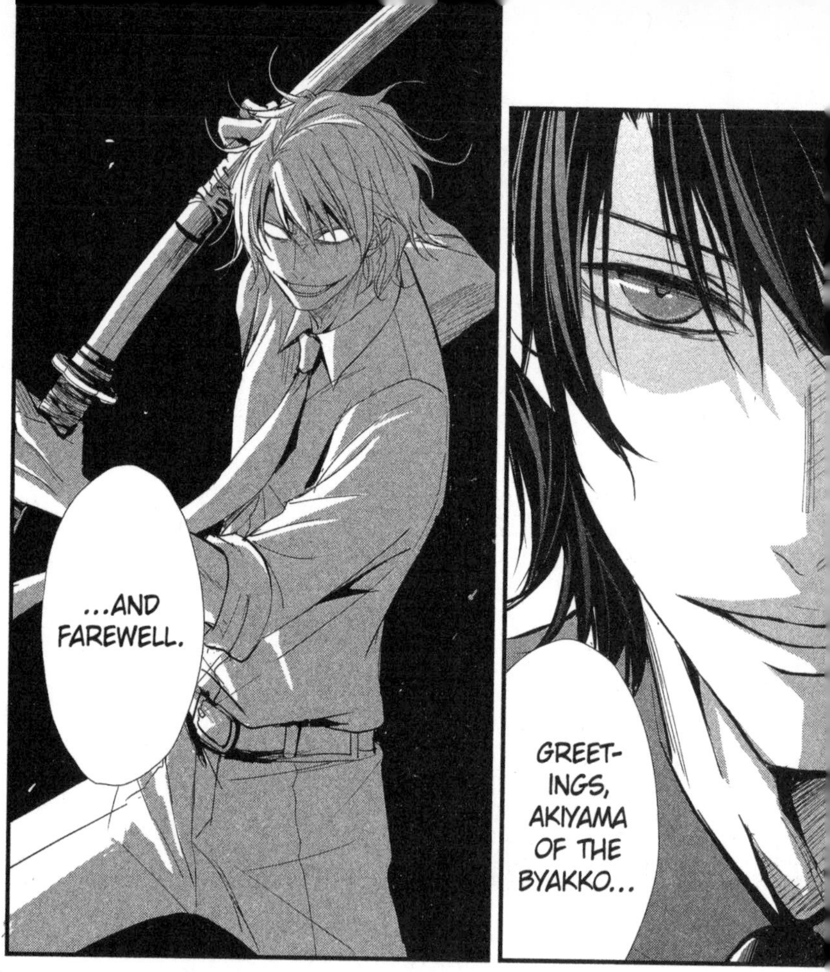
GREET-
INGS,
AKIYAMA
OF THE
BYAKKO...
...AND
FAREWELL.

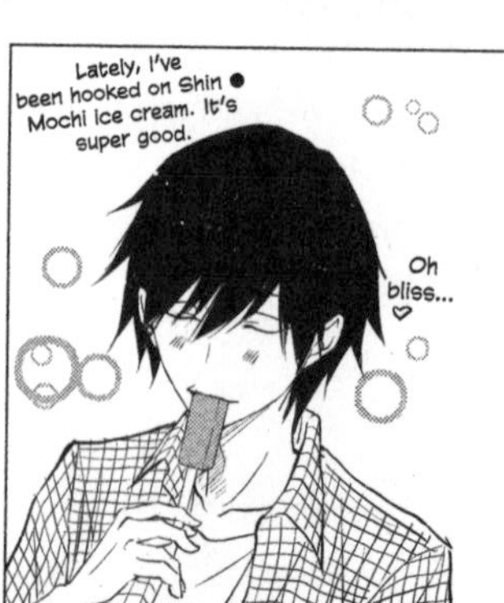
Lately, I've been hooked on Shin ● Mochi ice cream. It's super good.
Oh bliss...

My editor praised me for coming up with the line "I'm an old man. My teeth are sensitive," in chapter 26. My teeth are sensitive too, so the line came up naturally. But since I started using toothpaste with fluoride, they seem to be better.

I'm so excited that there's been a lot of new ice cream lately!

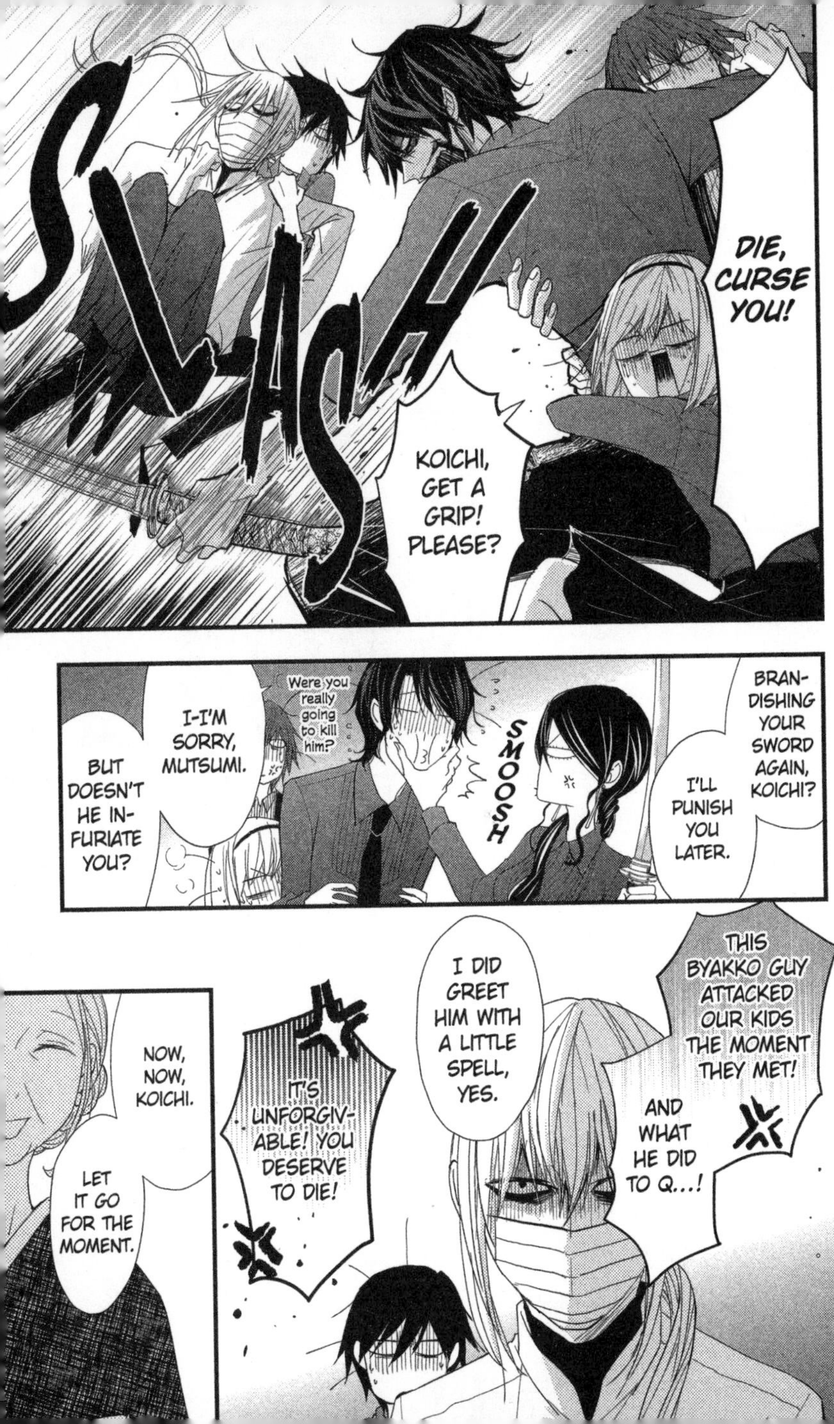
DIE, CURSE YOU!
KOICHI, GET A GRIP! PLEASE?
SLASH
BRAN-DISHING YOUR SWORD AGAIN, KOICHI?
I'LL PUNISH YOU LATER.
SMOOSH
Were you really going to kill him?
I-I'M SORRY, MUTSUMI.
BUT DOESN'T HE IN-FURIATE YOU?
THIS BYAKKO GUY ATTACKED OUR KIDS THE MOMENT THEY MET!
AND WHAT HE DID TO Q...!
I DID GREET HIM WITH A LITTLE SPELL, YES.
IT'S UNFORGIV-ABLE! YOU DESERVE TO DIE!
NOW, NOW, KOICHI.
LET IT GO FOR THE MOMENT.

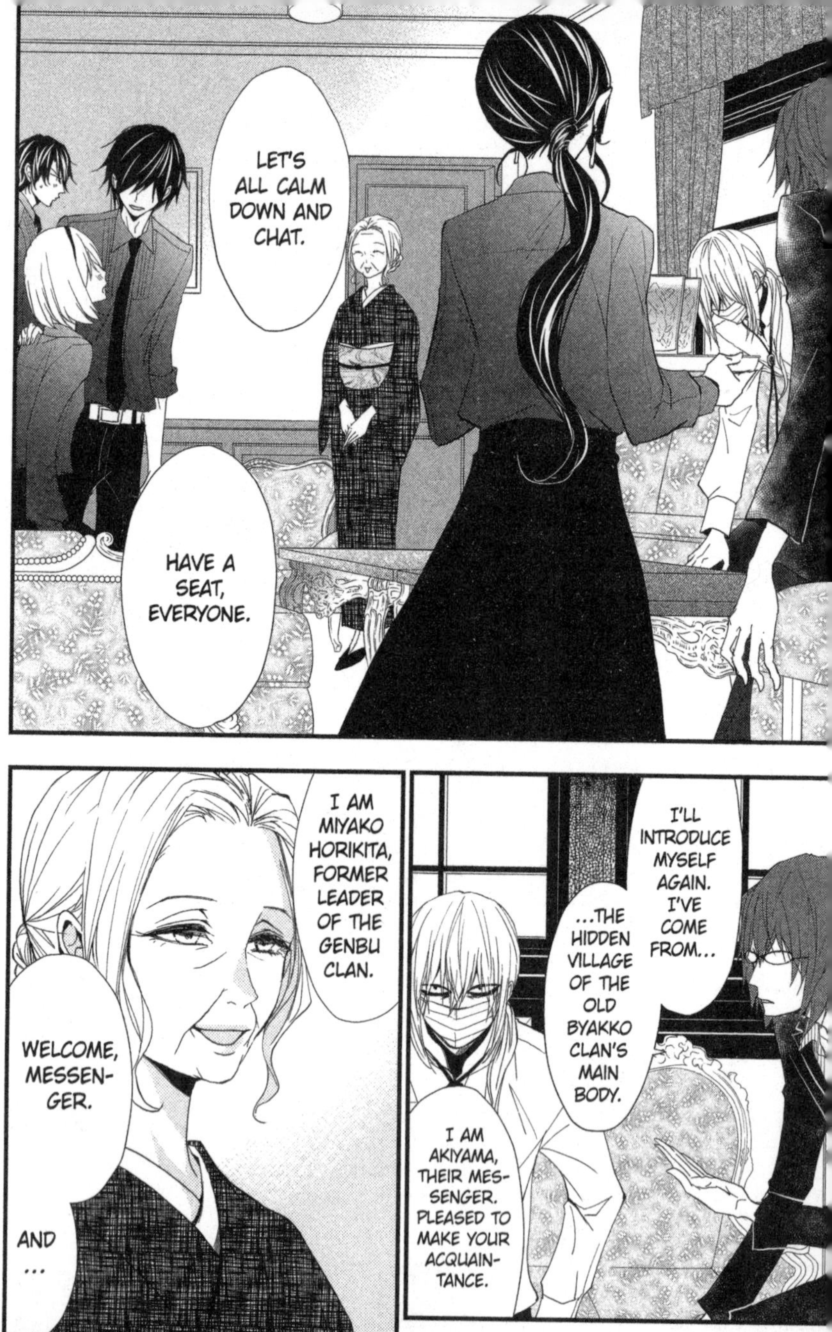

LET'S ALL CALM DOWN AND CHAT.
HAVE A SEAT, EVERYONE.
I'LL INTRODUCE MYSELF AGAIN. I'VE COME FROM...
...THE HIDDEN VILLAGE OF THE OLD BYAKKO CLAN'S MAIN BODY.
I AM AKIYAMA, THEIR MES-SENGER. PLEASED TO MAKE YOUR ACQUAIN-TANCE.
I AM MIYAKO HORIKITA, FORMER LEADER OF THE GENBU CLAN.
WELCOME, MESSEN-GER.
AND ...

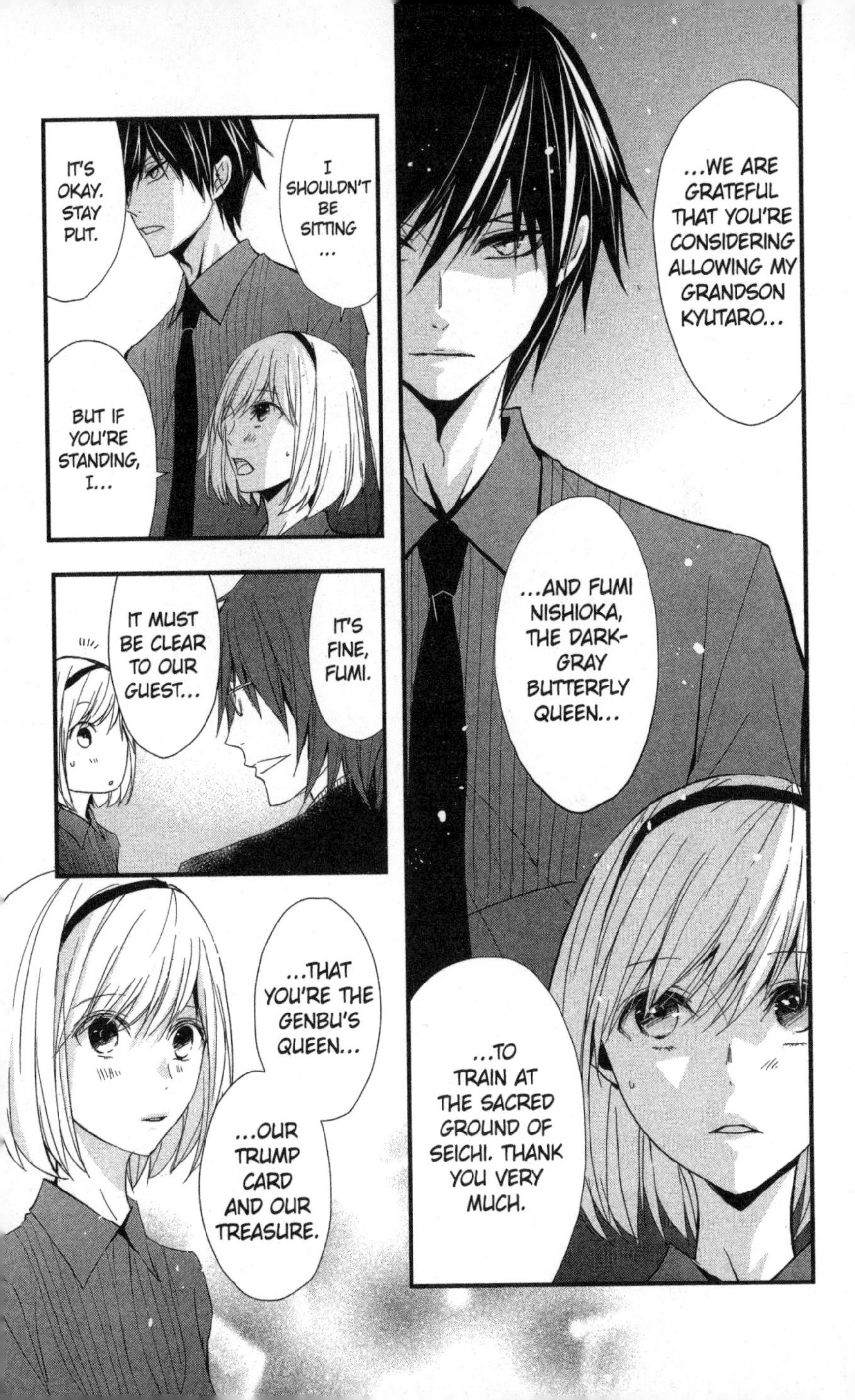
...WE ARE GRATEFUL THAT YOU'RE CONSIDERING ALLOWING MY GRANDSON KYUTARO...
...AND FUMI NISHIOKA, THE DARK-GRAY BUTTERFLY QUEEN...
...TO TRAIN AT THE SACRED GROUND OF SEICHI. THANK YOU VERY MUCH.
I SHOULDN'T BE SITTING ...
IT'S OKAY. STAY PUT.
BUT IF YOU'RE STANDING, I...
IT'S FINE, FUMI.
IT MUST BE CLEAR TO OUR GUEST...
...THAT YOU'RE THE GENBU'S QUEEN...
...OUR TRUMP CARD AND OUR TREASURE.

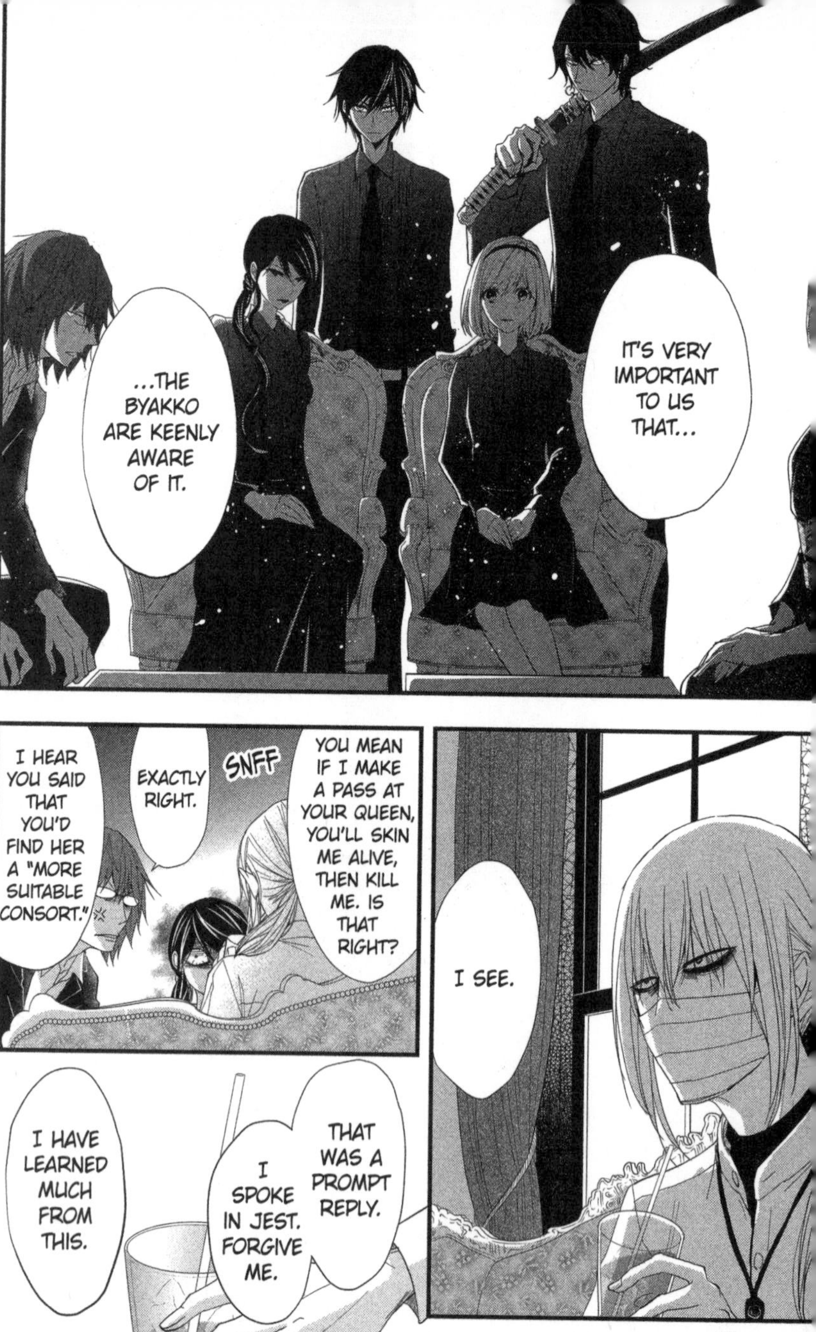
IT'S VERY IMPORTANT TO US THAT...
...THE BYAKKO ARE KEENLY AWARE OF IT.
I SEE.
YOU MEAN IF I MAKE A PASS AT YOUR QUEEN, YOU'LL SKIN ME ALIVE, THEN KILL ME. IS THAT RIGHT?
SNFF
EXACTLY RIGHT.
I HEAR YOU SAID THAT YOU'D FIND HER A "MORE SUITABLE CONSORT."
THAT WAS A PROMPT REPLY.
I SPOKE IN JEST. FORGIVE ME.
I HAVE LEARNED MUCH FROM THIS.

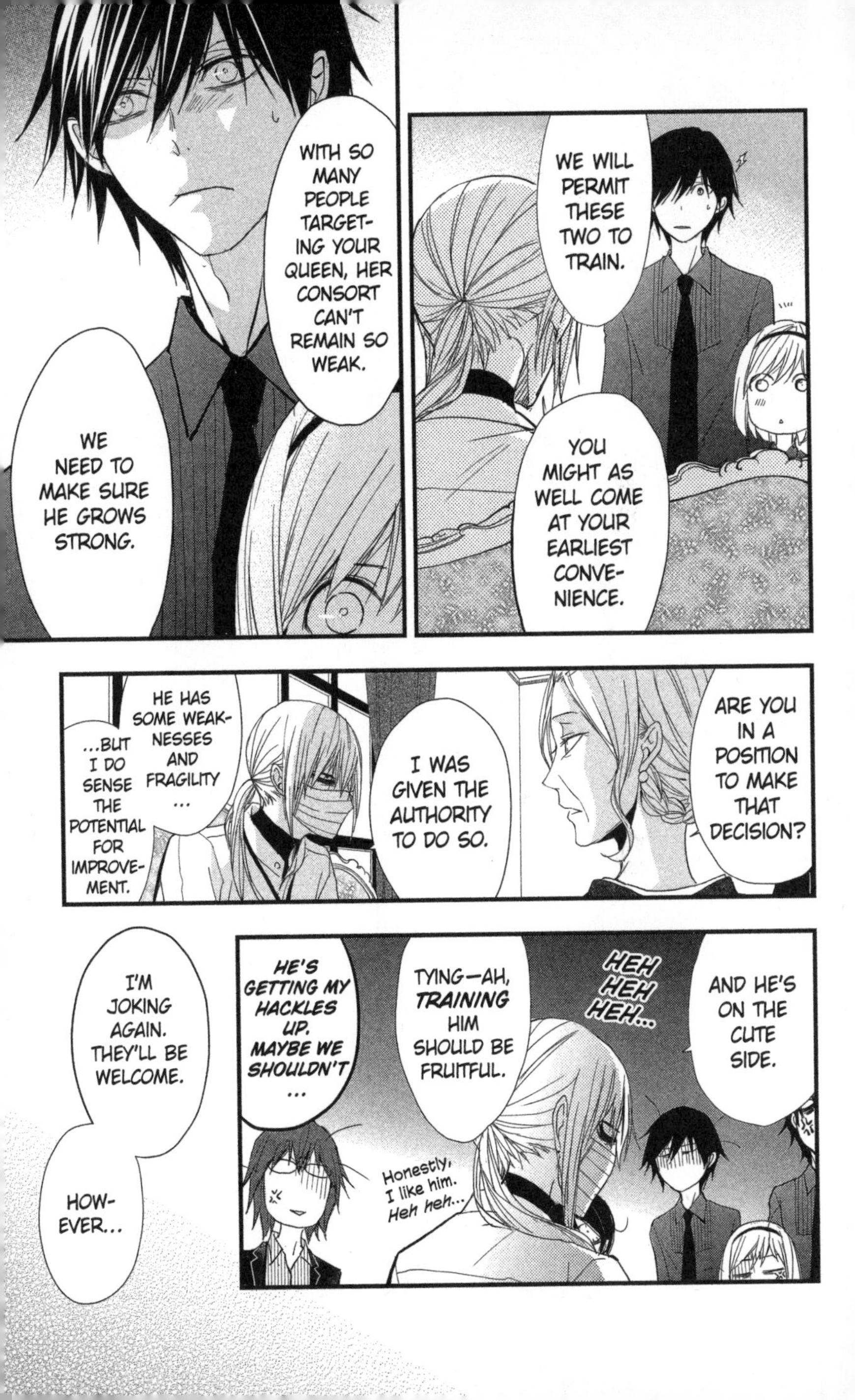
WE WILL PERMIT THESE TWO TO TRAIN.
YOU MIGHT AS WELL COME AT YOUR EARLIEST CONVENIENCE.
WITH SO MANY PEOPLE TARGETING YOUR QUEEN, HER CONSORT CAN'T REMAIN SO WEAK.
WE NEED TO MAKE SURE HE GROWS STRONG.
ARE YOU IN A POSITION TO MAKE THAT DECISION?
I WAS GIVEN THE AUTHORITY TO DO SO.
HE HAS SOME WEAKNESSES AND FRAGILITY...
...BUT I DO SENSE THE POTENTIAL FOR IMPROVEMENT.
AND HE'S ON THE CUTE SIDE.
HEH HEH HEH...
TYING—AH, *TRAINING* HIM SHOULD BE FRUITFUL.
HE'S GETTING MY HACKLES UP. MAYBE WE SHOULDN'T...
Honestly, I like him. Heh heh...
I'M JOKING AGAIN. THEY'LL BE WELCOME.
HOWEVER...

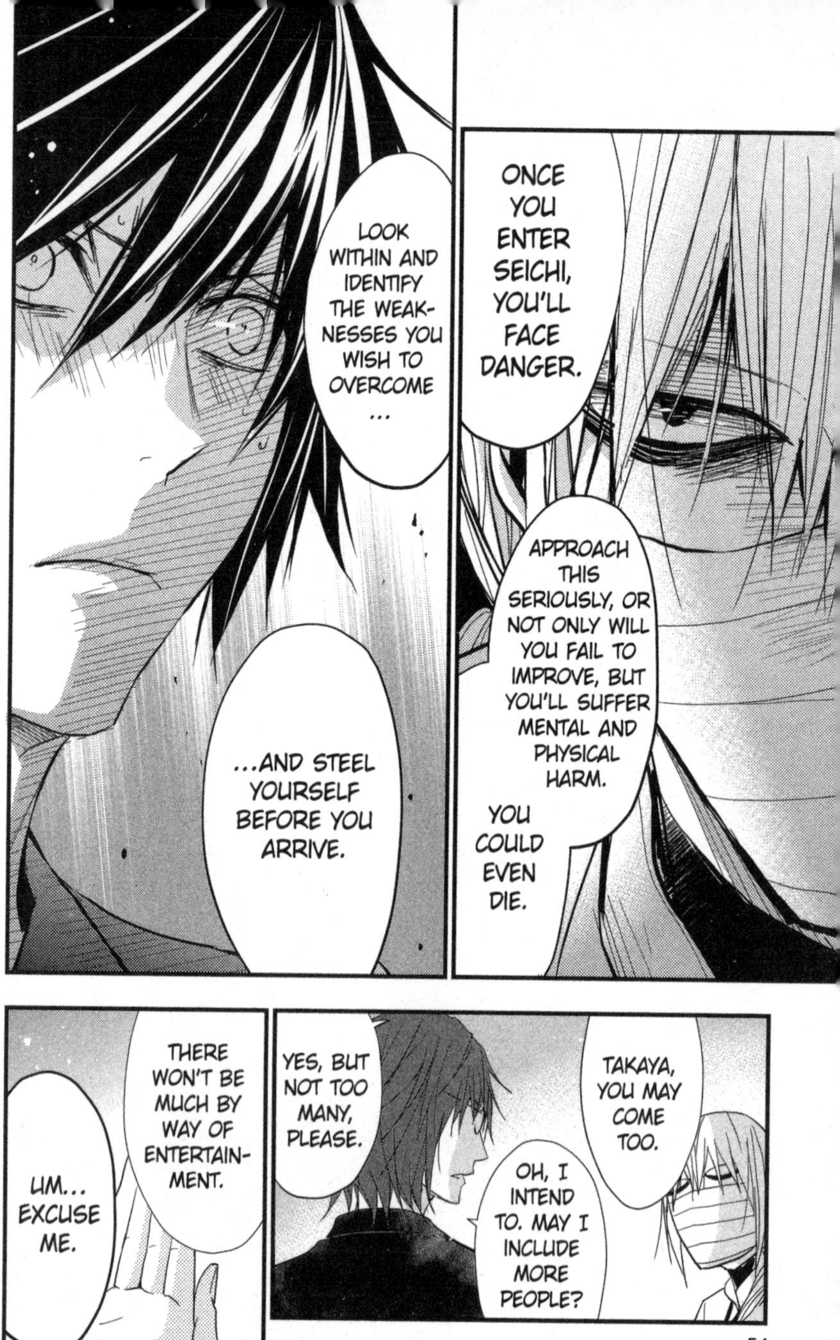
ONCE YOU ENTER SEICHI, YOU'LL FACE DANGER.
APPROACH THIS SERIOUSLY, OR NOT ONLY WILL YOU FAIL TO IMPROVE, BUT YOU'LL SUFFER MENTAL AND PHYSICAL HARM.
YOU COULD EVEN DIE.
LOOK WITHIN AND IDENTIFY THE WEAK-NESSES YOU WISH TO OVERCOME ...
...AND STEEL YOURSELF BEFORE YOU ARRIVE.
TAKAYA, YOU MAY COME TOO.
OH, I INTEND TO. MAY I INCLUDE MORE PEOPLE?
YES, BUT NOT TOO MANY, PLEASE.
THERE WON'T BE MUCH BY WAY OF ENTERTAIN-MENT.
UM... EXCUSE ME.

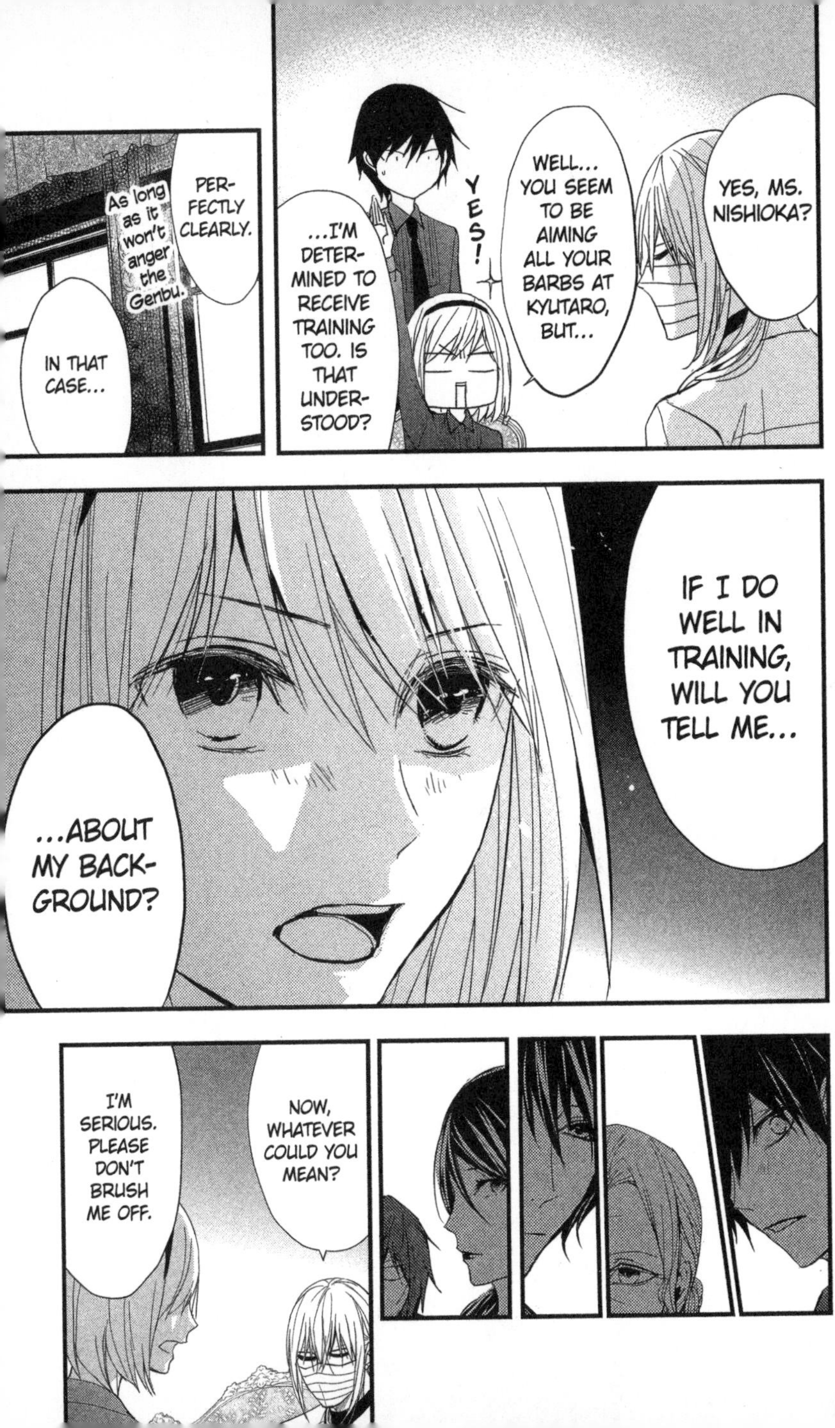
YES, MS. NISHIOKA?
WELL... YOU SEEM TO BE AIMING ALL YOUR BARBS AT KYUTARO, BUT...
YES!
...I'M DETERMINED TO RECEIVE TRAINING TOO. IS THAT UNDERSTOOD?
PERFECTLY CLEARLY.
As long as it won't anger the Genbu.
IN THAT CASE...
IF I DO WELL IN TRAINING, WILL YOU TELL ME...
...ABOUT MY BACKGROUND?
NOW, WHATEVER COULD YOU MEAN?
I'M SERIOUS. PLEASE DON'T BRUSH ME OFF.

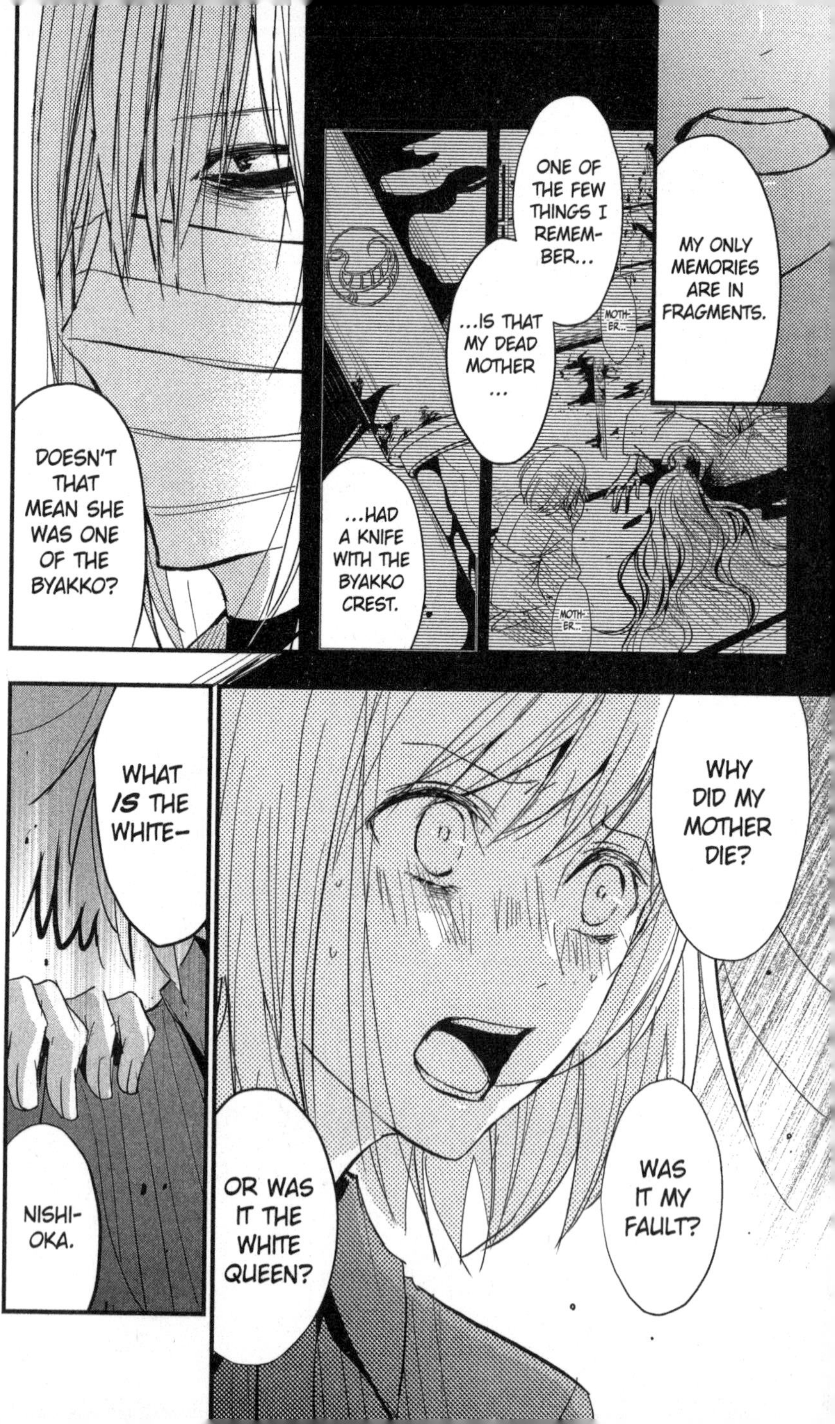
MY ONLY MEMORIES ARE IN FRAGMENTS.
ONE OF THE FEW THINGS I REMEMBER...
...IS THAT MY DEAD MOTHER...
MOTHER...
...HAD A KNIFE WITH THE BYAKKO CREST.
MOTHER...
DOESN'T THAT MEAN SHE WAS ONE OF THE BYAKKO?
WHY DID MY MOTHER DIE?
WAS IT MY FAULT?
OR WAS IT THE WHITE QUEEN?
WHAT *IS* THE WHITE-
NISHIOKA.

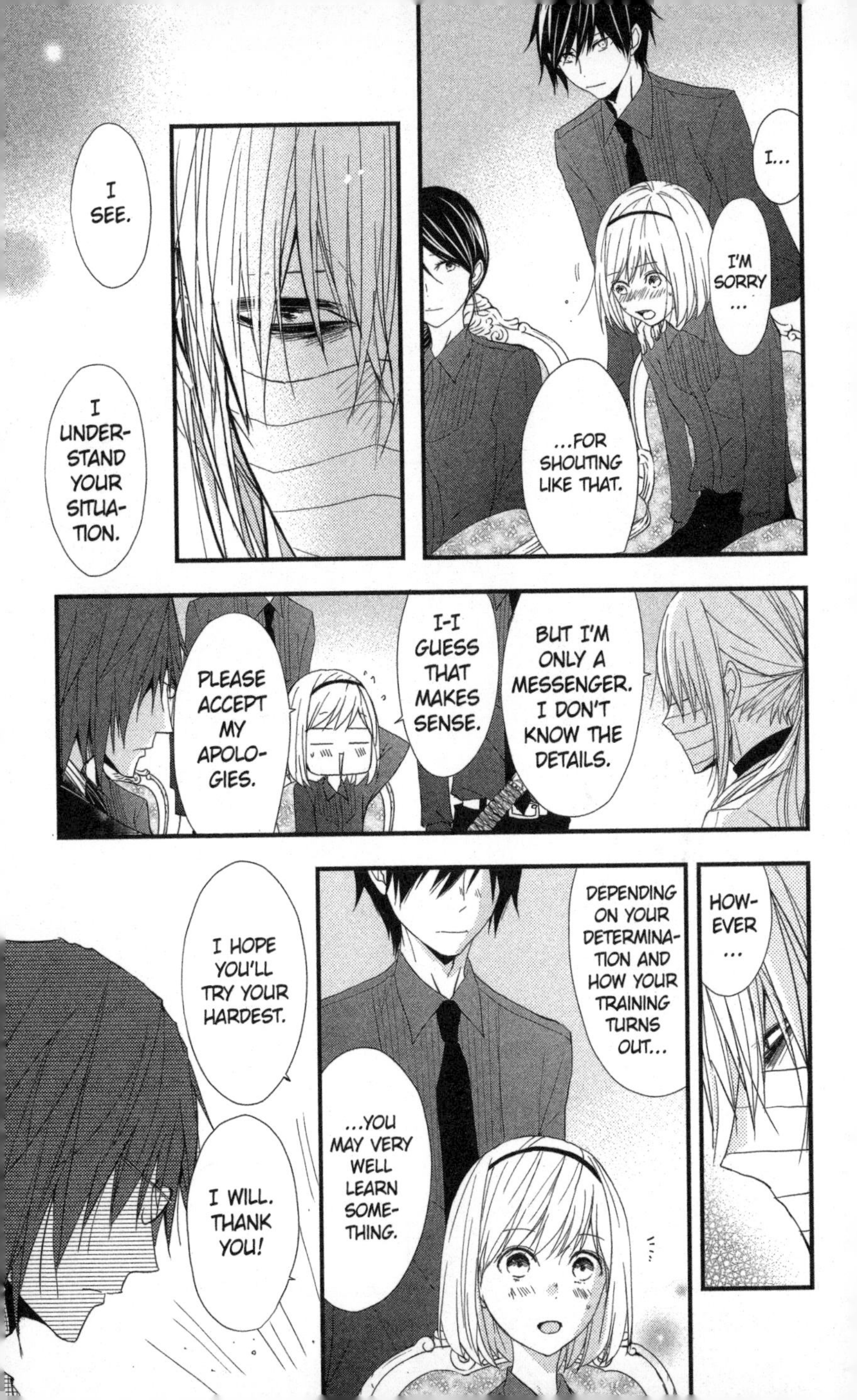
I...
I'M SORRY...
...FOR SHOUTING LIKE THAT.
I SEE.
I UNDERSTAND YOUR SITUATION.
BUT I'M ONLY A MESSENGER. I DON'T KNOW THE DETAILS.
I-I GUESS THAT MAKES SENSE.
PLEASE ACCEPT MY APOLOGIES.
HOW-EVER...
DEPENDING ON YOUR DETERMINATION AND HOW YOUR TRAINING TURNS OUT...
...YOU MAY VERY WELL LEARN SOMETHING.
I HOPE YOU'LL TRY YOUR HARDEST.
I WILL. THANK YOU!

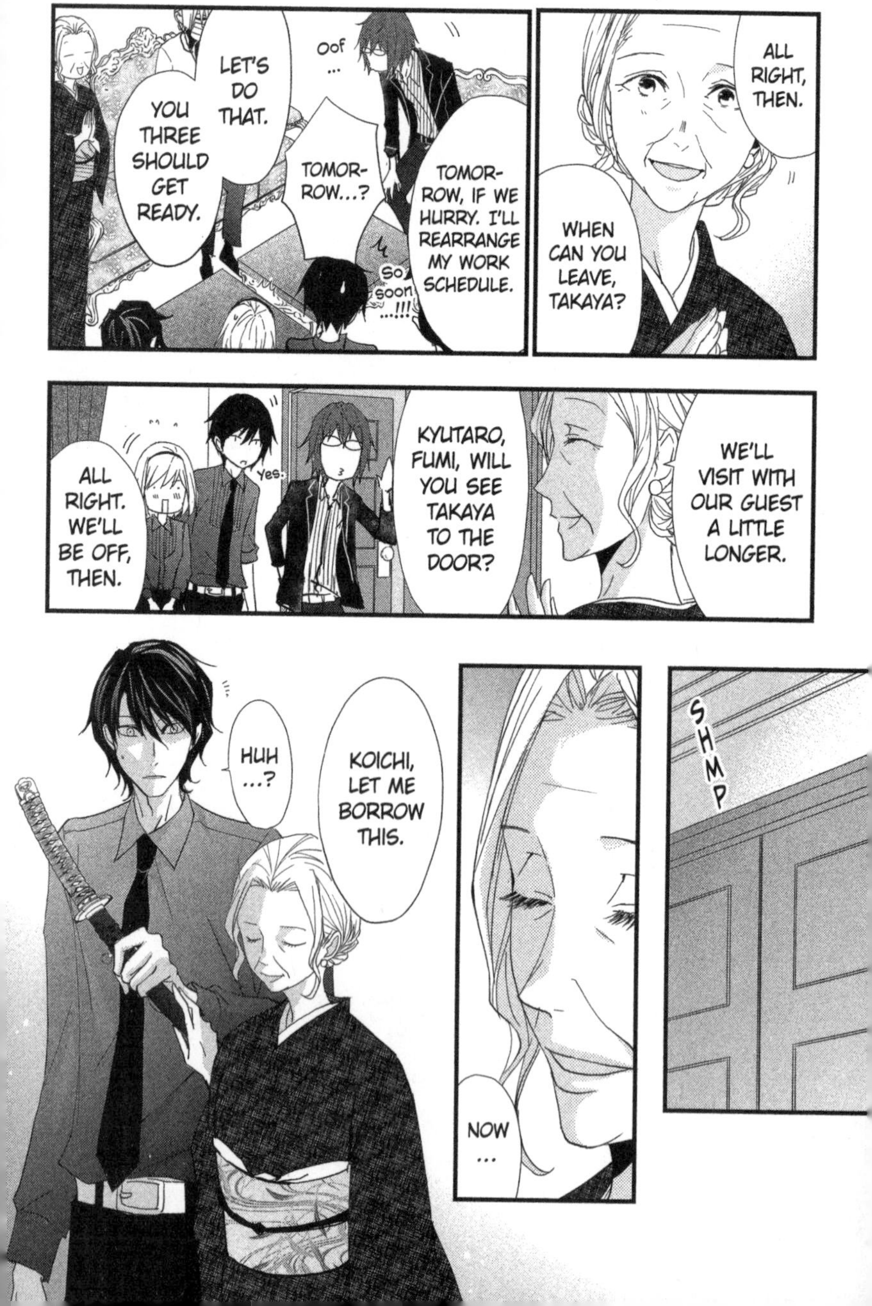
ALL RIGHT, THEN.
WHEN CAN YOU LEAVE, TAKAYA?
TOMORROW, IF WE HURRY. I'LL REARRANGE MY WORK SCHEDULE.
Oof ...
TOMORROW...?
So soon ...!!!
LET'S DO THAT.
YOU THREE SHOULD GET READY.
WE'LL VISIT WITH OUR GUEST A LITTLE LONGER.
KYUTARO, FUMI, WILL YOU SEE TAKAYA TO THE DOOR?
Yes.
ALL RIGHT. WE'LL BE OFF, THEN.
SHMP
NOW ...
KOICHI, LET ME BORROW THIS.
HUH ...?

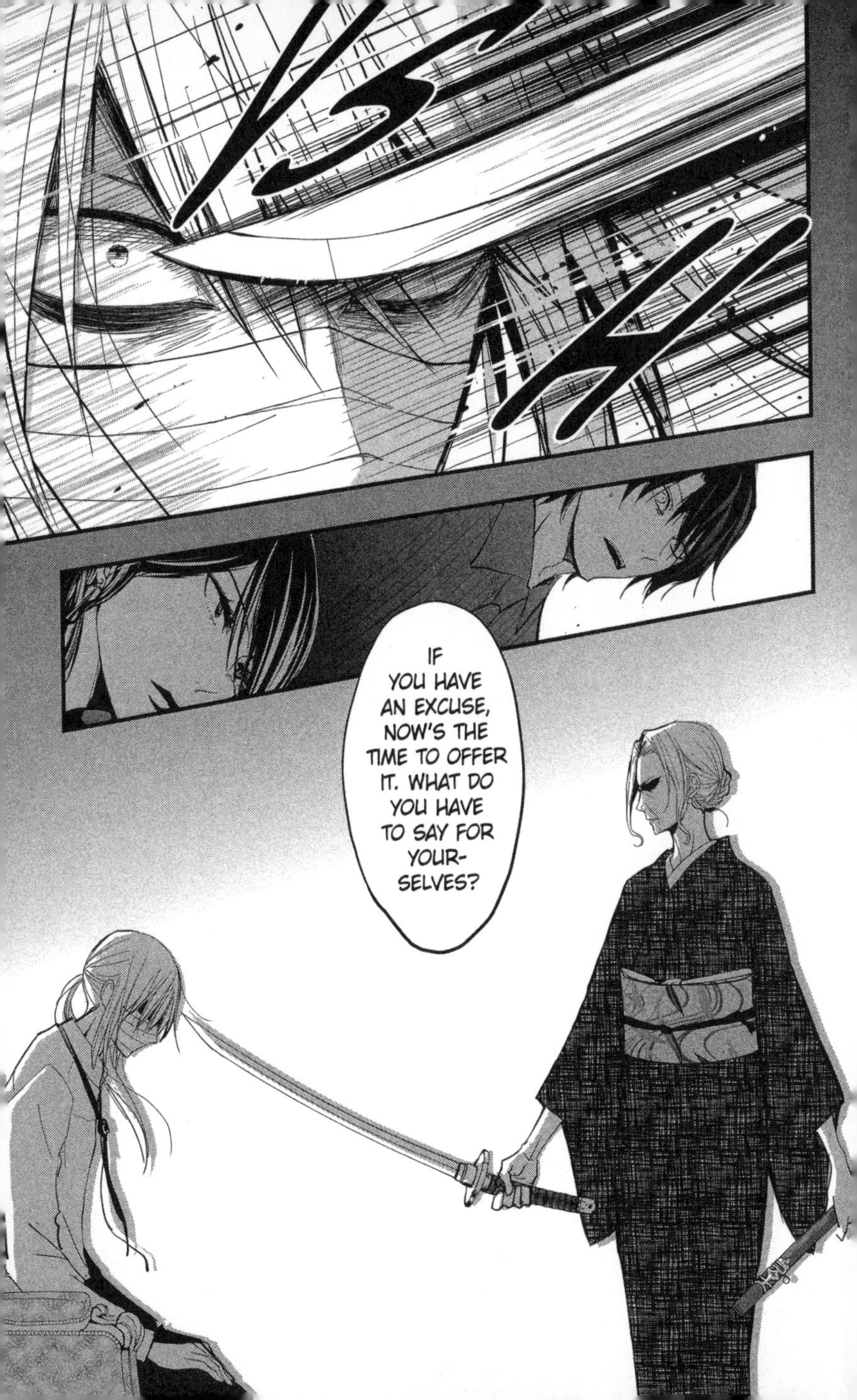
VSSH
IF YOU HAVE AN EXCUSE, NOW'S THE TIME TO OFFER IT. WHAT DO YOU HAVE TO SAY FOR YOUR-SELVES?

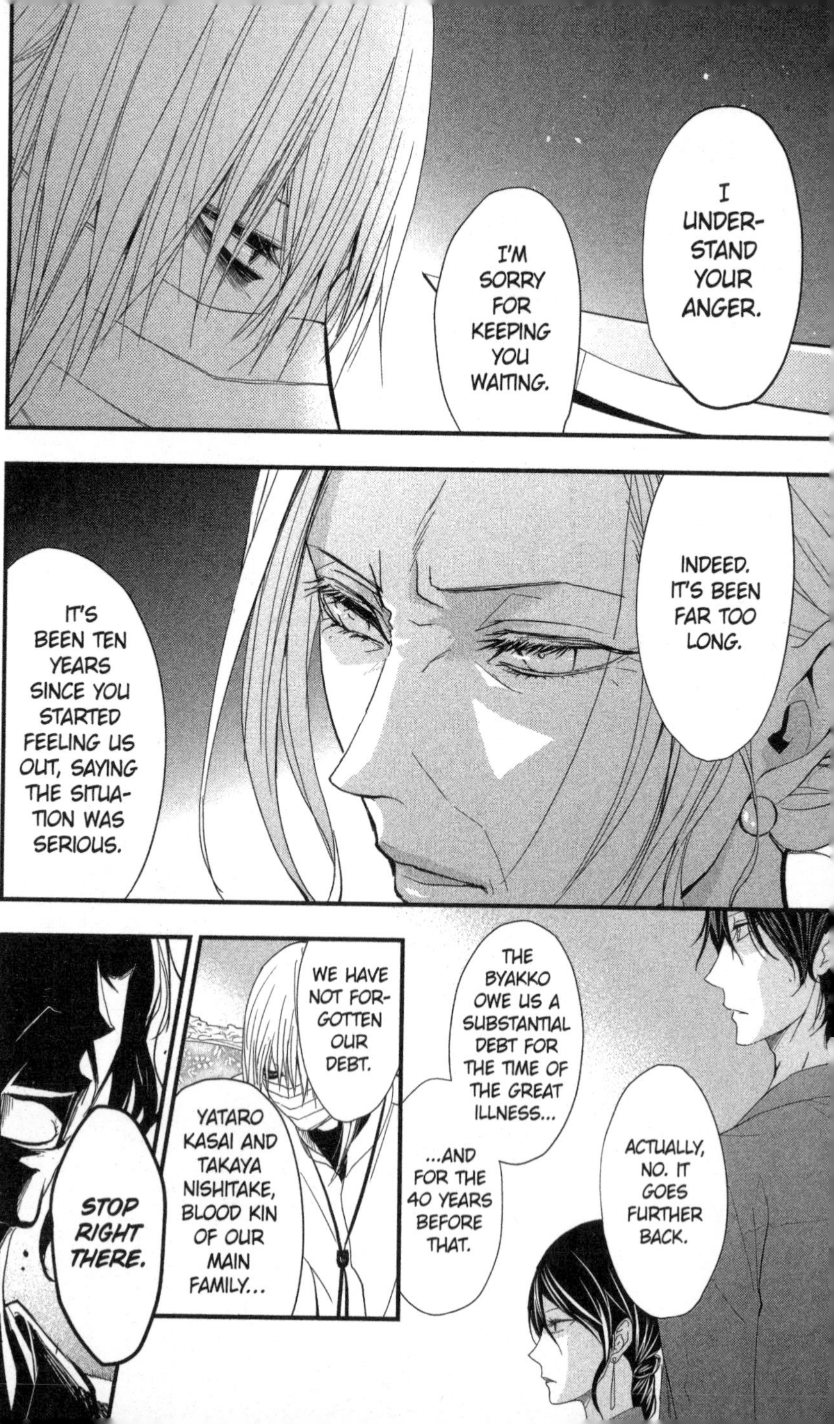
I UNDER-STAND YOUR ANGER.
I'M SORRY FOR KEEPING YOU WAITING.
INDEED. IT'S BEEN FAR TOO LONG.
IT'S BEEN TEN YEARS SINCE YOU STARTED FEELING US OUT, SAYING THE SITUA-TION WAS SERIOUS.
THE BYAKKO OWE US A SUBSTANTIAL DEBT FOR THE TIME OF THE GREAT ILLNESS...
ACTUALLY, NO. IT GOES FURTHER BACK.
...AND FOR THE 40 YEARS BEFORE THAT.
WE HAVE NOT FOR-GOTTEN OUR DEBT.
YATARO KASAI AND TAKAYA NISHITAKE, BLOOD KIN OF OUR MAIN FAMILY...
STOP RIGHT THERE.

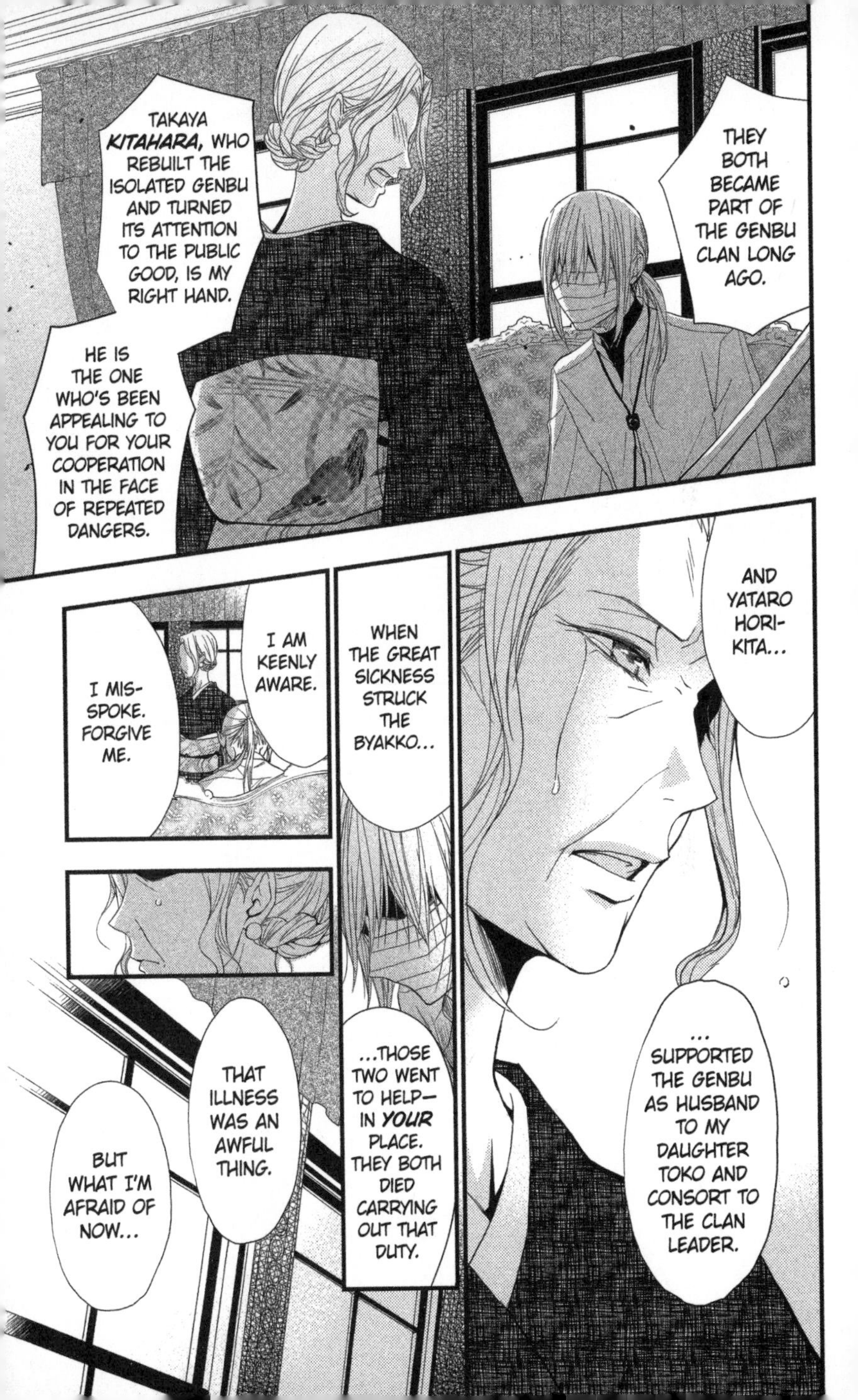
THEY BOTH BECAME PART OF THE GENBU CLAN LONG AGO.
TAKAYA **KITAHARA**, WHO REBUILT THE ISOLATED GENBU AND TURNED ITS ATTENTION TO THE PUBLIC GOOD, IS MY RIGHT HAND.
HE IS THE ONE WHO'S BEEN APPEALING TO YOU FOR YOUR COOPERATION IN THE FACE OF REPEATED DANGERS.
AND YATARO HORI-KITA...
...SUPPORTED THE GENBU AS HUSBAND TO MY DAUGHTER TOKO AND CONSORT TO THE CLAN LEADER.
WHEN THE GREAT SICKNESS STRUCK THE BYAKKO...
...THOSE TWO WENT TO HELP—IN **YOUR** PLACE. THEY BOTH DIED CARRYING OUT THAT DUTY.
I AM KEENLY AWARE.
I MIS-SPOKE. FORGIVE ME.
THAT ILLNESS WAS AN AWFUL THING.
BUT WHAT I'M AFRAID OF NOW...

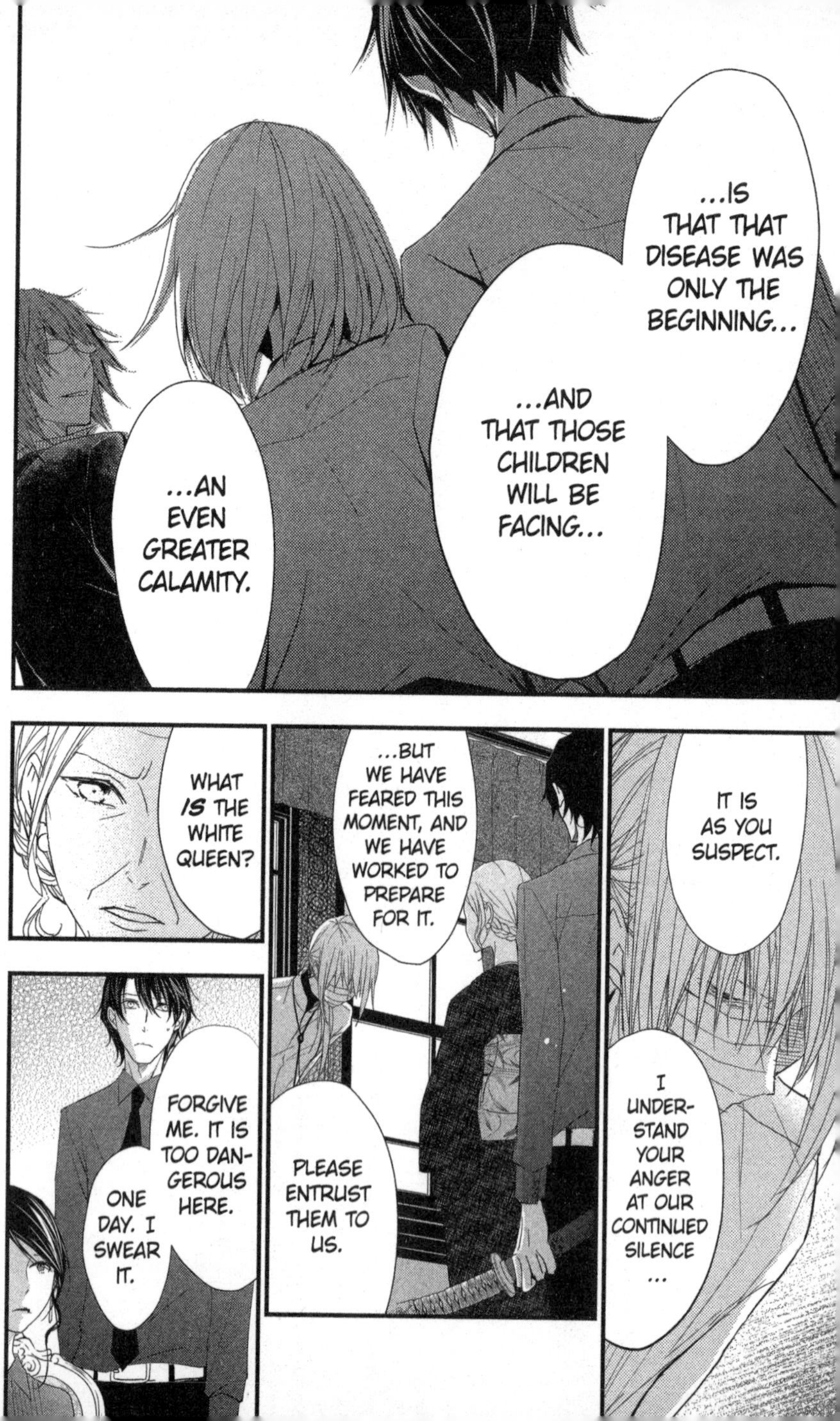
...IS THAT THAT DISEASE WAS ONLY THE BEGINNING...
...AND THAT THOSE CHILDREN WILL BE FACING...
...AN EVEN GREATER CALAMITY.
IT IS AS YOU SUSPECT.
I UNDERSTAND YOUR ANGER AT OUR CONTINUED SILENCE...
...BUT WE HAVE FEARED THIS MOMENT, AND WE HAVE WORKED TO PREPARE FOR IT.
PLEASE ENTRUST THEM TO US.
WHAT *IS* THE WHITE QUEEN?
FORGIVE ME. IT IS TOO DANGEROUS HERE.
ONE DAY. I SWEAR IT.

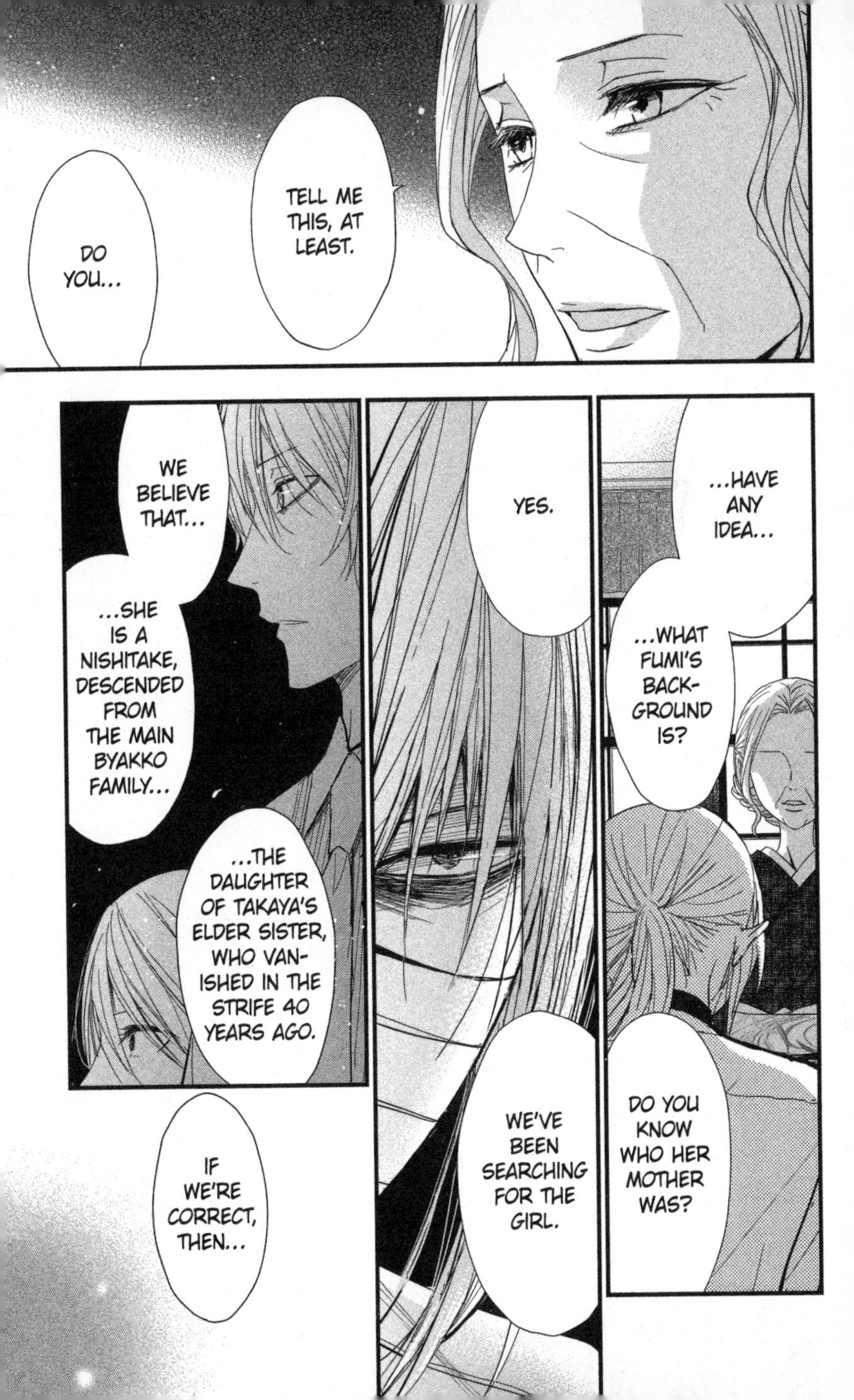
TELL ME THIS, AT LEAST.
DO YOU...
...HAVE ANY IDEA...
...WHAT FUMI'S BACKGROUND IS?
DO YOU KNOW WHO HER MOTHER WAS?
YES.
WE'VE BEEN SEARCHING FOR THE GIRL.
WE BELIEVE THAT...
...SHE IS A NISHITAKE, DESCENDED FROM THE MAIN BYAKKO FAMILY...
...THE DAUGHTER OF TAKAYA'S ELDER SISTER, WHO VANISHED IN THE STRIFE 40 YEARS AGO.
IF WE'RE CORRECT, THEN...

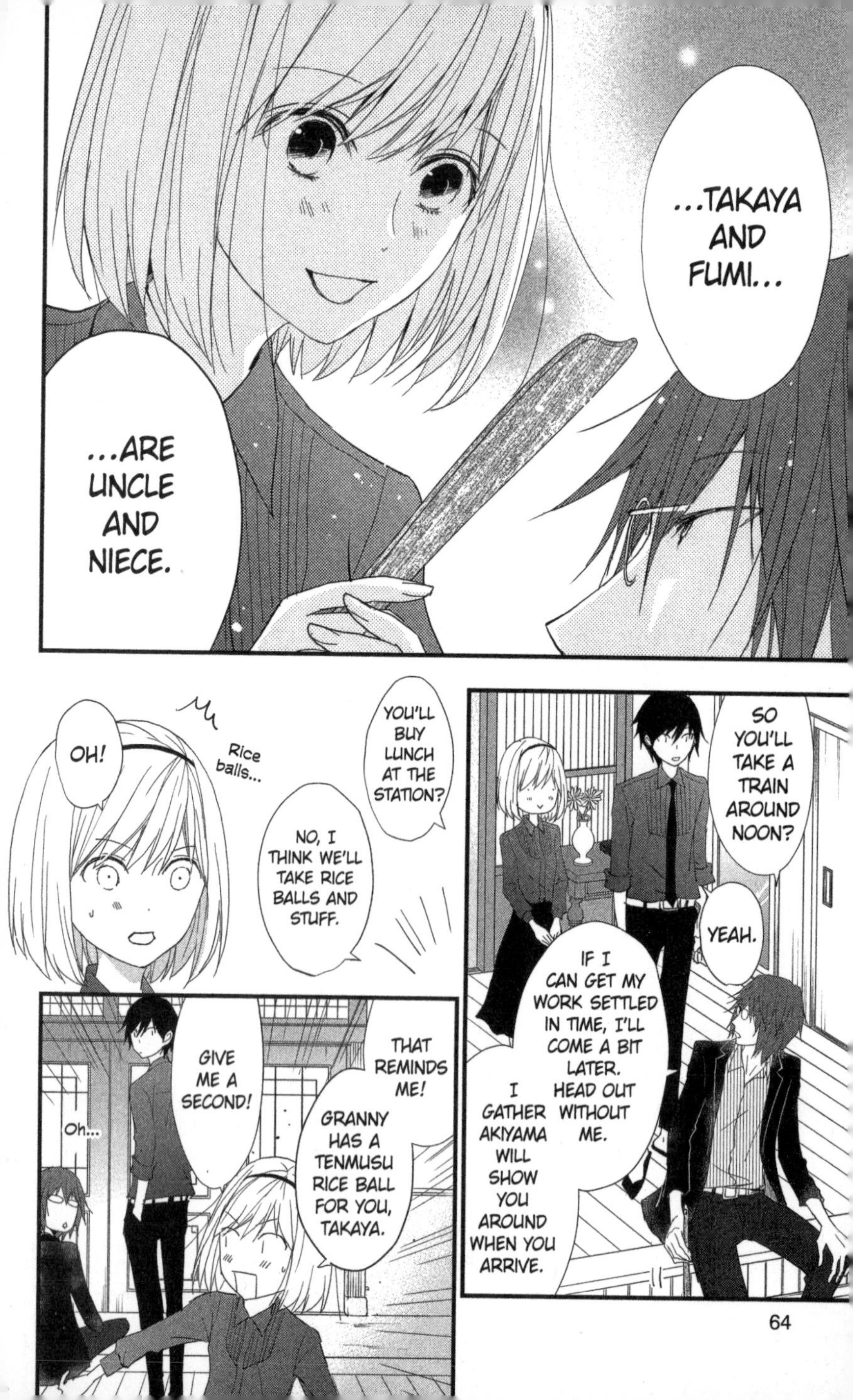
...TAKAYA AND FUMI...
...ARE UNCLE AND NIECE.
SO YOU'LL TAKE A TRAIN AROUND NOON?
YEAH.
IF I CAN GET MY WORK SETTLED IN TIME, I'LL COME A BIT LATER. HEAD OUT WITHOUT ME.
I GATHER AKIYAMA WILL SHOW YOU AROUND WHEN YOU ARRIVE.
YOU'LL BUY LUNCH AT THE STATION?
NO, I THINK WE'LL TAKE RICE BALLS AND STUFF.
OH!
Rice balls...
THAT REMINDS ME!
GRANNY HAS A TENMUSU RICE BALL FOR YOU, TAKAYA.
GIVE ME A SECOND!
Oh...

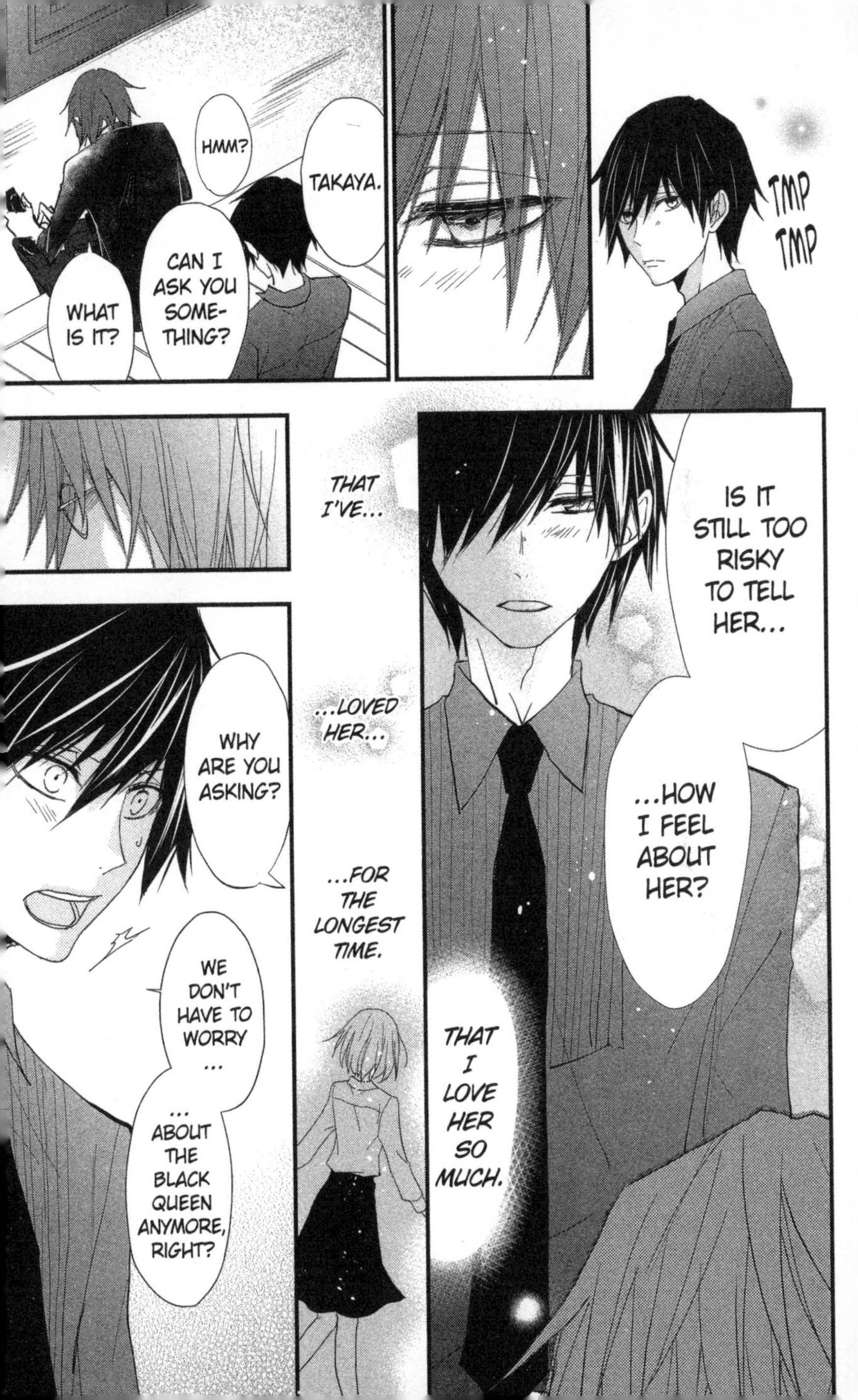
TMP TMP
TAKAYA.
HMM?
CAN I ASK YOU SOME-THING?
WHAT IS IT?
IS IT STILL TOO RISKY TO TELL HER...
...HOW I FEEL ABOUT HER?
THAT I'VE...
...LOVED HER...
...FOR THE LONGEST TIME.
THAT I LOVE HER SO MUCH.
WHY ARE YOU ASKING?
WE DON'T HAVE TO WORRY...
...ABOUT THE BLACK QUEEN ANYMORE, RIGHT?

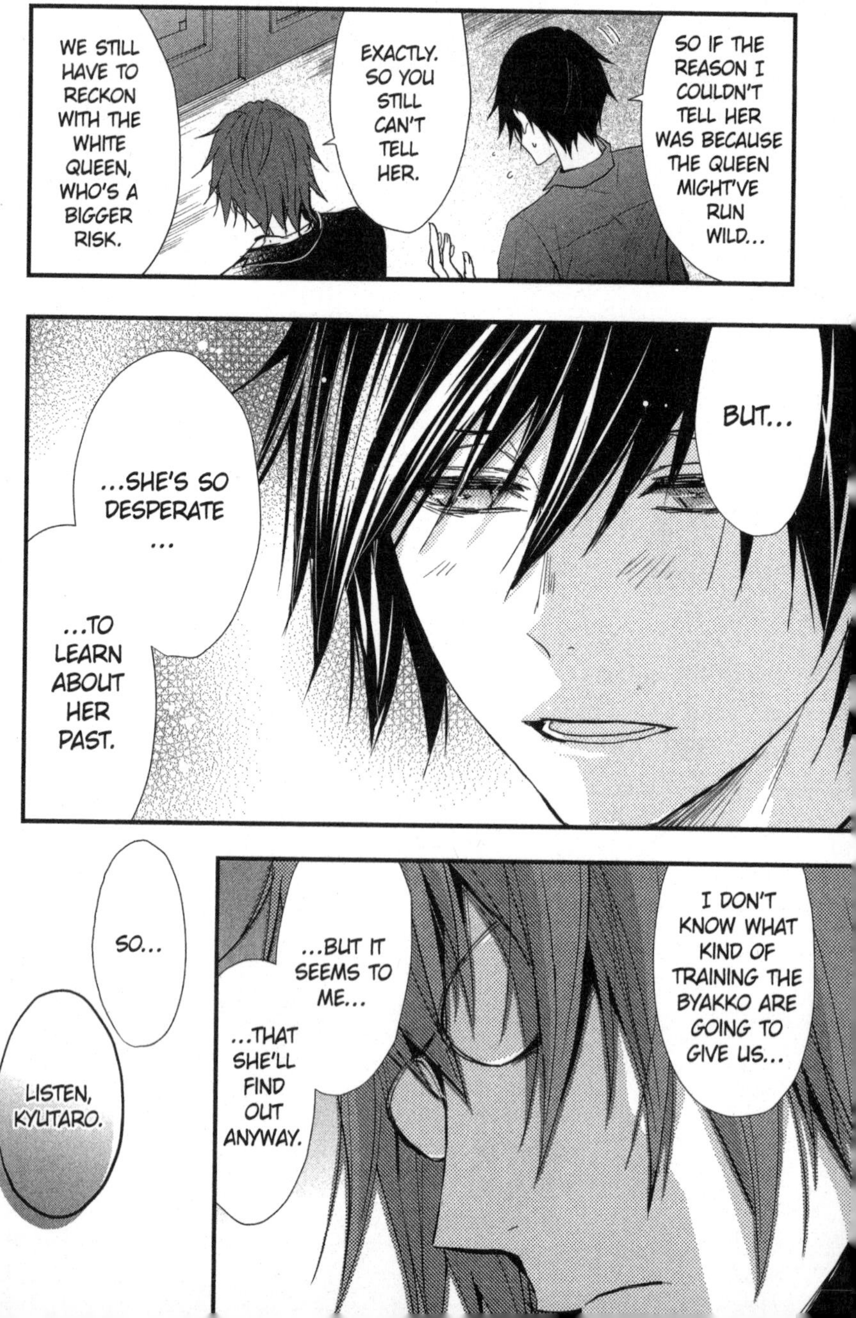
SO IF THE REASON I COULDN'T TELL HER WAS BECAUSE THE QUEEN MIGHT'VE RUN WILD...
EXACTLY. SO YOU STILL CAN'T TELL HER.
WE STILL HAVE TO RECKON WITH THE WHITE QUEEN, WHO'S A BIGGER RISK.
BUT...
...SHE'S SO DESPERATE...
...TO LEARN ABOUT HER PAST.
I DON'T KNOW WHAT KIND OF TRAINING THE BYAKKO ARE GOING TO GIVE US...
...BUT IT SEEMS TO ME...
...THAT SHE'LL FIND OUT ANYWAY.
SO...
LISTEN, KYUTARO.

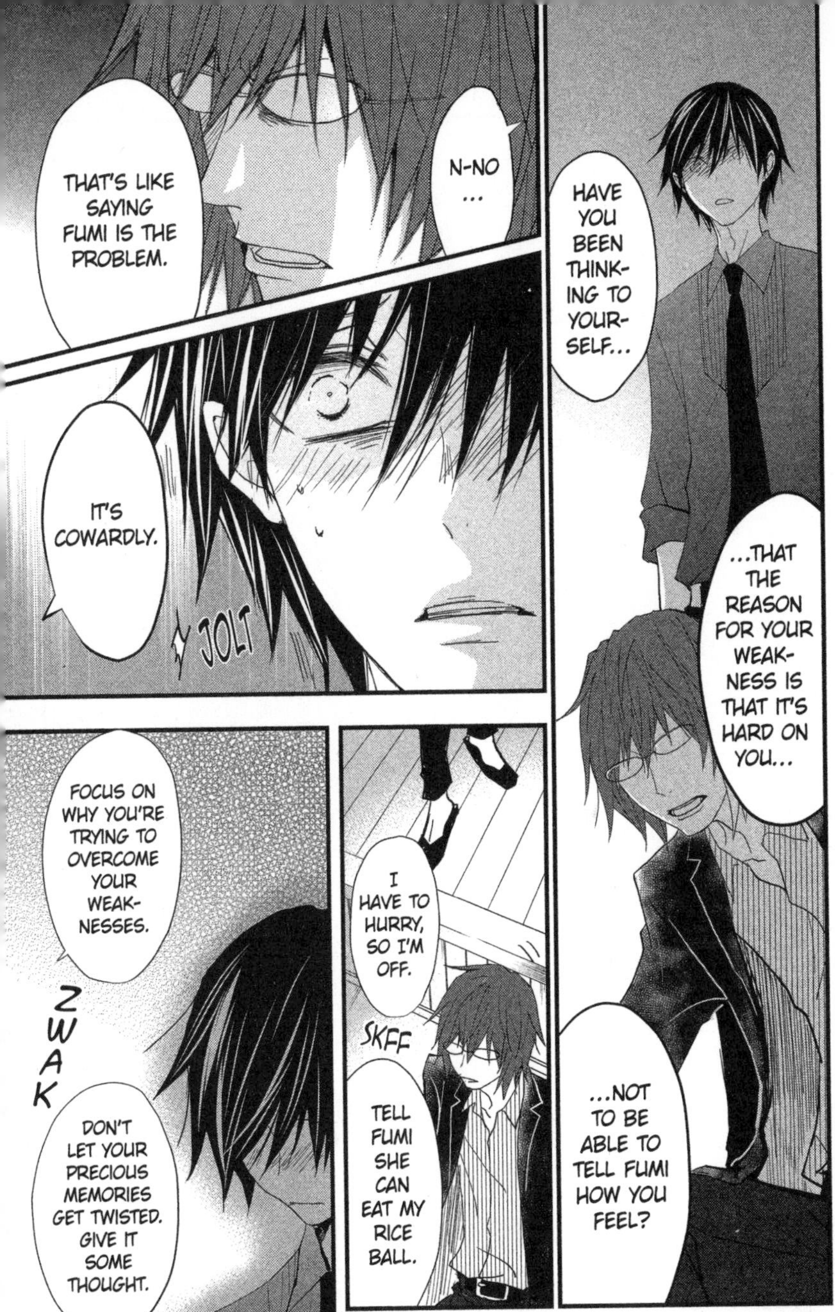
HAVE YOU BEEN THINKING TO YOURSELF...
...THAT THE REASON FOR YOUR WEAKNESS IS THAT IT'S HARD ON YOU...
...NOT TO BE ABLE TO TELL FUMI HOW YOU FEEL?
N-NO...
THAT'S LIKE SAYING FUMI IS THE PROBLEM.
IT'S COWARDLY.
JOLT
I HAVE TO HURRY, SO I'M OFF.
SKFF
TELL FUMI SHE CAN EAT MY RICE BALL.
FOCUS ON WHY YOU'RE TRYING TO OVERCOME YOUR WEAKNESSES.
ZWAK
DON'T LET YOUR PRECIOUS MEMORIES GET TWISTED. GIVE IT SOME THOUGHT.

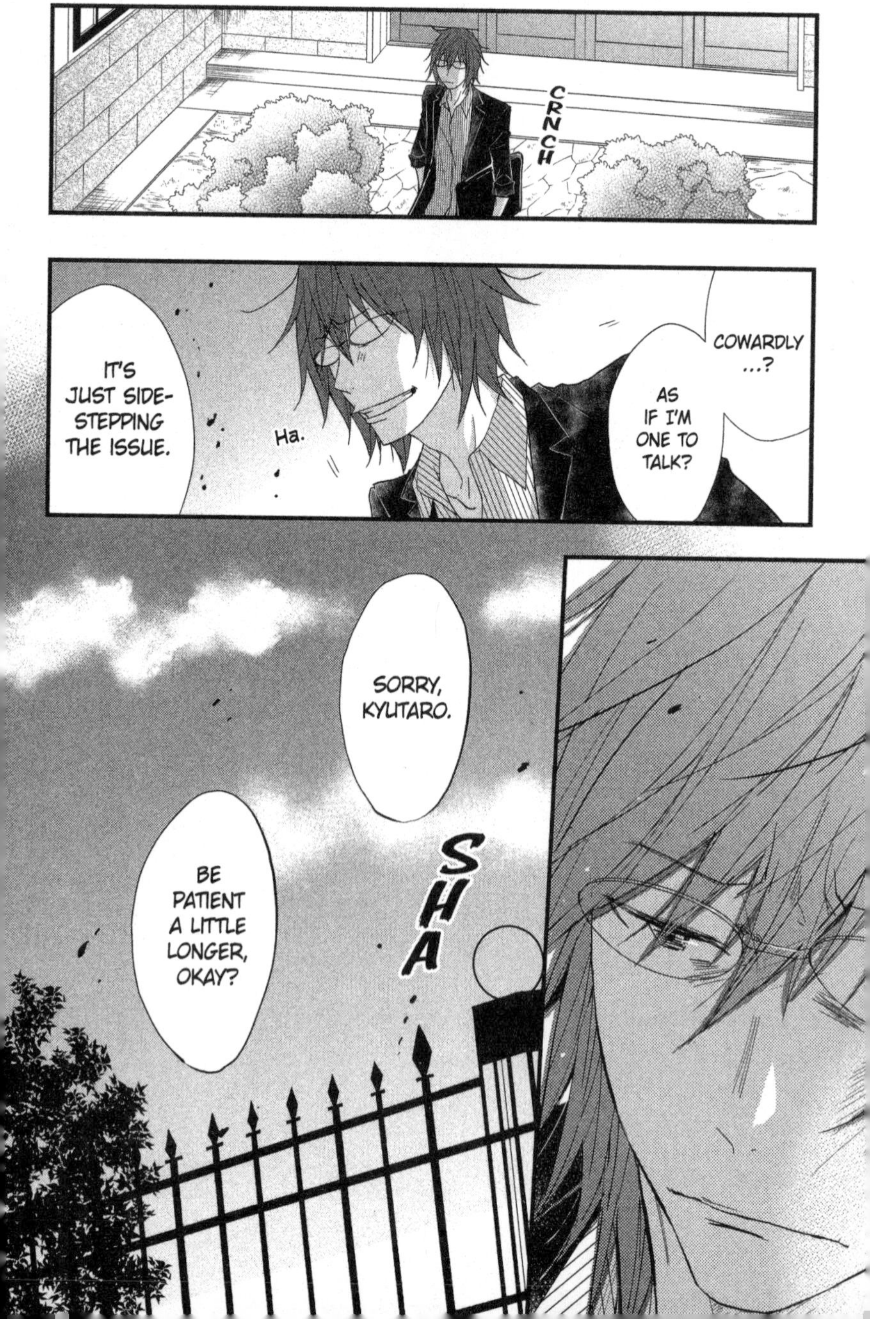
CRNCH
COWARDLY ...?
AS IF I'M ONE TO TALK?
Ha.
IT'S JUST SIDE-STEPPING THE ISSUE.
SORRY, KYUTARO.
SHA
BE PATIENT A LITTLE LONGER, OKAY?

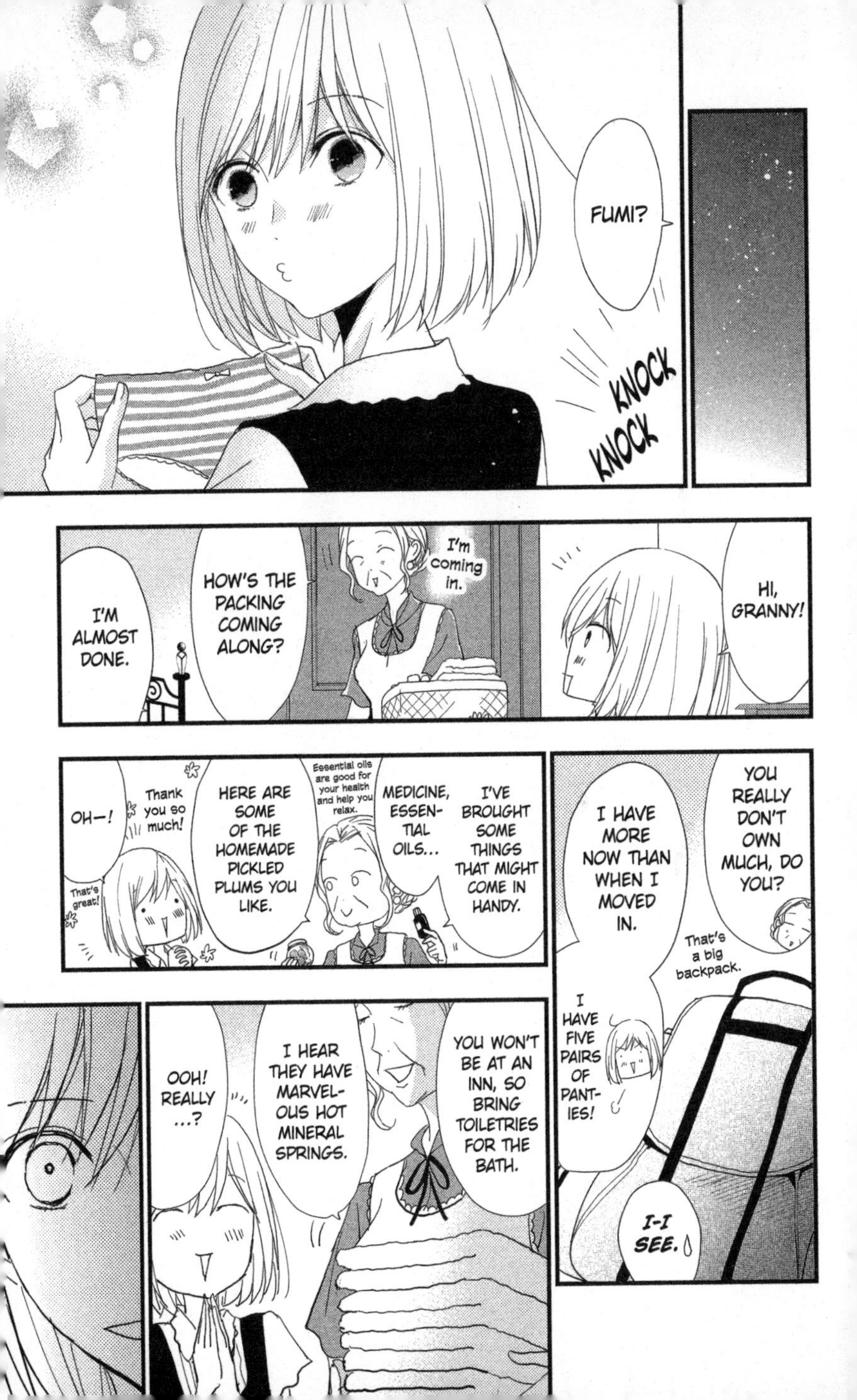
FUMI?
KNOCK KNOCK
HI, GRANNY!
I'm coming in.
HOW'S THE PACKING COMING ALONG?
I'M ALMOST DONE.
YOU REALLY DON'T OWN MUCH, DO YOU?
I HAVE MORE NOW THAN WHEN I MOVED IN.
That's a big backpack.
I HAVE FIVE PAIRS OF PANTIES!
I-I SEE.
I'VE BROUGHT SOME THINGS THAT MIGHT COME IN HANDY.
MEDICINE, ESSENTIAL OILS...
Essential oils are good for your health and help you relax.
HERE ARE SOME OF THE HOMEMADE PICKLED PLUMS YOU LIKE.
Thank you so much!
OH—!
That's great!
YOU WON'T BE AT AN INN, SO BRING TOILETRIES FOR THE BATH.
I HEAR THEY HAVE MARVELOUS HOT MINERAL SPRINGS.
OOH! REALLY ...?

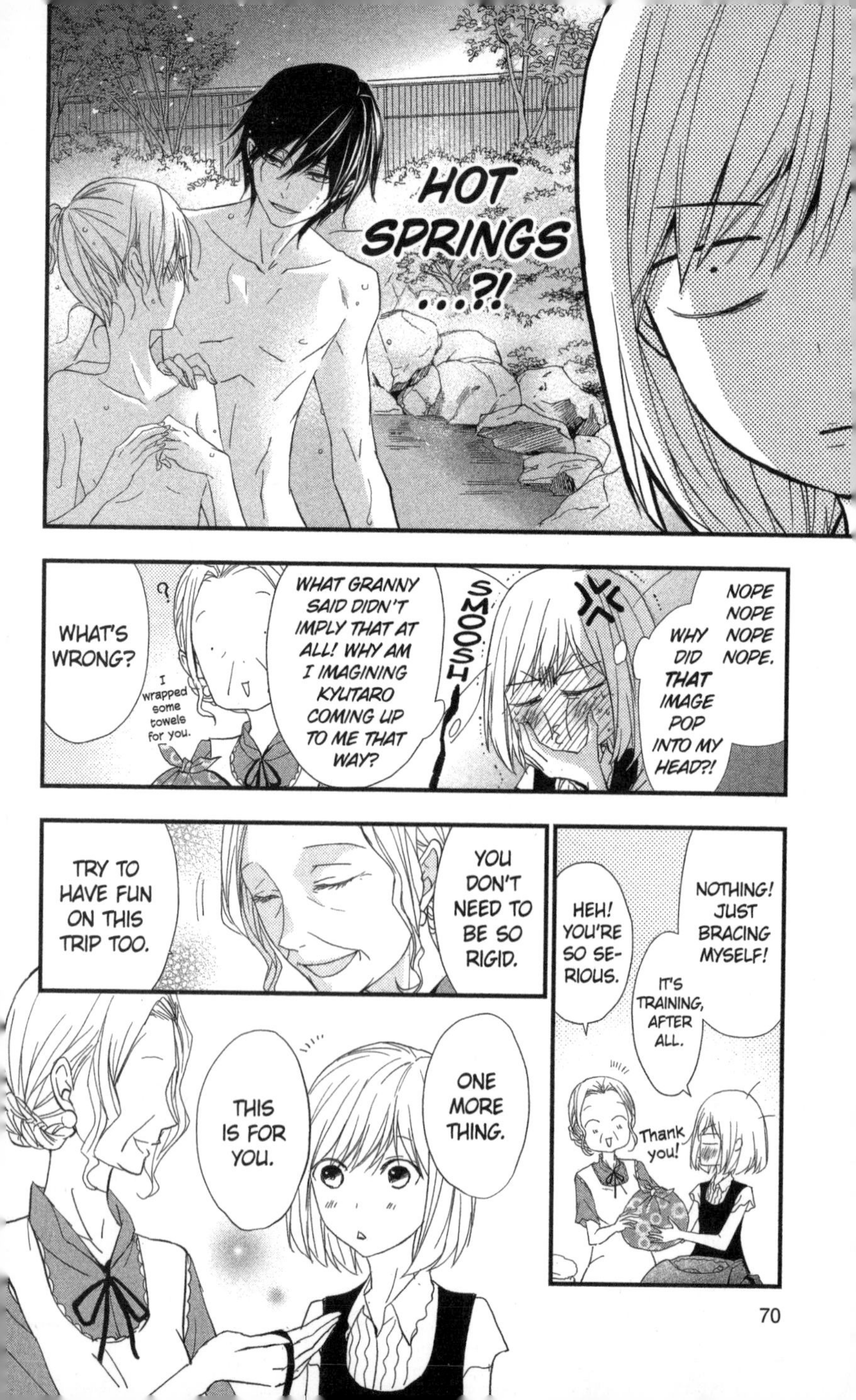
HOT SPRINGS ...?!
NOPE NOPE NOPE NOPE.
WHY DID THAT IMAGE POP INTO MY HEAD?!
SMOOSH
WHAT GRANNY SAID DIDN'T IMPLY THAT AT ALL! WHY AM I IMAGINING KYUTARO COMING UP TO ME THAT WAY?
I wrapped some towels for you.
WHAT'S WRONG?
NOTHING! JUST BRACING MYSELF!
IT'S TRAINING, AFTER ALL.
HEH! YOU'RE SO SE-RIOUS.
Thank you!
YOU DON'T NEED TO BE SO RIGID.
TRY TO HAVE FUN ON THIS TRIP TOO.
ONE MORE THING.
THIS IS FOR YOU.

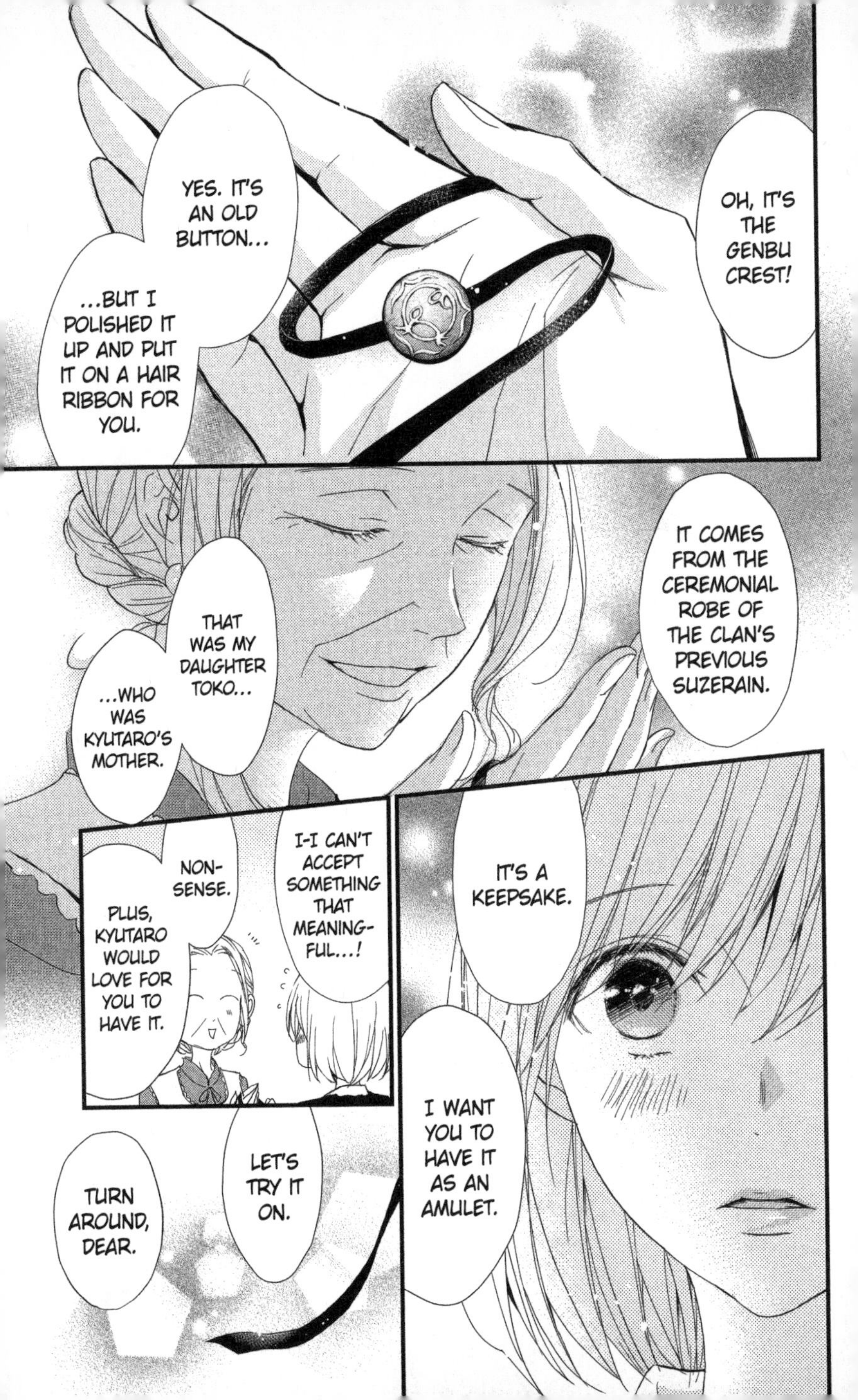

OH, IT'S THE GENBU CREST!
YES. IT'S AN OLD BUTTON...
...BUT I POLISHED IT UP AND PUT IT ON A HAIR RIBBON FOR YOU.
IT COMES FROM THE CEREMONIAL ROBE OF THE CLAN'S PREVIOUS SUZERAIN.
THAT WAS MY DAUGHTER TOKO...
...WHO WAS KYUTARO'S MOTHER.
IT'S A KEEPSAKE.
I WANT YOU TO HAVE IT AS AN AMULET.
I-I CAN'T ACCEPT SOMETHING THAT MEANING-FUL...!
NON-SENSE.
PLUS, KYUTARO WOULD LOVE FOR YOU TO HAVE IT.
LET'S TRY IT ON.
TURN AROUND, DEAR.

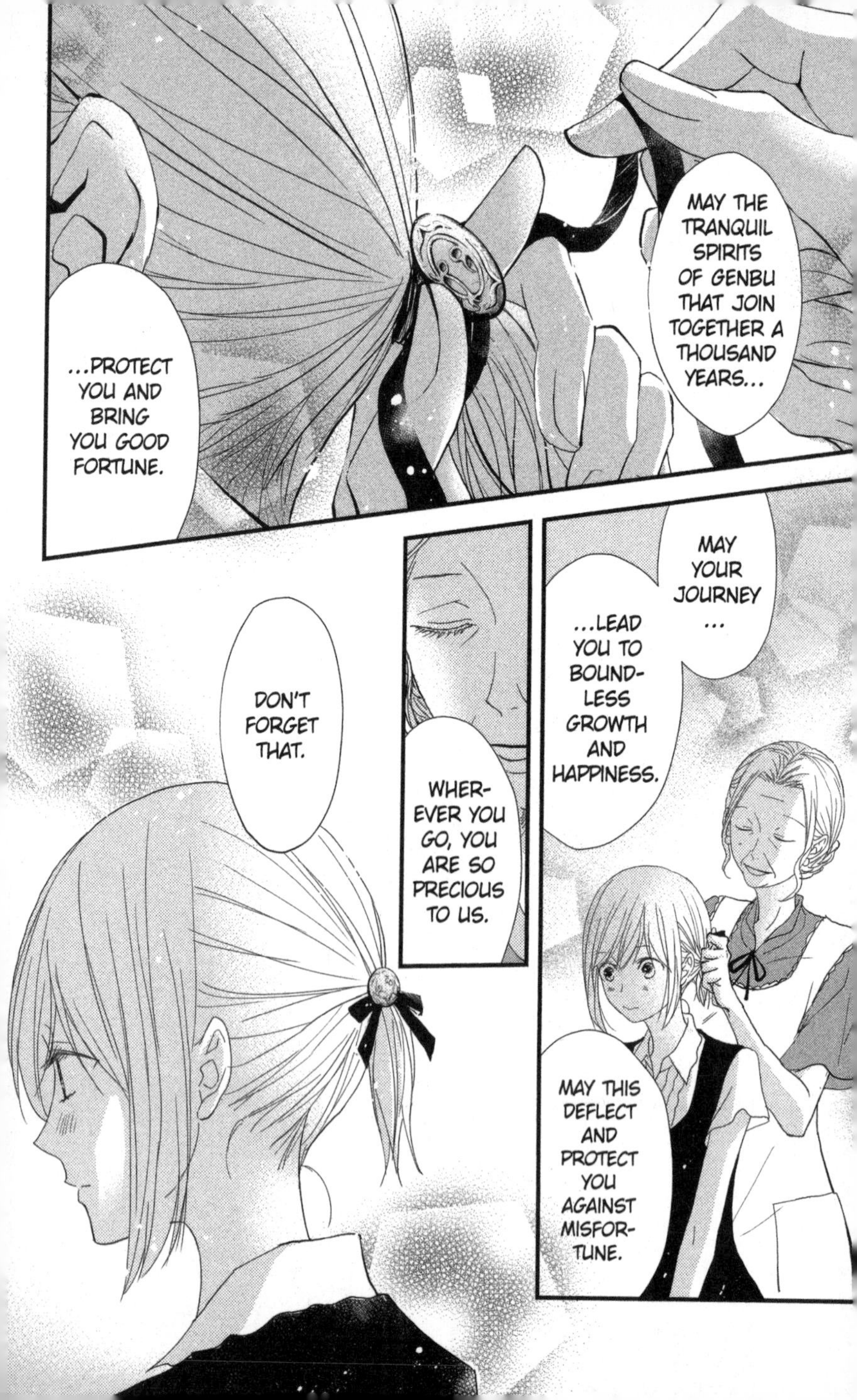
MAY THE TRANQUIL SPIRITS OF GENBU THAT JOIN TOGETHER A THOUSAND YEARS...
...PROTECT YOU AND BRING YOU GOOD FORTUNE.
MAY YOUR JOURNEY ...
...LEAD YOU TO BOUND-LESS GROWTH AND HAPPINESS.
MAY THIS DEFLECT AND PROTECT YOU AGAINST MISFOR-TUNE.
WHER-EVER YOU GO, YOU ARE SO PRECIOUS TO US.
DON'T FORGET THAT.

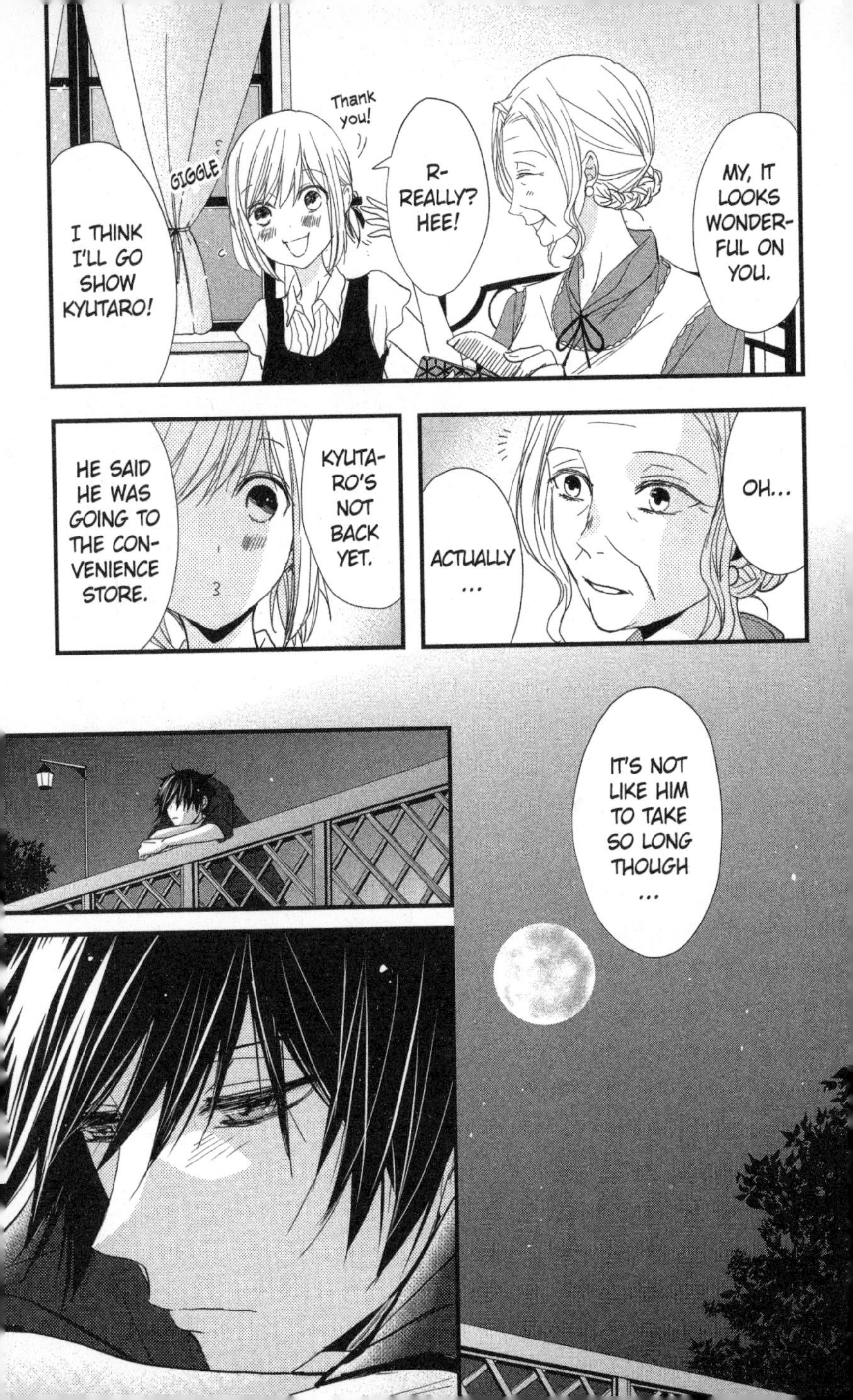
MY, IT LOOKS WONDERFUL ON YOU.
R-REALLY? HEE!
Thank you!
GIGGLE
I THINK I'LL GO SHOW KYUTARO!
OH...
ACTUALLY...
KYUTARO'S NOT BACK YET.
HE SAID HE WAS GOING TO THE CONVENIENCE STORE.
IT'S NOT LIKE HIM TO TAKE SO LONG THOUGH...

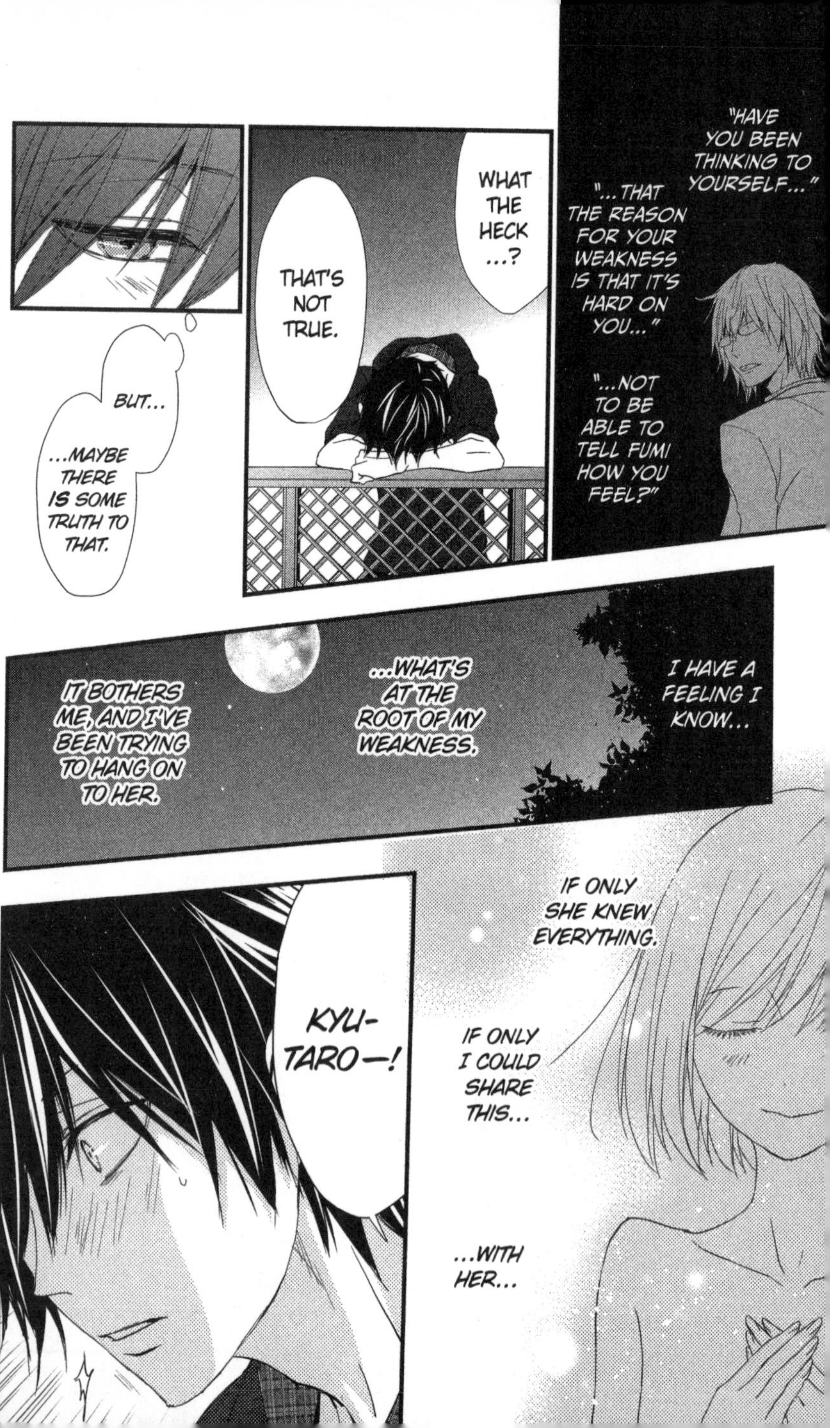
"HAVE YOU BEEN THINKING TO YOURSELF..."
"...THAT THE REASON FOR YOUR WEAKNESS IS THAT IT'S HARD ON YOU..."
"...NOT TO BE ABLE TO TELL FUMI HOW YOU FEEL?"
WHAT THE HECK ...?
THAT'S NOT TRUE.
BUT...
...MAYBE THERE **IS** SOME TRUTH TO THAT.
I HAVE A FEELING I KNOW...
...WHAT'S AT THE ROOT OF MY WEAKNESS.
IT BOTHERS ME, AND I'VE BEEN TRYING TO HANG ON TO HER.
IF ONLY SHE KNEW EVERYTHING.
IF ONLY I COULD SHARE THIS...
...WITH HER...
KYU-TARO—!

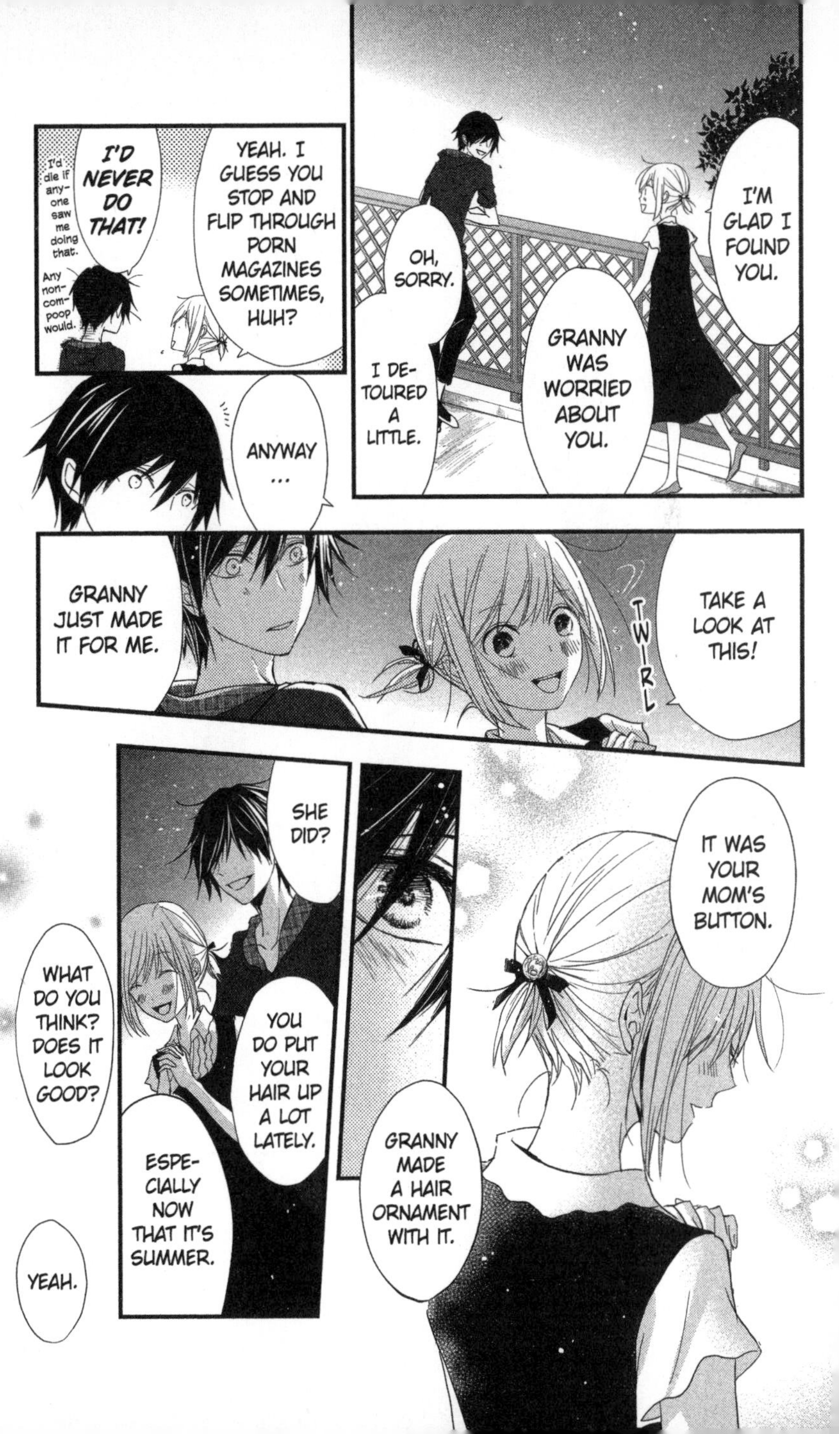
I'M GLAD I FOUND YOU.
GRANNY WAS WORRIED ABOUT YOU.
OH, SORRY.
I DE-TOURED A LITTLE.
YEAH. I GUESS YOU STOP AND FLIP THROUGH PORN MAGAZINES SOMETIMES, HUH?
I'D NEVER DO THAT!
I'd die if any-one saw me doing that.
Any non-com-poop would.
ANYWAY ...
TAKE A LOOK AT THIS!
TWIRL
GRANNY JUST MADE IT FOR ME.
IT WAS YOUR MOM'S BUTTON.
GRANNY MADE A HAIR ORNAMENT WITH IT.
SHE DID?
WHAT DO YOU THINK? DOES IT LOOK GOOD?
YOU DO PUT YOUR HAIR UP A LOT LATELY.
ESPE-CIALLY NOW THAT IT'S SUMMER.
YEAH.

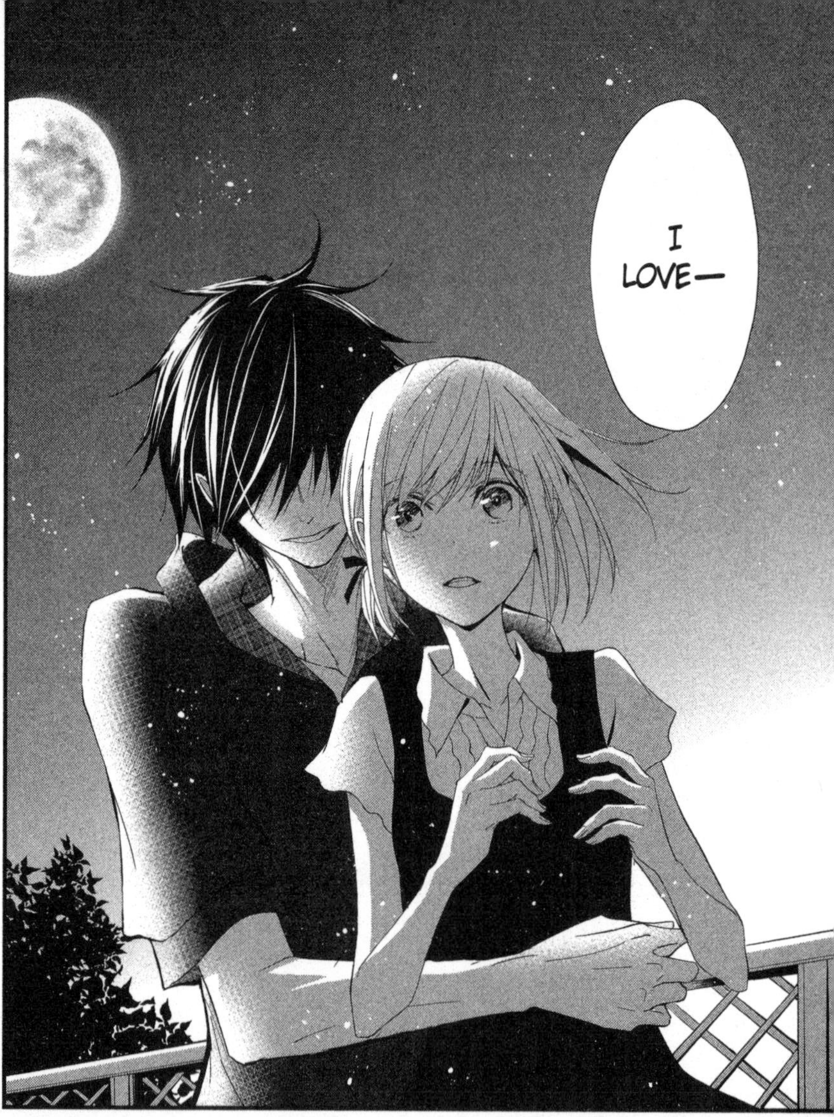
I LOVE—
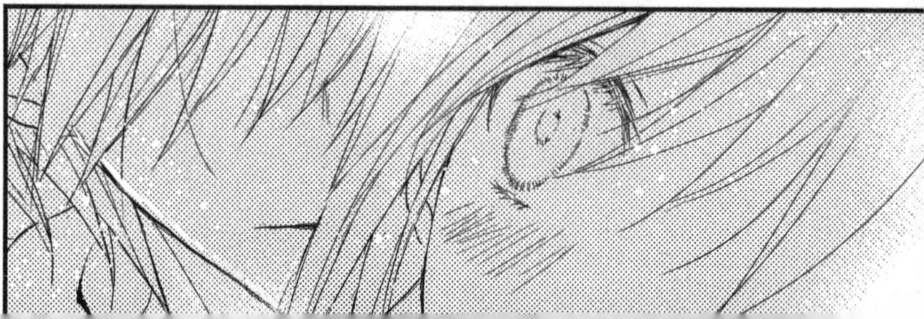

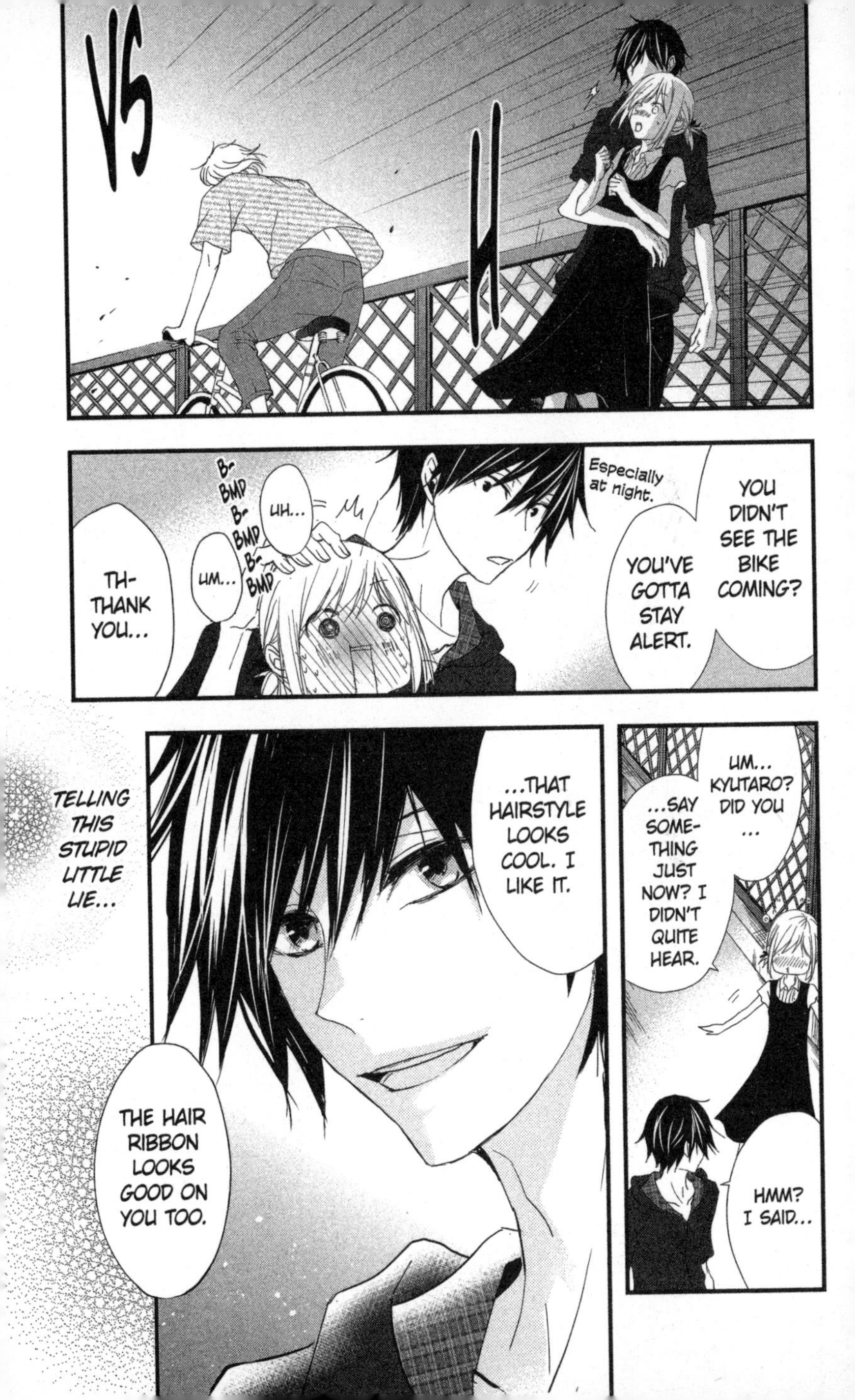
VS
H
YOU DIDN'T SEE THE BIKE COMING?
Especially at night.
YOU'VE GOTTA STAY ALERT.
UH...
B-BMP B-BMP B-BMP
UM...
TH-THANK YOU...
UM... KYUTARO? DID YOU ...
...SAY SOMETHING JUST NOW? I DIDN'T QUITE HEAR.
HMM? I SAID...
...THAT HAIRSTYLE LOOKS COOL. I LIKE IT.
THE HAIR RIBBON LOOKS GOOD ON YOU TOO.
TELLING THIS STUPID LITTLE LIE...

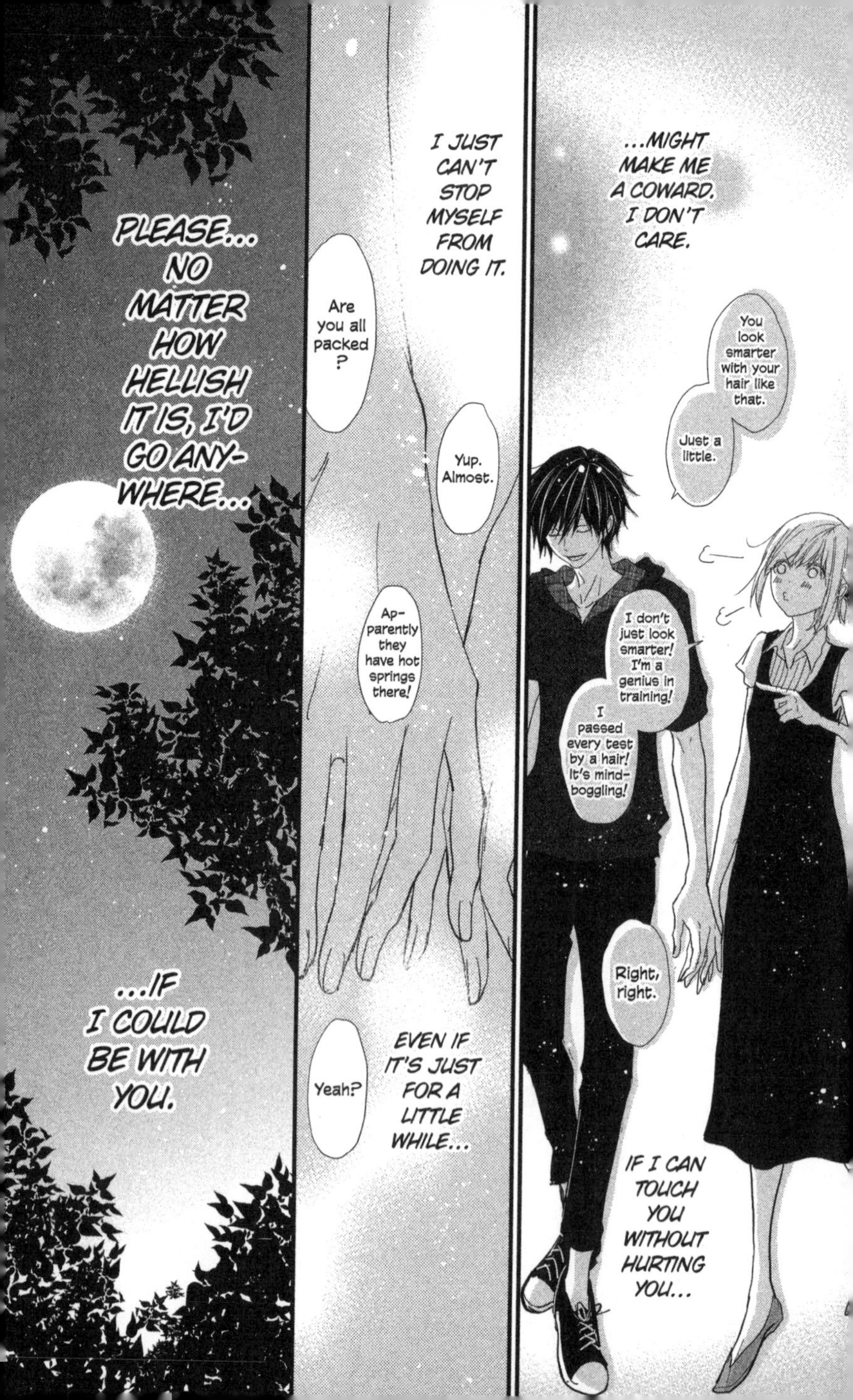
...MIGHT MAKE ME A COWARD. I DON'T CARE.
You look smarter with your hair like that.
Just a little.
I don't just look smarter! I'm a genius in training!
I passed every test by a hair! It's mind-boggling!
Right, right.
IF I CAN TOUCH YOU WITHOUT HURTING YOU...
I JUST CAN'T STOP MYSELF FROM DOING IT.
Are you all packed?
Yup. Almost.
Ap-parently they have hot springs there!
EVEN IF IT'S JUST FOR A LITTLE WHILE...
Yeah?
PLEASE... NO MATTER HOW HELLISH IT IS, I'D GO ANY-WHERE...
...IF I COULD BE WITH YOU.

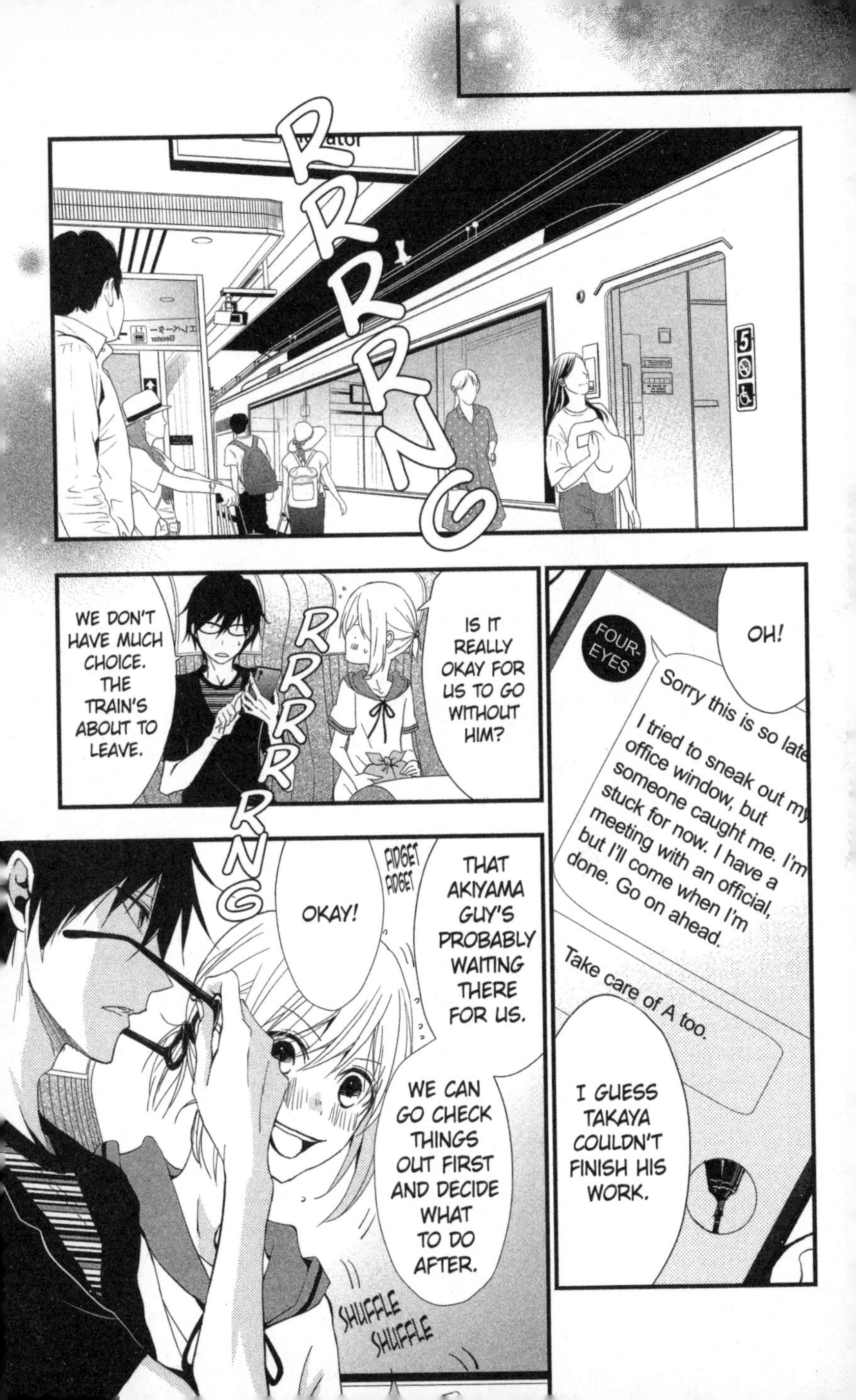
RRRRNG
OH!
FOUR-EYES
Sorry this is so late
I tried to sneak out my office window, but someone caught me. I'm stuck for now. I have a meeting with an official, but I'll come when I'm done. Go on ahead.
Take care of A too.
I GUESS TAKAYA COULDN'T FINISH HIS WORK.
RRRRNG
IS IT REALLY OKAY FOR US TO GO WITHOUT HIM?
WE DON'T HAVE MUCH CHOICE. THE TRAIN'S ABOUT TO LEAVE.
THAT AKIYAMA GUY'S PROBABLY WAITING THERE FOR US.
FIDGET FIDGET
OKAY!
WE CAN GO CHECK THINGS OUT FIRST AND DECIDE WHAT TO DO AFTER.
SHUFFLE SHUFFLE

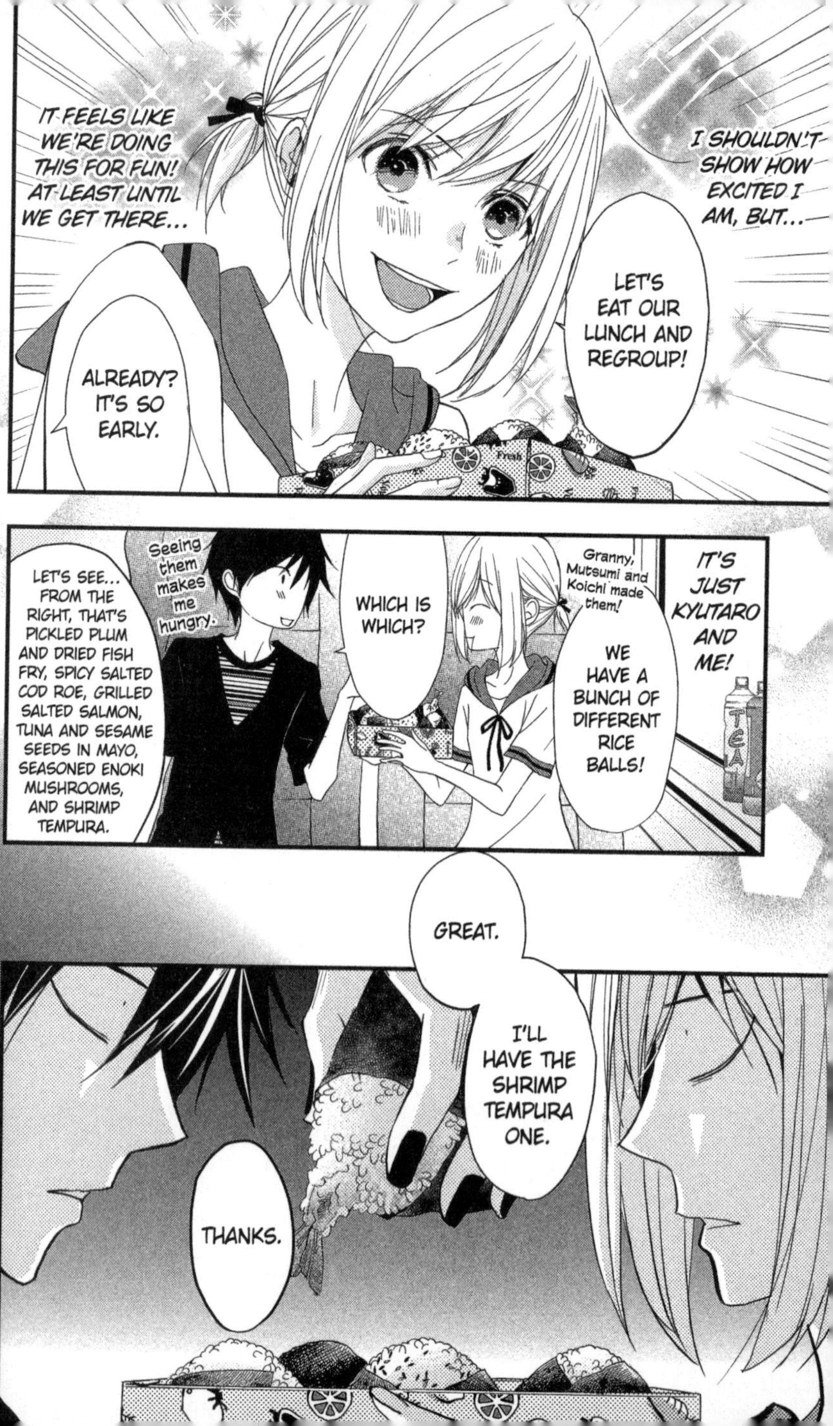
I SHOULDN'T SHOW HOW EXCITED I AM, BUT...
IT FEELS LIKE WE'RE DOING THIS FOR FUN! AT LEAST UNTIL WE GET THERE...
LET'S EAT OUR LUNCH AND REGROUP!
ALREADY? IT'S SO EARLY.
Fresh
IT'S JUST KYUTARO AND ME!
Granny, Mutsumi and Koichi made them!
WE HAVE A BUNCH OF DIFFERENT RICE BALLS!
TEA
WHICH IS WHICH?
Seeing them makes me hungry.
LET'S SEE... FROM THE RIGHT, THAT'S PICKLED PLUM AND DRIED FISH FRY, SPICY SALTED COD ROE, GRILLED SALTED SALMON, TUNA AND SESAME SEEDS IN MAYO, SEASONED ENOKI MUSHROOMS, AND SHRIMP TEMPURA.
GREAT.
I'LL HAVE THE SHRIMP TEMPURA ONE.
THANKS.

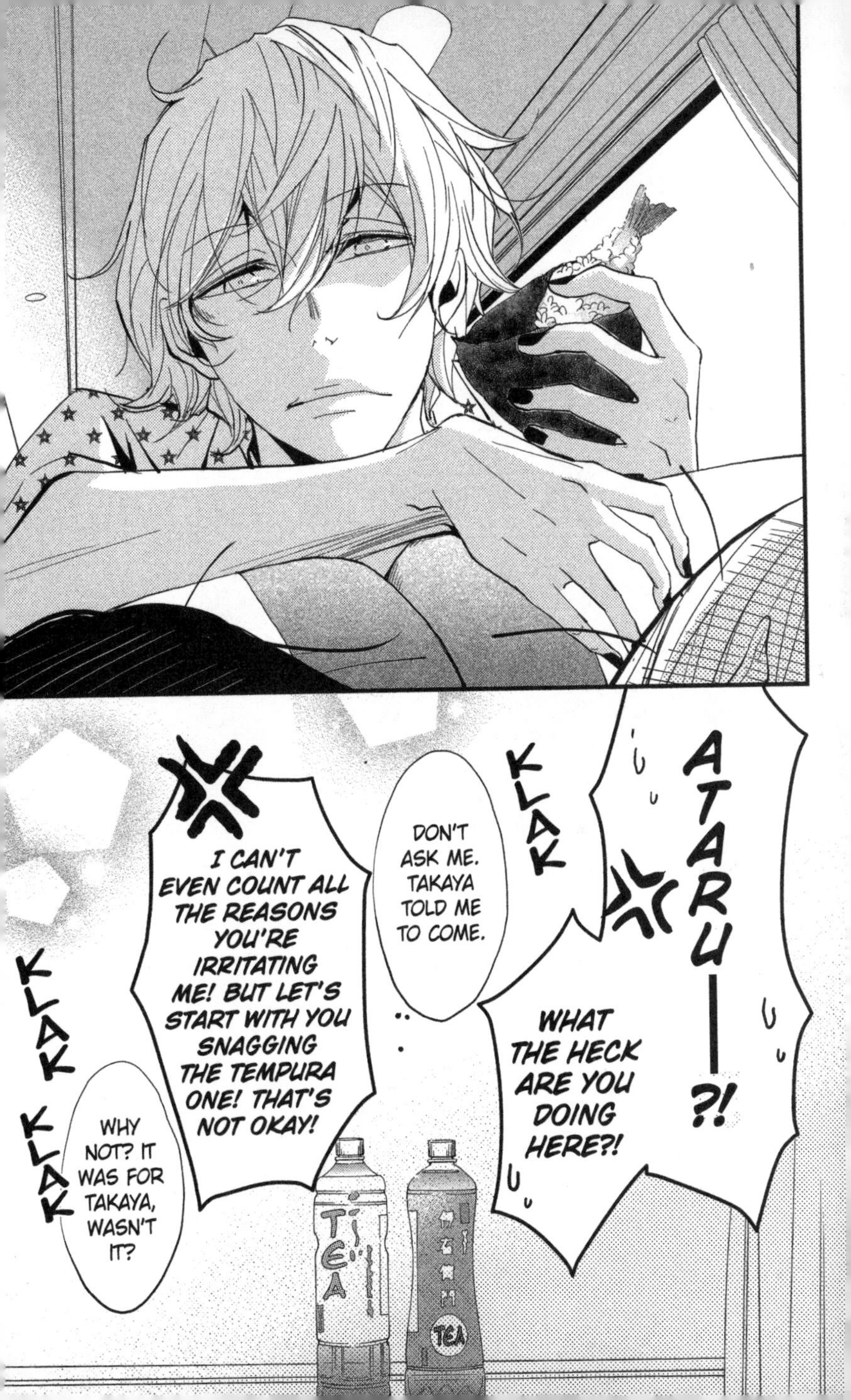
ATARU—?!
WHAT THE HECK ARE YOU DOING HERE?!
KLAK
DON'T ASK ME. TAKAYA TOLD ME TO COME.
..
I CAN'T EVEN COUNT ALL THE REASONS YOU'RE IRRITATING ME! BUT LET'S START WITH YOU SNAGGING THE TEMPURA ONE! THAT'S NOT OKAY!
KLAK KLAK KLAK
WHY NOT? IT WAS FOR TAKAYA, WASN'T IT?
TEA
TEA

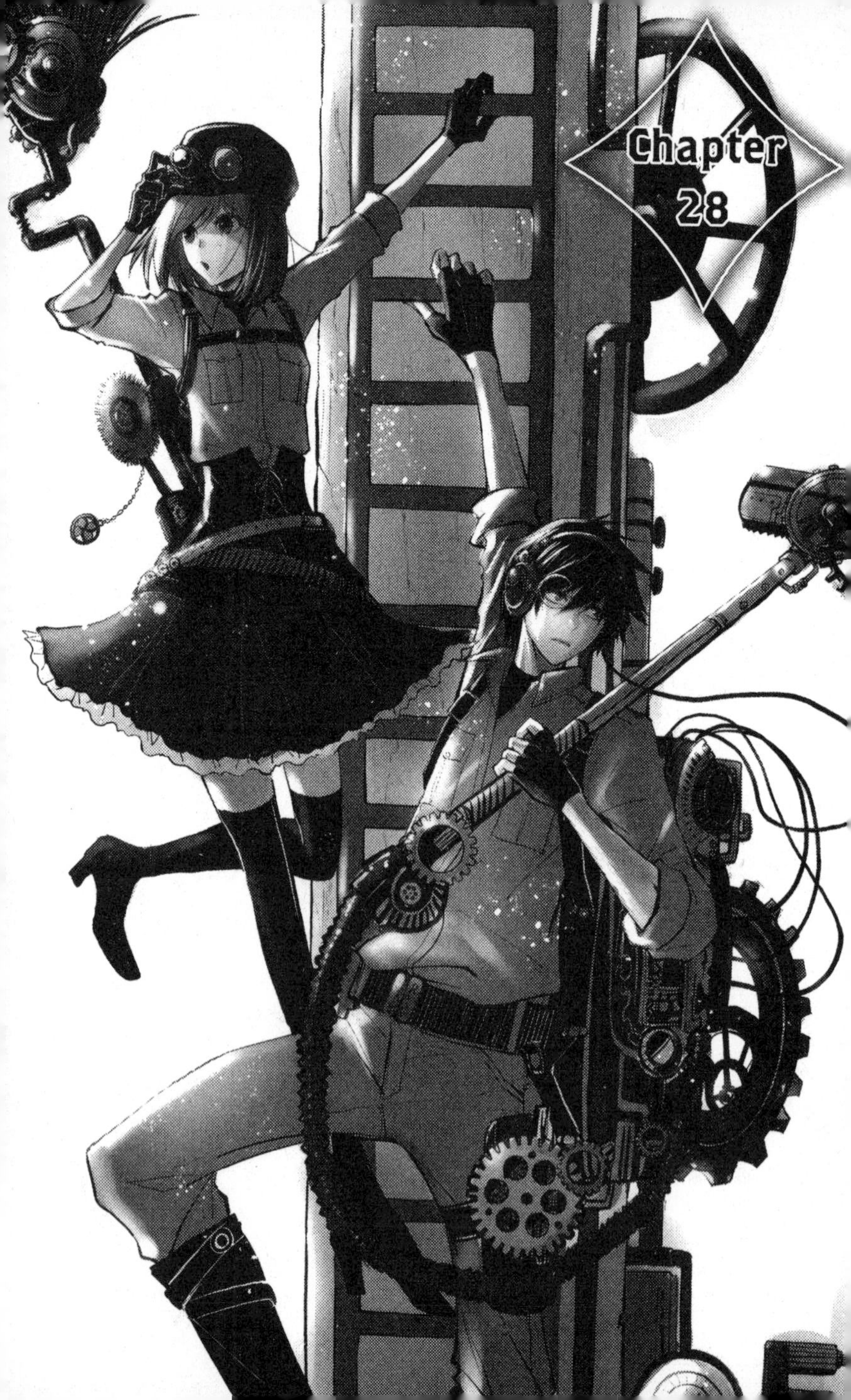
Chapter
28

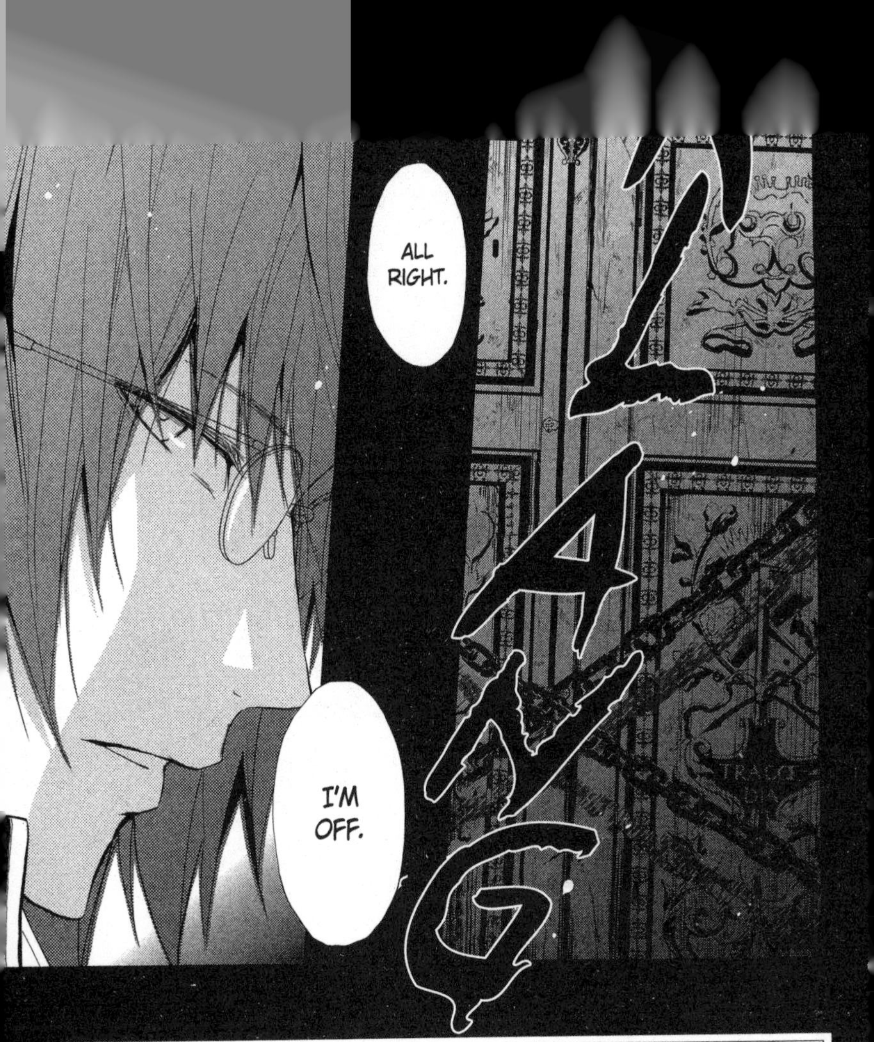
ALL RIGHT.
I'M OFF.
CLANG

Ataru reappeared much sooner than I, the author, anticipated. I'm so relieved to hear that many readers are fairly sympathetic to him. I suspected you would be, but now that he's fighting on our side, it's easy to use him. I'm glad he, Kyutaro and Fumi play off each other so well.

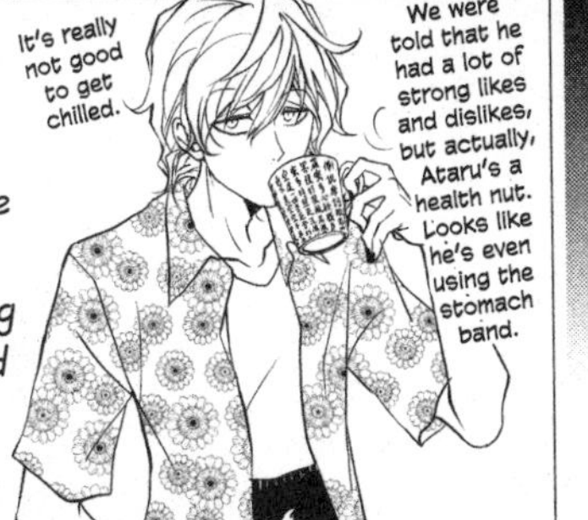
We were told that he had a lot of strong likes and dislikes, but actually, Ataru's a health nut. Looks like he's even using the stomach band.
It's really not good to get chilled.

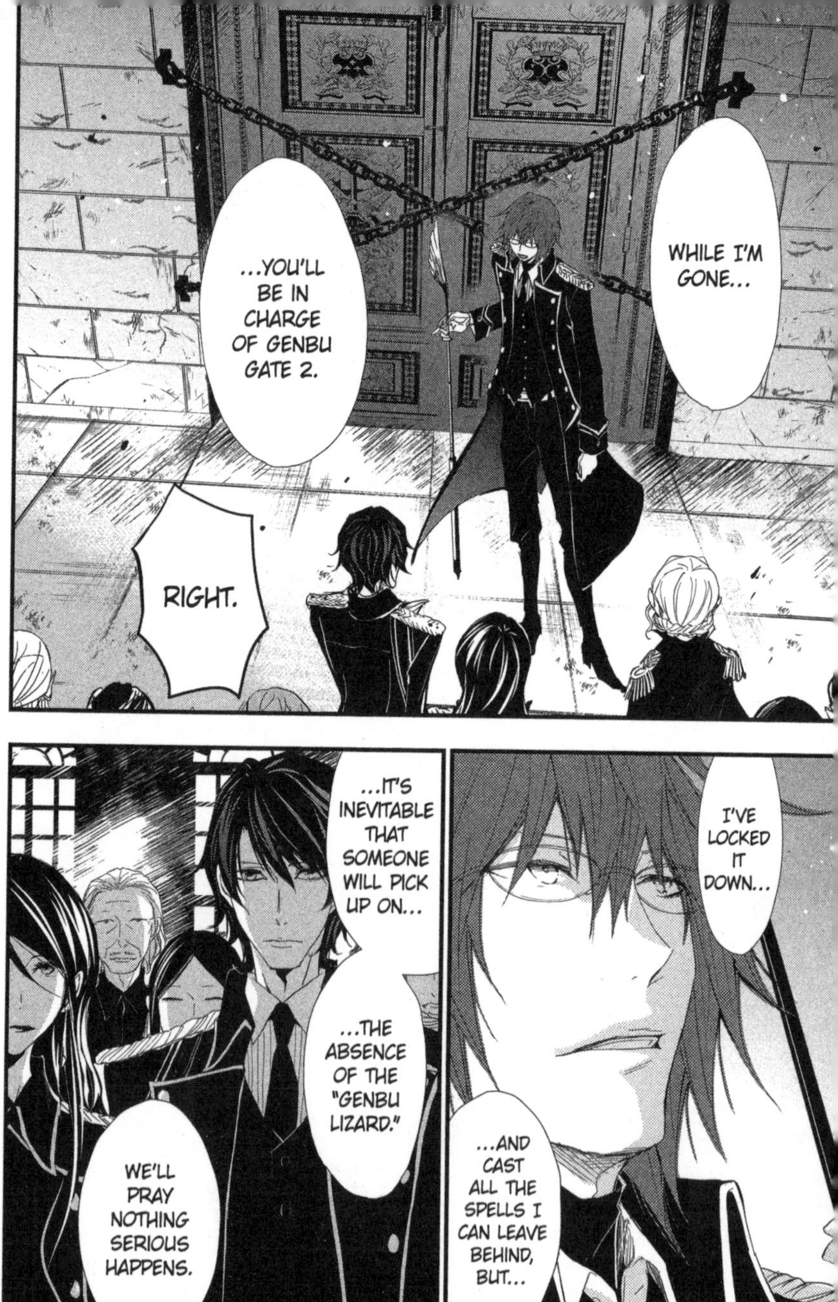
WHILE I'M GONE...
...YOU'LL BE IN CHARGE OF GENBU GATE 2.
RIGHT.
I'VE LOCKED IT DOWN...
...AND CAST ALL THE SPELLS I CAN LEAVE BEHIND, BUT...
...IT'S INEVITABLE THAT SOMEONE WILL PICK UP ON...
...THE ABSENCE OF THE "GENBU LIZARD."
WE'LL PRAY NOTHING SERIOUS HAPPENS.

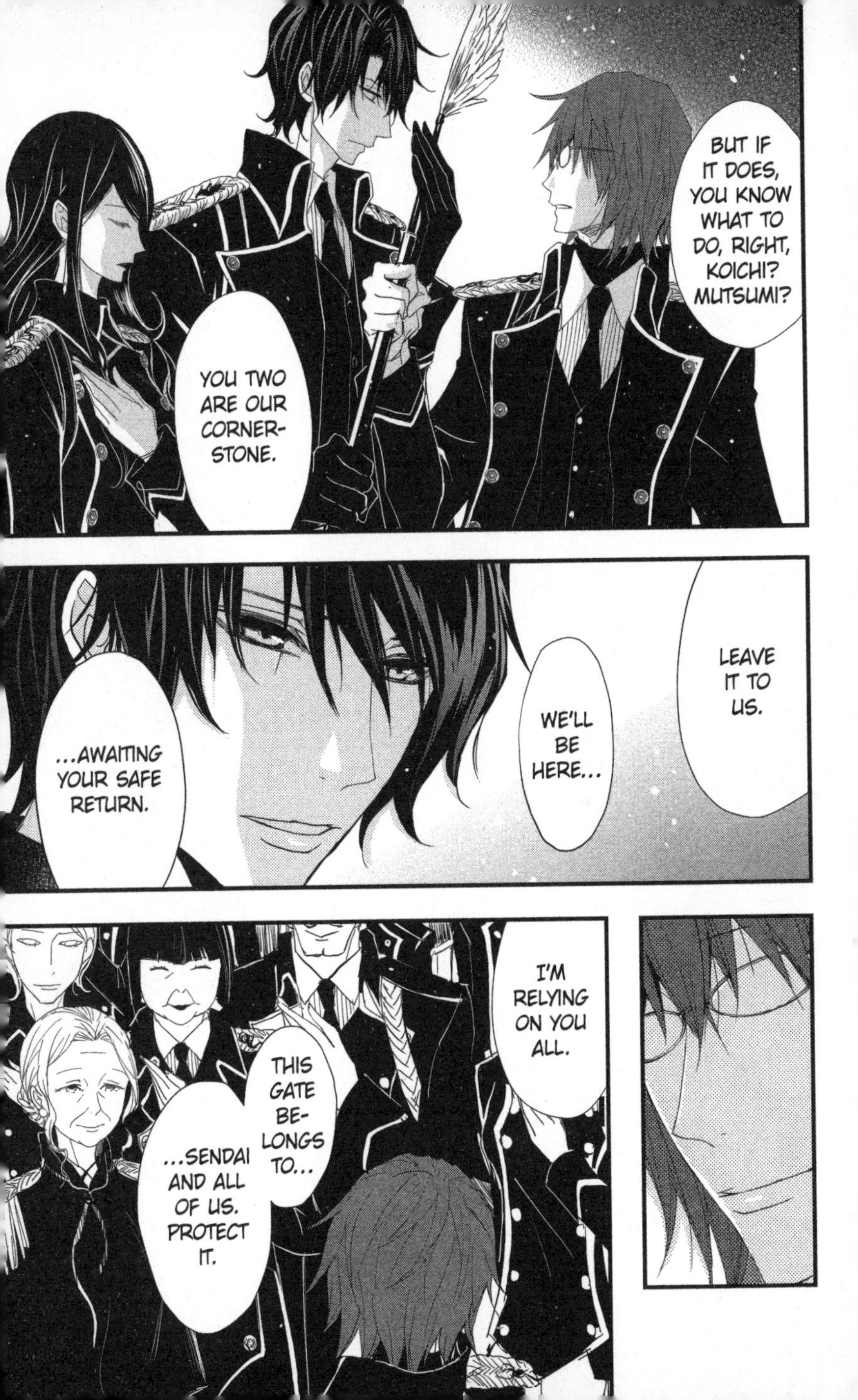
BUT IF IT DOES, YOU KNOW WHAT TO DO, RIGHT, KOICHI? MUTSUMI?
YOU TWO ARE OUR CORNER-STONE.
LEAVE IT TO US.
WE'LL BE HERE...
...AWAITING YOUR SAFE RETURN.
I'M RELYING ON YOU ALL.
THIS GATE BE-LONGS TO...
...SENDAI AND ALL OF US. PROTECT IT.

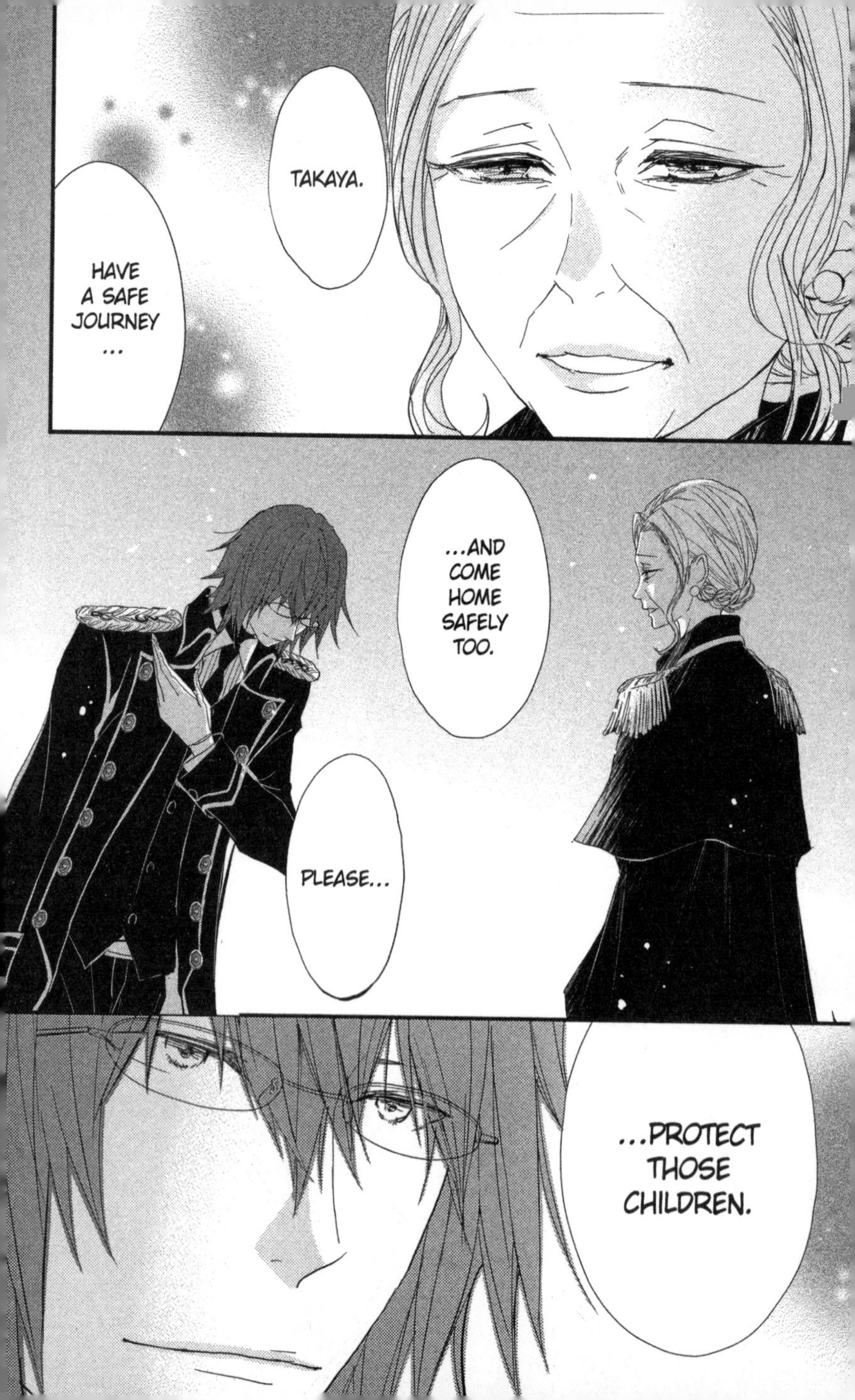
TAKAYA.
HAVE A SAFE JOURNEY ...
...AND COME HOME SAFELY TOO.
PLEASE...
...PROTECT THOSE CHILDREN.

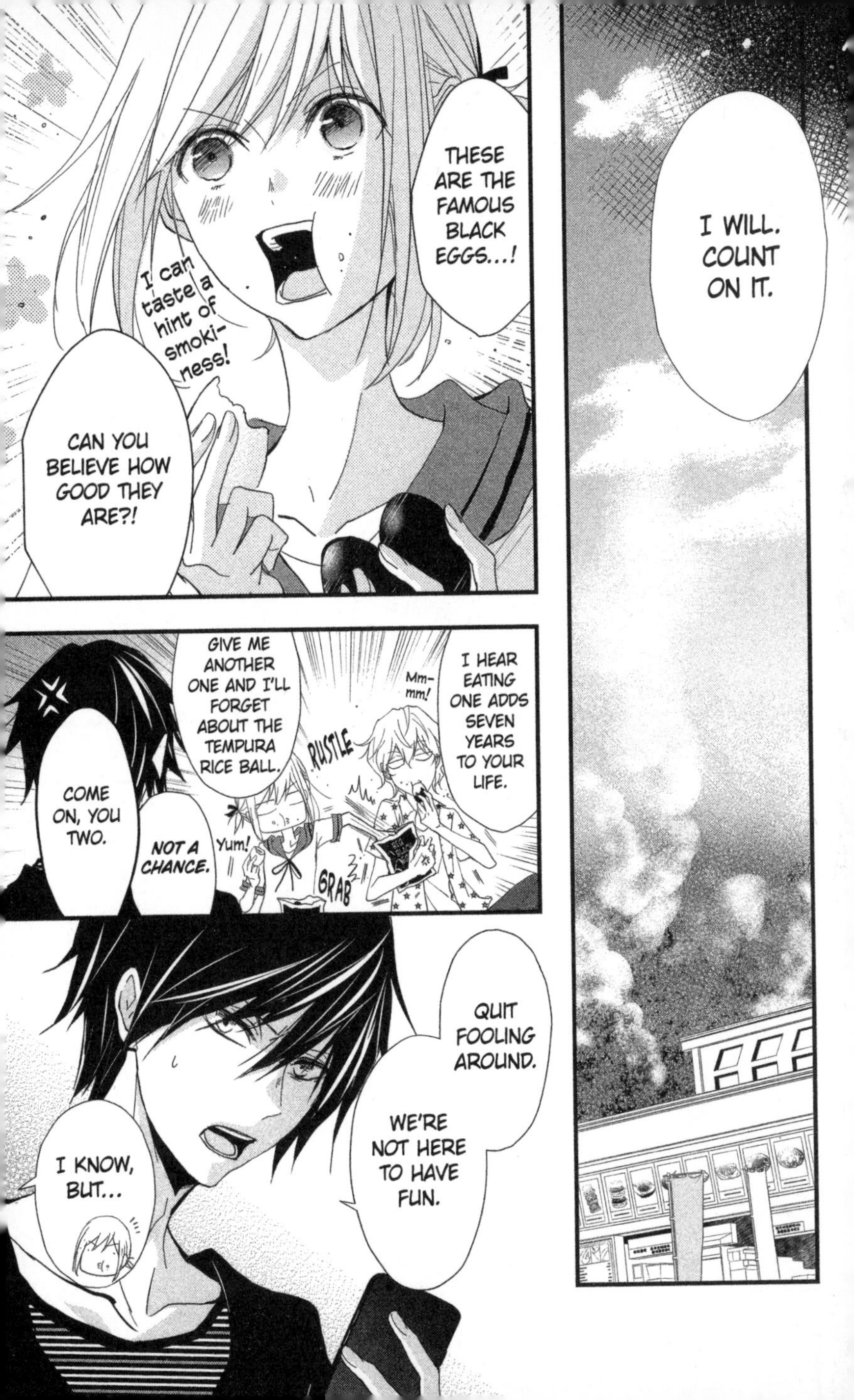
I WILL. COUNT ON IT.
THESE ARE THE FAMOUS BLACK EGGS...!
I can taste a hint of smoki-ness!
CAN YOU BELIEVE HOW GOOD THEY ARE?!
I HEAR EATING ONE ADDS SEVEN YEARS TO YOUR LIFE.
Mm-mm!
GIVE ME ANOTHER ONE AND I'LL FORGET ABOUT THE TEMPURA RICE BALL.
RUSTLE
Yum!
GRAB
NOT A CHANCE.
COME ON, YOU TWO.
QUIT FOOLING AROUND.
WE'RE NOT HERE TO HAVE FUN.
I KNOW, BUT...

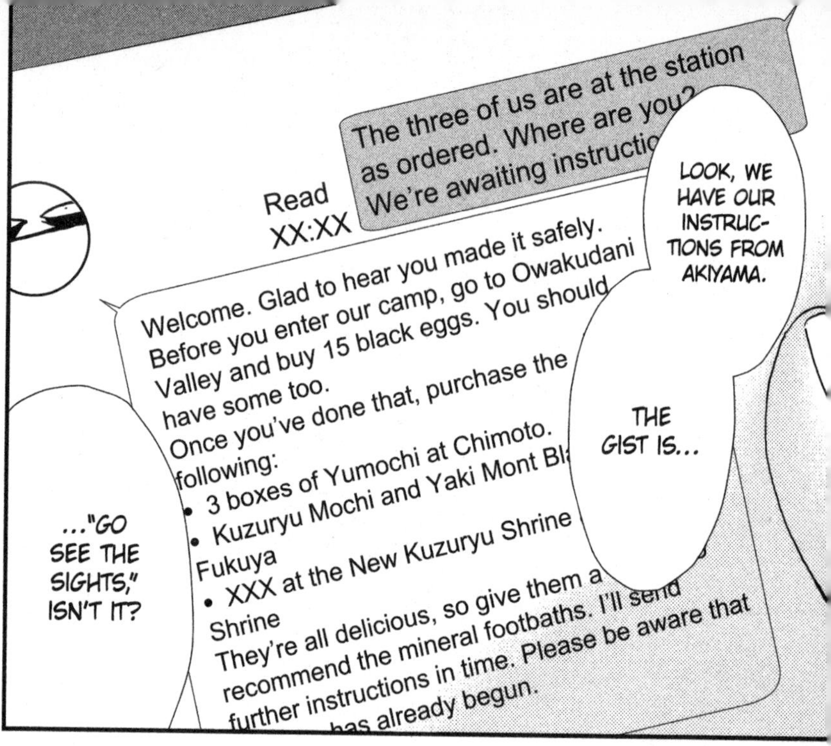
LOOK, WE HAVE OUR INSTRUCTIONS FROM AKIYAMA.
The three of us are at the station as ordered. Where are you? We're awaiting instructio
Read XX:XX
Welcome. Glad to hear you made it safely. Before you enter our camp, go to Owakudani Valley and buy 15 black eggs. You should have some too.
Once you've done that, purchase the following:
• 3 boxes of Yumochi at Chimoto.
• Kuzuryu Mochi and Yaki Mont Bl
Fukuya
• XXX at the New Kuzuryu Shrine
Shrine
They're all delicious, so give them a
recommend the mineral footbaths. I'll send further instructions in time. Please be aware that
has already begun.
THE GIST IS...
..."GO SEE THE SIGHTS," ISN'T IT?

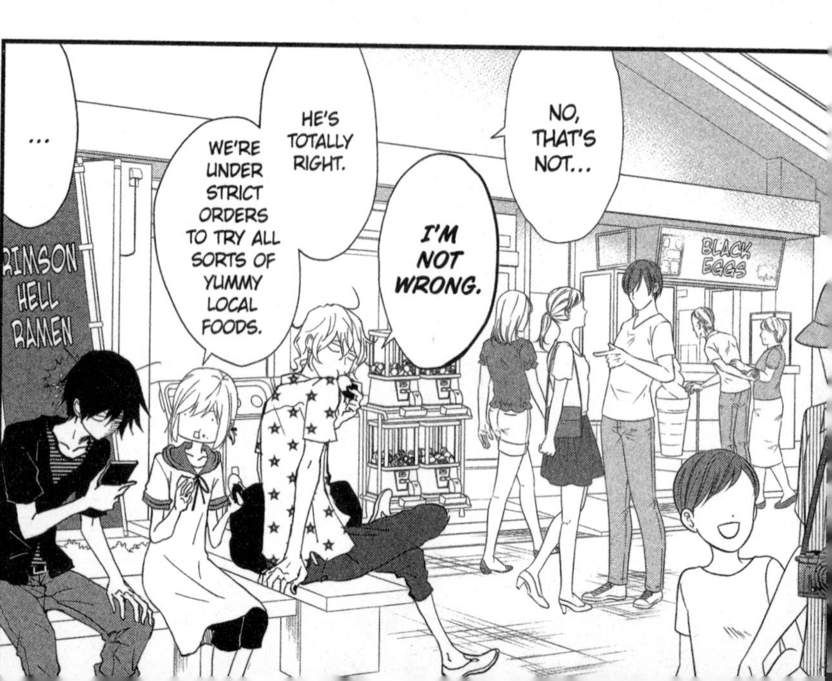
NO, THAT'S NOT...
BLACK EGGS
I'M NOT WRONG.
HE'S TOTALLY RIGHT.
WE'RE UNDER STRICT ORDERS TO TRY ALL SORTS OF YUMMY LOCAL FOODS.
...
RIMSON HELL RAMEN

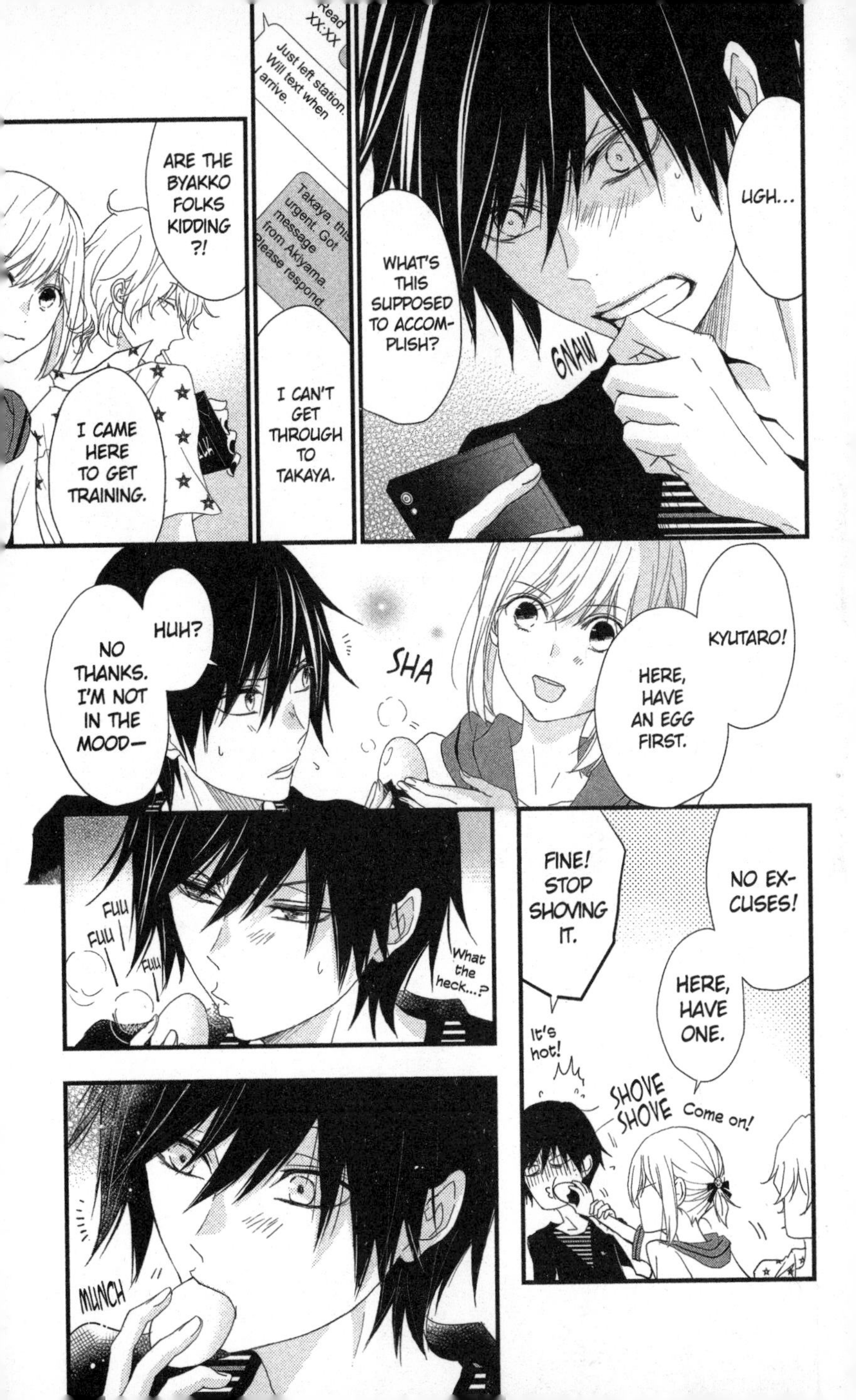
UGH...
WHAT'S THIS SUPPOSED TO ACCOMPLISH?
GNAW
Read XX:XX
Just left station. Will text when I arrive.
Takaya, this urgent. Got message from Akiyama. Please respond.
I CAN'T GET THROUGH TO TAKAYA.
ARE THE BYAKKO FOLKS KIDDING?!
I CAME HERE TO GET TRAINING.
KYUTARO!
HERE, HAVE AN EGG FIRST.
SHA
HUH?
NO THANKS. I'M NOT IN THE MOOD—
NO EX-CUSES!
HERE, HAVE ONE.
FINE! STOP SHOVING IT.
Come on!
SHOVE SHOVE
It's hot!
What the heck...?
FUU FUU FUU
MUNCH

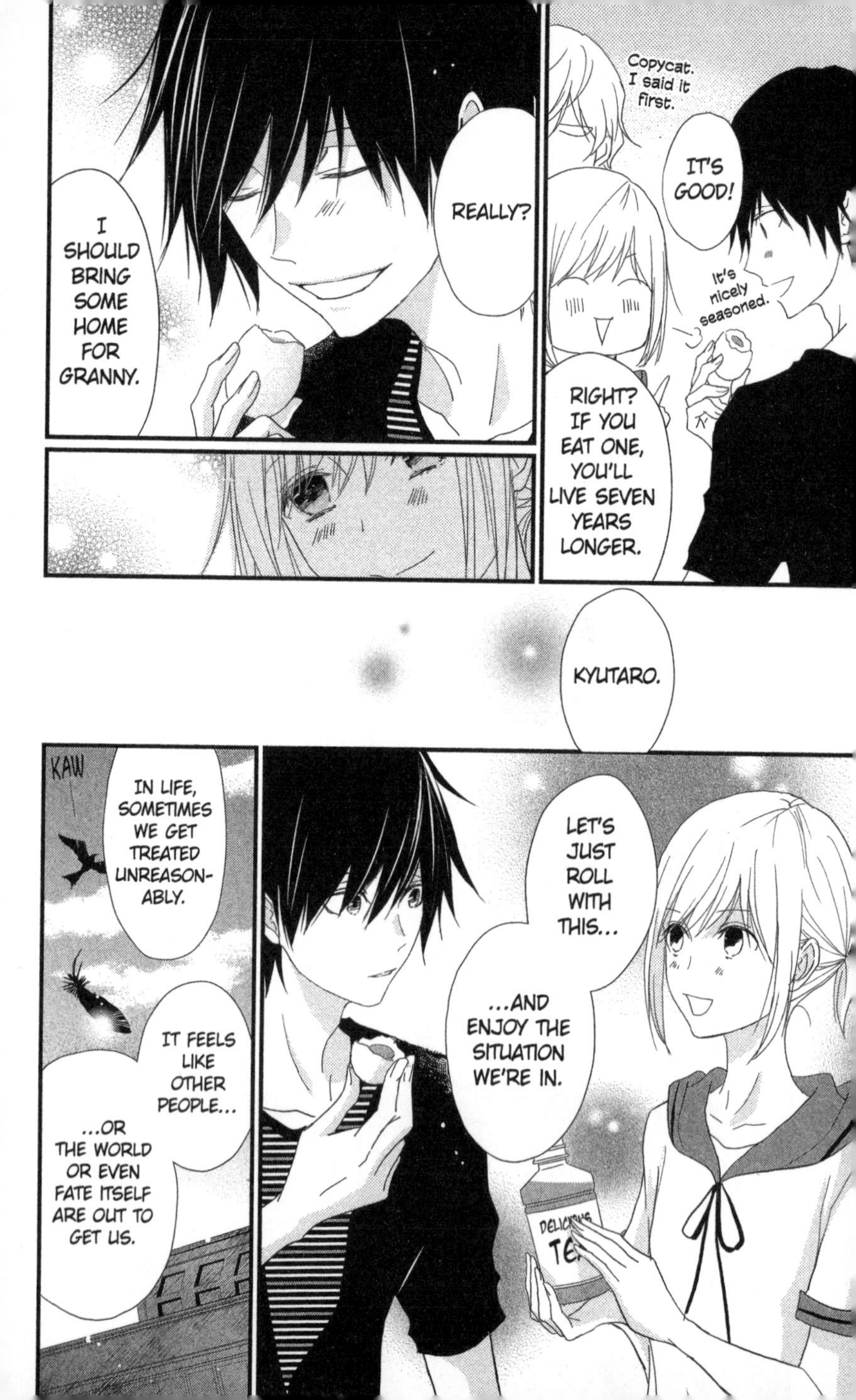
Copycat. I said it first.
IT'S GOOD!
It's nicely seasoned.
RIGHT? IF YOU EAT ONE, YOU'LL LIVE SEVEN YEARS LONGER.
REALLY?
I SHOULD BRING SOME HOME FOR GRANNY.
KYUTARO.
LET'S JUST ROLL WITH THIS...
...AND ENJOY THE SITUATION WE'RE IN.
KAW
IN LIFE, SOMETIMES WE GET TREATED UNREASON-ABLY.
IT FEELS LIKE OTHER PEOPLE...
...OR THE WORLD OR EVEN FATE ITSELF ARE OUT TO GET US.

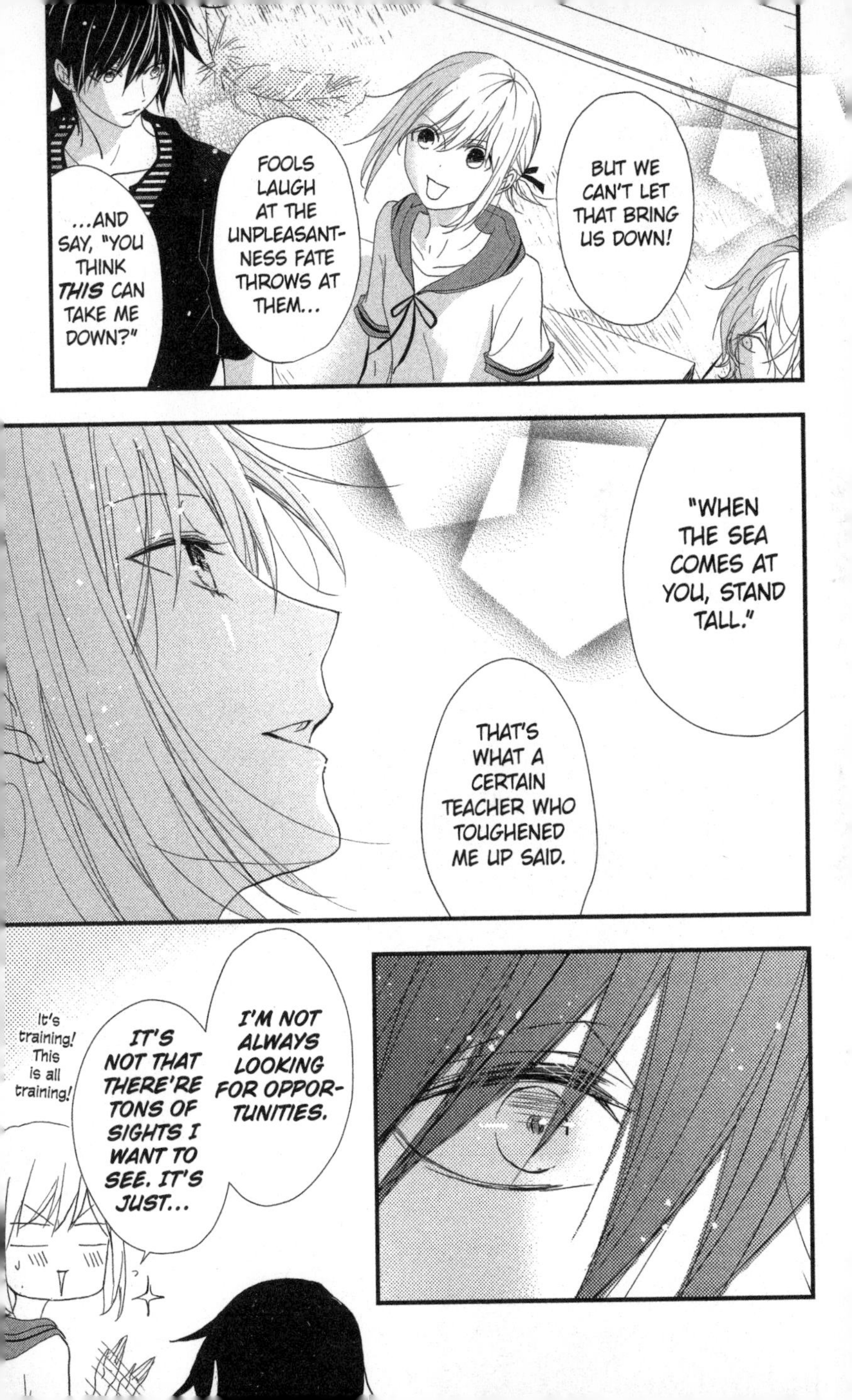
BUT WE CAN'T LET THAT BRING US DOWN!
FOOLS LAUGH AT THE UNPLEASANTNESS FATE THROWS AT THEM...
...AND SAY, "YOU THINK *THIS* CAN TAKE ME DOWN?"
"WHEN THE SEA COMES AT YOU, STAND TALL."
THAT'S WHAT A CERTAIN TEACHER WHO TOUGHENED ME UP SAID.
I'M NOT ALWAYS LOOKING FOR OPPORTUNITIES.
IT'S NOT THAT THERE'RE TONS OF SIGHTS I WANT TO SEE. IT'S JUST...
It's training! This is all training!

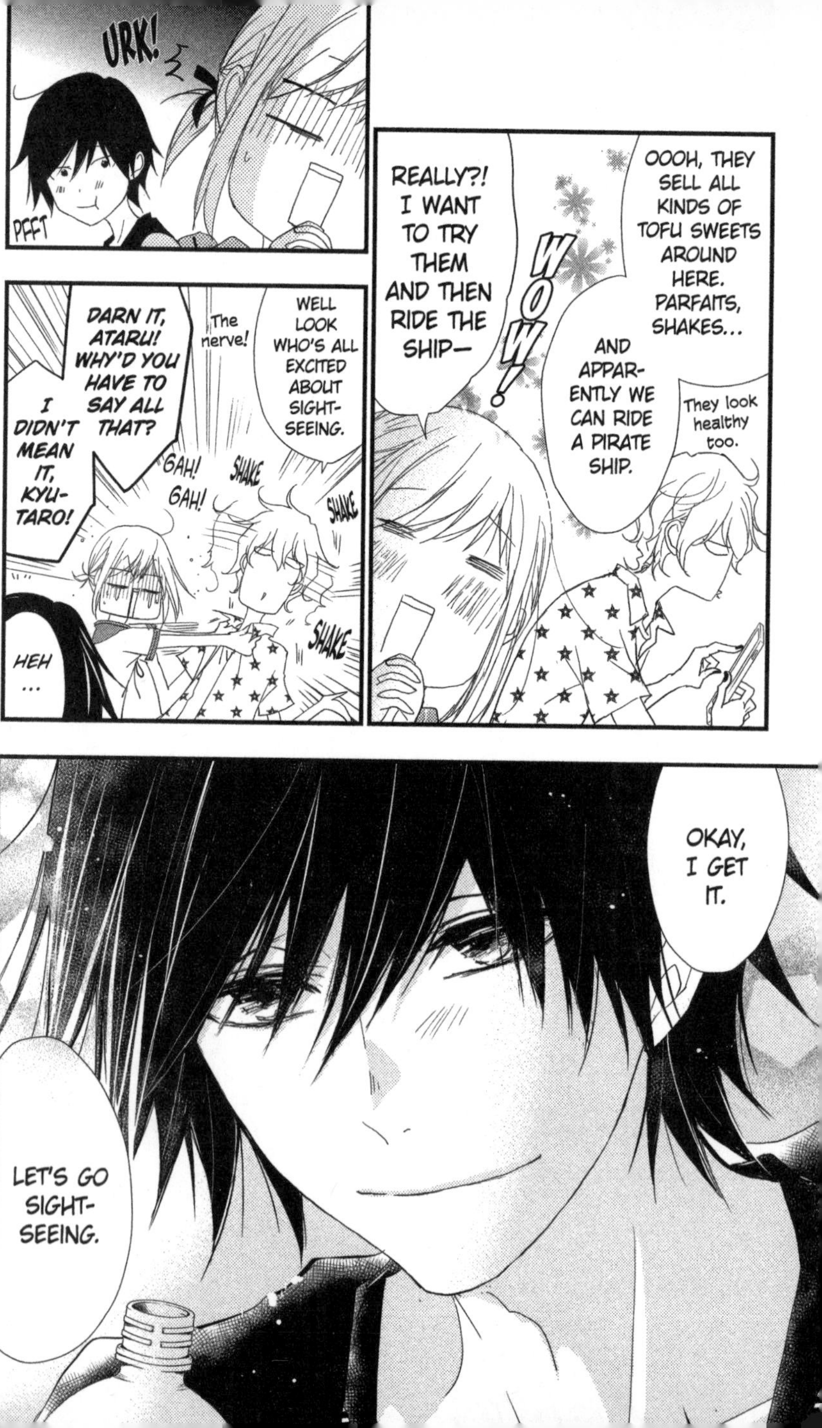
OOOH, THEY SELL ALL KINDS OF TOFU SWEETS AROUND HERE. PARFAITS, SHAKES...
AND APPARENTLY WE CAN RIDE A PIRATE SHIP.
They look healthy too.
WOW!
REALLY?! I WANT TO TRY THEM AND THEN RIDE THE SHIP—
URK!
PFFT
WELL LOOK WHO'S ALL EXCITED ABOUT SIGHT-SEEING.
The nerve!
SHAKE
SHAKE
SHAKE
DARN IT, ATARU! WHY'D YOU HAVE TO SAY ALL THAT?
GAH! GAH!
I DIDN'T MEAN IT, KYU-TARO!
HEH...
OKAY, I GET IT.
LET'S GO SIGHT-SEEING.

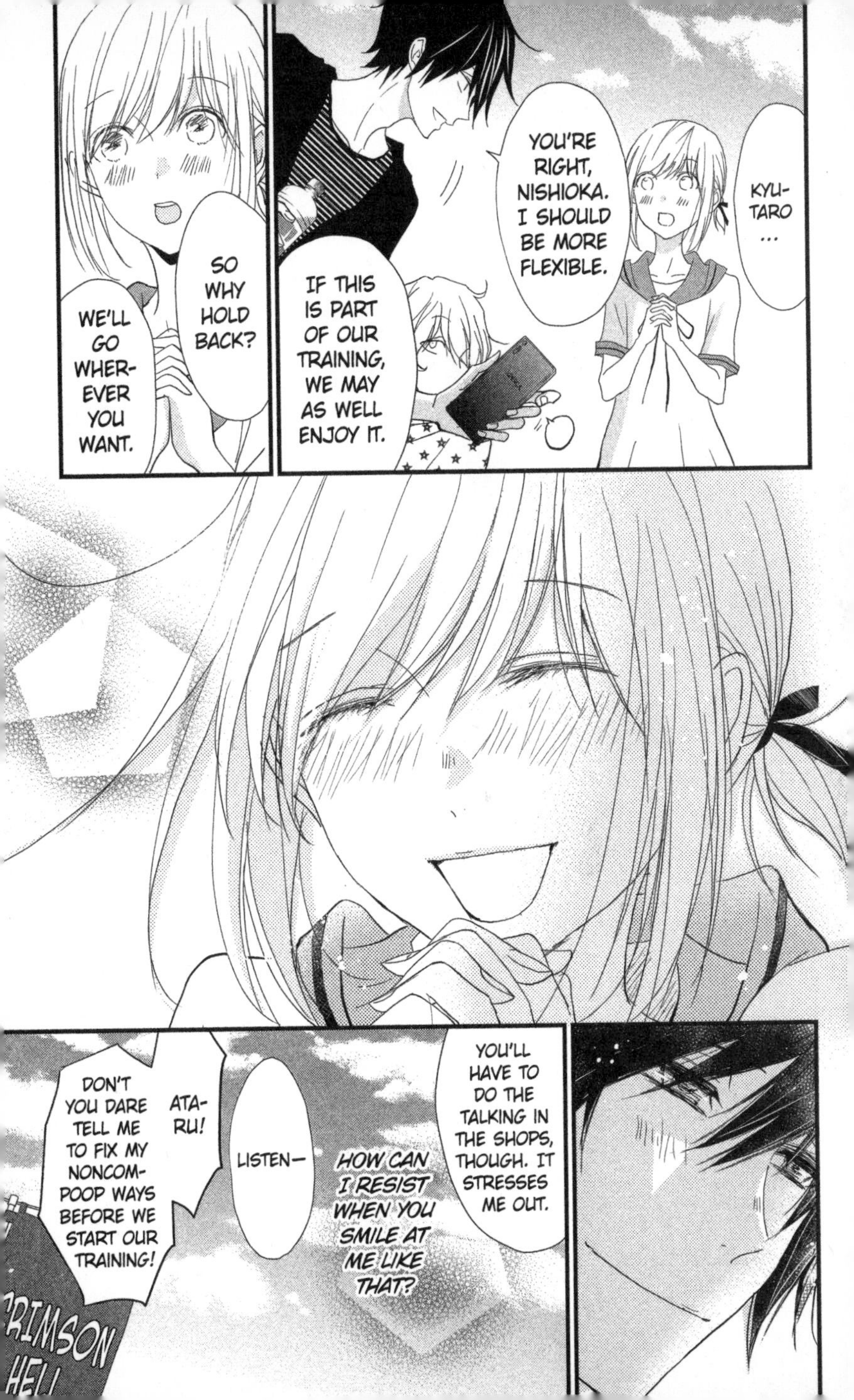
KYU-TARO...
YOU'RE RIGHT, NISHIOKA. I SHOULD BE MORE FLEXIBLE.
IF THIS IS PART OF OUR TRAINING, WE MAY AS WELL ENJOY IT.
SO WHY HOLD BACK?
WE'LL GO WHEREVER YOU WANT.
YOU'LL HAVE TO DO THE TALKING IN THE SHOPS, THOUGH. IT STRESSES ME OUT.
HOW CAN I RESIST WHEN YOU SMILE AT ME LIKE THAT?
LISTEN—
ATARU!
DON'T YOU DARE TELL ME TO FIX MY NONCOMPOOP WAYS BEFORE WE START OUR TRAINING!
CRIMSON HELL

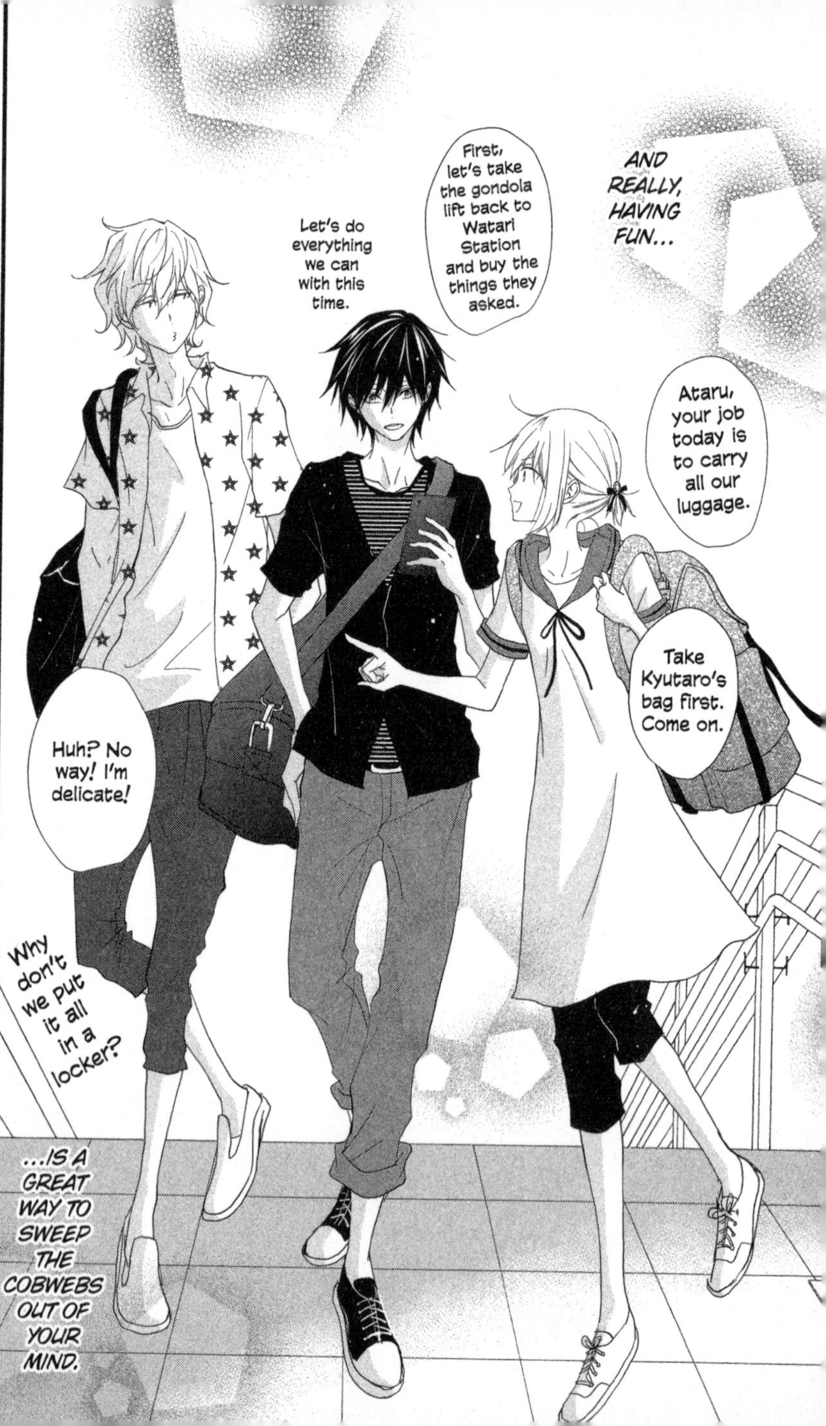
AND REALLY, HAVING FUN...
First, let's take the gondola lift back to Watari Station and buy the things they asked.
Let's do everything we can with this time.
Ataru, your job today is to carry all our luggage.
Take Kyutaro's bag first. Come on.
Huh? No way! I'm delicate!
Why don't we put it all in a locker?
...IS A GREAT WAY TO SWEEP THE COBWEBS OUT OF YOUR MIND.

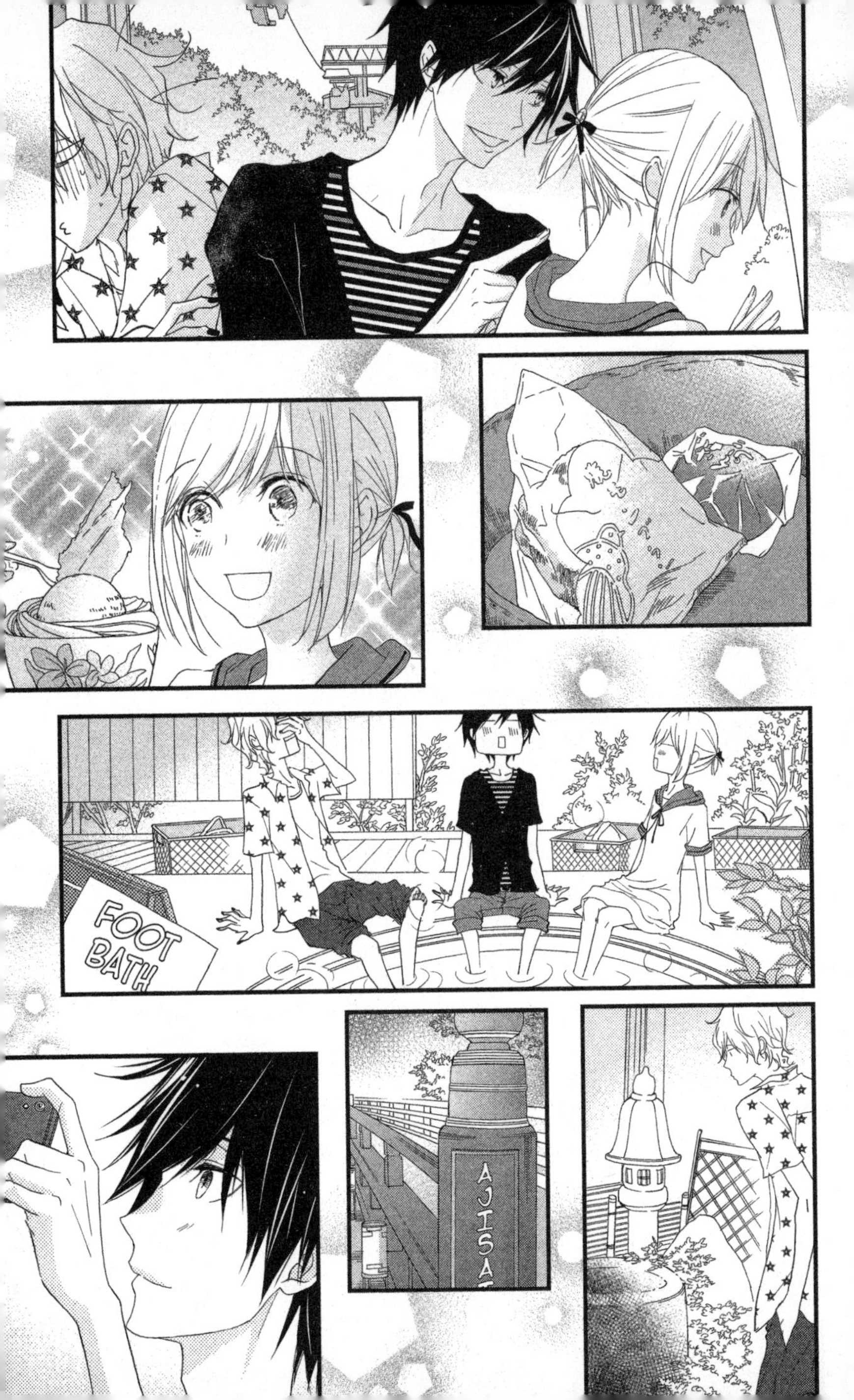
FOOT BATH
AJISA

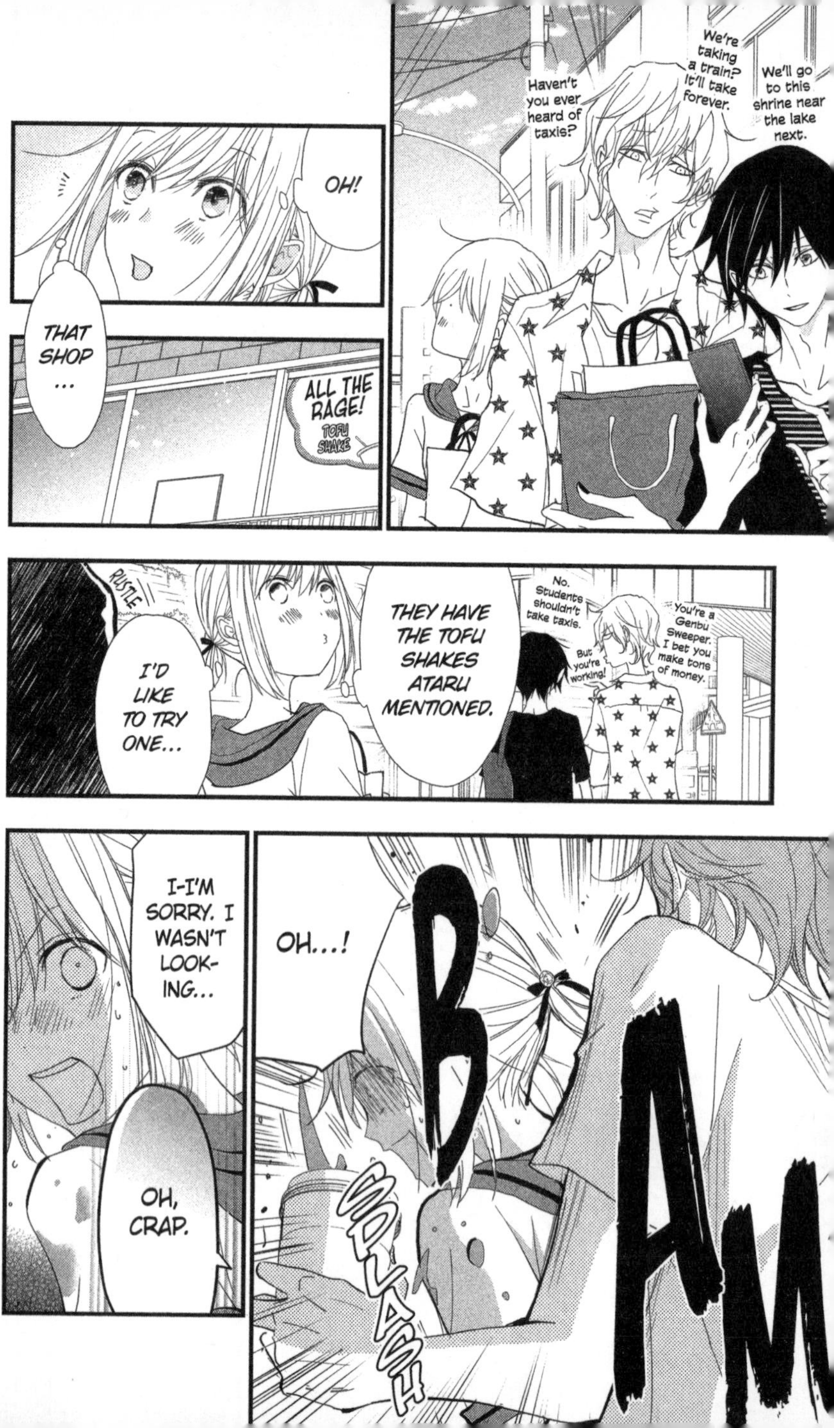
We'll go to this shrine near the lake next.
We're taking a train? It'll take forever.
Haven't you ever heard of taxis?
OH!
THAT SHOP...
ALL THE RAGE!
TOFU SHAKE
You're a Genbu Sweeper. I bet you make tons of money.
No. Students shouldn't take taxis.
But you're working!
THEY HAVE THE TOFU SHAKES ATARU MENTIONED.
I'D LIKE TO TRY ONE...
RUSTLE
OH...!
BAM
SPLASH
I-I'M SORRY. I WASN'T LOOKING...
OH, CRAP.

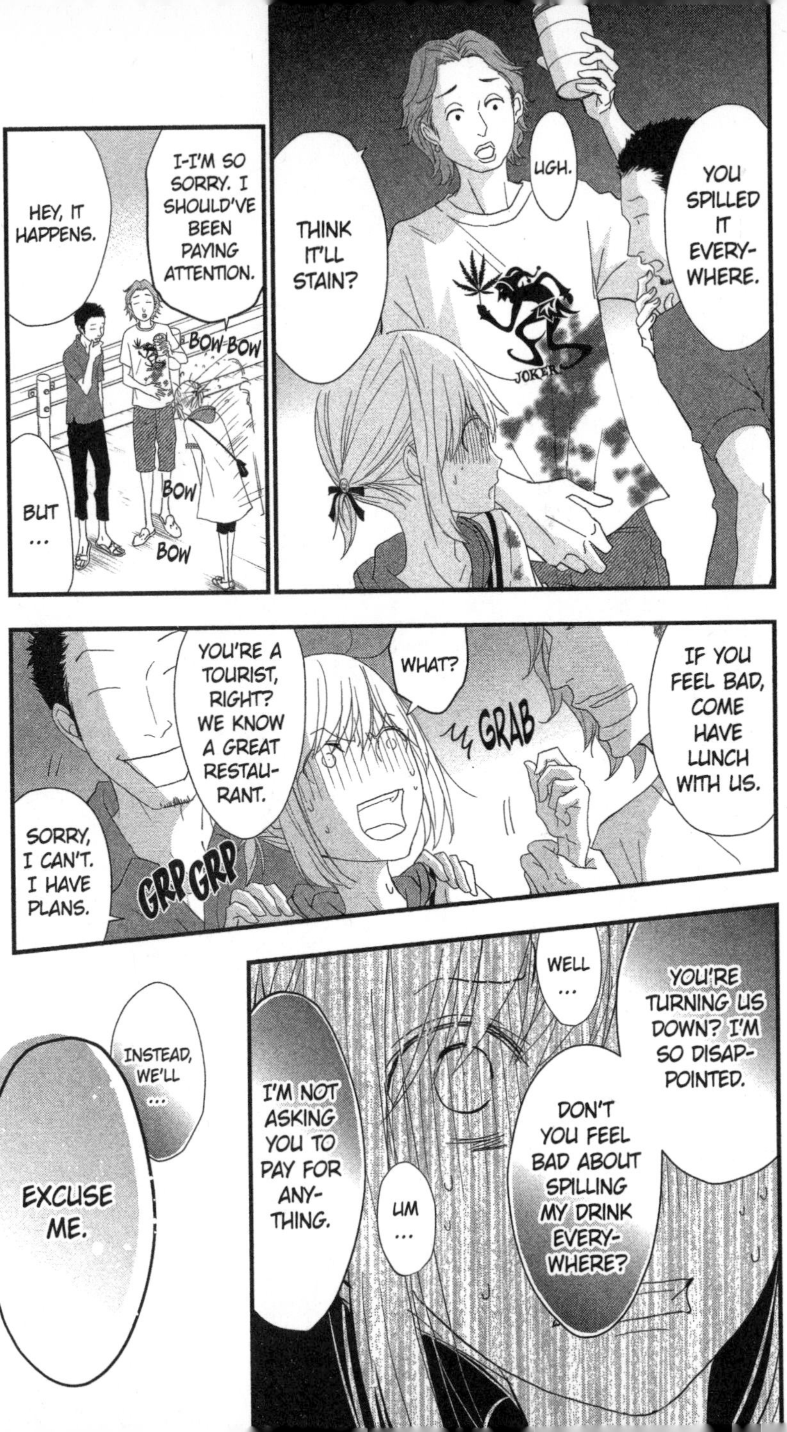
YOU SPILLED IT EVERY-WHERE.
UGH.
THINK IT'LL STAIN?
JOKER
I-I'M SO SORRY. I SHOULD'VE BEEN PAYING ATTENTION.
BOW BOW
HEY, IT HAPPENS.
BOW
BOW
BUT ...
IF YOU FEEL BAD, COME HAVE LUNCH WITH US.
GRAB
WHAT?
YOU'RE A TOURIST, RIGHT? WE KNOW A GREAT RESTAU-RANT.
GRP GRP
SORRY, I CAN'T. I HAVE PLANS.
YOU'RE TURNING US DOWN? I'M SO DISAP-POINTED.
WELL ...
DON'T YOU FEEL BAD ABOUT SPILLING MY DRINK EVERY-WHERE?
I'M NOT ASKING YOU TO PAY FOR ANY-THING.
UM ...
INSTEAD, WE'LL ...
EXCUSE ME.

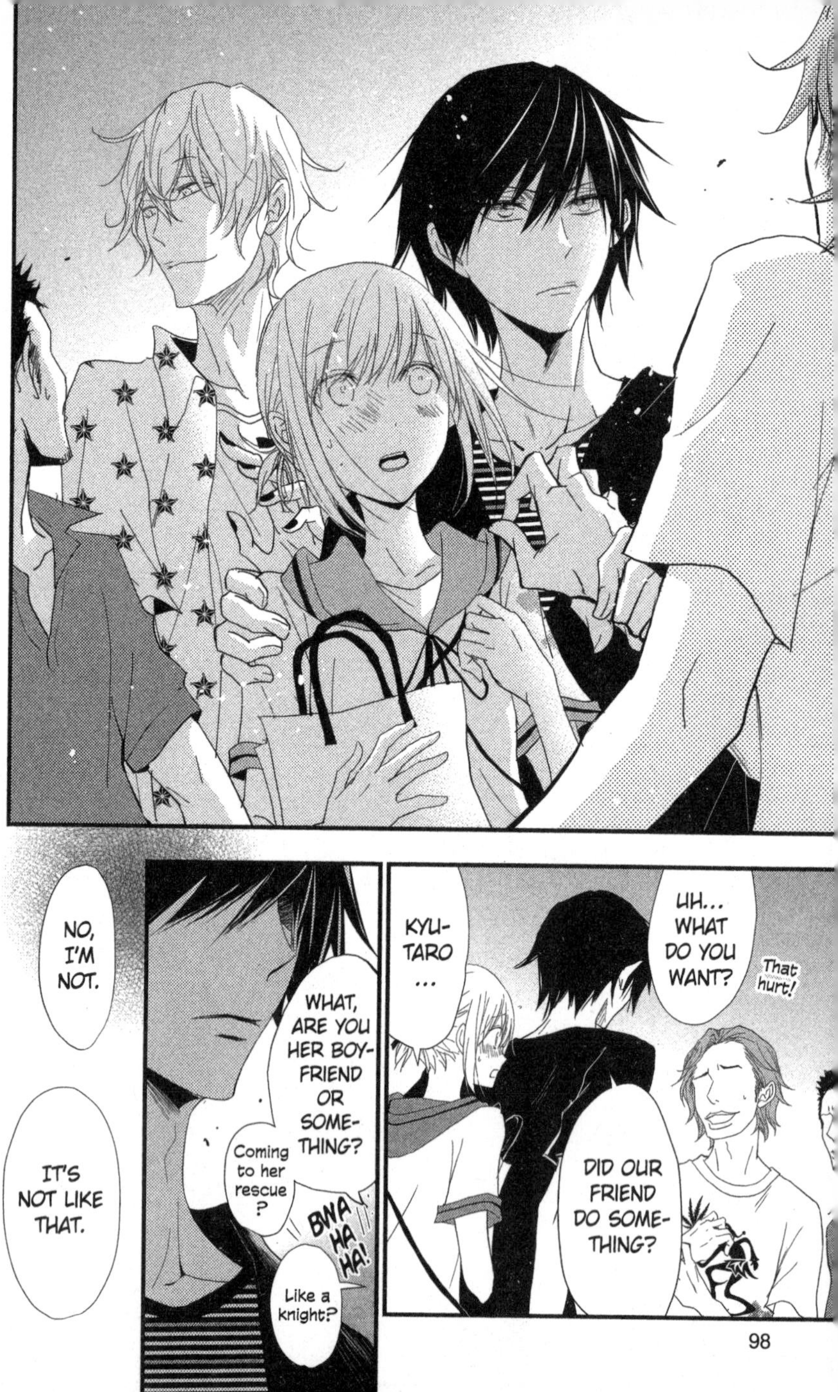
That hurt!
UH... WHAT DO YOU WANT?
KYU-TARO ...
DID OUR FRIEND DO SOME-THING?
WHAT, ARE YOU HER BOY-FRIEND OR SOME-THING?
Coming to her rescue?
BWA HA HA!
Like a knight?
NO, I'M NOT.
IT'S NOT LIKE THAT.

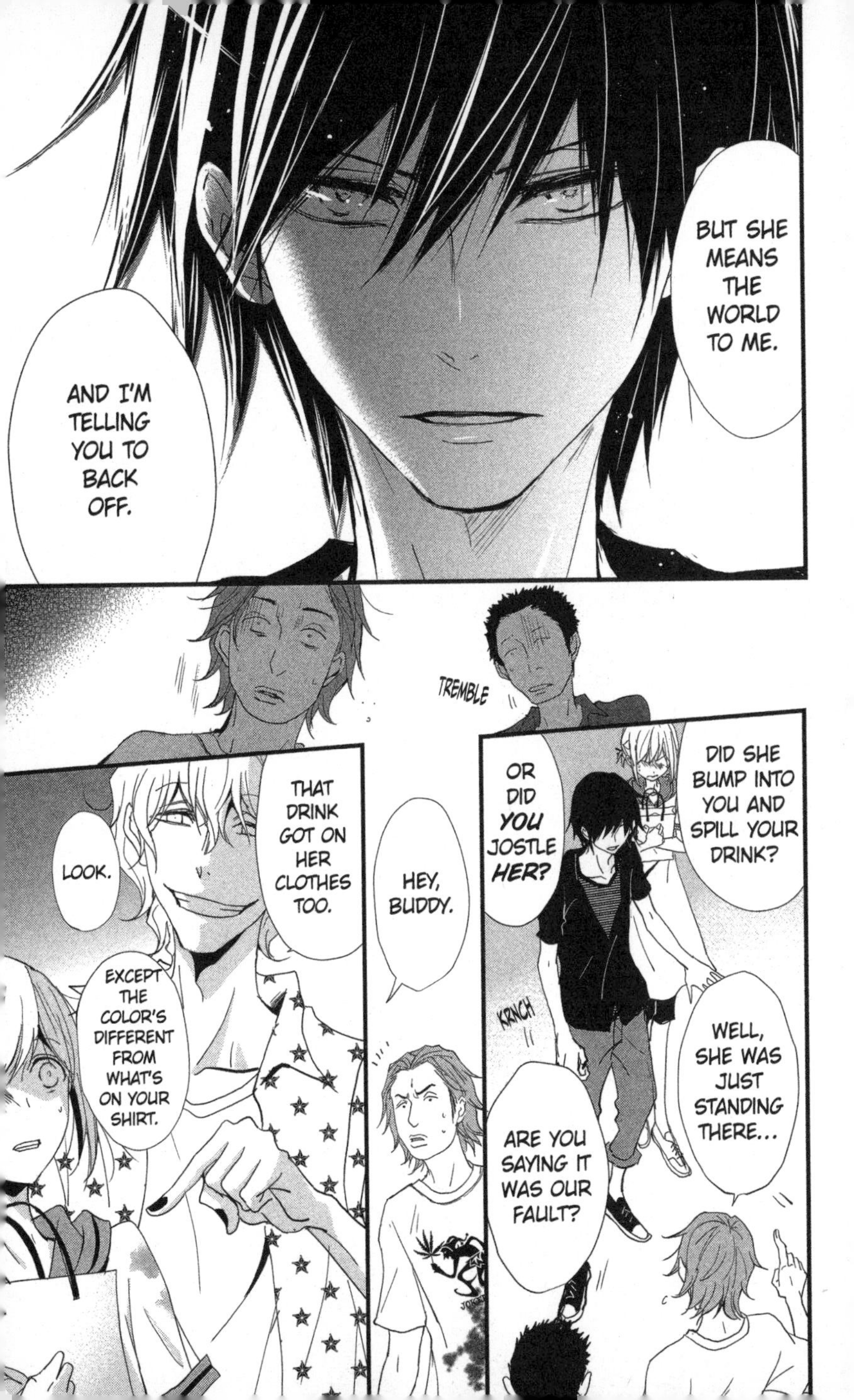
BUT SHE MEANS THE WORLD TO ME.
AND I'M TELLING YOU TO BACK OFF.
TREMBLE
DID SHE BUMP INTO YOU AND SPILL YOUR DRINK?
OR DID *YOU* JOSTLE *HER*?
KRNCH
WELL, SHE WAS JUST STANDING THERE...
ARE YOU SAYING IT WAS OUR FAULT?
HEY, BUDDY.
THAT DRINK GOT ON HER CLOTHES TOO.
LOOK.
EXCEPT THE COLOR'S DIFFERENT FROM WHAT'S ON YOUR SHIRT.

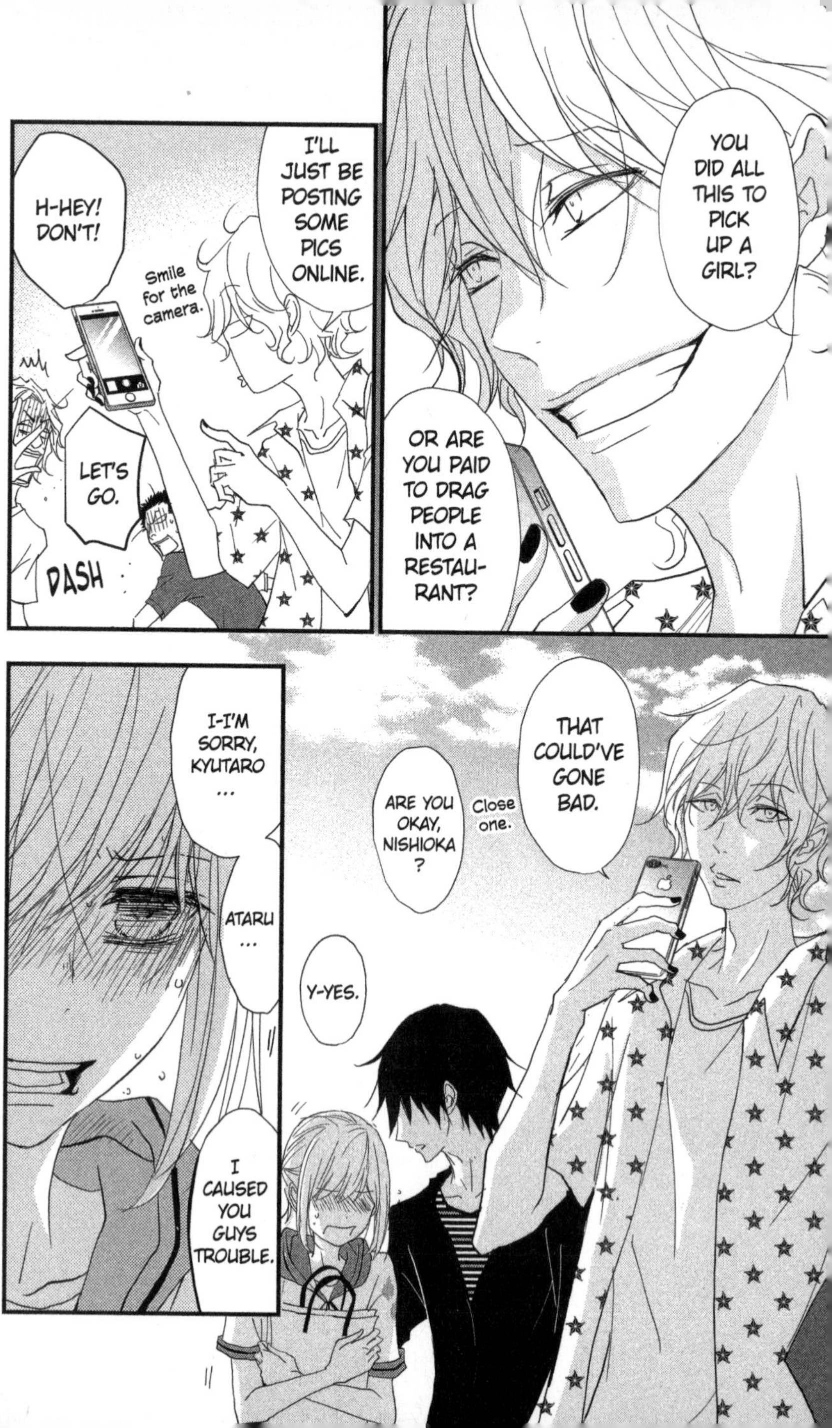

YOU DID ALL THIS TO PICK UP A GIRL?
OR ARE YOU PAID TO DRAG PEOPLE INTO A RESTAU-RANT?
I'LL JUST BE POSTING SOME PICS ONLINE.
Smile for the camera.
H-HEY! DON'T!
LET'S GO.
DASH
THAT COULD'VE GONE BAD.
Close one.
ARE YOU OKAY, NISHIOKA?
Y-YES.
I-I'M SORRY, KYUTARO...
ATARU...
I CAUSED YOU GUYS TROUBLE.

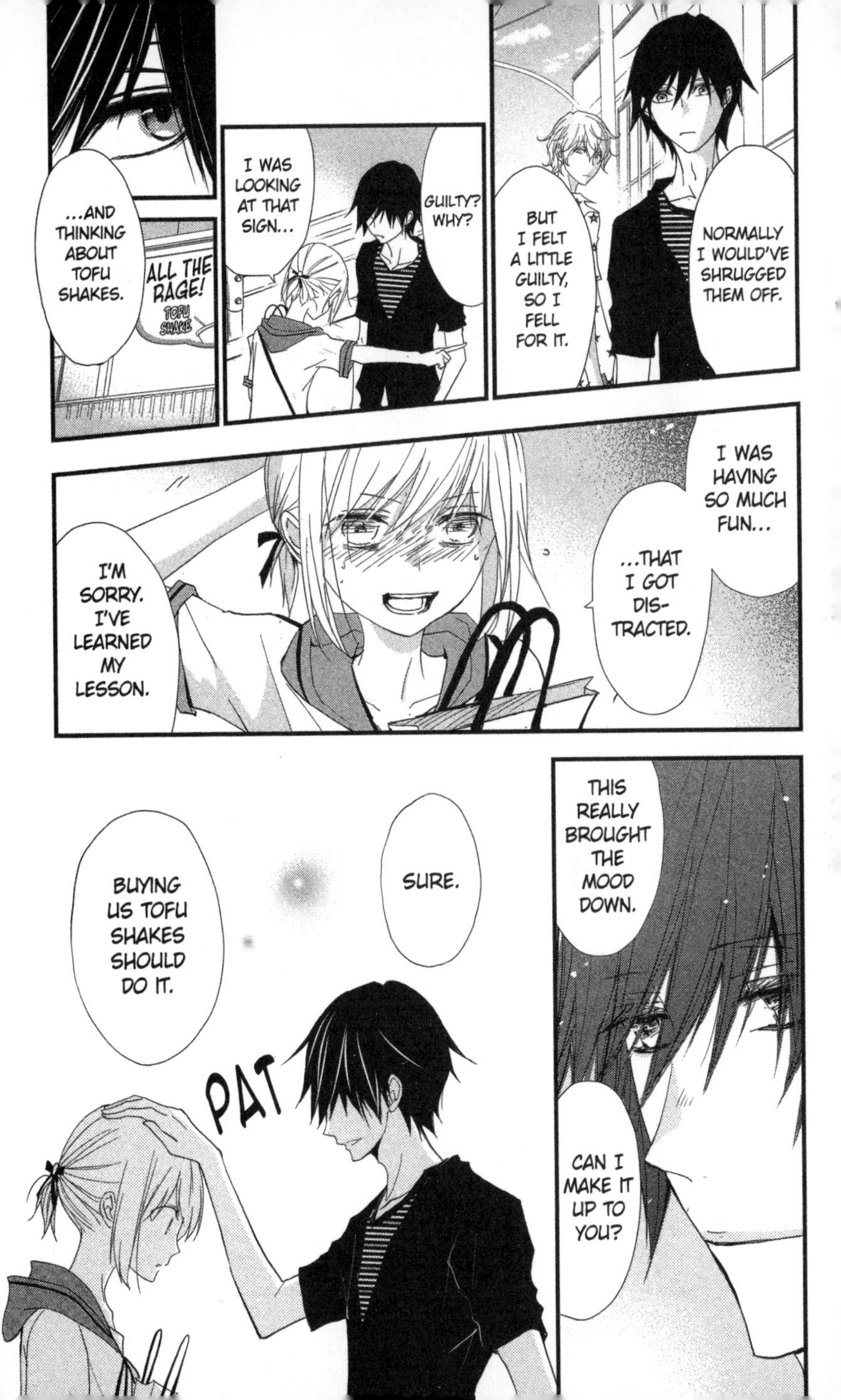
NORMALLY I WOULD'VE SHRUGGED THEM OFF.
BUT I FELT A LITTLE GUILTY, SO I FELL FOR IT.
GUILTY? WHY?
I WAS LOOKING AT THAT SIGN...
...AND THINKING ABOUT TOFU SHAKES.
ALL THE RAGE!
TOFU SHAKE
I WAS HAVING SO MUCH FUN...
...THAT I GOT DIS-TRACTED.
I'M SORRY. I'VE LEARNED MY LESSON.
THIS REALLY BROUGHT THE MOOD DOWN.
CAN I MAKE IT UP TO YOU?
SURE.
BUYING US TOFU SHAKES SHOULD DO IT.
PAT

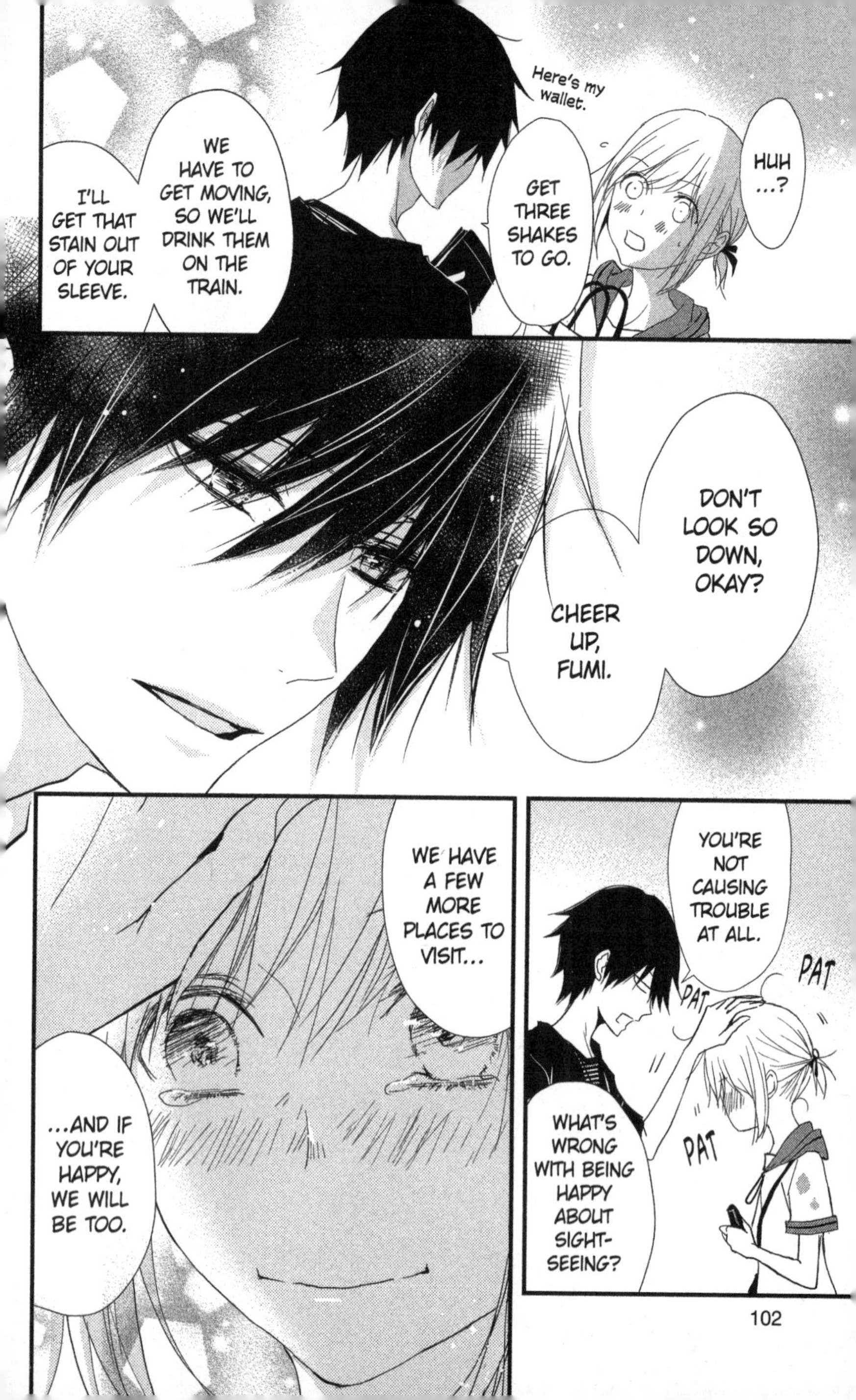
HUH ...?
Here's my wallet.
GET THREE SHAKES TO GO.
WE HAVE TO GET MOVING, SO WE'LL DRINK THEM ON THE TRAIN.
I'LL GET THAT STAIN OUT OF YOUR SLEEVE.
DON'T LOOK SO DOWN, OKAY?
CHEER UP, FUMI.
YOU'RE NOT CAUSING TROUBLE AT ALL.
PAT
PAT
PAT
WHAT'S WRONG WITH BEING HAPPY ABOUT SIGHT-SEEING?
WE HAVE A FEW MORE PLACES TO VISIT...
...AND IF YOU'RE HAPPY, WE WILL BE TOO.

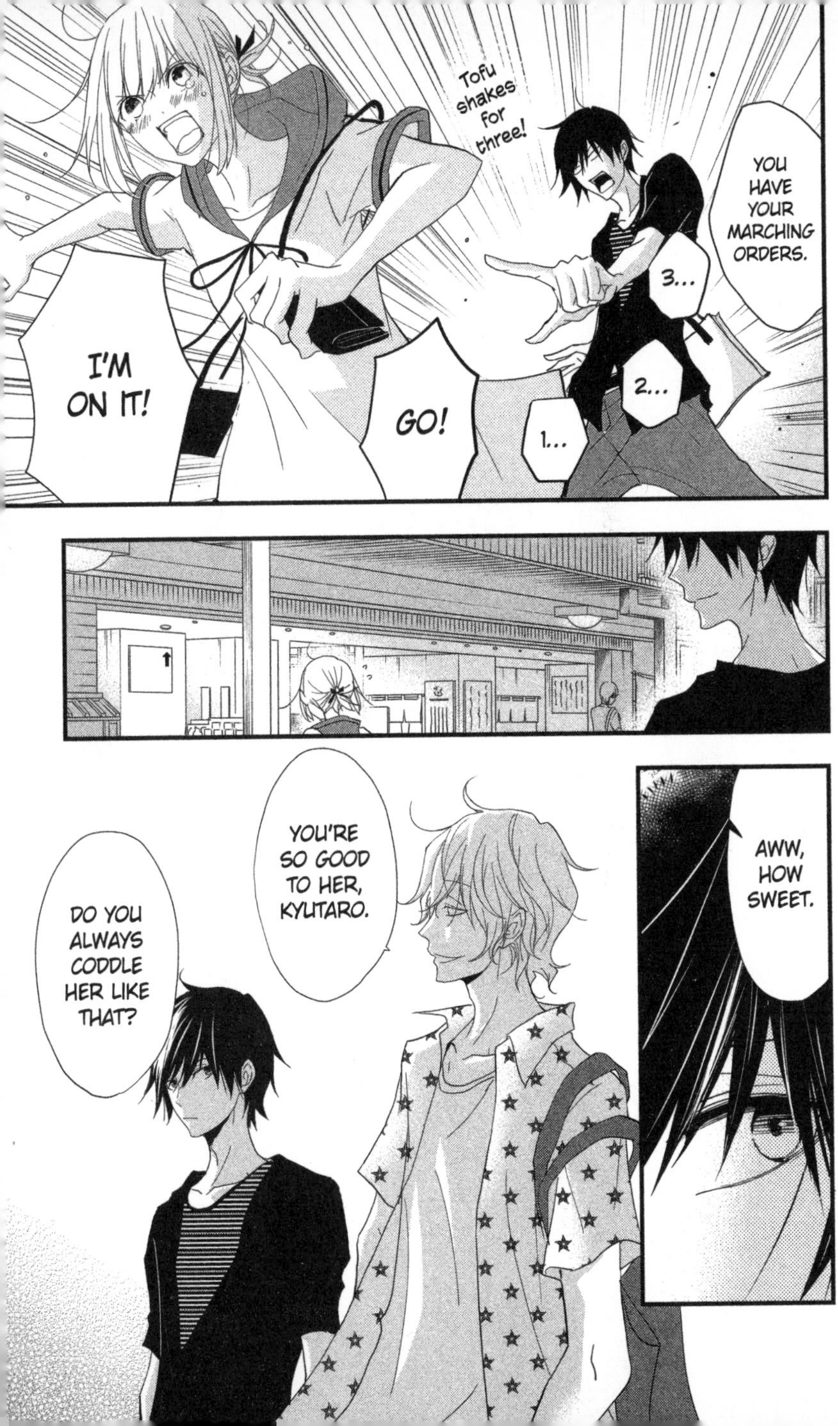
YOU HAVE YOUR MARCHING ORDERS.
Tofu shakes for three!
3...
2...
1...
GO!
I'M ON IT!
AWW, HOW SWEET.
YOU'RE SO GOOD TO HER, KYUTARO.
DO YOU ALWAYS CODDLE HER LIKE THAT?

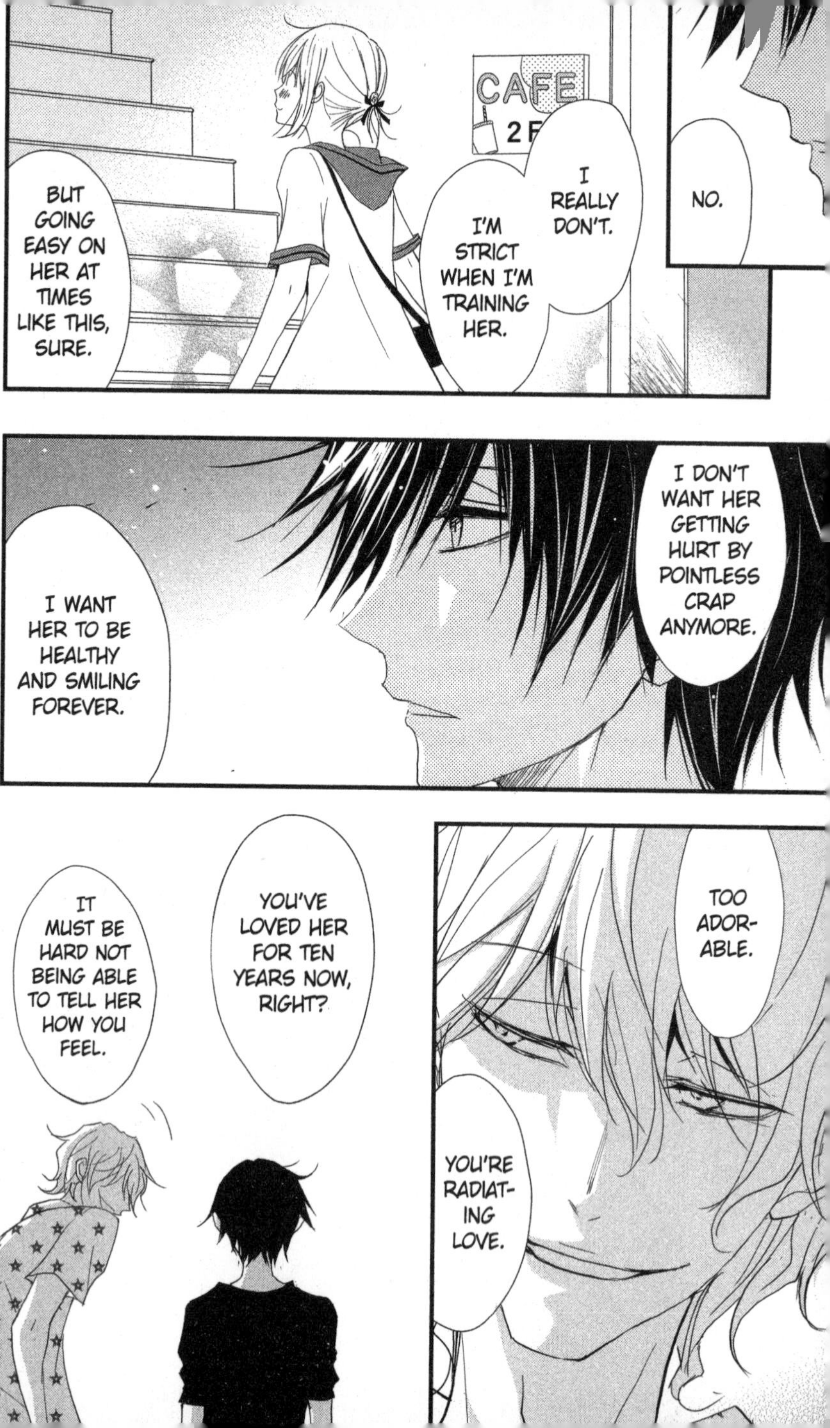
NO.
CAFE
I REALLY DON'T.
I'M STRICT WHEN I'M TRAINING HER.
BUT GOING EASY ON HER AT TIMES LIKE THIS, SURE.
I DON'T WANT HER GETTING HURT BY POINTLESS CRAP ANYMORE.
I WANT HER TO BE HEALTHY AND SMILING FOREVER.
TOO ADORABLE.
YOU'RE RADIATING LOVE.
YOU'VE LOVED HER FOR TEN YEARS NOW, RIGHT?
IT MUST BE HARD NOT BEING ABLE TO TELL HER HOW YOU FEEL.

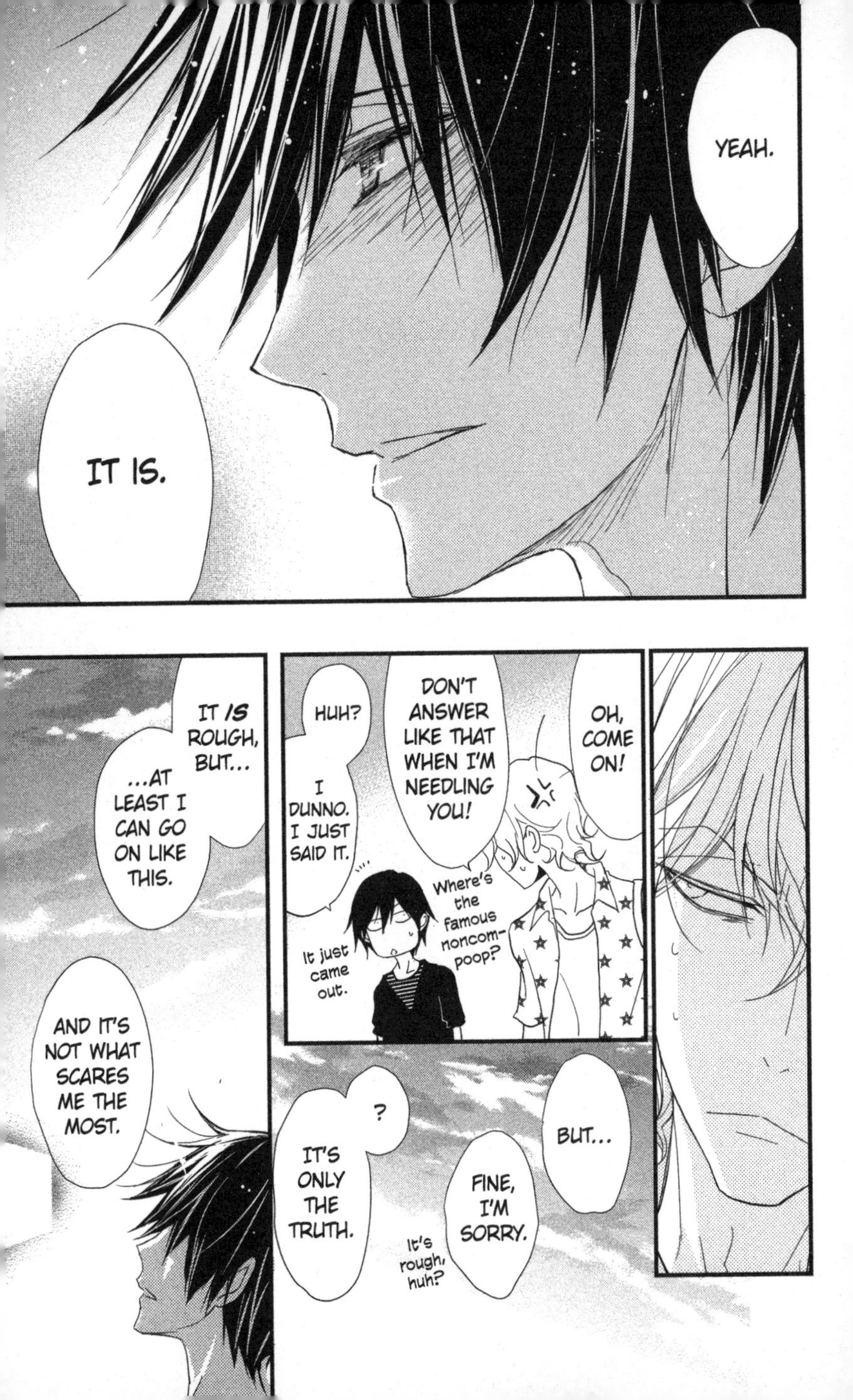
YEAH.
IT IS.
OH, COME ON!
DON'T ANSWER LIKE THAT WHEN I'M NEEDLING YOU!
Where's the famous noncom-poop?
HUH?
I DUNNO. I JUST SAID IT.
It just came out.
BUT...
FINE, I'M SORRY.
It's rough, huh?
?
IT'S ONLY THE TRUTH.
IT *IS* ROUGH, BUT...
...AT LEAST I CAN GO ON LIKE THIS.
AND IT'S NOT WHAT SCARES ME THE MOST.

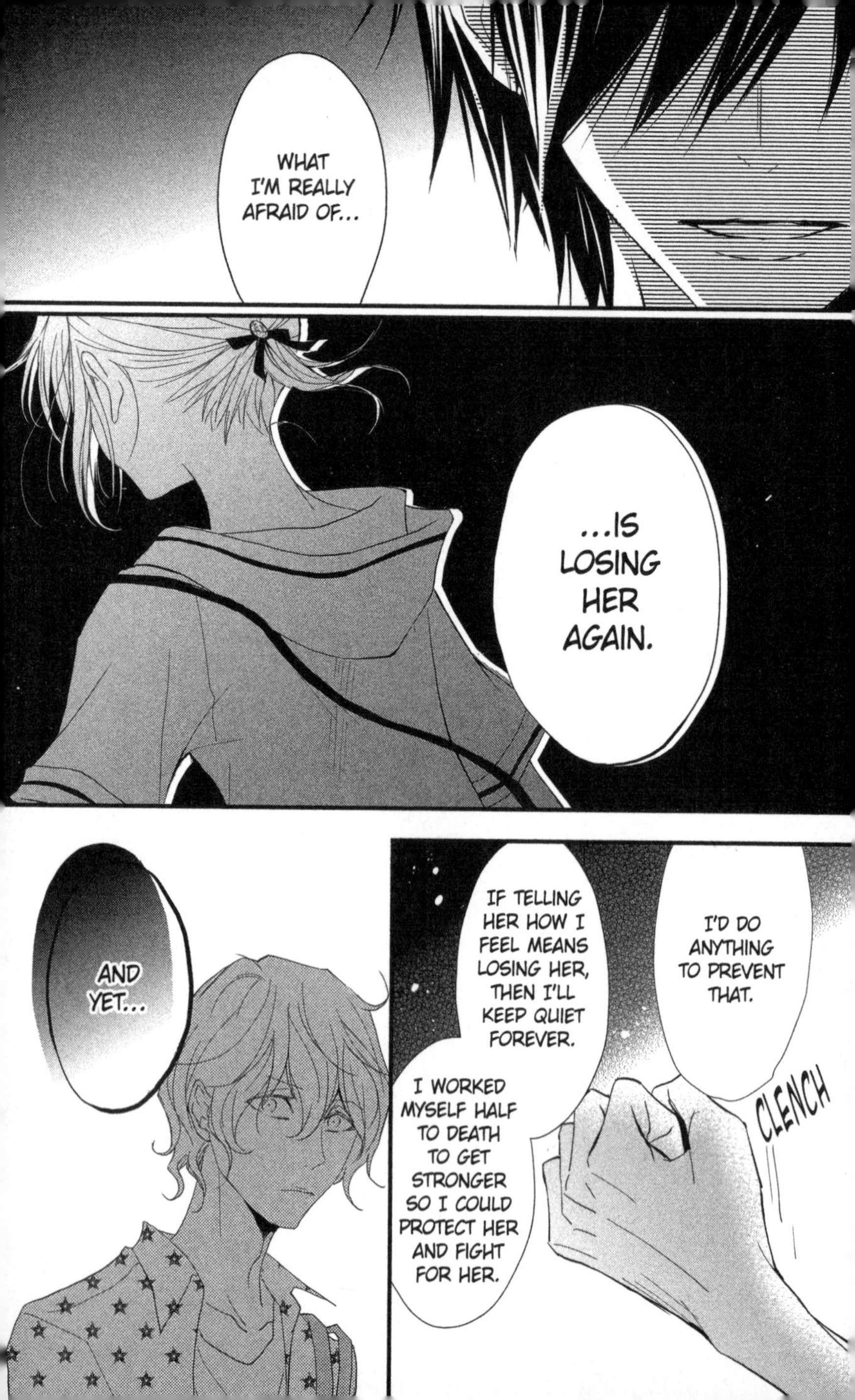
WHAT I'M REALLY AFRAID OF...
...IS LOSING HER AGAIN.
I'D DO ANYTHING TO PREVENT THAT.
IF TELLING HER HOW I FEEL MEANS LOSING HER, THEN I'LL KEEP QUIET FOREVER.
CLENCH
I WORKED MYSELF HALF TO DEATH TO GET STRONGER SO I COULD PROTECT HER AND FIGHT FOR HER.
AND YET...

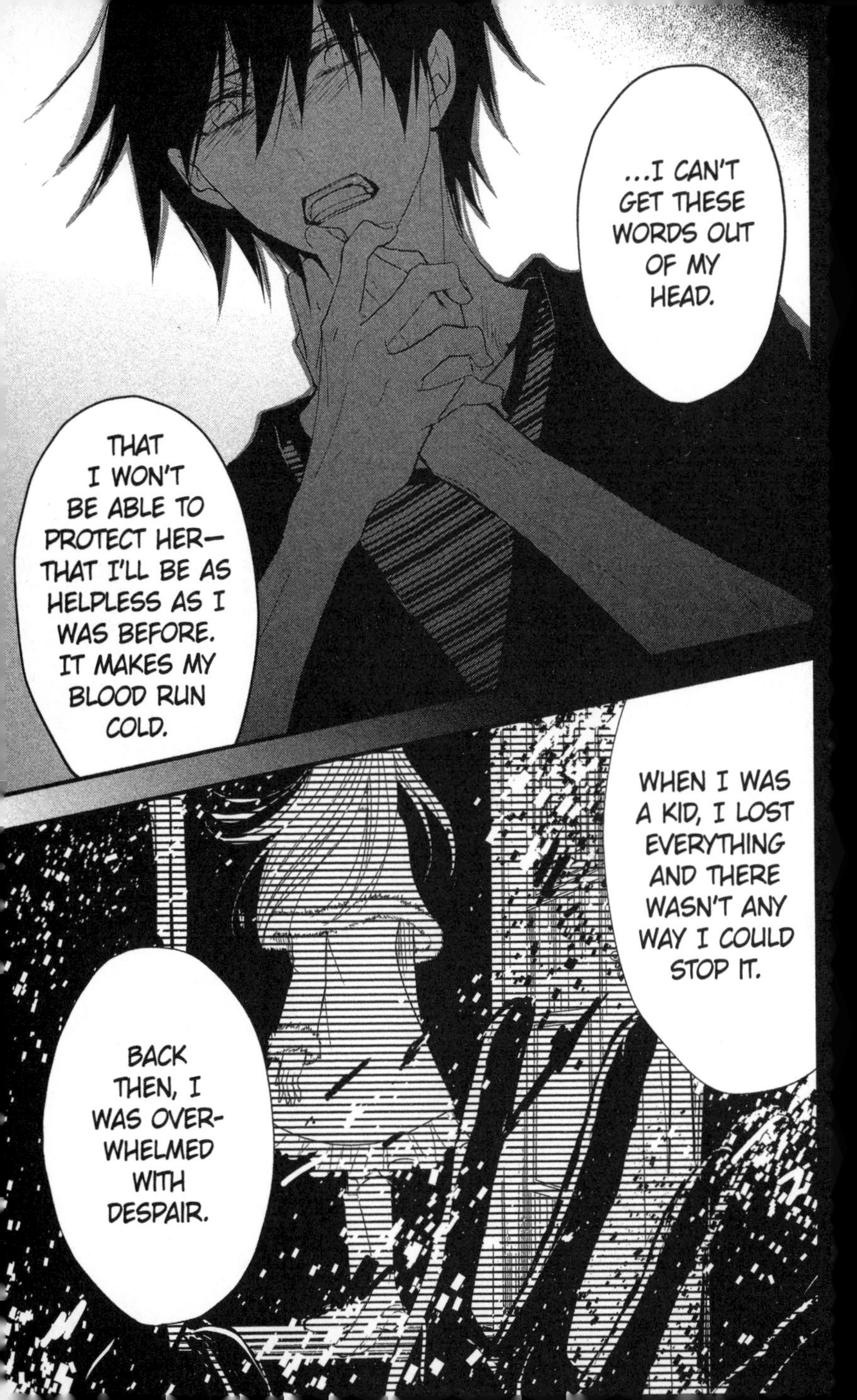
...I CAN'T GET THESE WORDS OUT OF MY HEAD.
THAT I WON'T BE ABLE TO PROTECT HER— THAT I'LL BE AS HELPLESS AS I WAS BEFORE. IT MAKES MY BLOOD RUN COLD.
WHEN I WAS A KID, I LOST EVERYTHING AND THERE WASN'T ANY WAY I COULD STOP IT.
BACK THEN, I WAS OVER-WHELMED WITH DESPAIR.

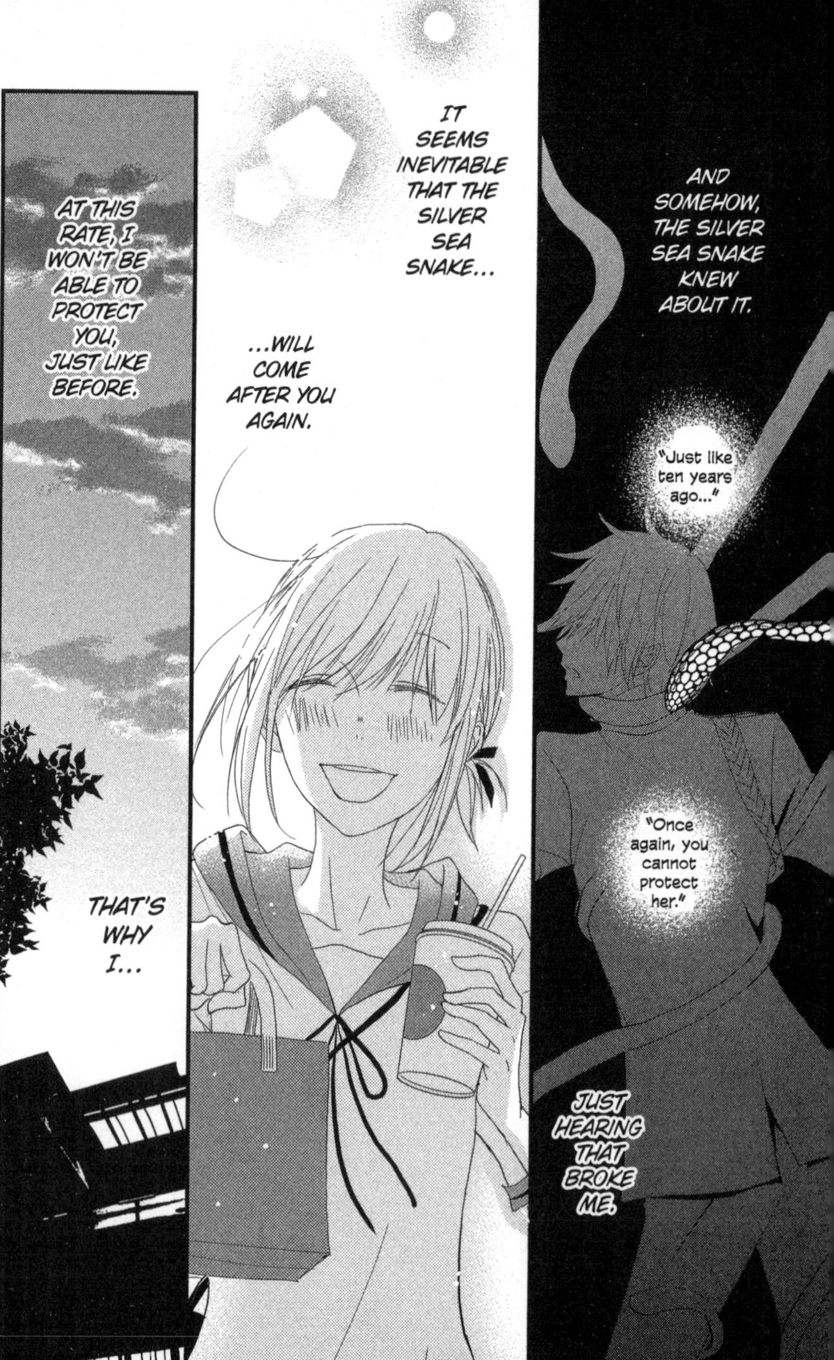
AND SOMEHOW, THE SILVER SEA SNAKE KNEW ABOUT IT.
"Just like ten years ago..."
"Once again, you cannot protect her."
JUST HEARING THAT BROKE ME.
IT SEEMS INEVITABLE THAT THE SILVER SEA SNAKE...
...WILL COME AFTER YOU AGAIN.
AT THIS RATE, I WON'T BE ABLE TO PROTECT YOU, JUST LIKE BEFORE.
THAT'S WHY I...

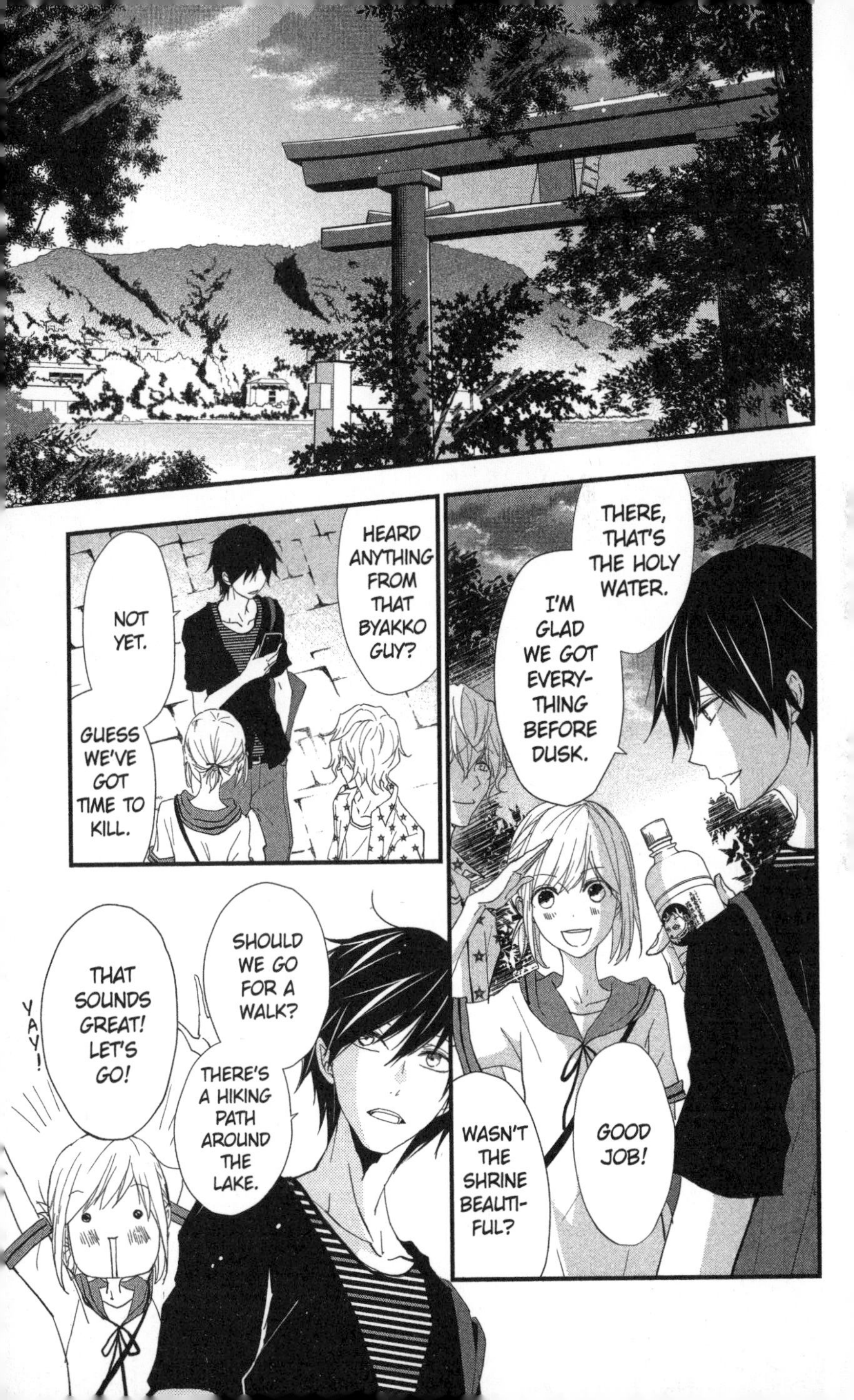
THERE, THAT'S THE HOLY WATER.
I'M GLAD WE GOT EVERY-THING BEFORE DUSK.
GOOD JOB!
WASN'T THE SHRINE BEAUTI-FUL?
HEARD ANYTHING FROM THAT BYAKKO GUY?
NOT YET.
GUESS WE'VE GOT TIME TO KILL.
SHOULD WE GO FOR A WALK?
THERE'S A HIKING PATH AROUND THE LAKE.
THAT SOUNDS GREAT! LET'S GO!
YAY!

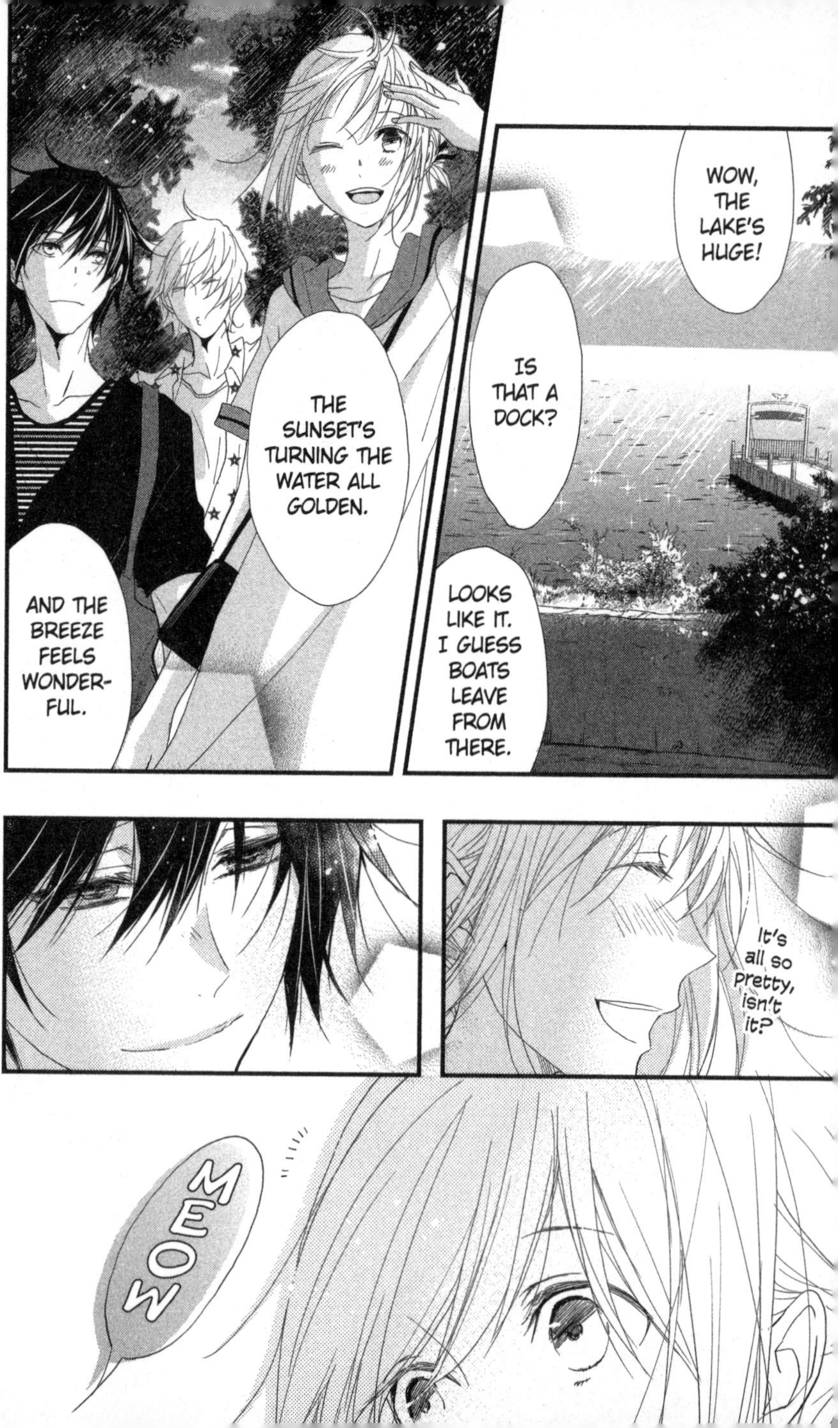
WOW, THE LAKE'S HUGE!
IS THAT A DOCK?
LOOKS LIKE IT. I GUESS BOATS LEAVE FROM THERE.
THE SUNSET'S TURNING THE WATER ALL GOLDEN.
AND THE BREEZE FEELS WONDER-FUL.
It's all so pretty, isn't it?
MEOW

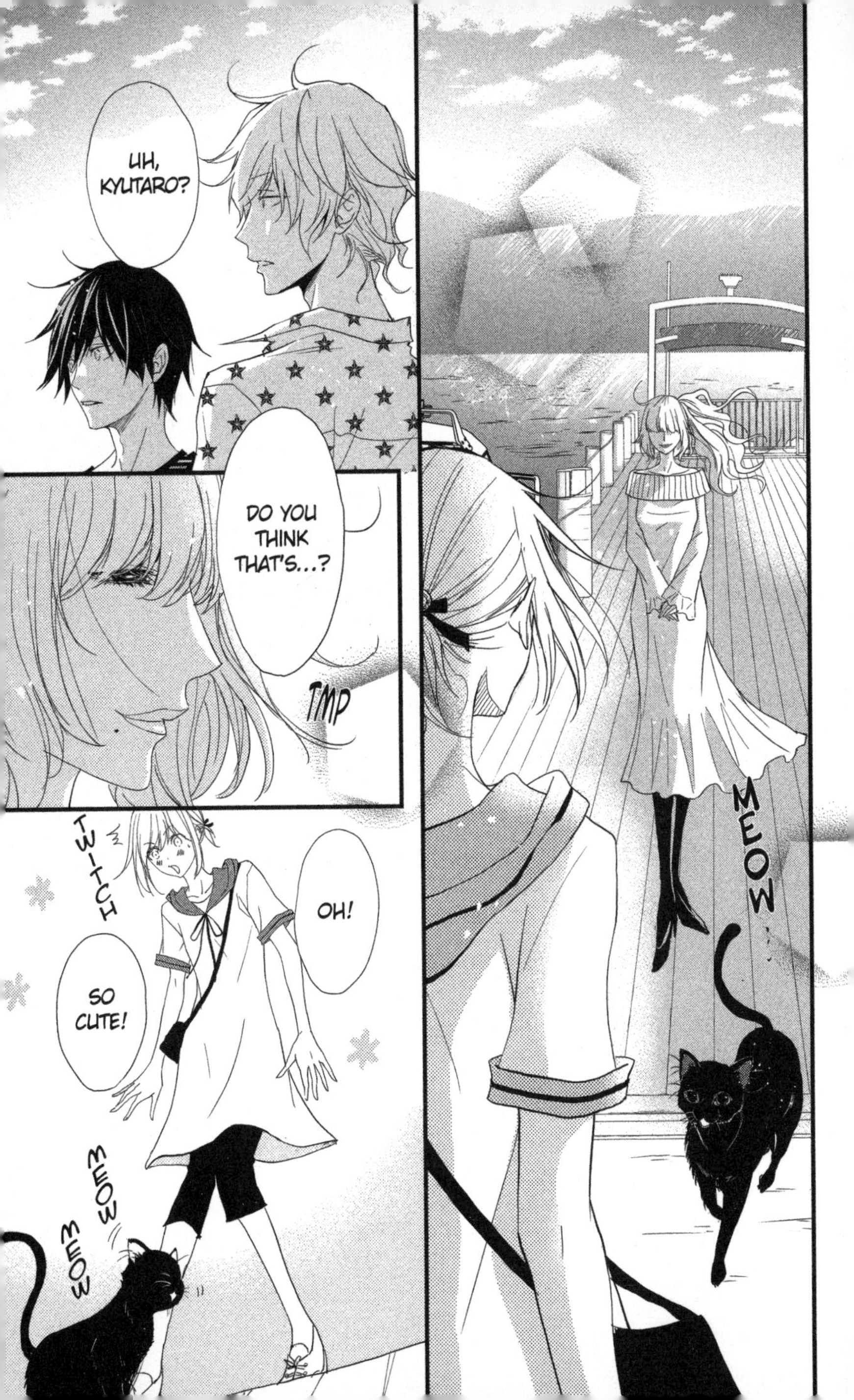
MEOW
UH, KYUTARO?
DO YOU THINK THAT'S...?
TMP
OH!
SO CUTE!
TWITCH
MEOW
MEOW

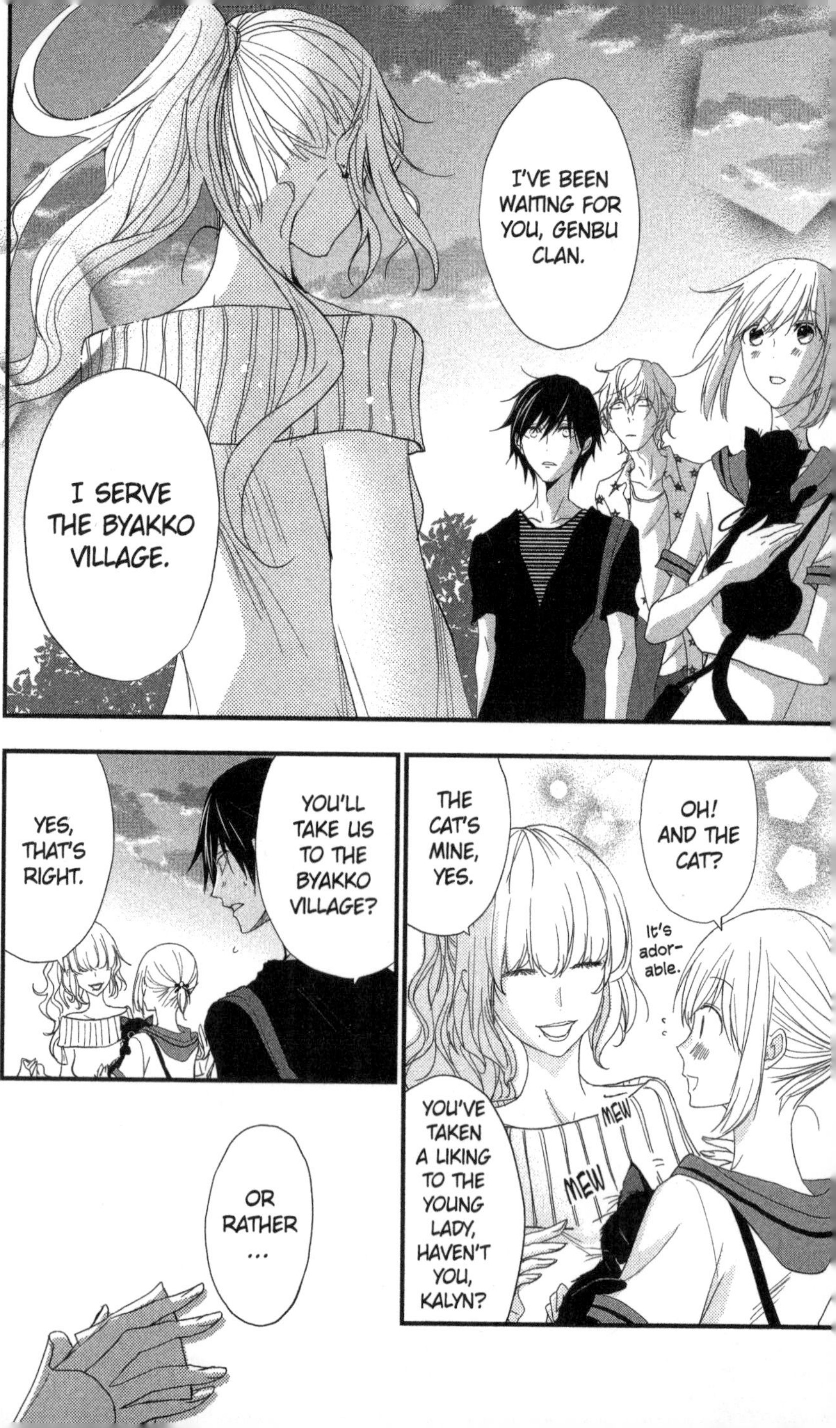

I'VE BEEN WAITING FOR YOU, GENBU CLAN.
I SERVE THE BYAKKO VILLAGE.
OH! AND THE CAT?
THE CAT'S MINE, YES.
It's adorable.
MEW
MEW
YOU'VE TAKEN A LIKING TO THE YOUNG LADY, HAVEN'T YOU, KALYN?
YOU'LL TAKE US TO THE BYAKKO VILLAGE?
YES, THAT'S RIGHT.
OR RATHER...

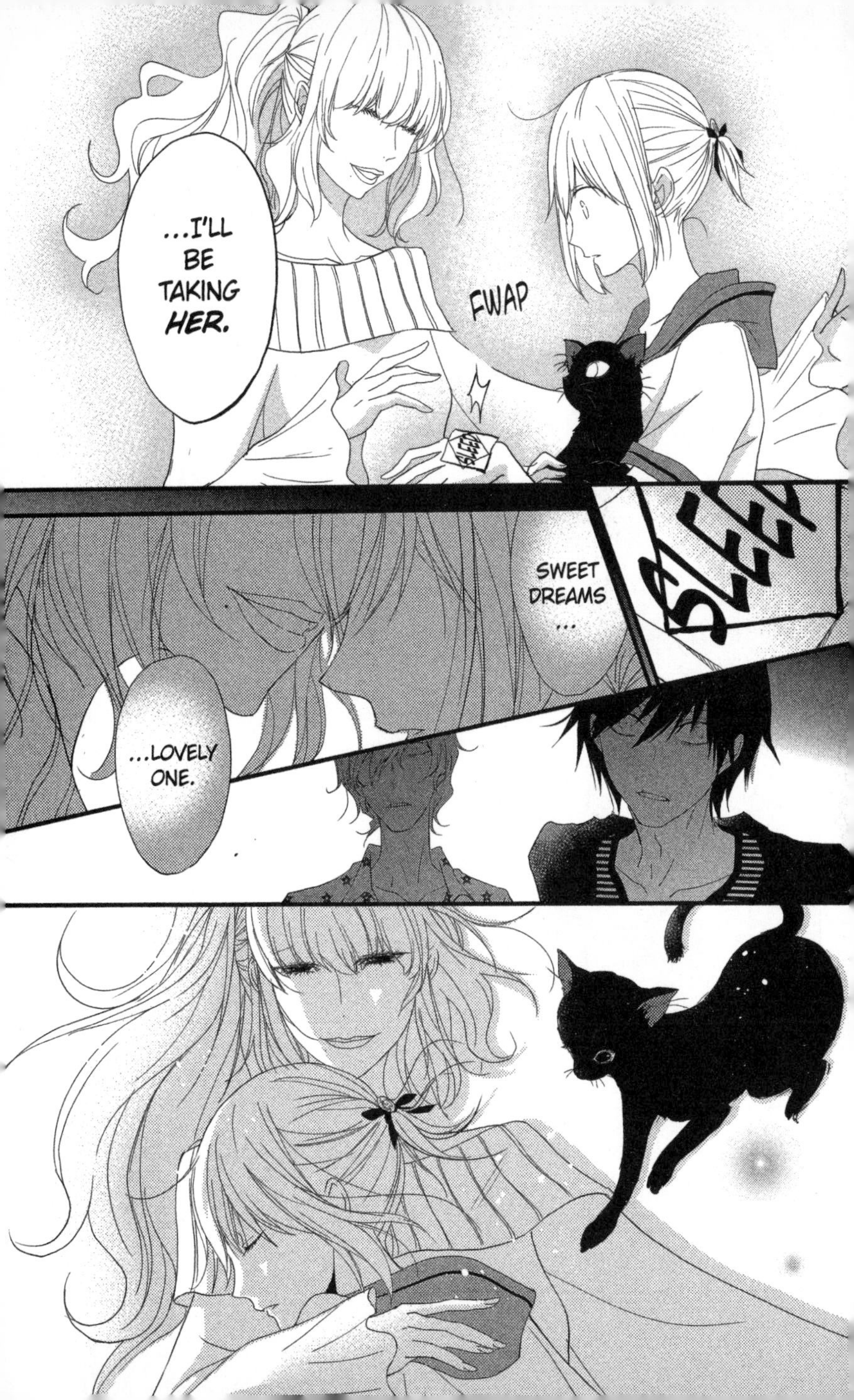
FWAP
...I'LL BE TAKING HER.
SLEEP
SLEEP
SWEET DREAMS ...
...LOVELY ONE.

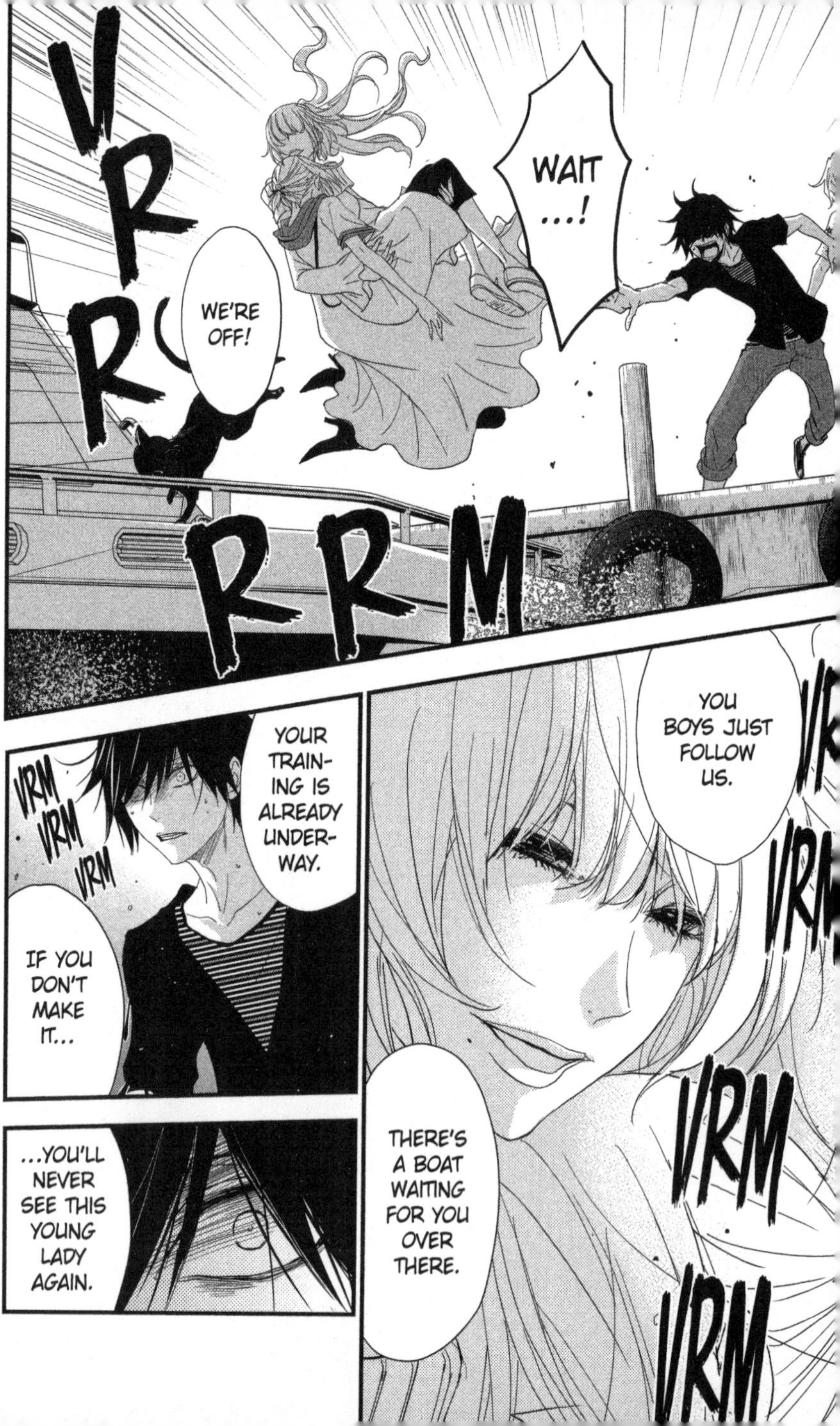
WAIT...!
WE'RE OFF!
VRRRRM
YOU BOYS JUST FOLLOW US.
THERE'S A BOAT WAITING FOR YOU OVER THERE.
VRM
VRM
YOUR TRAINING IS ALREADY UNDERWAY.
VRM VRM VRM
IF YOU DON'T MAKE IT...
...YOU'LL NEVER SEE THIS YOUNG LADY AGAIN.

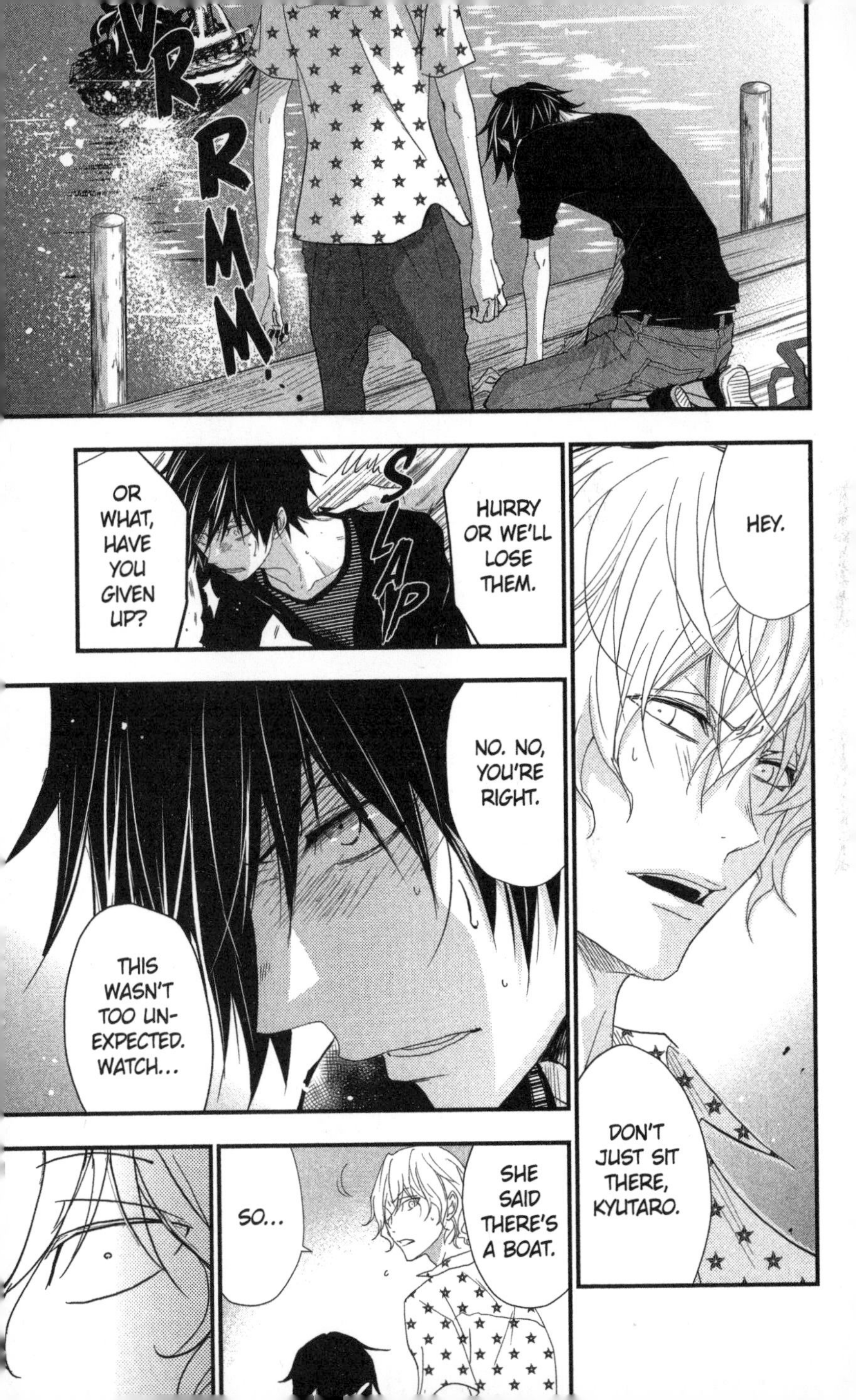
VRRMM!
HEY.
DON'T JUST SIT THERE, KYUTARO.
SLAP
HURRY OR WE'LL LOSE THEM.
OR WHAT, HAVE YOU GIVEN UP?
NO. NO, YOU'RE RIGHT.
THIS WASN'T TOO UN-EXPECTED. WATCH...
SHE SAID THERE'S A BOAT.
SO...

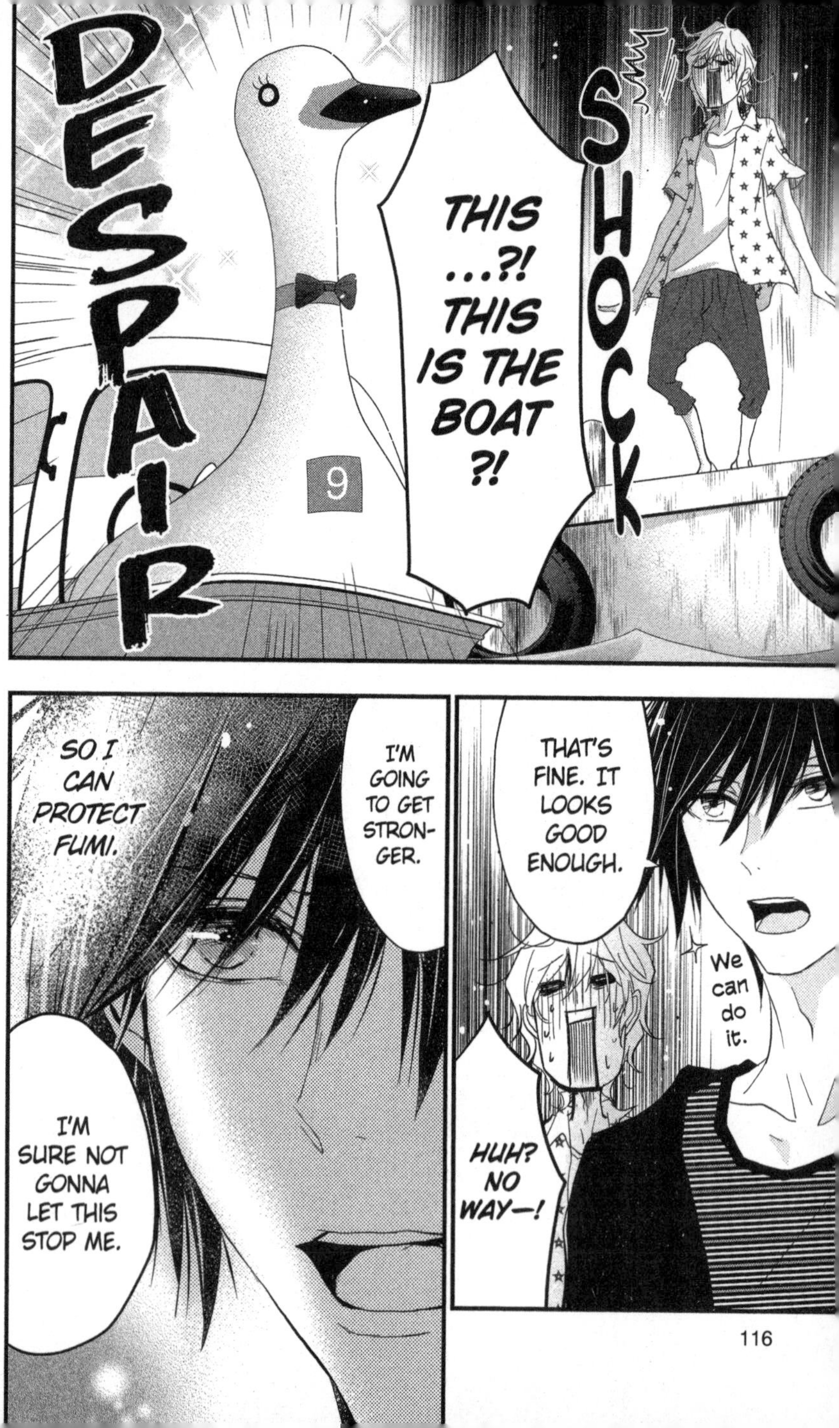
SHOCK
THIS ...?! THIS IS THE BOAT ?!
DESPAIR
THAT'S FINE. IT LOOKS GOOD ENOUGH.
We can do it.
HUH? NO WAY—!
I'M GOING TO GET STRON-GER.
SO I CAN PROTECT FUMI.
I'M SURE NOT GONNA LET THIS STOP ME.

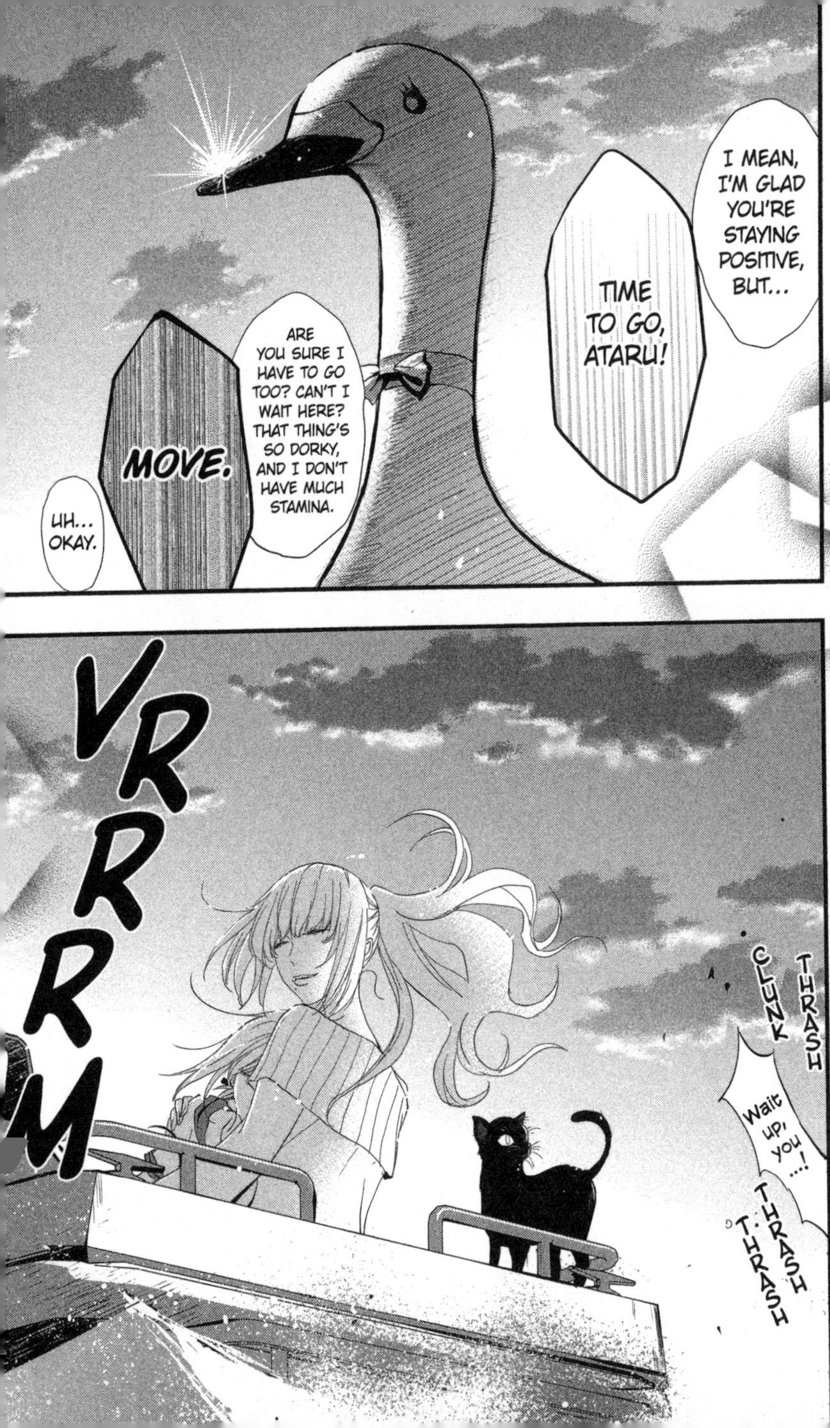
I MEAN, I'M GLAD YOU'RE STAYING POSITIVE, BUT...
TIME TO GO, ATARU!
ARE YOU SURE I HAVE TO GO TOO? CAN'T I WAIT HERE? THAT THING'S SO DORKY, AND I DON'T HAVE MUCH STAMINA.
MOVE.
UH... OKAY.
THRASH
CLUNK
Wait up, you...!
THRASH
THRASH
VRRRM

MONTHLY BETSUCOMI SALE DATE NOTICE ON TWITTER

CHAPTER 29

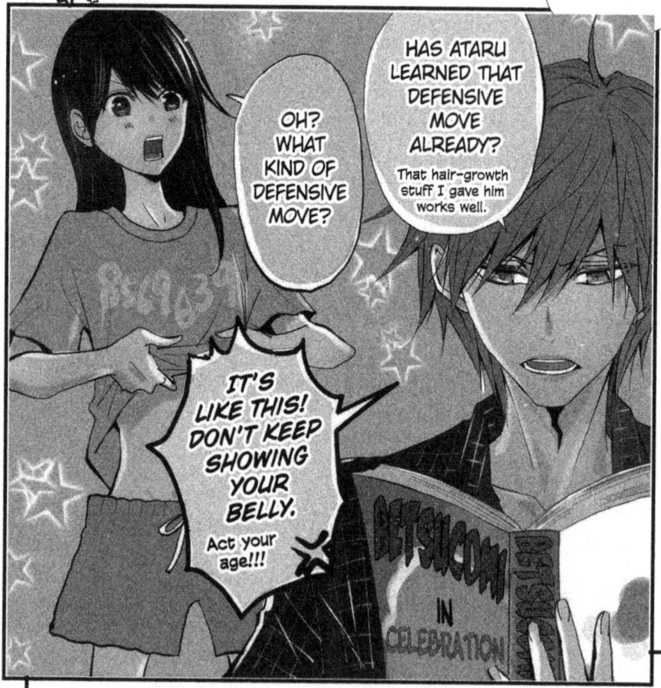
HAS ATARU LEARNED THAT DEFENSIVE MOVE ALREADY?
That hair-growth stuff I gave him works well.
OH? WHAT KIND OF DEFENSIVE MOVE?
IT'S LIKE THIS! DON'T KEEP SHOWING YOUR BELLY.
Act your age!!!
BETSUCOMI
IN CELEBRATION

WHAT'S UP IN *QUEEN'S QUALITY* THIS MONTH?
(1) I HEAR THE *ROSALIA BATESI* IS VERY PRETTY.
(2) THOSE SWEETS ARE PROBABLY THE KIND THAT FUMI AND THE GUYS BOUGHT. (DELICIOUS!)
(3) BOTH KYUTARO AND KUROSAKI HAVE USED THAT DEFENSIVE MOVE TO PROTECT QUITE A FEW THINGS.
CHAPTER 29 INTRODUCES A NEW CHARACTER AND HAS SOME NOT-SO-PLEASANT UNDRESSING SCENES!

KUROSAKI AND TERU FROM *DENGEKI DAISY* ARE BACK AGAIN. I'M GLAD THERE ARE STILL PEOPLE READING IT. WE HAVE SOME STAMPS WITH *DENGEKI DAISY* AND *QUEEN'S QUALITY* CHARACTERS FOR SALE ON LINE. SEARCH CREATORS' STAMPS ON "KYOUSUKE MOTOMI'S WHITE-EYED PEOPLE." (BIT.LY/2FVMC.E4)

THEY'RE FAIRLY EASY TO USE, AND I THINK THEY'LL MAKE INTERPERSONAL RELATIONS SMOOTHER. THEY'RE ALL ORIGINAL DESIGNS.

40 LIKE THIS ONE! →

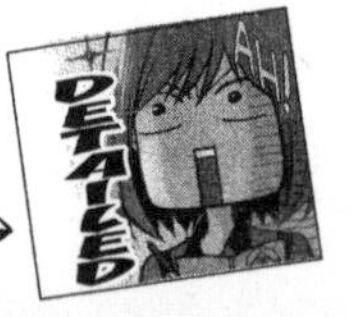
DETAILED

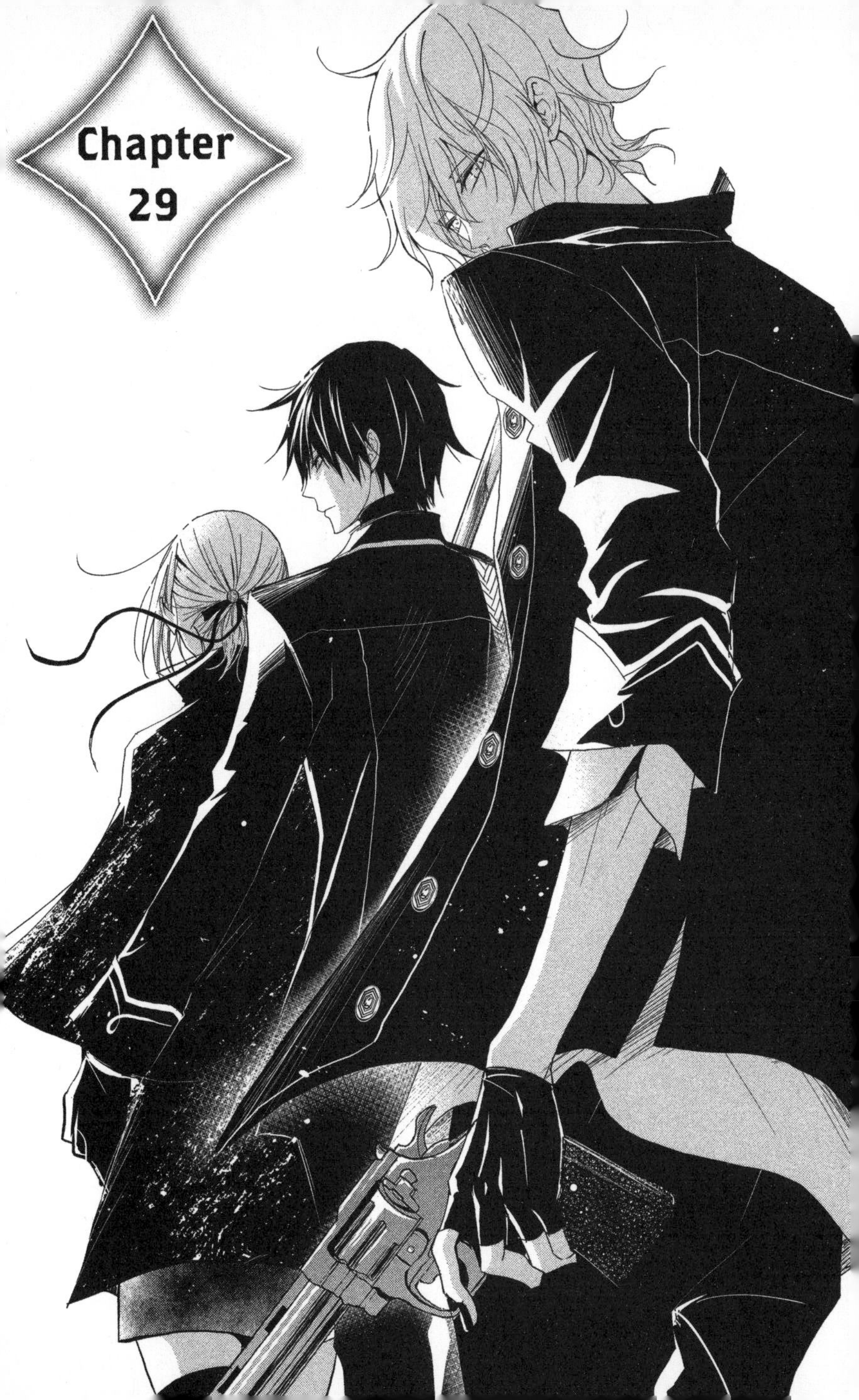
Chapter
29

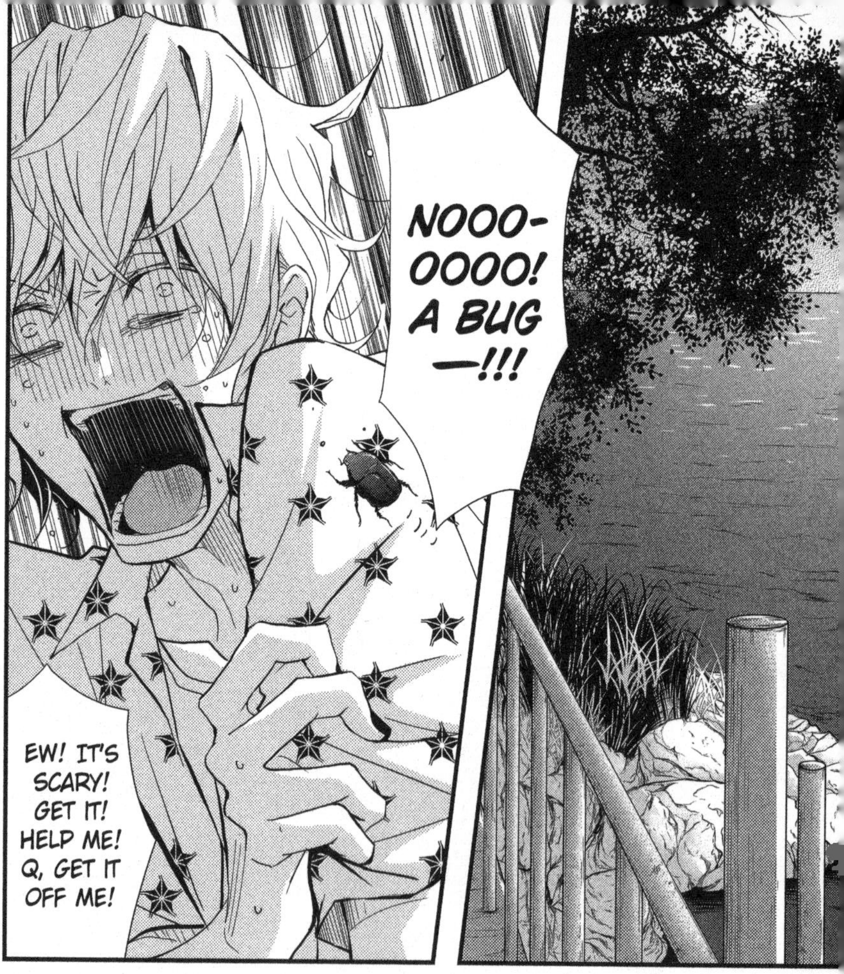
NOOO-OOOO! A BUG—!!!
EW! IT'S SCARY! GET IT! HELP ME! Q, GET IT OFF ME!

I love that thing that men pulling rickshaws wear—the one that looks like a short apron or a long bib.

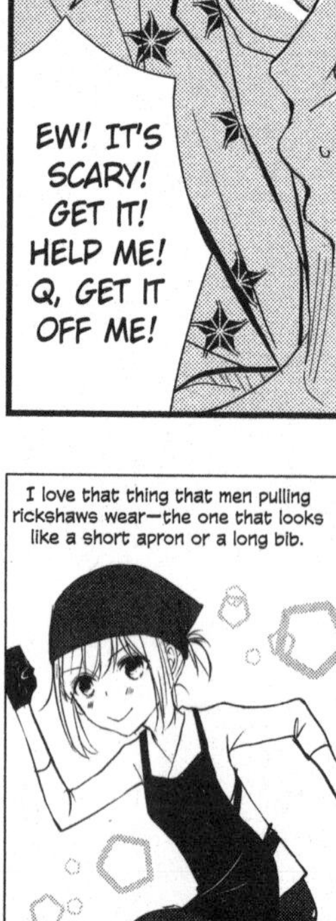

While developing the story that begins in this volume, I researched this area, which is famous for hot springs and long-distance relay racing. I ate a lot of tasty food too. It's a lovely place where everything tastes good. I even rode a rickshaw, after which I considered including a scene where Kyutaro's in a rickshaw and Fumi's pulling it along with all her might... but alas, I couldn't use it. I'd still like to draw a rickshaw someday.

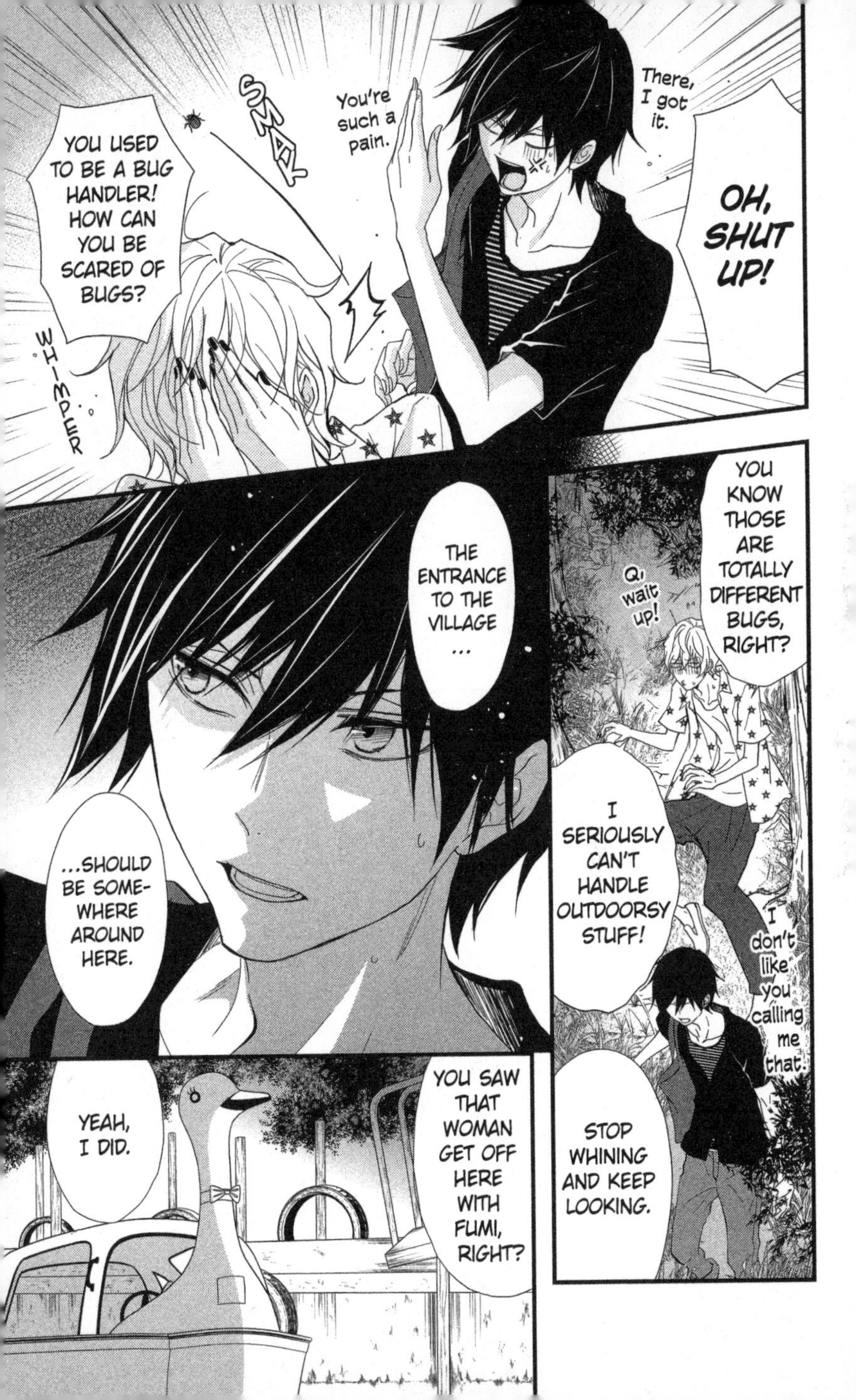
There, I got it.
OH, SHUT UP!
You're such a pain.
SMACK
YOU USED TO BE A BUG HANDLER! HOW CAN YOU BE SCARED OF BUGS?
WHIMPER
YOU KNOW THOSE ARE TOTALLY DIFFERENT BUGS, RIGHT?
Q, wait up!
I SERIOUSLY CAN'T HANDLE OUTDOORSY STUFF!
I don't like you calling me that.
STOP WHINING AND KEEP LOOKING.
THE ENTRANCE TO THE VILLAGE...
...SHOULD BE SOME-WHERE AROUND HERE.
YOU SAW THAT WOMAN GET OFF HERE WITH FUMI, RIGHT?
YEAH, I DID.

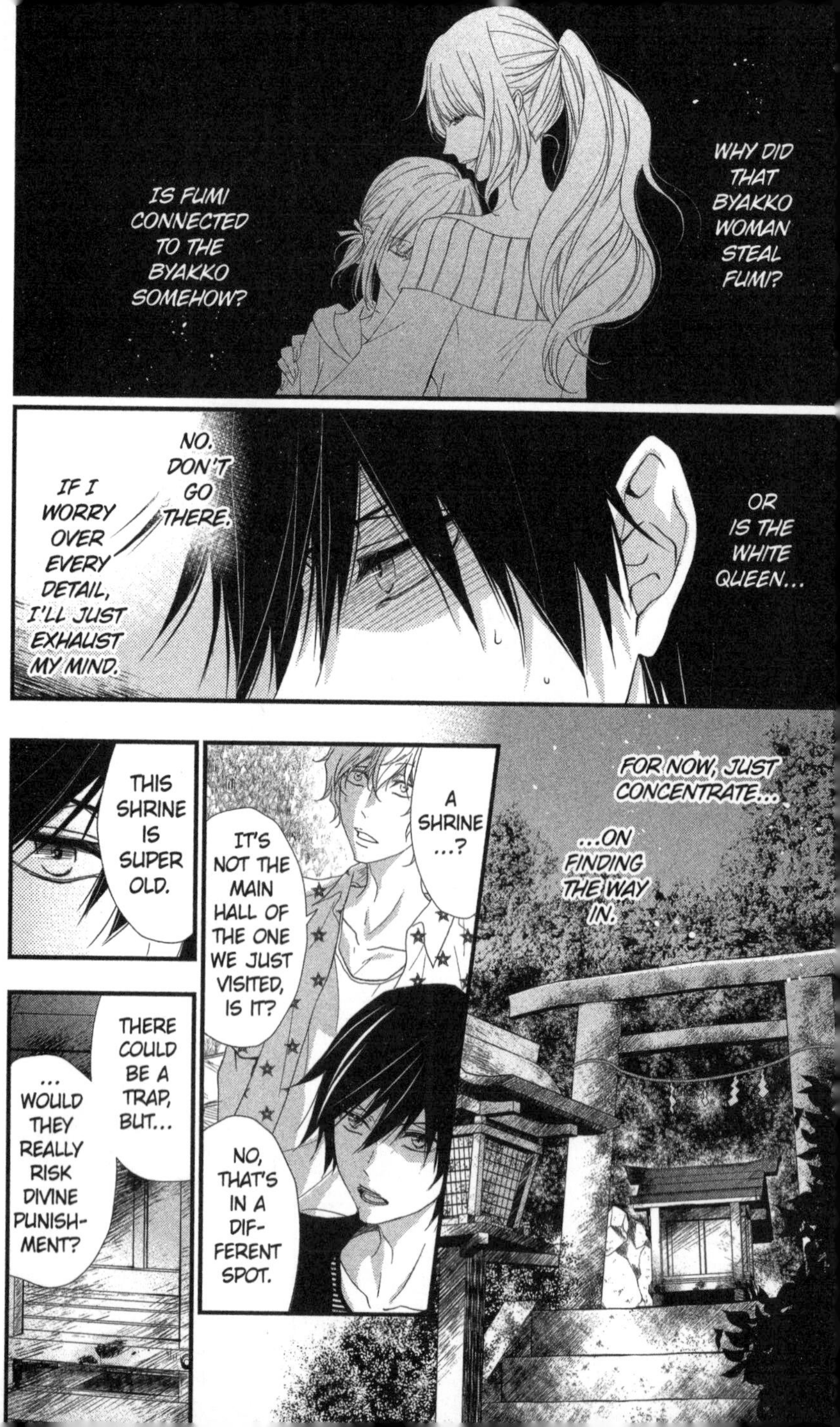
WHY DID THAT BYAKKO WOMAN STEAL FUMI?
IS FUMI CONNECTED TO THE BYAKKO SOMEHOW?
OR IS THE WHITE QUEEN...
NO. DON'T GO THERE.
IF I WORRY OVER EVERY DETAIL, I'LL JUST EXHAUST MY MIND.
FOR NOW, JUST CONCENTRATE...
...ON FINDING THE WAY IN.
A SHRINE...?
IT'S NOT THE MAIN HALL OF THE ONE WE JUST VISITED, IS IT?
NO, THAT'S IN A DIFFERENT SPOT.
THIS SHRINE IS SUPER OLD.
THERE COULD BE A TRAP, BUT...
...WOULD THEY REALLY RISK DIVINE PUNISHMENT?

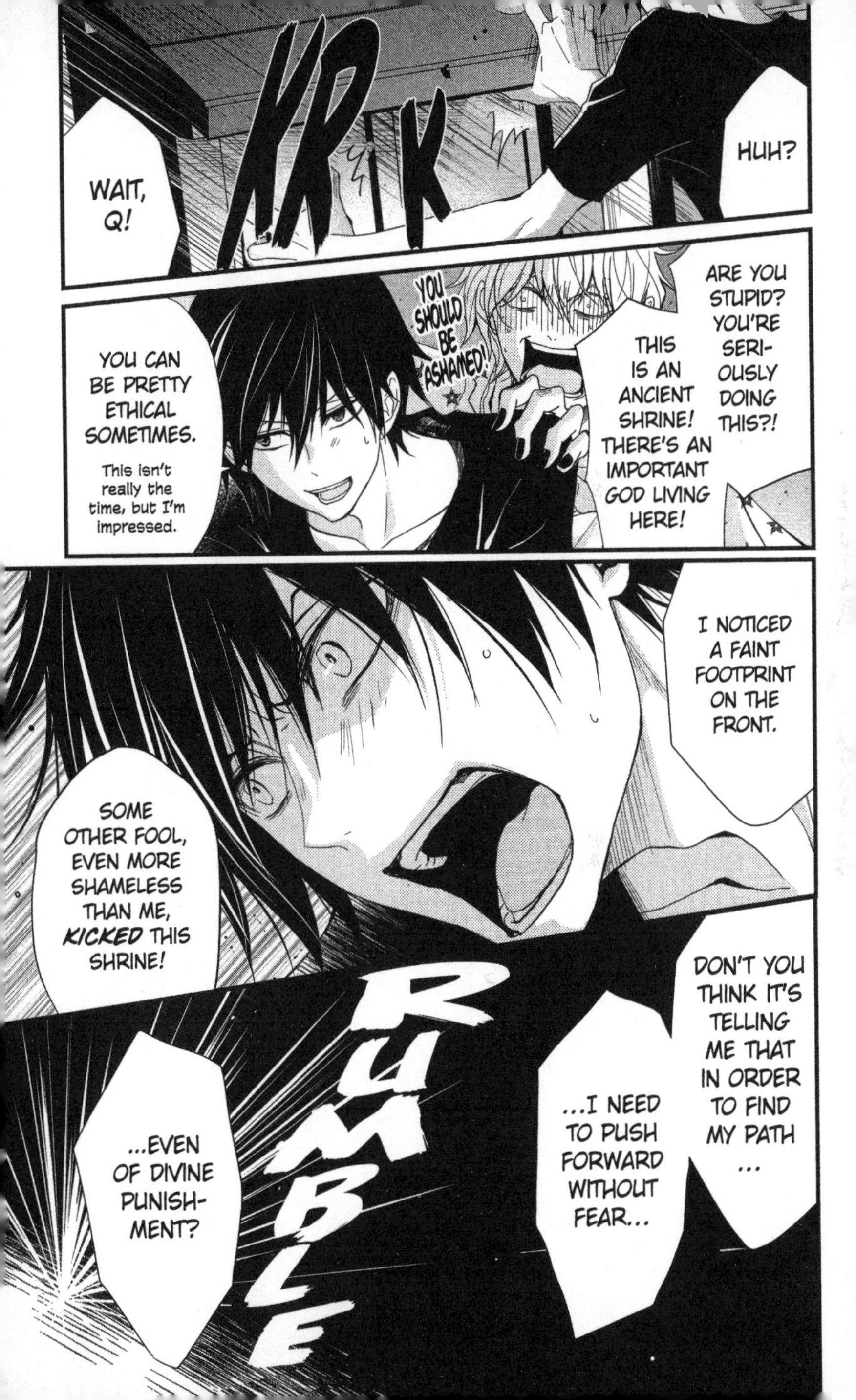
HUH?
KRIK
WAIT, Q!
ARE YOU STUPID? YOU'RE SERIOUSLY DOING THIS?!
THIS IS AN ANCIENT SHRINE! THERE'S AN IMPORTANT GOD LIVING HERE!
YOU SHOULD BE ASHAMED!
YOU CAN BE PRETTY ETHICAL SOMETIMES.
This isn't really the time, but I'm impressed.
I NOTICED A FAINT FOOTPRINT ON THE FRONT.
SOME OTHER FOOL, EVEN MORE SHAMELESS THAN ME, *KICKED* THIS SHRINE!
DON'T YOU THINK IT'S TELLING ME THAT IN ORDER TO FIND MY PATH…
…I NEED TO PUSH FORWARD WITHOUT FEAR…
RUMBLE
…EVEN OF DIVINE PUNISHMENT?

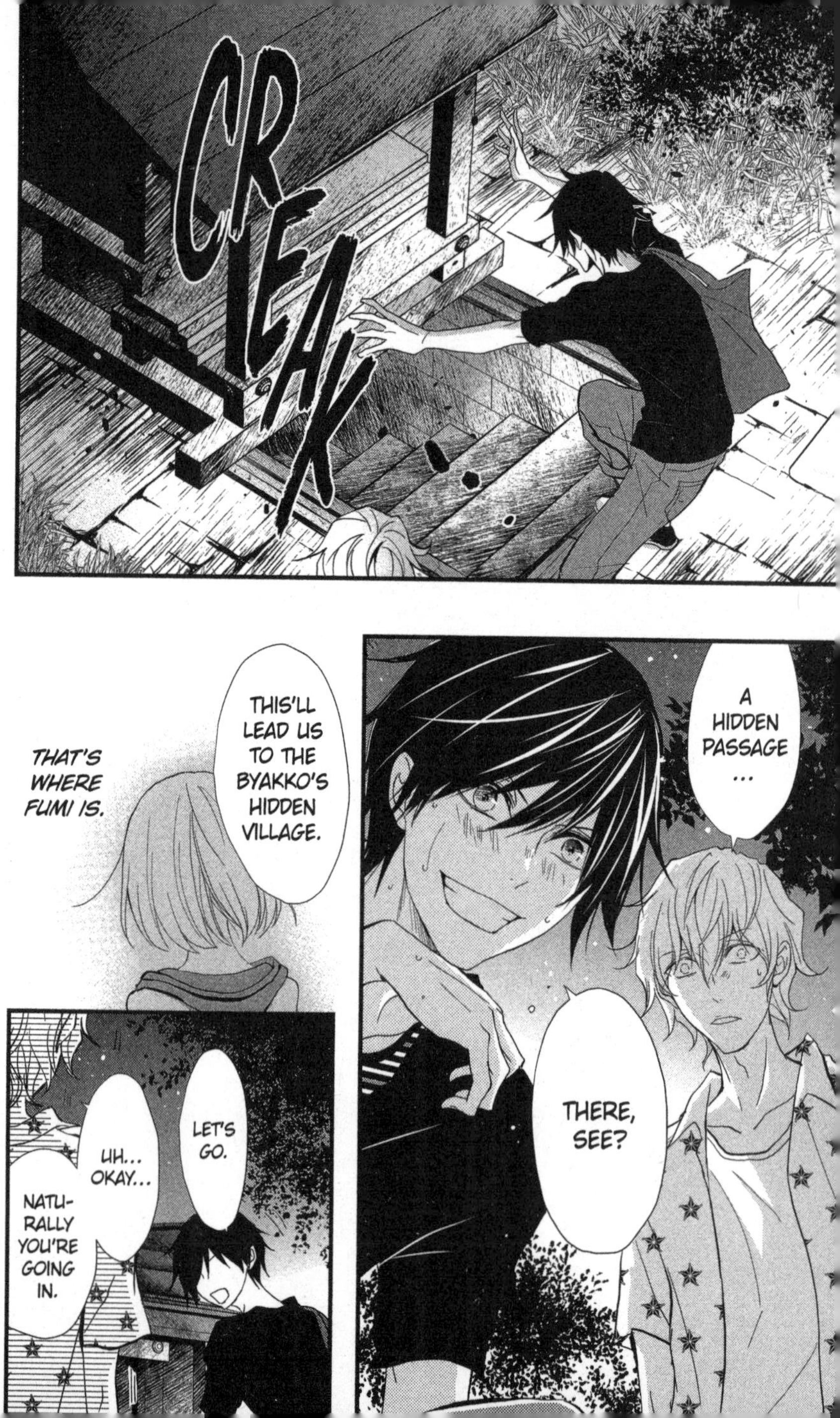
CREAK
A HIDDEN PASSAGE...
THERE, SEE?
THIS'LL LEAD US TO THE BYAKKO'S HIDDEN VILLAGE.
THAT'S WHERE FUMI IS.
LET'S GO.
UH... OKAY...
NATURALLY YOU'RE GOING IN.

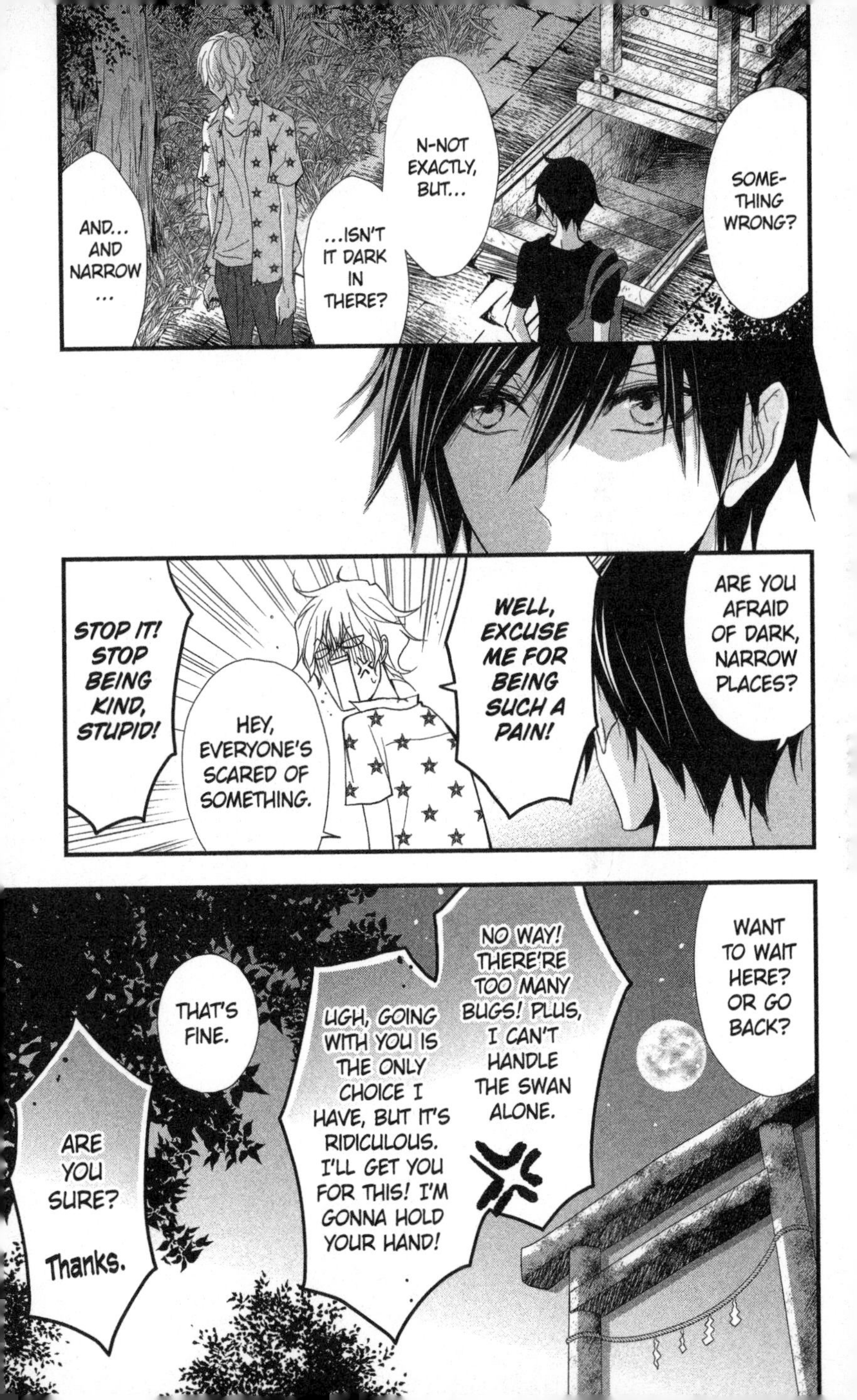
SOME-THING WRONG?
N-NOT EXACTLY, BUT...
...ISN'T IT DARK IN THERE?
AND... AND NARROW ...
ARE YOU AFRAID OF DARK, NARROW PLACES?
WELL, EXCUSE ME FOR BEING SUCH A PAIN!
HEY, EVERYONE'S SCARED OF SOMETHING.
STOP IT! STOP BEING KIND, STUPID!
WANT TO WAIT HERE? OR GO BACK?
NO WAY! THERE'RE TOO MANY BUGS! PLUS, I CAN'T HANDLE THE SWAN ALONE.
THAT'S FINE.
UGH, GOING WITH YOU IS THE ONLY CHOICE I HAVE, BUT IT'S RIDICULOUS. I'LL GET YOU FOR THIS! I'M GONNA HOLD YOUR HAND!
ARE YOU SURE?
Thanks.

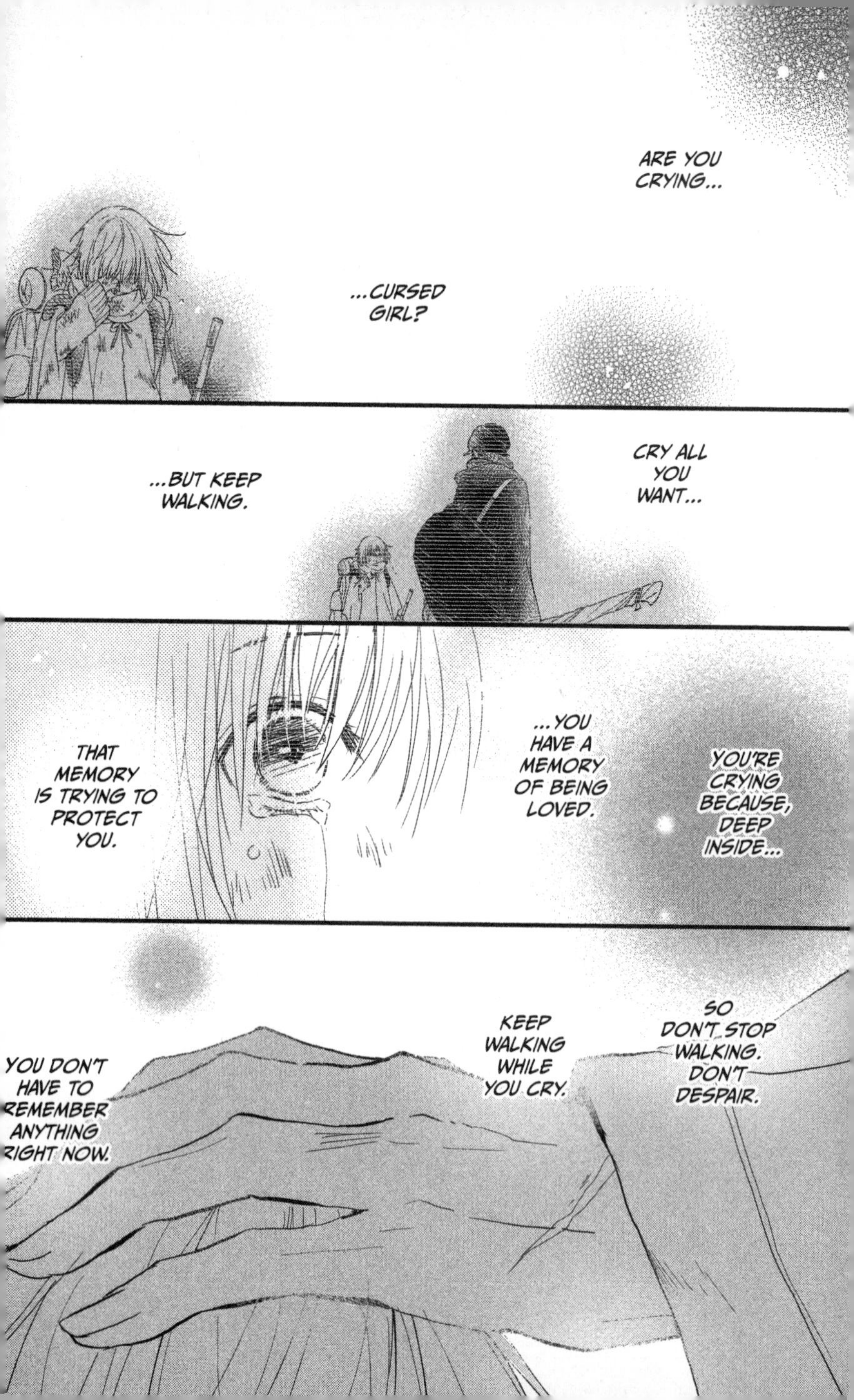
ARE YOU CRYING...
...CURSED GIRL?
CRY ALL YOU WANT...
...BUT KEEP WALKING.
YOU'RE CRYING BECAUSE, DEEP INSIDE...
...YOU HAVE A MEMORY OF BEING LOVED.
THAT MEMORY IS TRYING TO PROTECT YOU.
SO DON'T STOP WALKING. DON'T DESPAIR.
KEEP WALKING WHILE YOU CRY.
YOU DON'T HAVE TO REMEMBER ANYTHING RIGHT NOW.

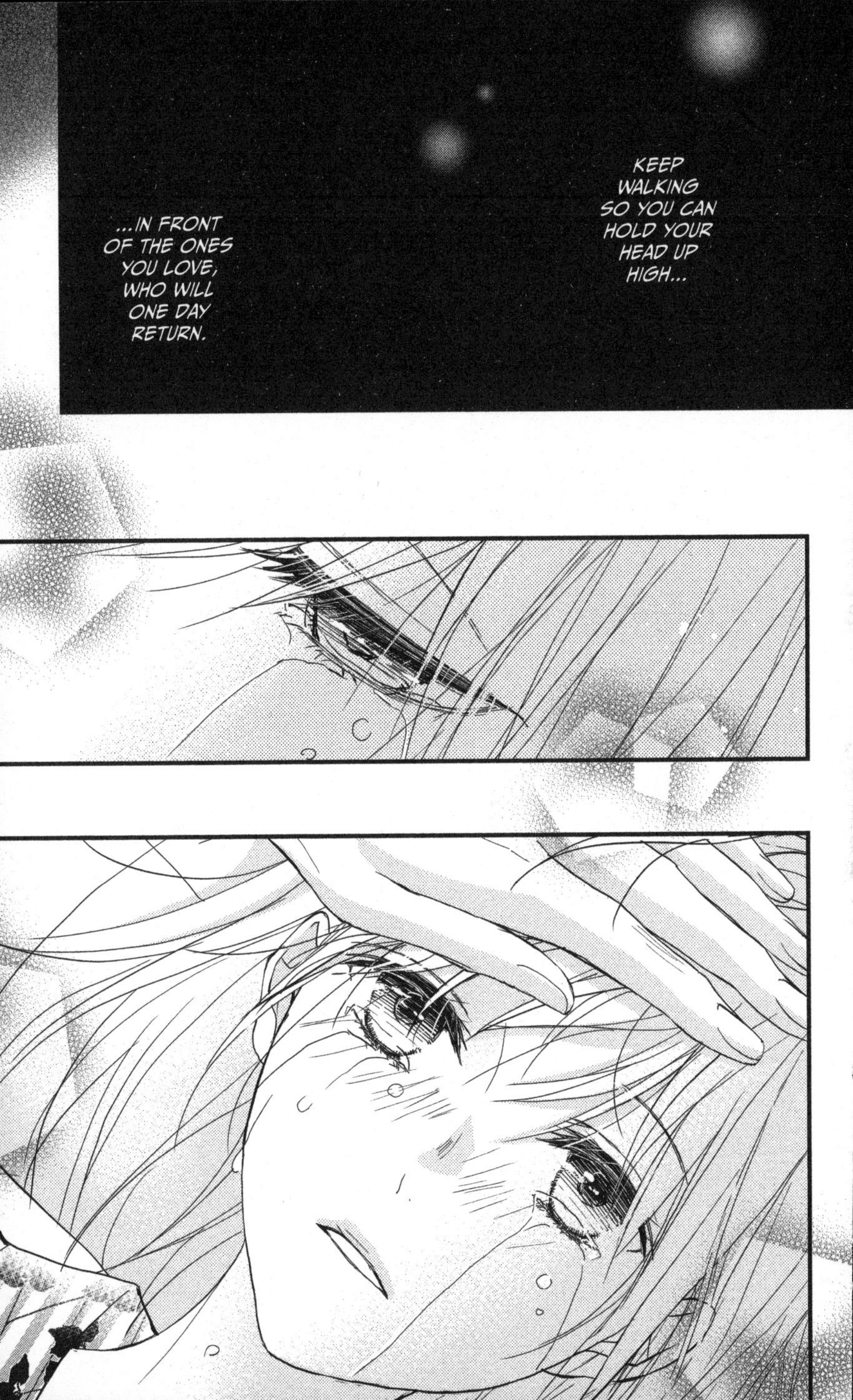
KEEP WALKING SO YOU CAN HOLD YOUR HEAD UP HIGH...
...IN FRONT OF THE ONES YOU LOVE, WHO WILL ONE DAY RETURN.

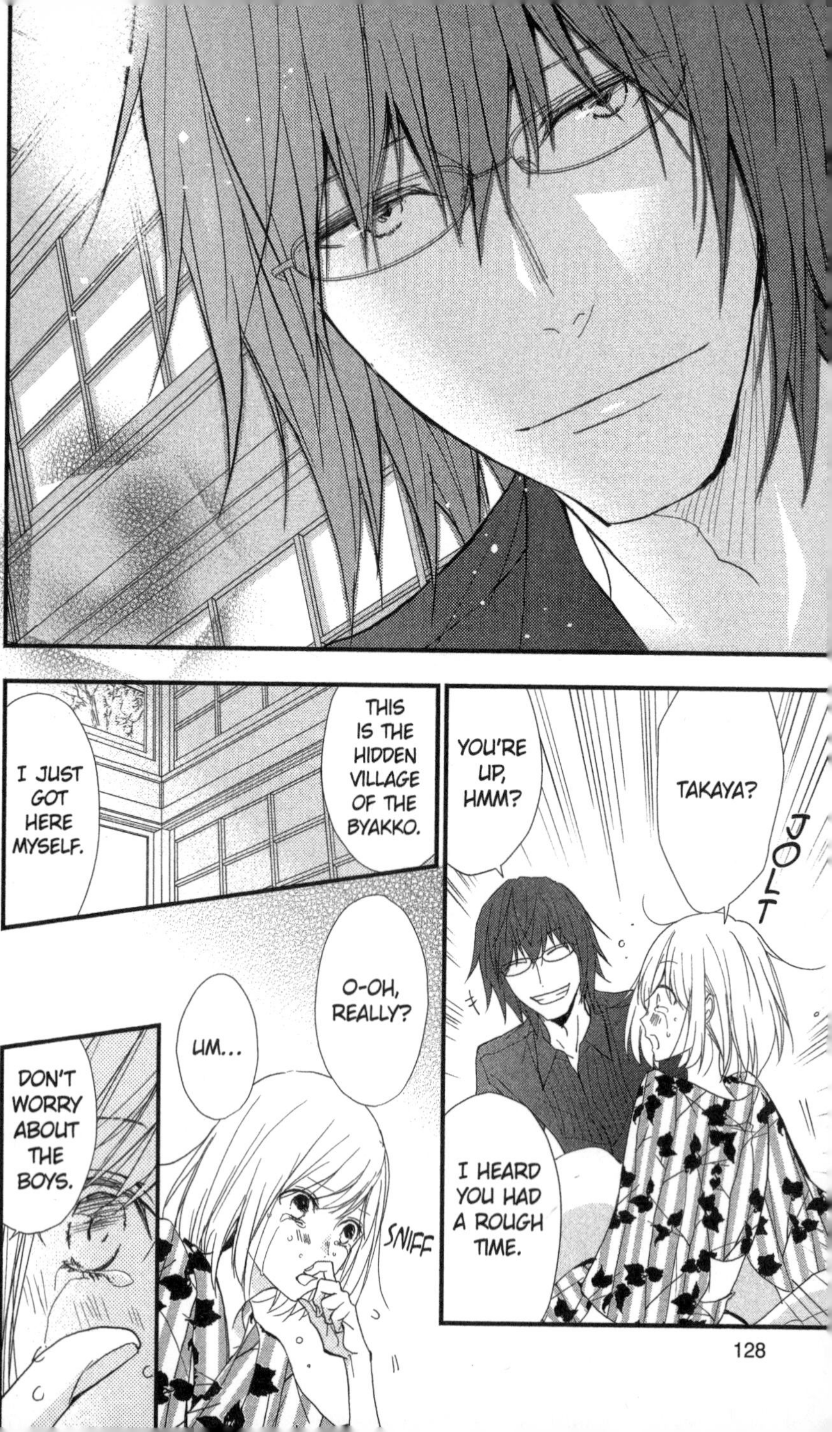
TAKAYA?
JOLT
YOU'RE UP, HMM?
I HEARD YOU HAD A ROUGH TIME.
THIS IS THE HIDDEN VILLAGE OF THE BYAKKO.
I JUST GOT HERE MYSELF.
O-OH, REALLY?
UM...
SNIFF
DON'T WORRY ABOUT THE BOYS.

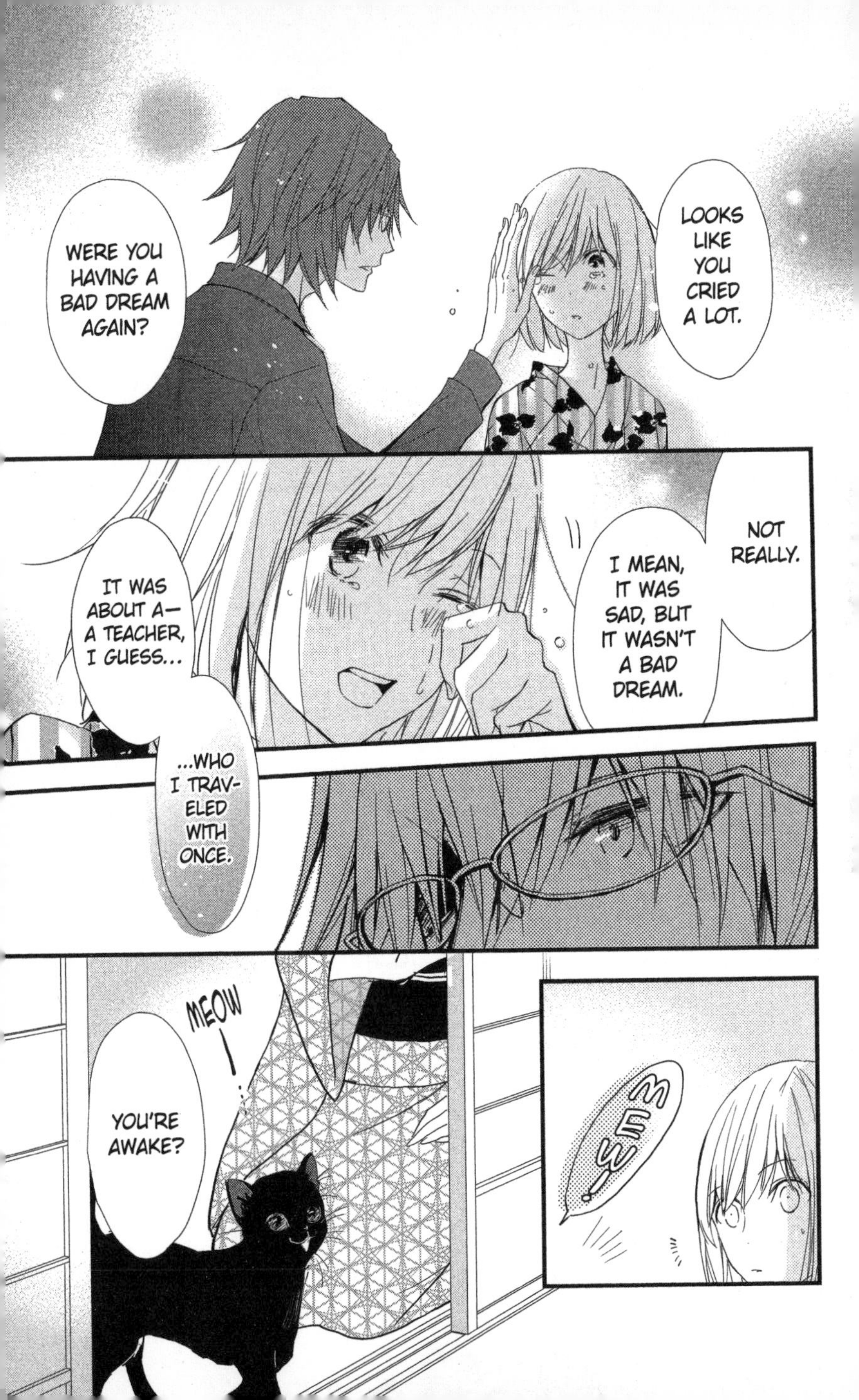
LOOKS LIKE YOU CRIED A LOT.
WERE YOU HAVING A BAD DREAM AGAIN?
NOT REALLY.
I MEAN, IT WAS SAD, BUT IT WASN'T A BAD DREAM.
IT WAS ABOUT A— A TEACHER, I GUESS...
...WHO I TRAV-ELED WITH ONCE.
MEW—!
MEOW
YOU'RE AWAKE?

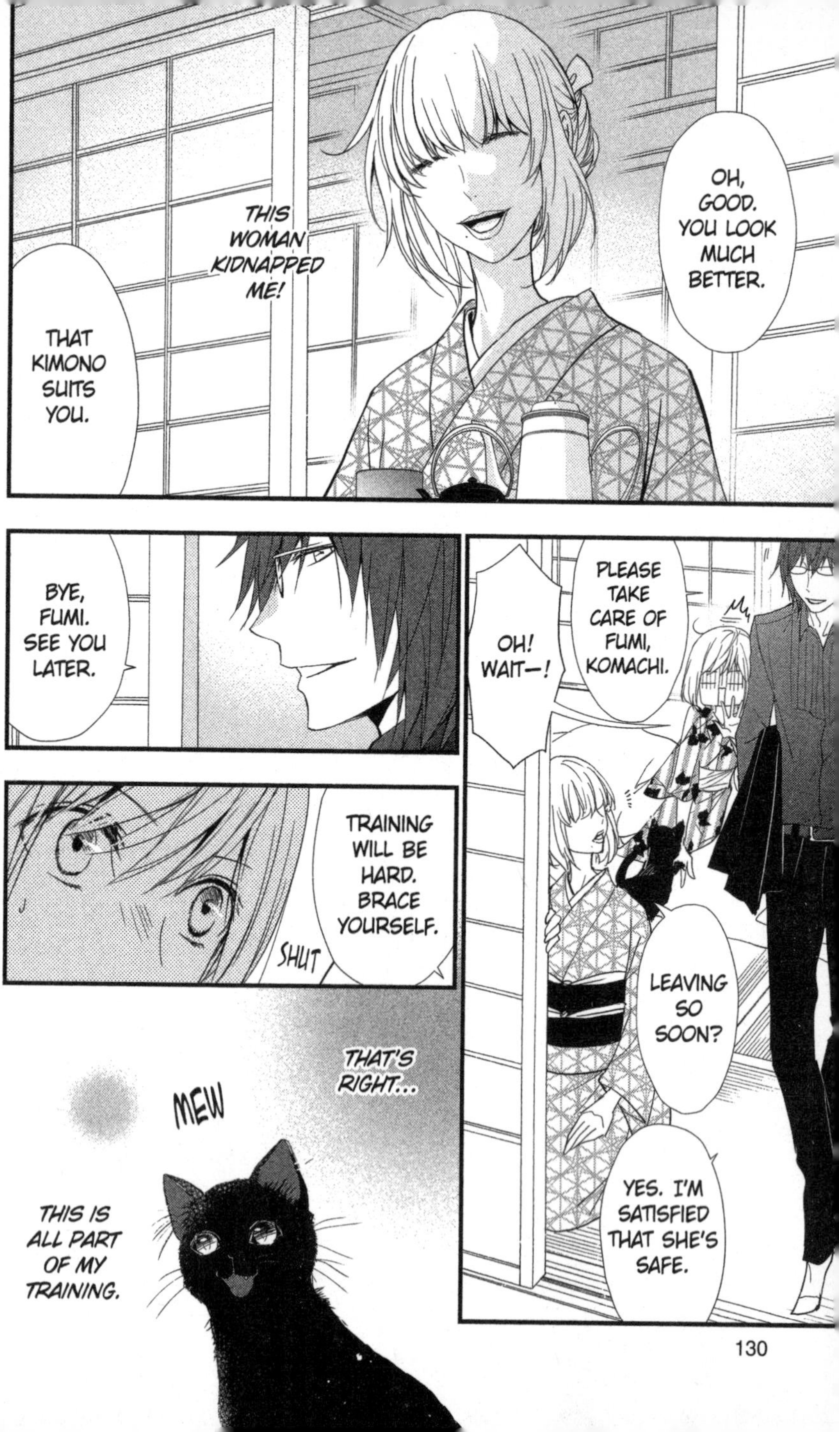
OH, GOOD. YOU LOOK MUCH BETTER.
THIS WOMAN KIDNAPPED ME!
THAT KIMONO SUITS YOU.
PLEASE TAKE CARE OF FUMI, KOMACHI.
OH! WAIT—!
LEAVING SO SOON?
YES. I'M SATISFIED THAT SHE'S SAFE.
BYE, FUMI. SEE YOU LATER.
TRAINING WILL BE HARD. BRACE YOURSELF.
SHUT
THAT'S RIGHT...
MEW
THIS IS ALL PART OF MY TRAINING.

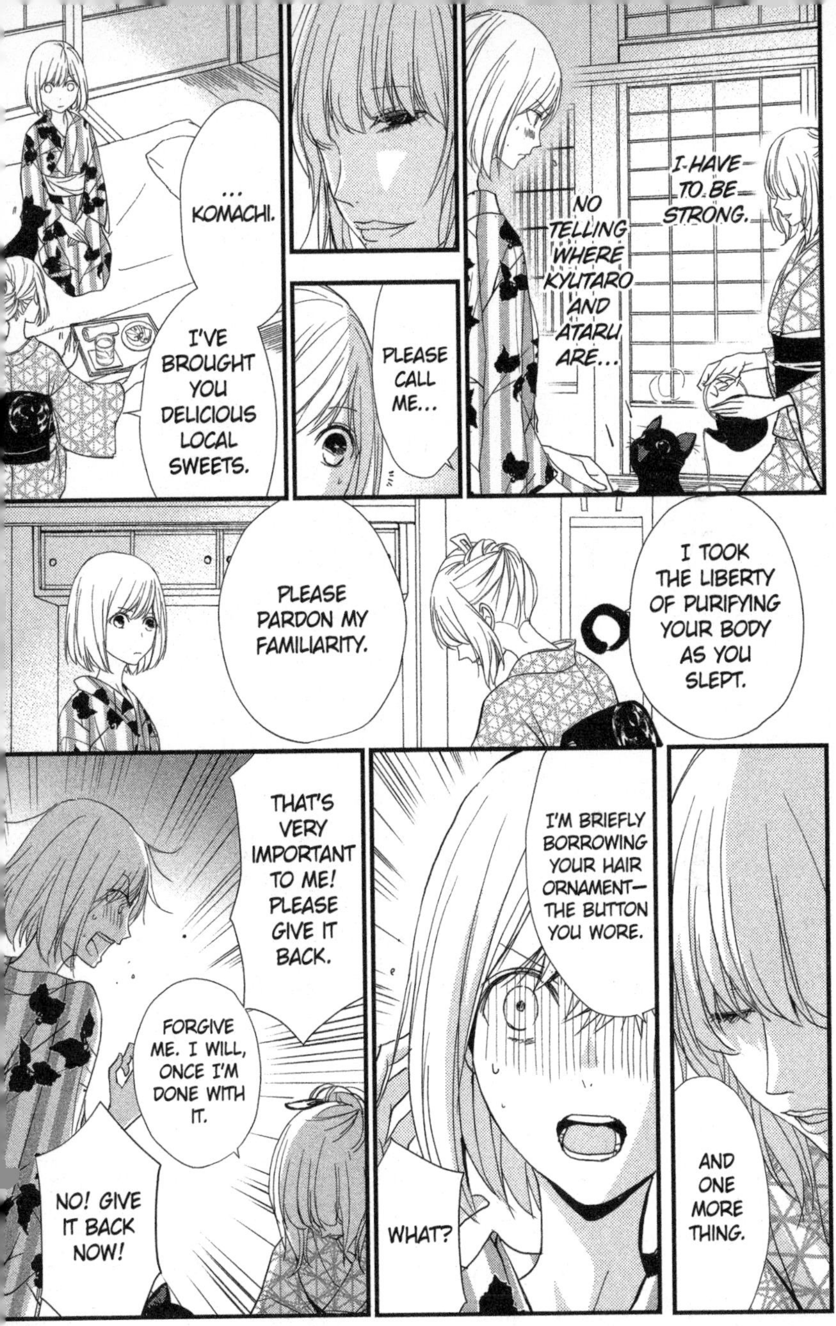
I HAVE TO BE STRONG.
NO TELLING WHERE KYUTARO AND ATARU ARE...
PLEASE CALL ME...
... KOMACHI.
I'VE BROUGHT YOU DELICIOUS LOCAL SWEETS.
I TOOK THE LIBERTY OF PURIFYING YOUR BODY AS YOU SLEPT.
PLEASE PARDON MY FAMILIARITY.
AND ONE MORE THING.
I'M BRIEFLY BORROWING YOUR HAIR ORNAMENT— THE BUTTON YOU WORE.
WHAT?
THAT'S VERY IMPORTANT TO ME! PLEASE GIVE IT BACK.
FORGIVE ME. I WILL, ONCE I'M DONE WITH IT.
NO! GIVE IT BACK NOW!

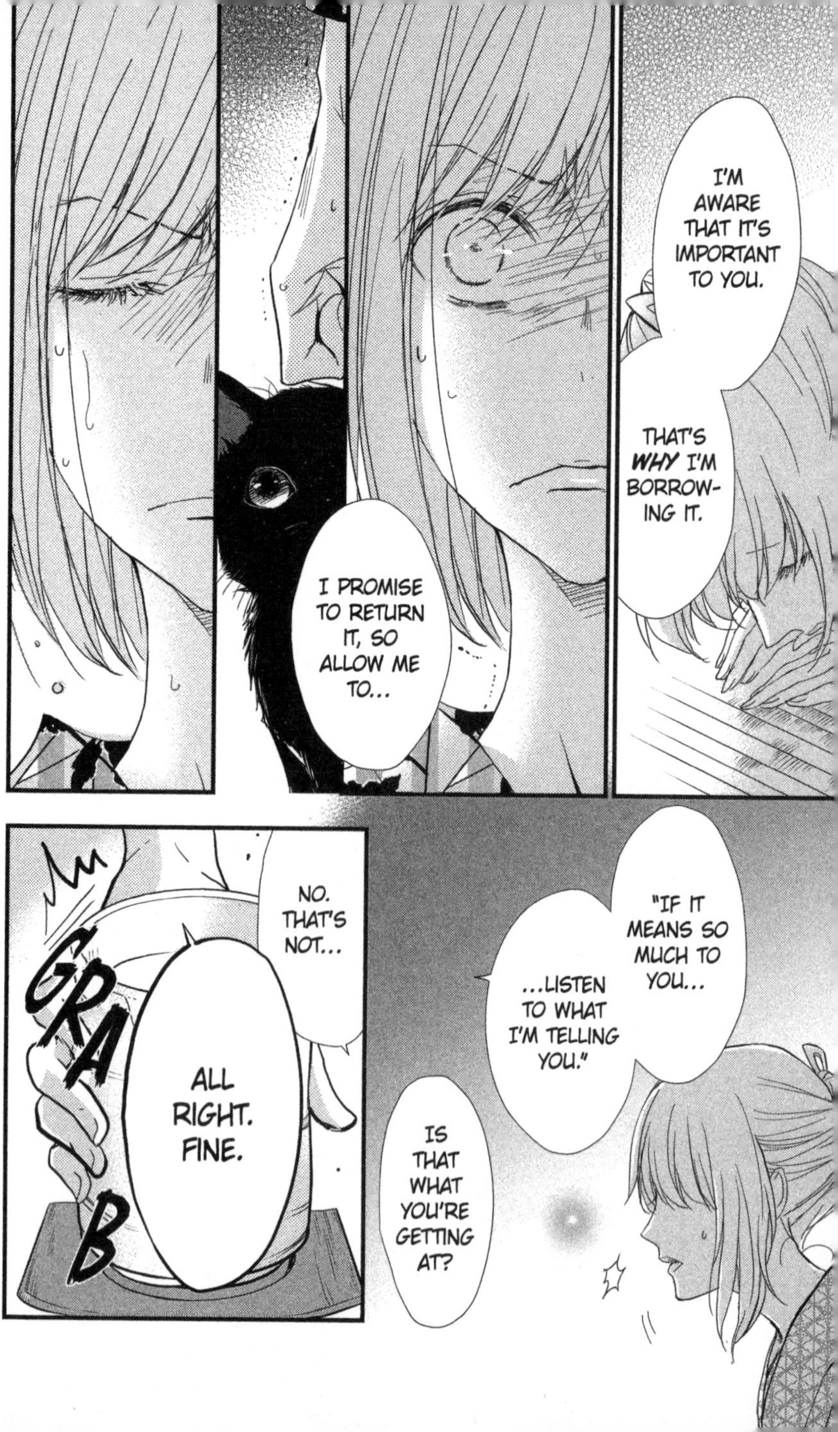
I'M AWARE THAT IT'S IMPORTANT TO YOU.
THAT'S *WHY* I'M BORROW-ING IT.
I PROMISE TO RETURN IT, SO ALLOW ME TO...
"IF IT MEANS SO MUCH TO YOU...
...LISTEN TO WHAT I'M TELLING YOU."
IS THAT WHAT YOU'RE GETTING AT?
NO. THAT'S NOT...
GRAB
ALL RIGHT. FINE.

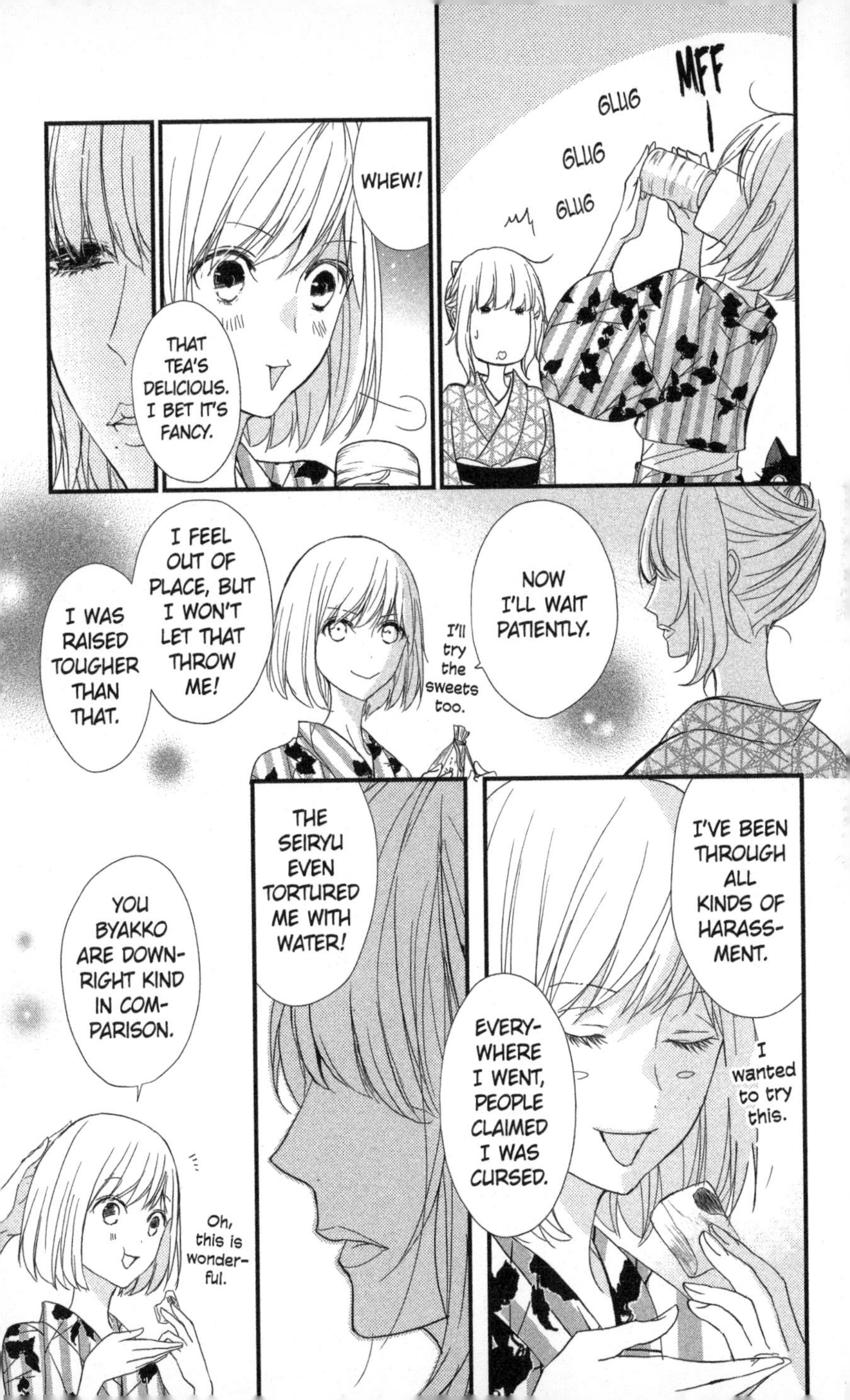
MFF
GLUG
GLUG
GLUG
WHEW!
THAT TEA'S DELICIOUS. I BET IT'S FANCY.
NOW I'LL WAIT PATIENTLY.
I'll try the sweets too.
I FEEL OUT OF PLACE, BUT I WON'T LET THAT THROW ME!
I WAS RAISED TOUGHER THAN THAT.
I'VE BEEN THROUGH ALL KINDS OF HARASS-MENT.
I wanted to try this.
EVERY-WHERE I WENT, PEOPLE CLAIMED I WAS CURSED.
THE SEIRYU EVEN TORTURED ME WITH WATER!
YOU BYAKKO ARE DOWN-RIGHT KIND IN COM-PARISON.
Oh, this is wonder-ful.

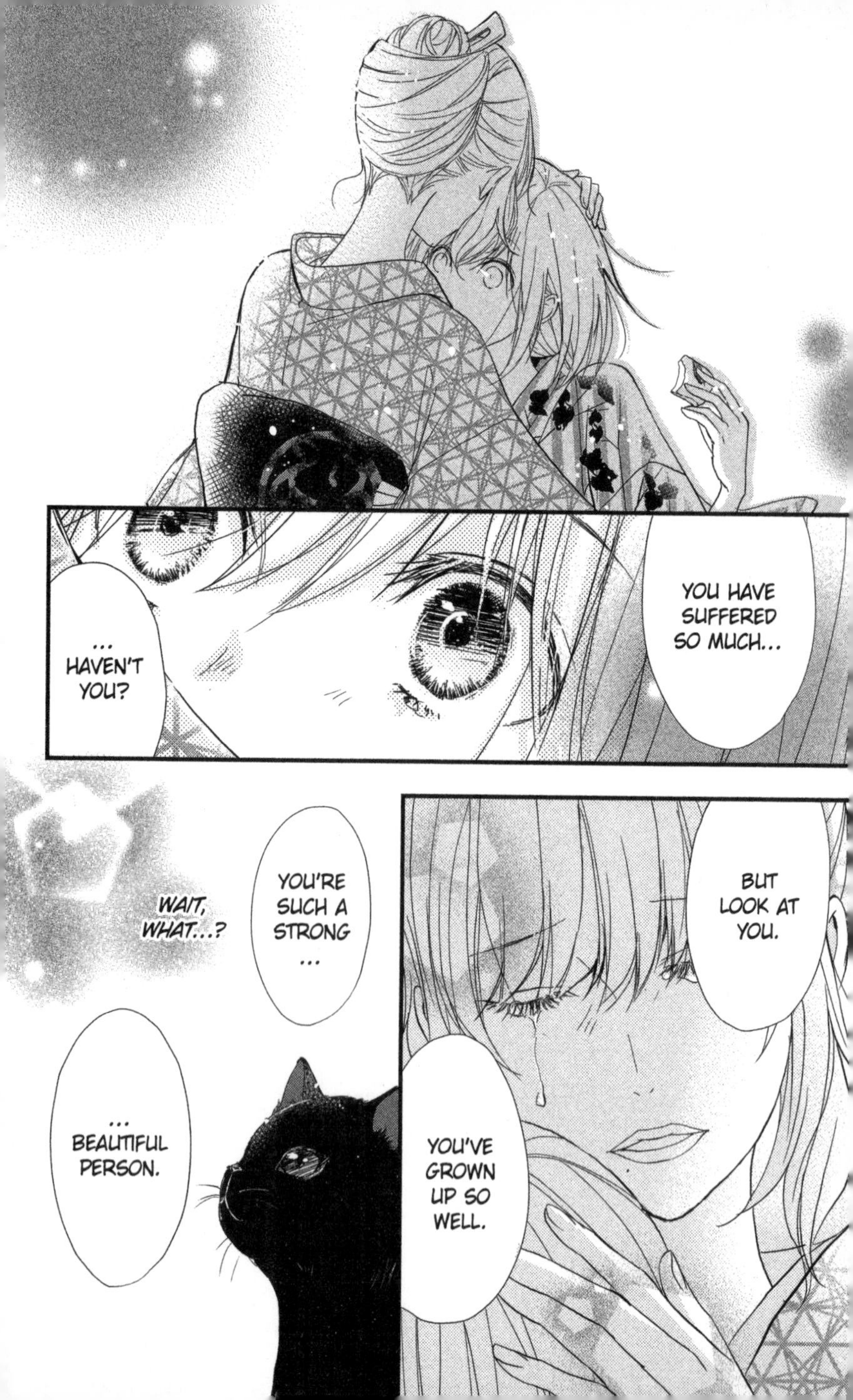
YOU HAVE SUFFERED SO MUCH...
... HAVEN'T YOU?
BUT LOOK AT YOU.
YOU'VE GROWN UP SO WELL.
YOU'RE SUCH A STRONG ...
WAIT, WHAT...?
... BEAUTIFUL PERSON.

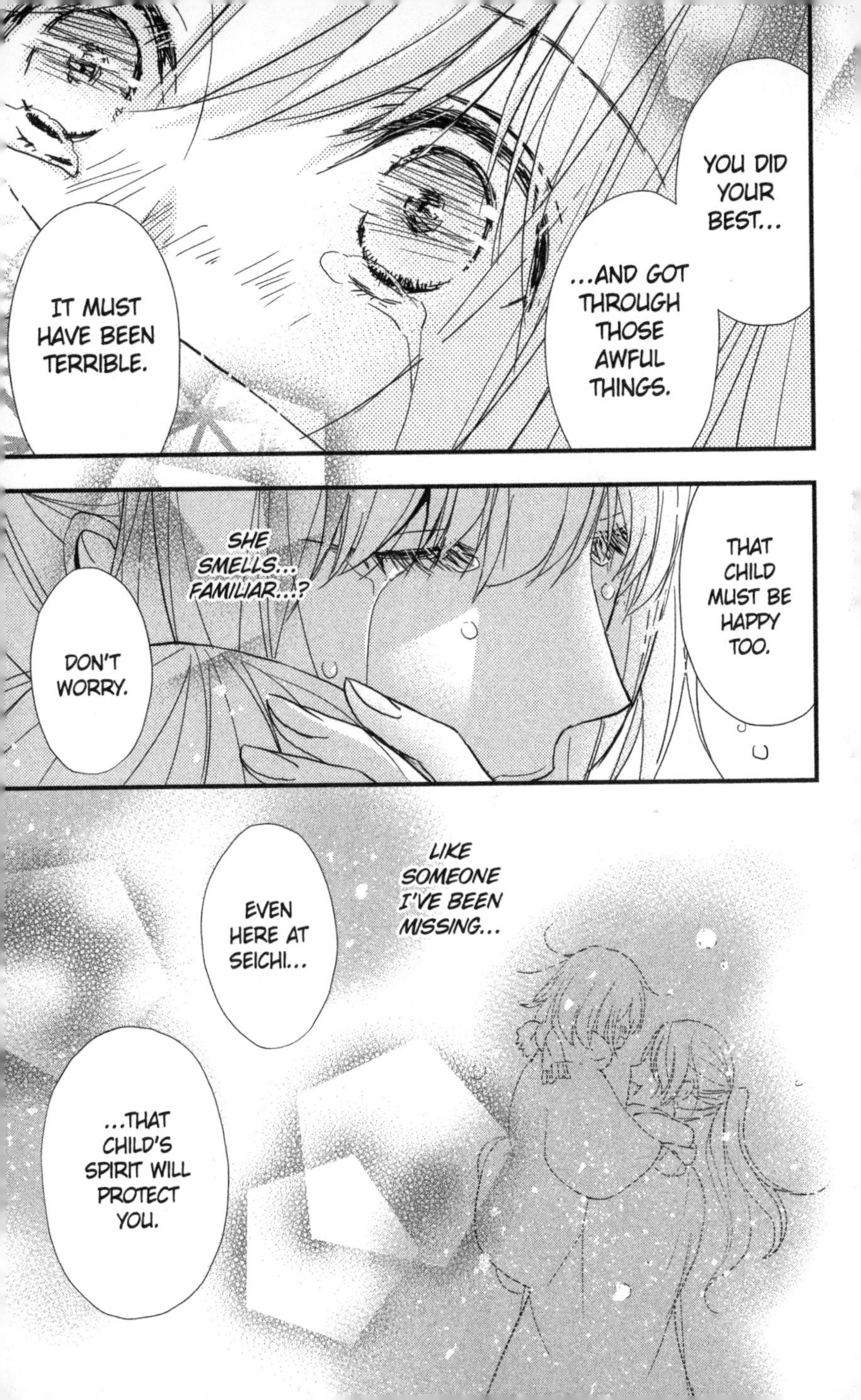
YOU DID YOUR BEST...
...AND GOT THROUGH THOSE AWFUL THINGS.
IT MUST HAVE BEEN TERRIBLE.
THAT CHILD MUST BE HAPPY TOO.
SHE SMELLS... FAMILIAR...?
DON'T WORRY.
LIKE SOMEONE I'VE BEEN MISSING...
EVEN HERE AT SEICHI...
...THAT CHILD'S SPIRIT WILL PROTECT YOU.

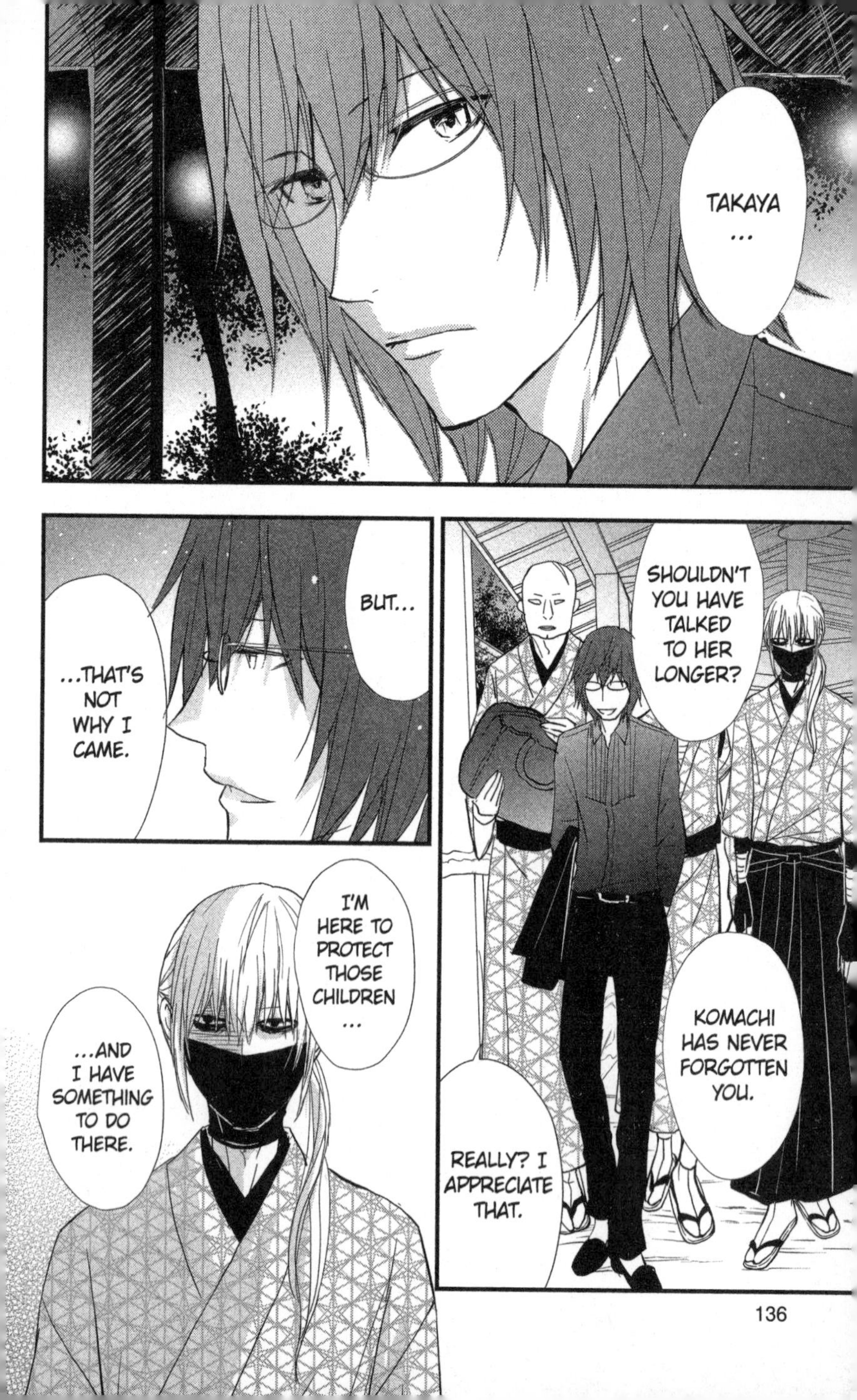
TAKAYA ...
SHOULDN'T YOU HAVE TALKED TO HER LONGER?
KOMACHI HAS NEVER FORGOTTEN YOU.
REALLY? I APPRECIATE THAT.
BUT...
...THAT'S NOT WHY I CAME.
I'M HERE TO PROTECT THOSE CHILDREN ...
...AND I HAVE SOMETHING TO DO THERE.

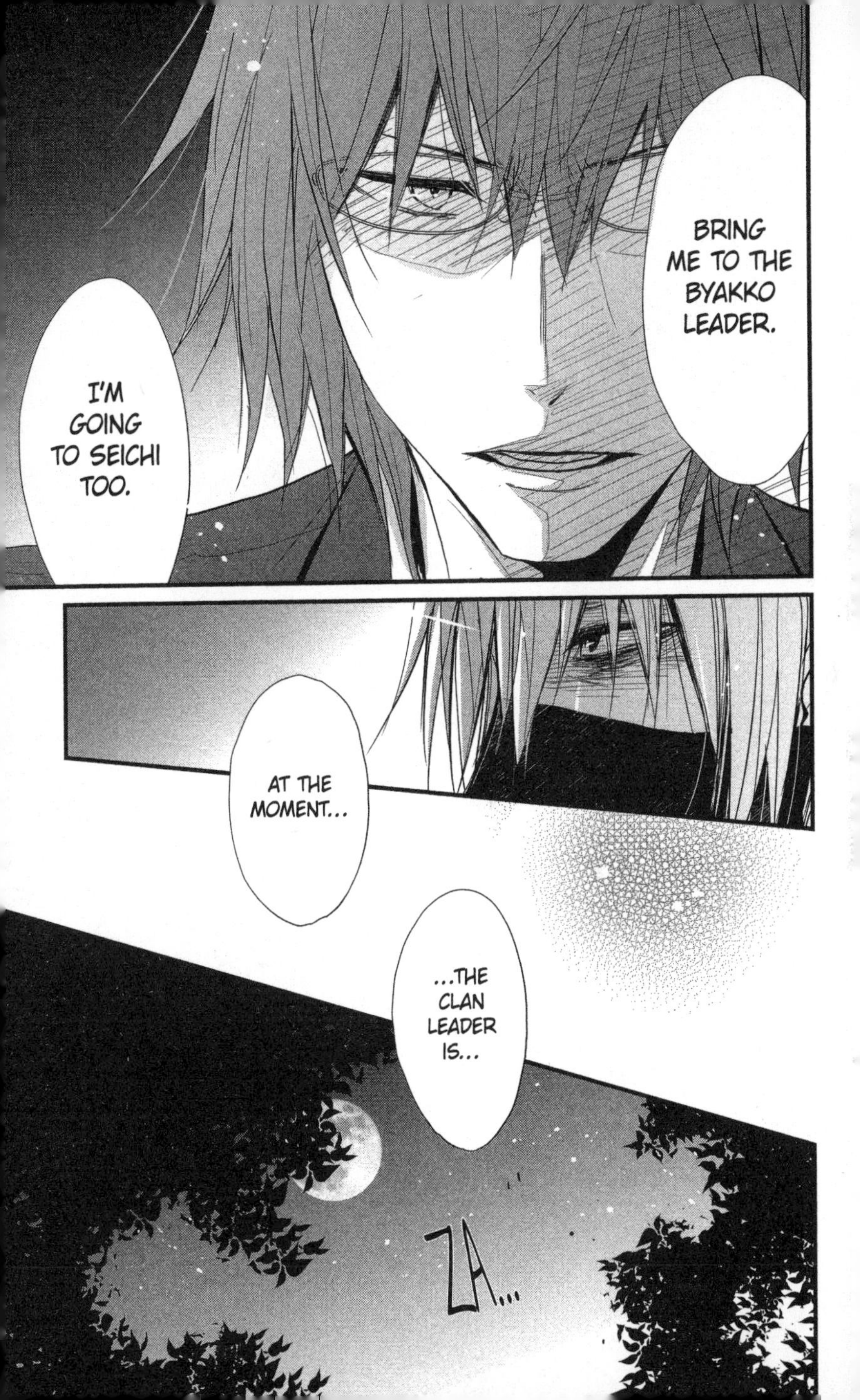
BRING ME TO THE BYAKKO LEADER.
I'M GOING TO SEICHI TOO.
AT THE MOMENT...
...THE CLAN LEADER IS...
ZA...

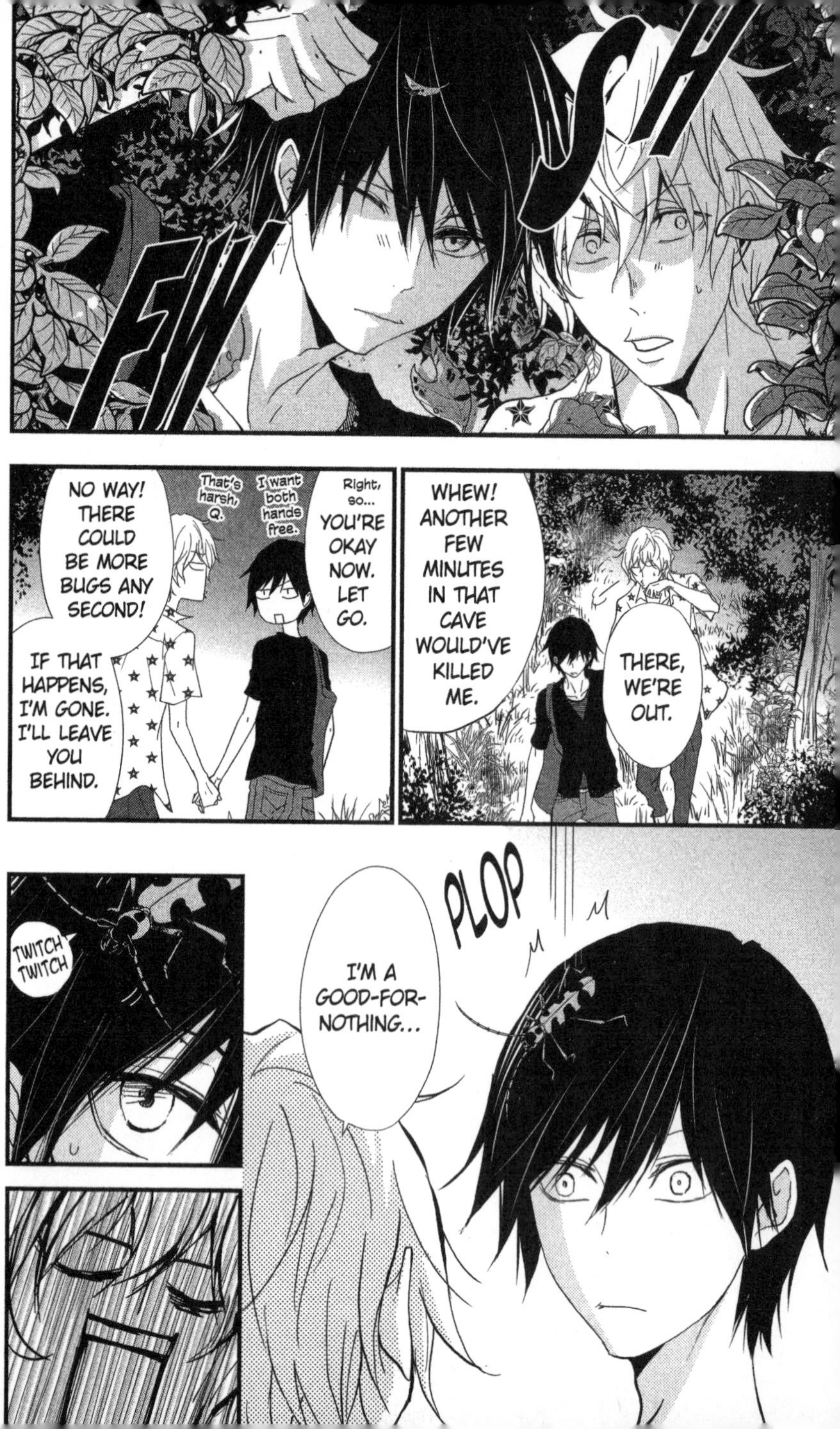
FWSH
THERE, WE'RE OUT.
WHEW! ANOTHER FEW MINUTES IN THAT CAVE WOULD'VE KILLED ME.
Right, so... YOU'RE OKAY NOW. LET GO.
I want both hands free.
NO WAY! THERE COULD BE MORE BUGS ANY SECOND!
IF THAT HAPPENS, I'M GONE. I'LL LEAVE YOU BEHIND.
That's harsh, Q.
PLOP
I'M A GOOD-FOR-NOTHING...
TWITCH TWITCH

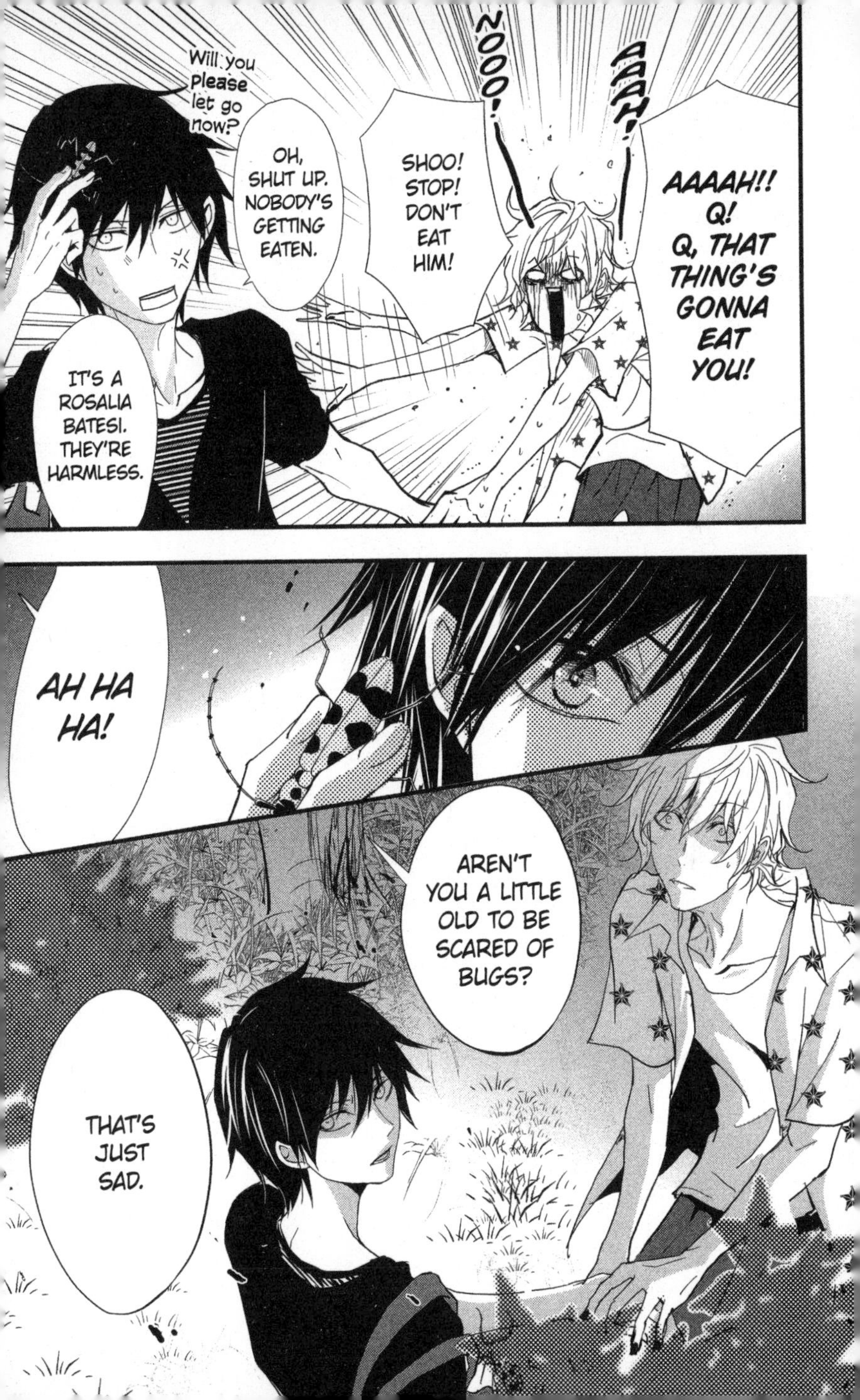
AAAAH!! Q! Q, THAT THING'S GONNA EAT YOU!
AAAH!
NOOO!
SHOO! STOP! DON'T EAT HIM!
OH, SHUT UP. NOBODY'S GETTING EATEN.
Will you please let go now?
IT'S A ROSALIA BATESI. THEY'RE HARMLESS.
AH HA HA!
AREN'T YOU A LITTLE OLD TO BE SCARED OF BUGS?
THAT'S JUST SAD.

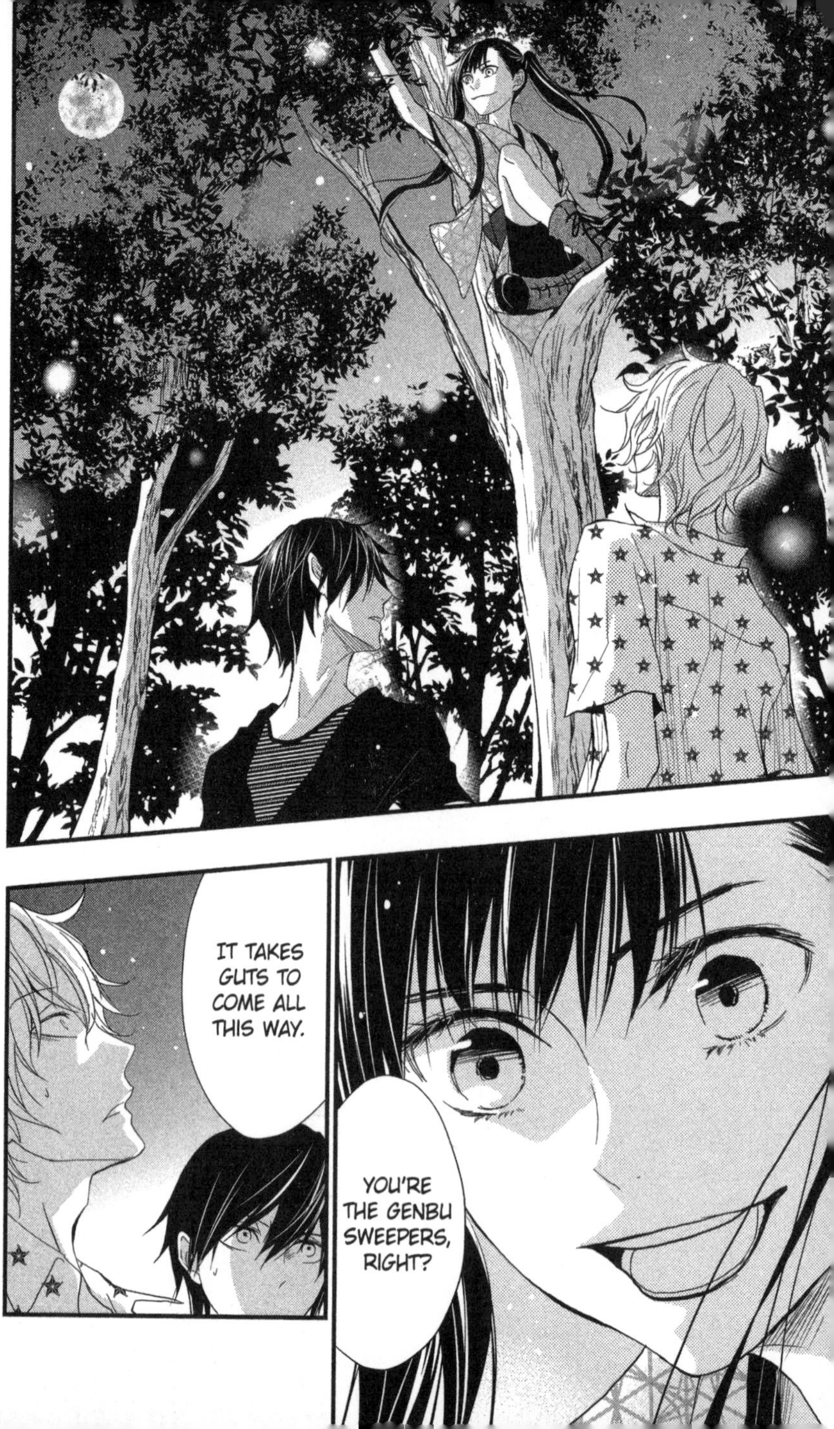
IT TAKES GUTS TO COME ALL THIS WAY.
YOU'RE THE GENBU SWEEPERS, RIGHT?

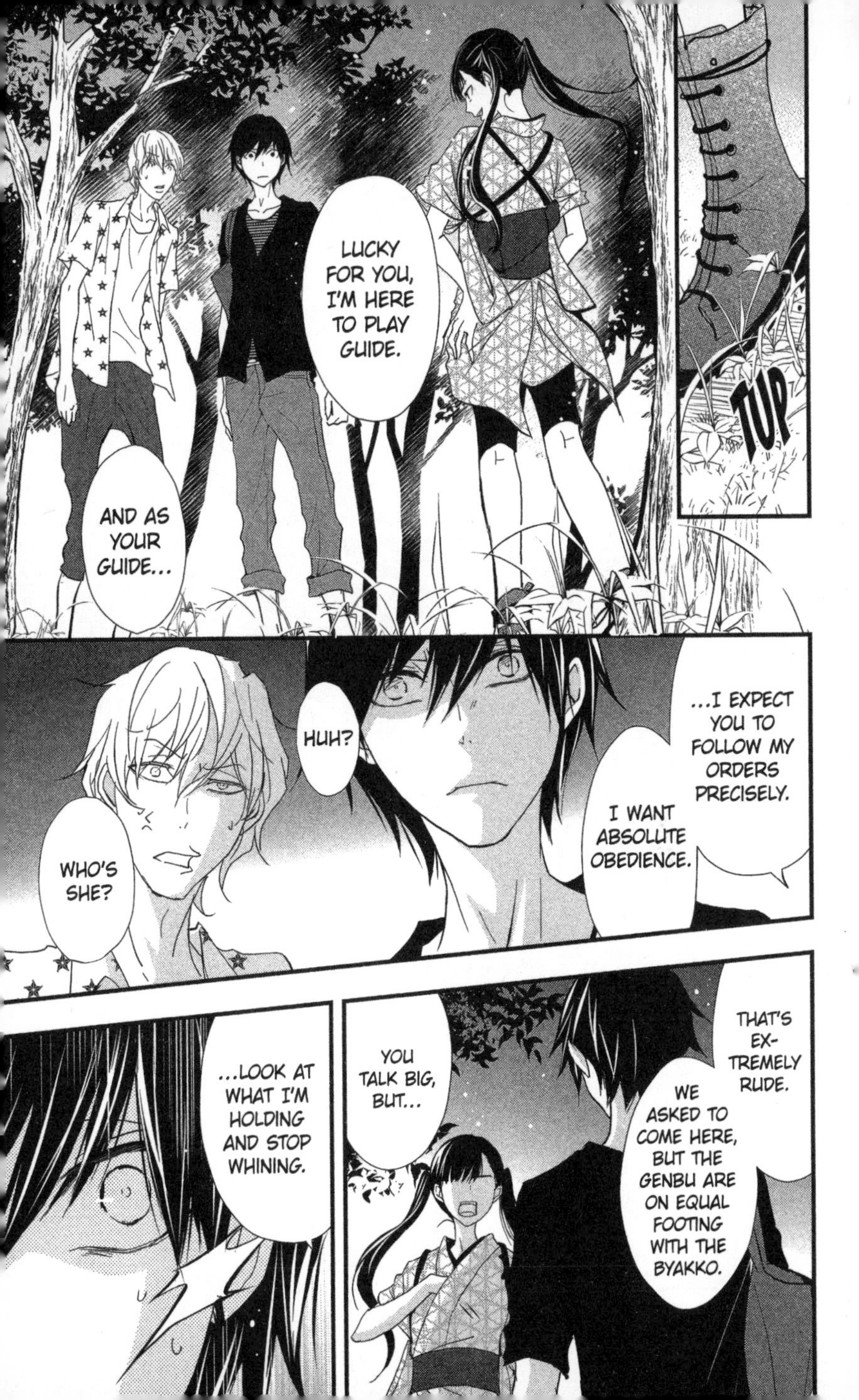
TUP
LUCKY FOR YOU, I'M HERE TO PLAY GUIDE.
AND AS YOUR GUIDE...
...I EXPECT YOU TO FOLLOW MY ORDERS PRECISELY.
I WANT ABSOLUTE OBEDIENCE.
HUH?
WHO'S SHE?
THAT'S EX-TREMELY RUDE.
WE ASKED TO COME HERE, BUT THE GENBU ARE ON EQUAL FOOTING WITH THE BYAKKO.
YOU TALK BIG, BUT...
...LOOK AT WHAT I'M HOLDING AND STOP WHINING.

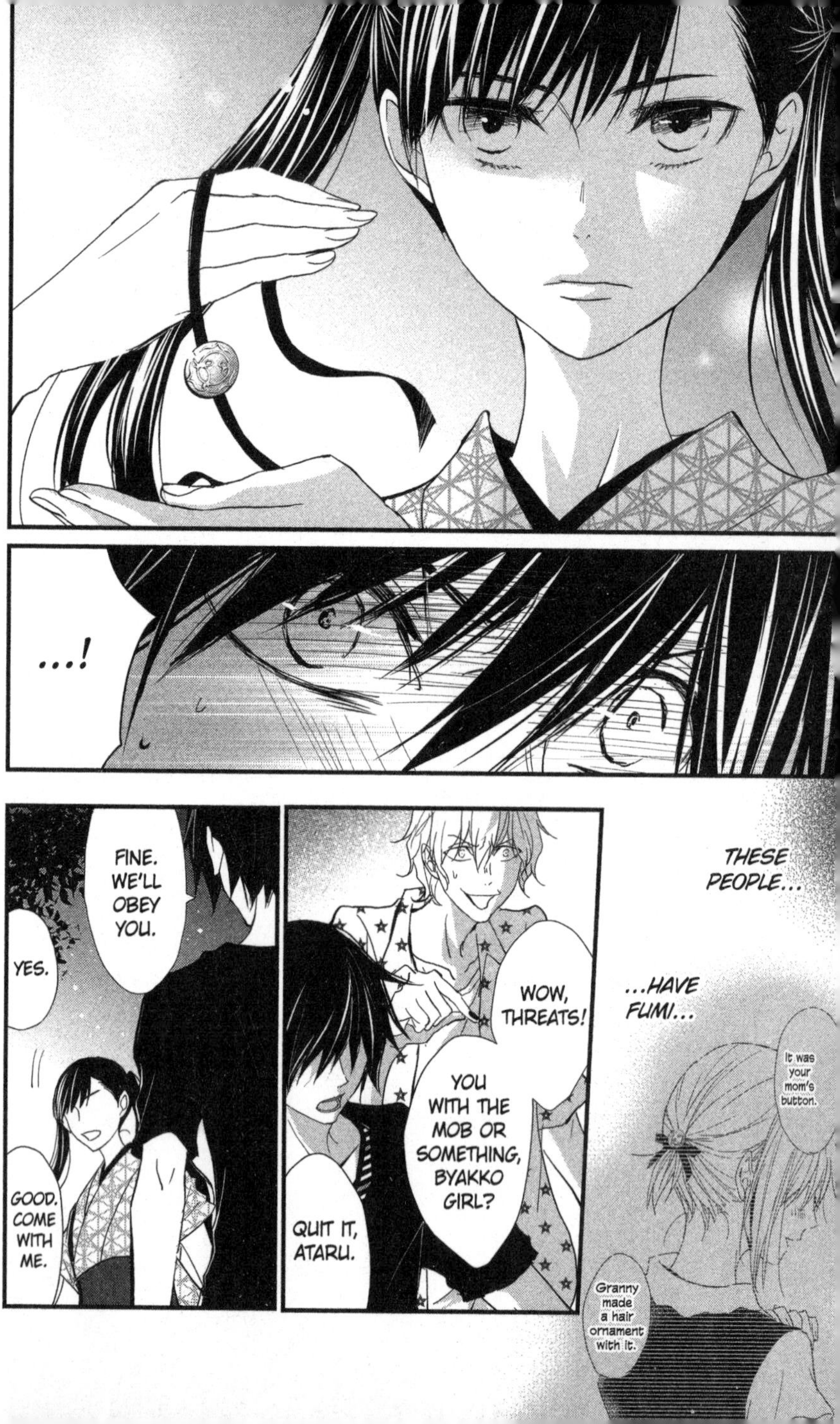
...!
THESE PEOPLE...
...HAVE FUMI...
It was your mom's button.
Granny made a hair ornament with it.
WOW, THREATS!
YOU WITH THE MOB OR SOMETHING, BYAKKO GIRL?
QUIT IT, ATARU.
FINE. WE'LL OBEY YOU.
YES.
GOOD. COME WITH ME.

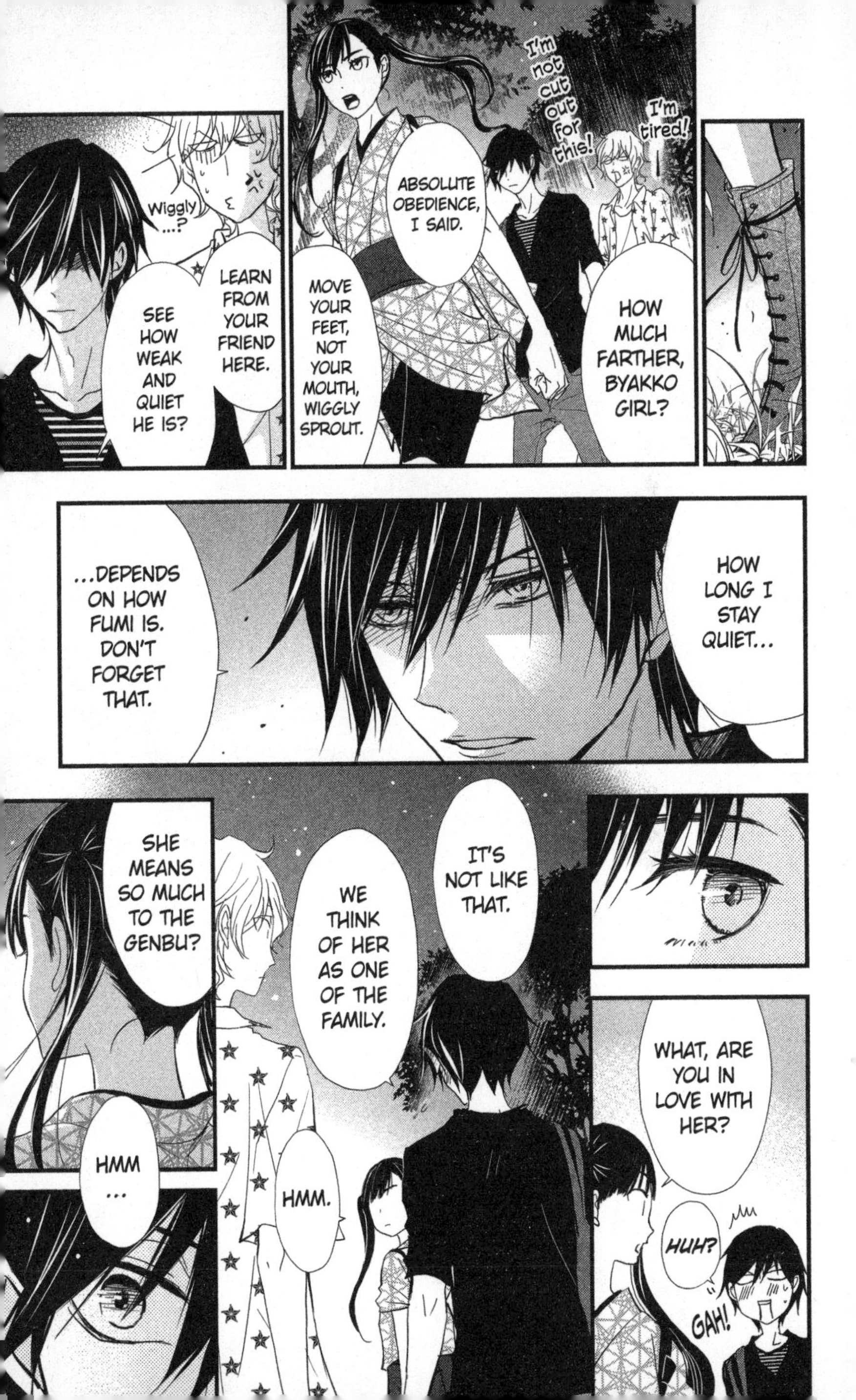
HOW MUCH FARTHER, BYAKKO GIRL?
I'm tired!
I'm not cut out for this!
ABSOLUTE OBEDIENCE, I SAID.
MOVE YOUR FEET, NOT YOUR MOUTH, WIGGLY SPROUT.
LEARN FROM YOUR FRIEND HERE.
SEE HOW WEAK AND QUIET HE IS?
Wiggly ...?
HOW LONG I STAY QUIET...
...DEPENDS ON HOW FUMI IS. DON'T FORGET THAT.
WHAT, ARE YOU IN LOVE WITH HER?
HUH?
GAH!
IT'S NOT LIKE THAT.
WE THINK OF HER AS ONE OF THE FAMILY.
HMM.
SHE MEANS SO MUCH TO THE GENBU?
HMM ...

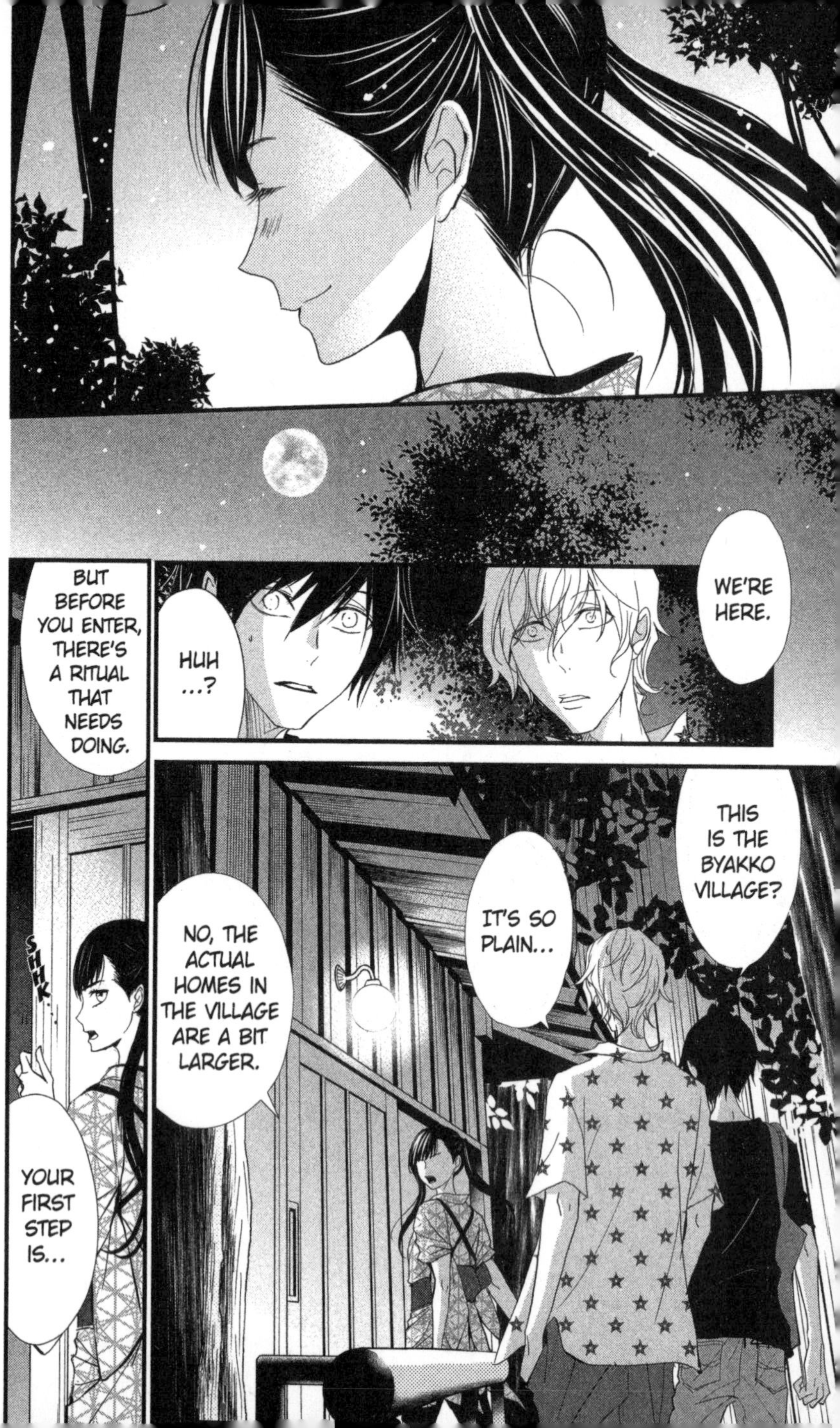
WE'RE HERE.
HUH ...?
THIS IS THE BYAKKO VILLAGE?
IT'S SO PLAIN...
NO, THE ACTUAL HOMES IN THE VILLAGE ARE A BIT LARGER.
BUT BEFORE YOU ENTER, THERE'S A RITUAL THAT NEEDS DOING.
SHHK
YOUR FIRST STEP IS...

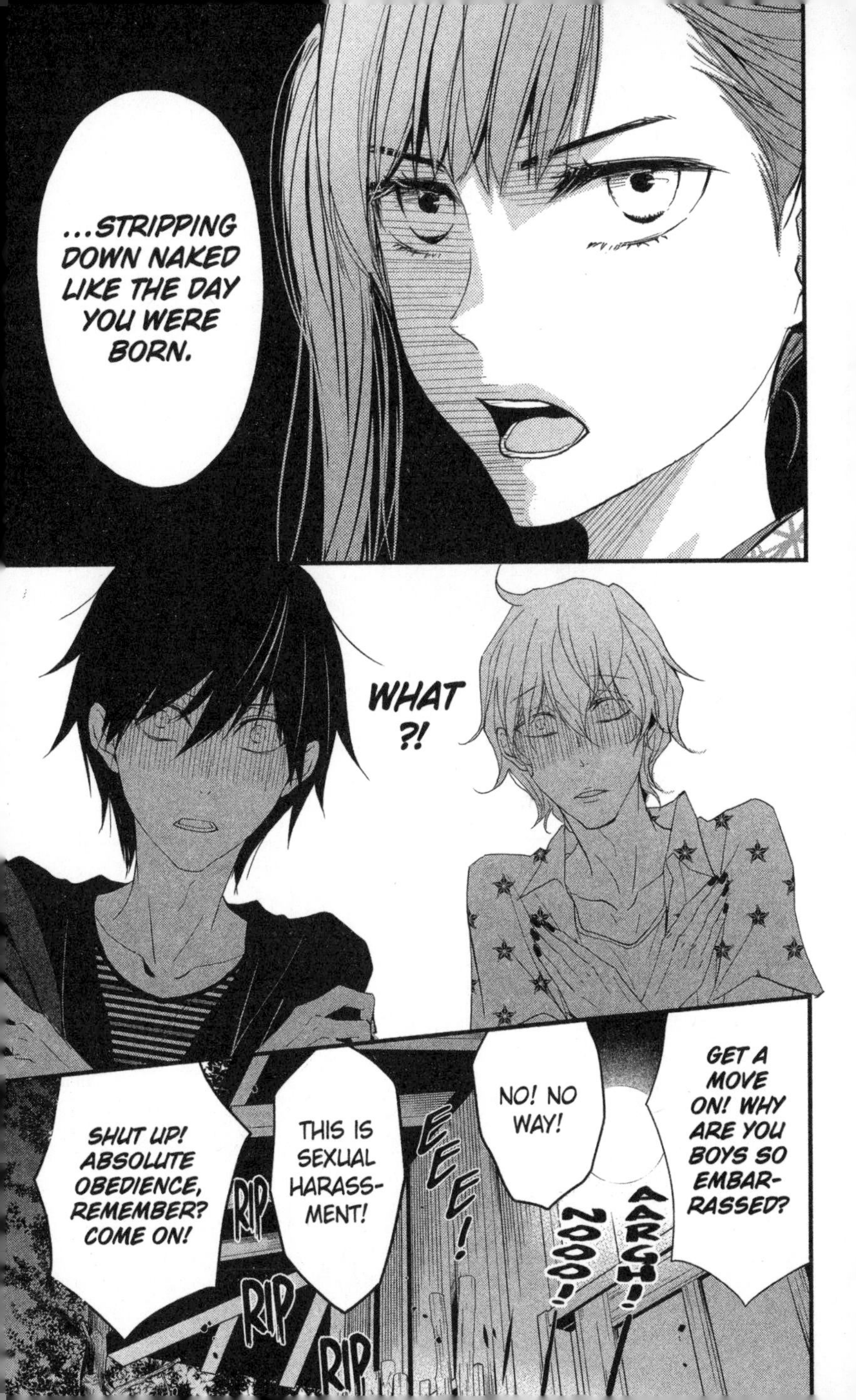
...STRIPPING DOWN NAKED LIKE THE DAY YOU WERE BORN.
WHAT ?!
GET A MOVE ON! WHY ARE YOU BOYS SO EMBARRASSED?
AARGH!
NO! NO WAY!
ZOOO!
EEEE!
THIS IS SEXUAL HARASSMENT!
SHUT UP! ABSOLUTE OBEDIENCE, REMEMBER? COME ON!
RIP
RIP
RIP

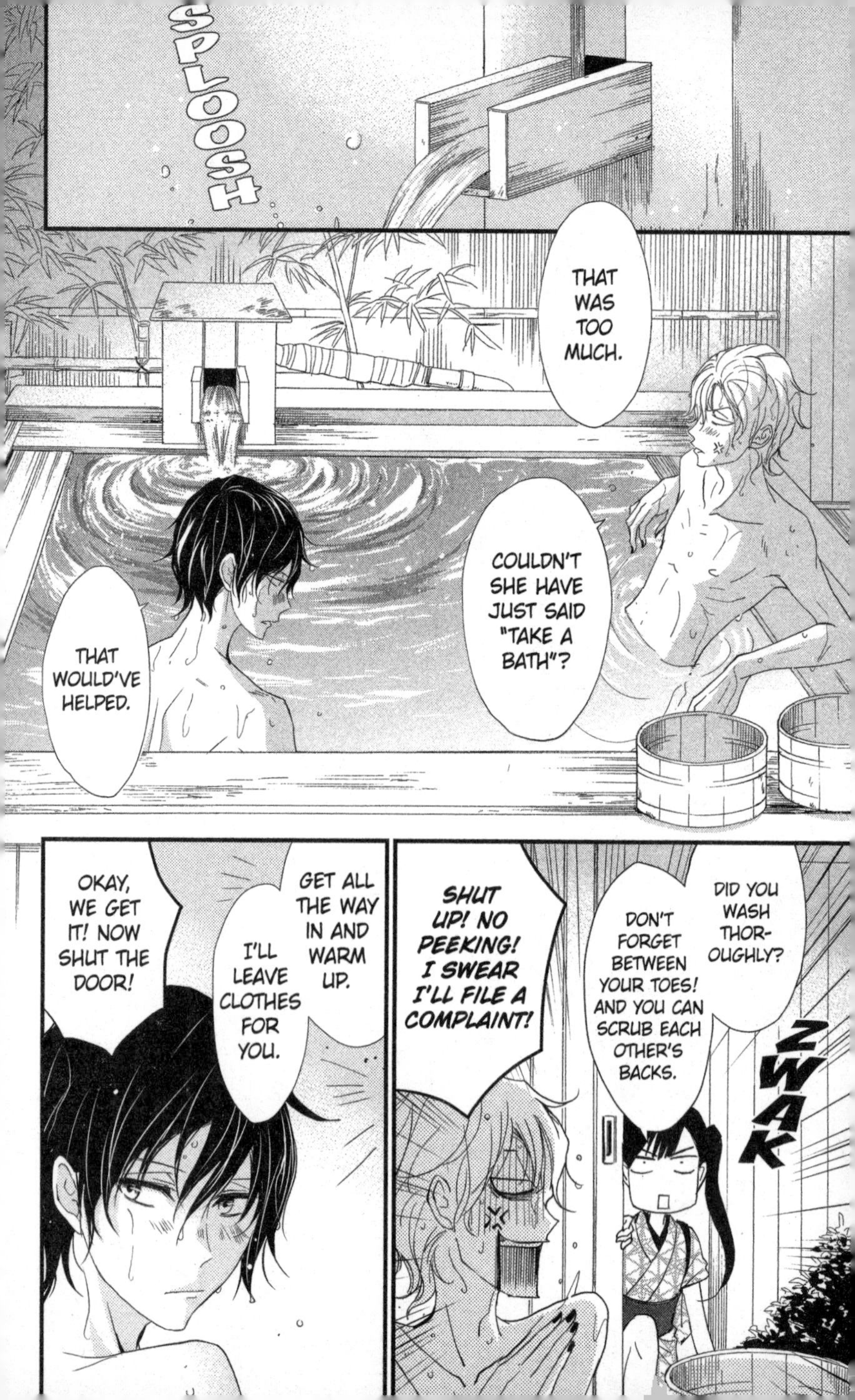
SPLOOSH
THAT WAS TOO MUCH.
COULDN'T SHE HAVE JUST SAID "TAKE A BATH"?
THAT WOULD'VE HELPED.
DID YOU WASH THOR-OUGHLY?
DON'T FORGET BETWEEN YOUR TOES! AND YOU CAN SCRUB EACH OTHER'S BACKS.
ZWAK
SHUT UP! NO PEEKING! I SWEAR I'LL FILE A COMPLAINT!
GET ALL THE WAY IN AND WARM UP.
I'LL LEAVE CLOTHES FOR YOU.
OKAY, WE GET IT! NOW SHUT THE DOOR!

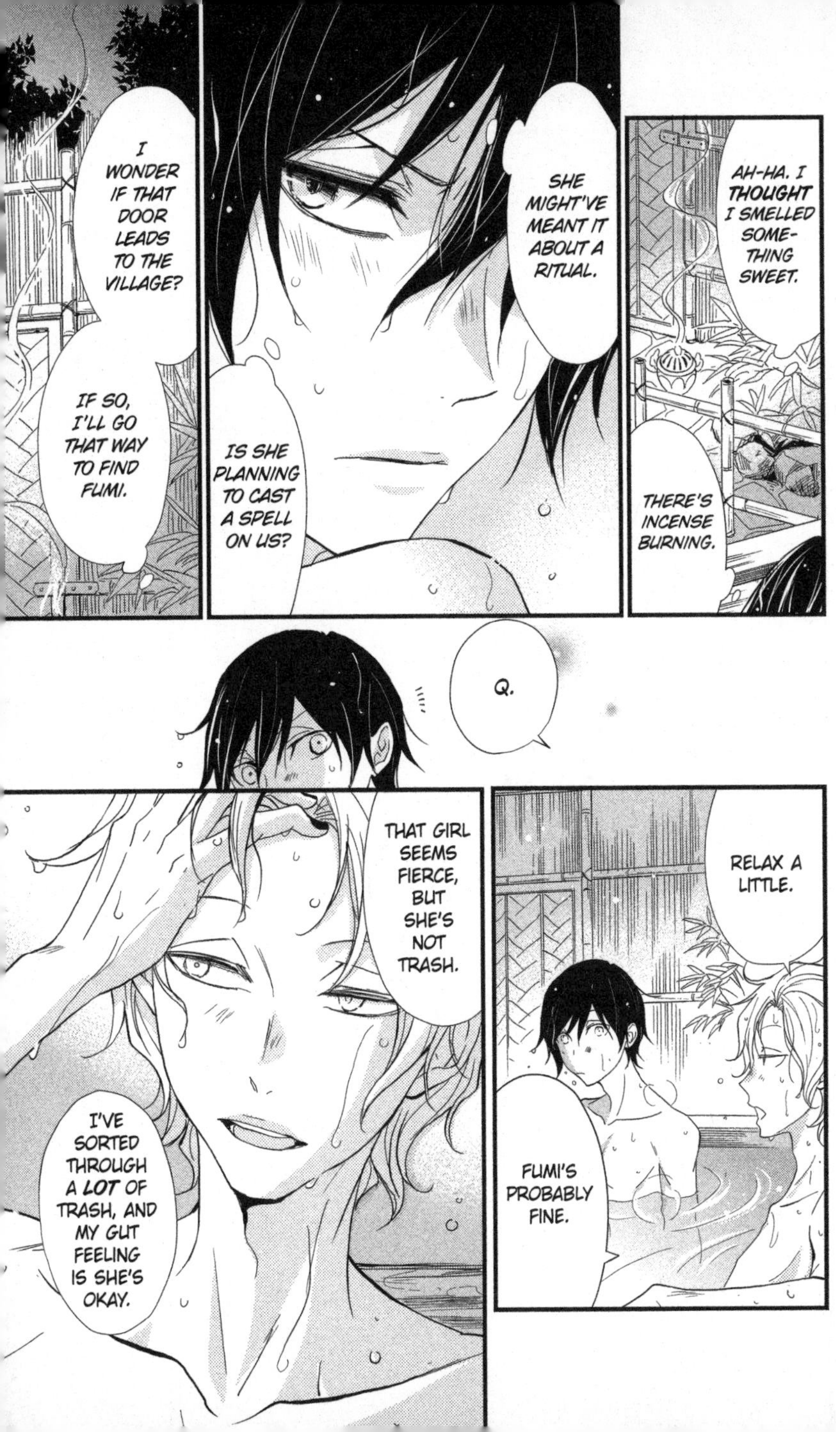
AH-HA. I **THOUGHT** I SMELLED SOME-THING SWEET.
THERE'S INCENSE BURNING.
SHE MIGHT'VE MEANT IT ABOUT A RITUAL.
IS SHE PLANNING TO CAST A SPELL ON US?
I WONDER IF THAT DOOR LEADS TO THE VILLAGE?
IF SO, I'LL GO THAT WAY TO FIND FUMI.
Q.
RELAX A LITTLE.
FUMI'S PROBABLY FINE.
THAT GIRL SEEMS FIERCE, BUT SHE'S NOT TRASH.
I'VE SORTED THROUGH A ***LOT*** OF TRASH, AND MY GUT FEELING IS SHE'S OKAY.

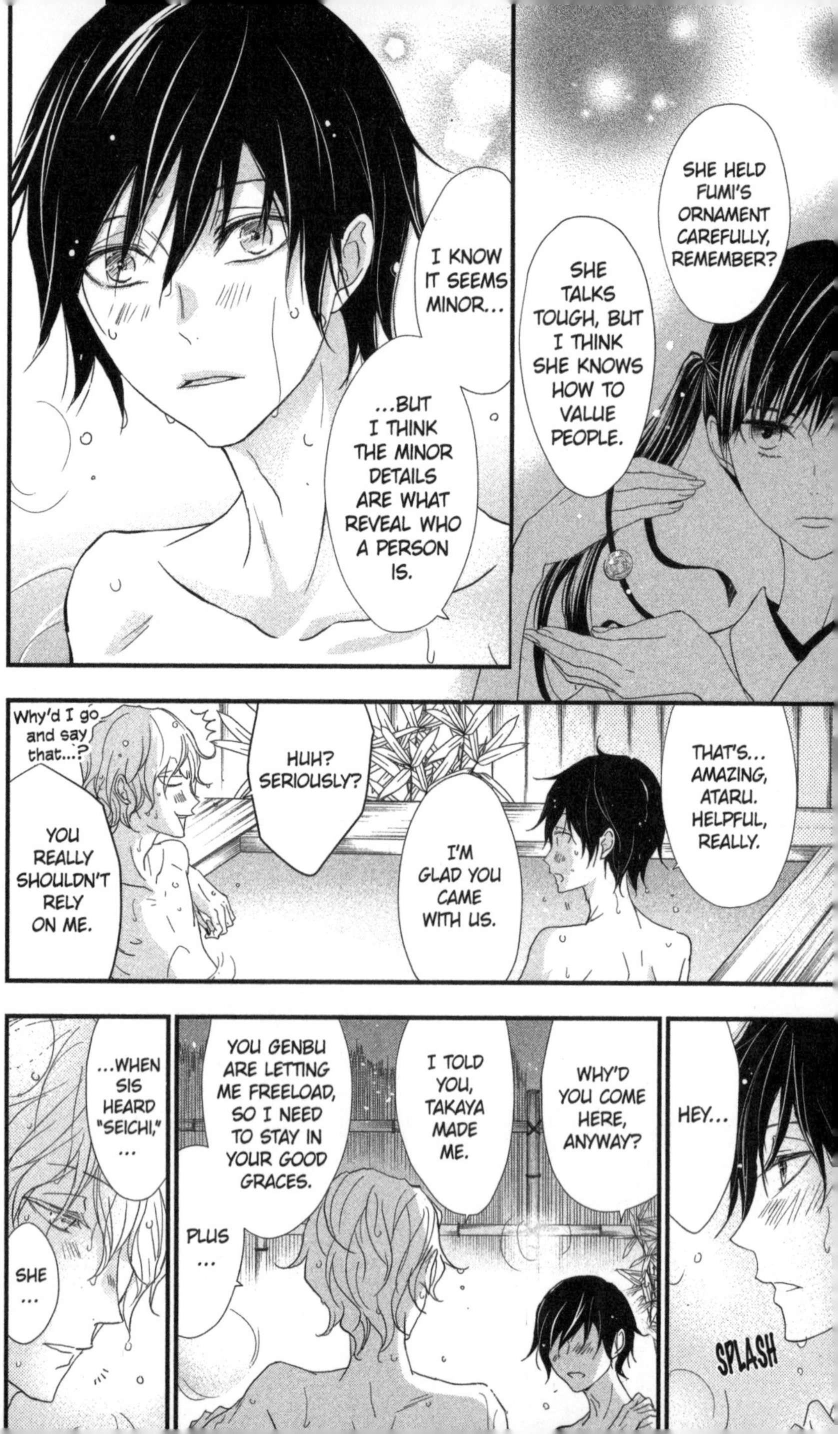
SHE HELD FUMI'S ORNAMENT CAREFULLY, REMEMBER?
SHE TALKS TOUGH, BUT I THINK SHE KNOWS HOW TO VALUE PEOPLE.
I KNOW IT SEEMS MINOR...
...BUT I THINK THE MINOR DETAILS ARE WHAT REVEAL WHO A PERSON IS.
THAT'S... AMAZING, ATARU. HELPFUL, REALLY.
I'M GLAD YOU CAME WITH US.
HUH? SERIOUSLY?
Why'd I go and say that...?
YOU REALLY SHOULDN'T RELY ON ME.
HEY...
SPLASH
WHY'D YOU COME HERE, ANYWAY?
I TOLD YOU, TAKAYA MADE ME.
YOU GENBU ARE LETTING ME FREELOAD, SO I NEED TO STAY IN YOUR GOOD GRACES.
PLUS ...
...WHEN SIS HEARD "SEICHI," ...
SHE ...

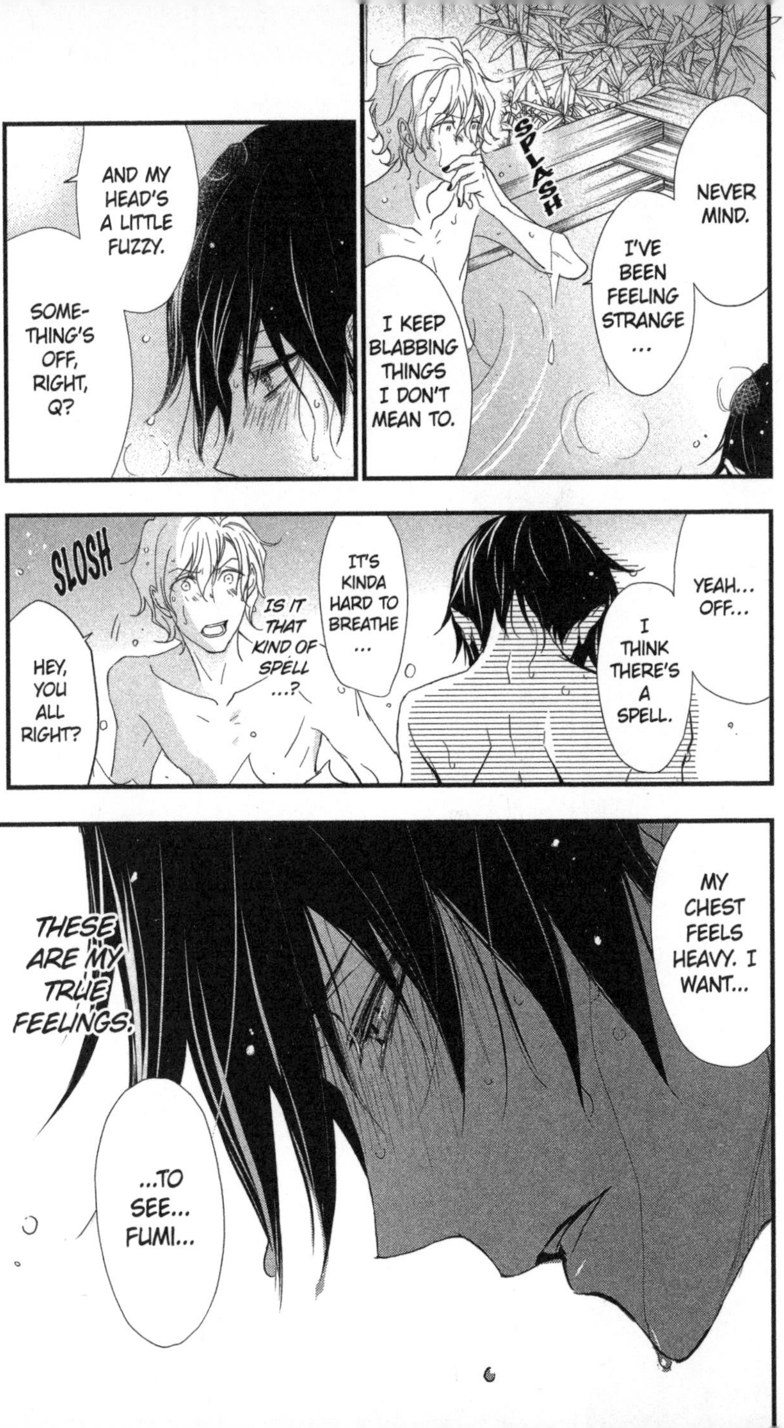
NEVER MIND.
I'VE BEEN FEELING STRANGE...
SPLASH
I KEEP BLABBING THINGS I DON'T MEAN TO.
AND MY HEAD'S A LITTLE FUZZY.
SOME-THING'S OFF, RIGHT, Q?
YEAH... OFF...
I THINK THERE'S A SPELL.
IT'S KINDA HARD TO BREATHE...
IS IT THAT KIND OF SPELL...?
SLOSH
HEY, YOU ALL RIGHT?
MY CHEST FEELS HEAVY. I WANT...
THESE ARE MY TRUE FEELINGS.
...TO SEE... FUMI...

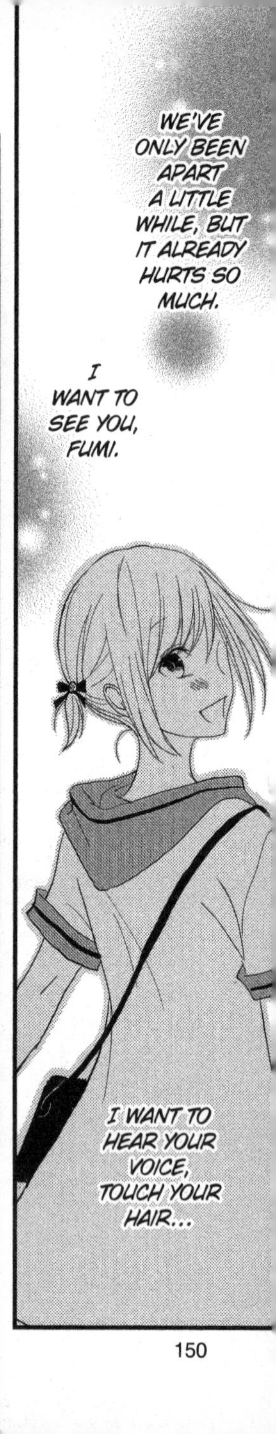
WE'VE ONLY BEEN APART A LITTLE WHILE, BUT IT ALREADY HURTS SO MUCH.
I WANT TO SEE YOU, FUMI.
I WANT TO HEAR YOUR VOICE, TOUCH YOUR HAIR...

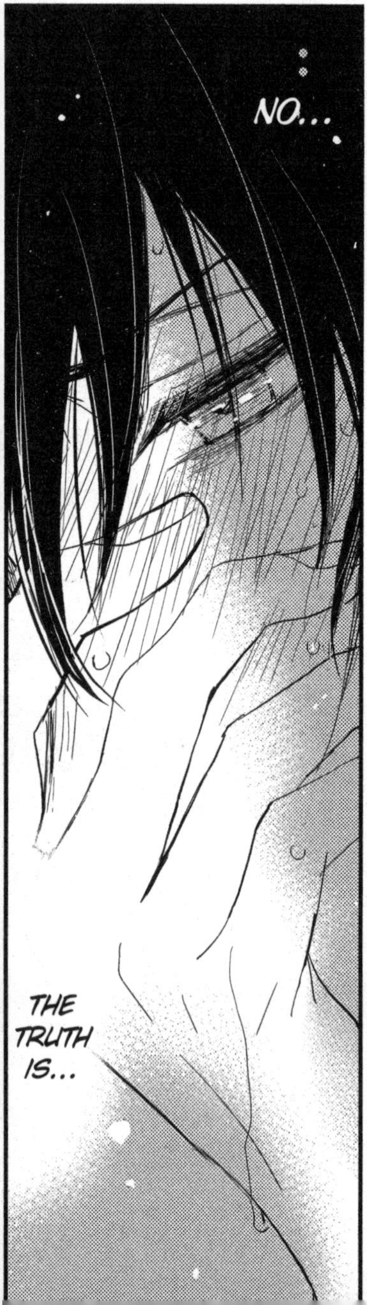
NO...
THE TRUTH IS...

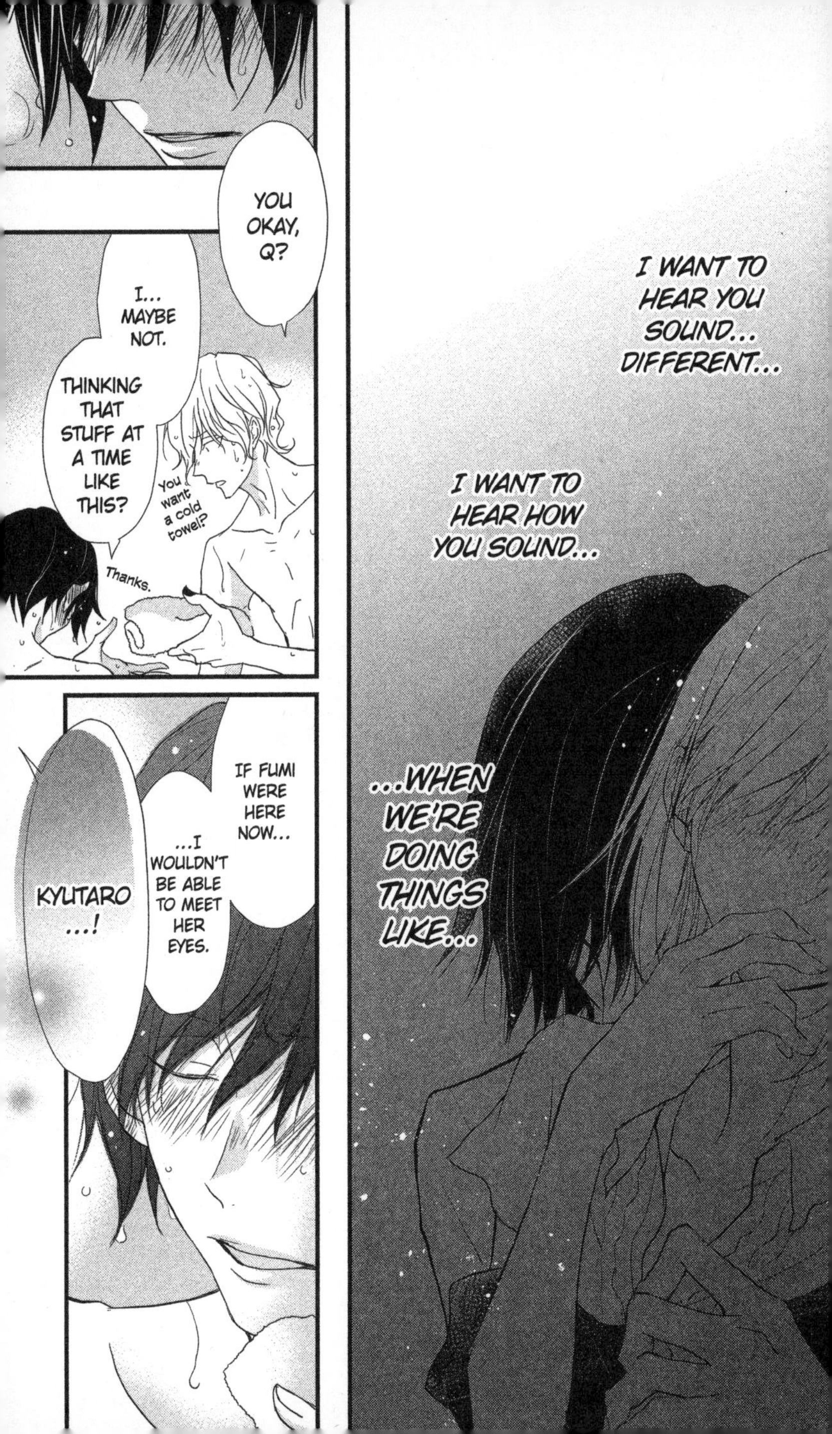
I WANT TO HEAR YOU SOUND... DIFFERENT...
I WANT TO HEAR HOW YOU SOUND...
...WHEN WE'RE DOING THINGS LIKE...
YOU OKAY, Q?
I... MAYBE NOT.
THINKING THAT STUFF AT A TIME LIKE THIS?
You want a cold towel?
Thanks.
IF FUMI WERE HERE NOW...
...I WOULDN'T BE ABLE TO MEET HER EYES.
KYUTARO ...!

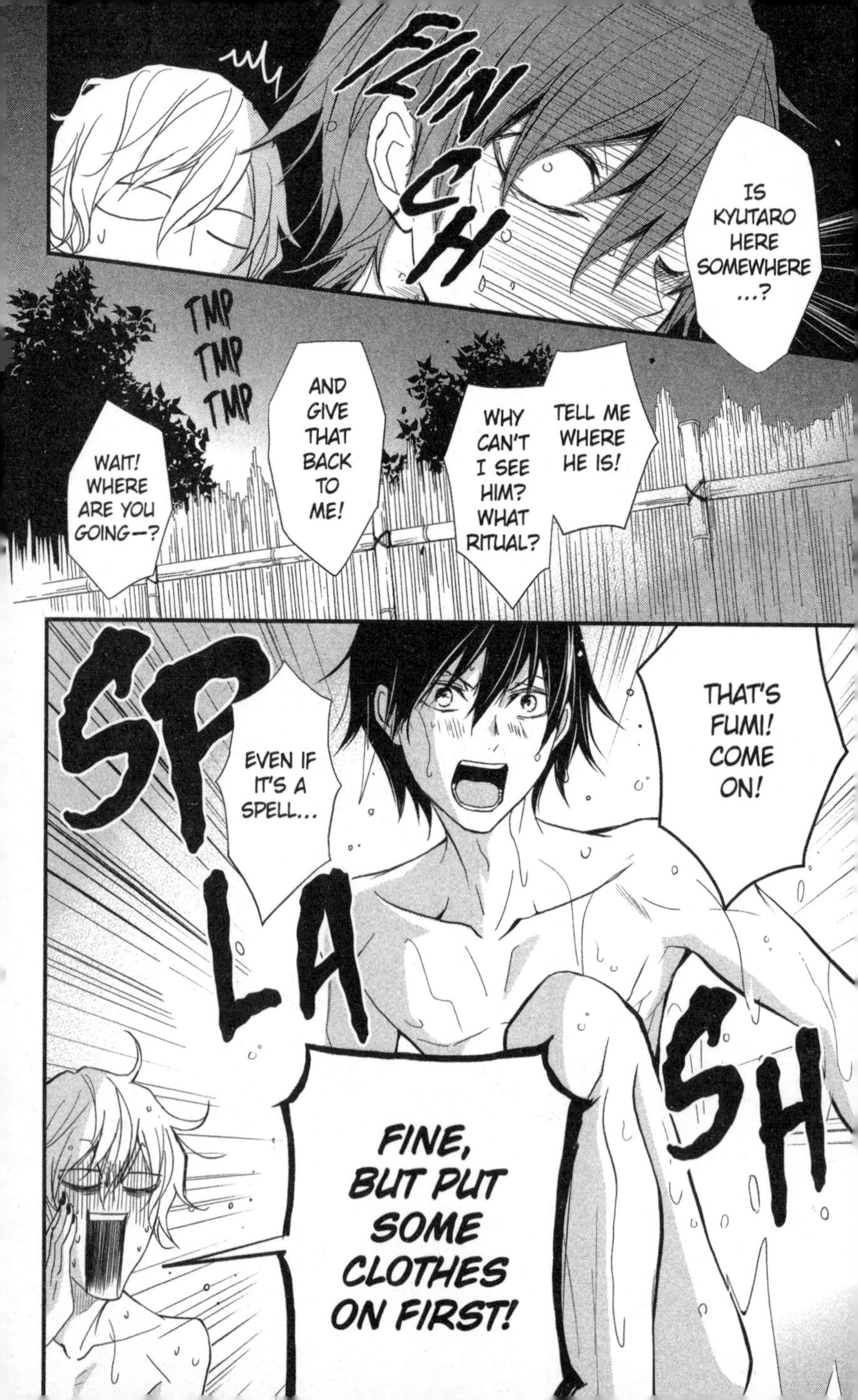
FLINCH
IS KYUTARO HERE SOMEWHERE ...?
TELL ME WHERE HE IS!
WHY CAN'T I SEE HIM? WHAT RITUAL?
AND GIVE THAT BACK TO ME!
TMP TMP TMP
WAIT! WHERE ARE YOU GOING—?
THAT'S FUMI! COME ON!
EVEN IF IT'S A SPELL...
SPLASH
FINE, BUT PUT SOME CLOTHES ON FIRST!

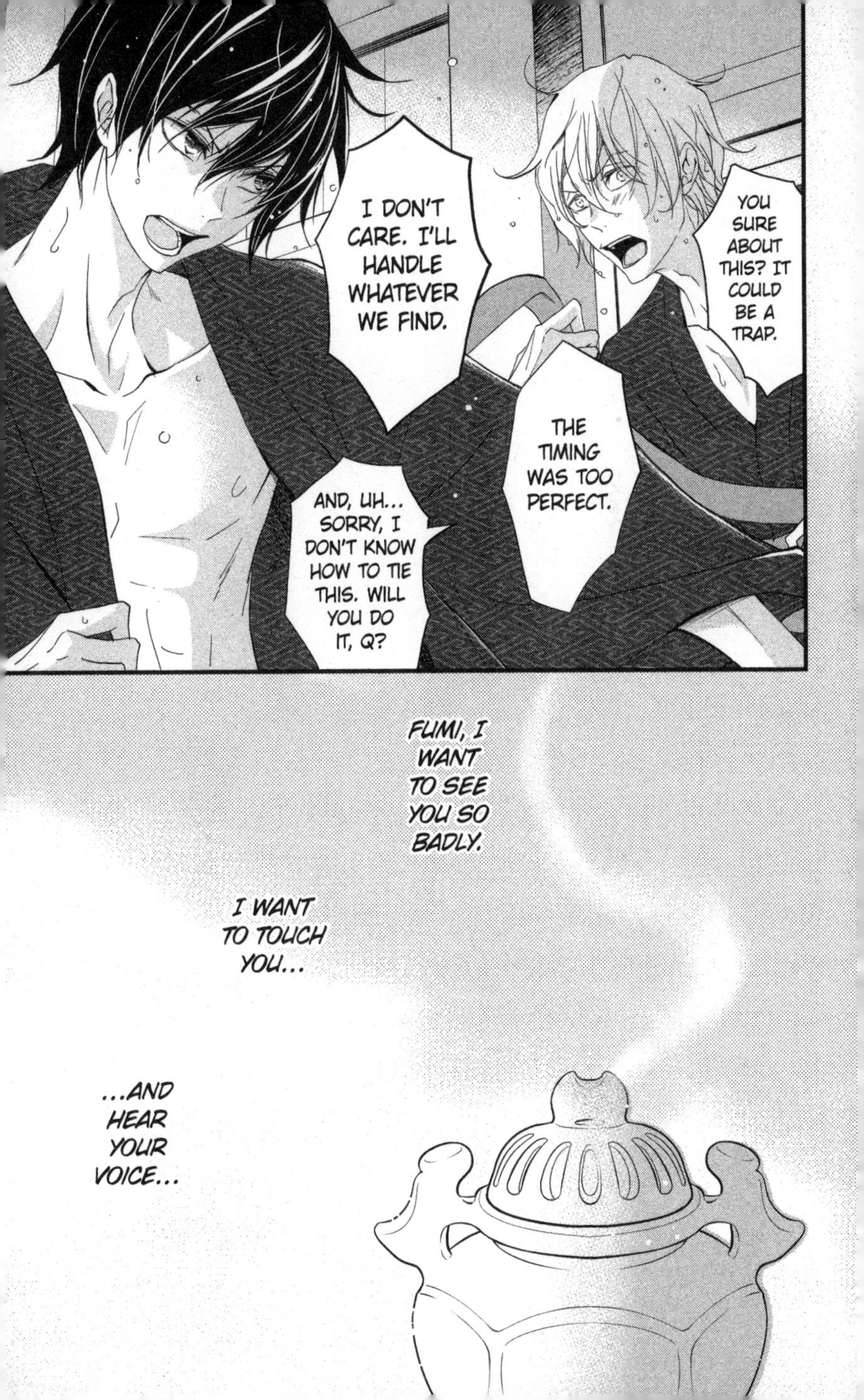
YOU SURE ABOUT THIS? IT COULD BE A TRAP.
THE TIMING WAS TOO PERFECT.
I DON'T CARE. I'LL HANDLE WHATEVER WE FIND.
AND, UH... SORRY, I DON'T KNOW HOW TO TIE THIS. WILL YOU DO IT, Q?
FUMI, I WANT TO SEE YOU SO BADLY.
I WANT TO TOUCH YOU...
...AND HEAR YOUR VOICE...

MONTHLY BETSUCOMI SALE DATE NOTICE ON TWITTER

CHAPTER 30

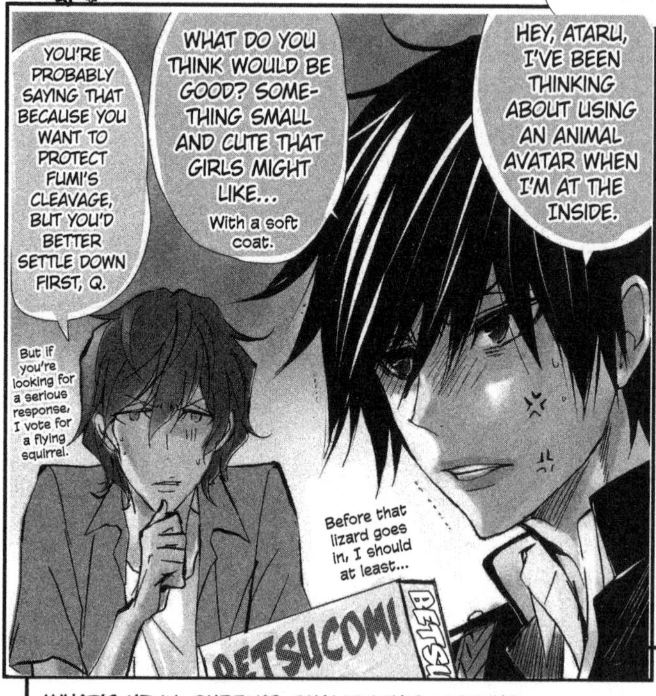
HEY, ATARU, I'VE BEEN THINKING ABOUT USING AN ANIMAL AVATAR WHEN I'M AT THE INSIDE.
WHAT DO YOU THINK WOULD BE GOOD? SOMETHING SMALL AND CUTE THAT GIRLS MIGHT LIKE...
With a soft coat.
YOU'RE PROBABLY SAYING THAT BECAUSE YOU WANT TO PROTECT FUMI'S CLEAVAGE, BUT YOU'D BETTER SETTLE DOWN FIRST, Q.
But if you're looking for a serious response, I vote for a flying squirrel.
Before that lizard goes in, I should at least...
BETSUCOMI

WHAT'S UP IN *QUEEN'S QUALITY* THIS MONTH?
(1) LATER, I'D LIKE TO ASK ATARU HOW HE GOT DRESSED.
(2) ISN'T HE A LITTLE CUTER THAN THE REAL FOUR-EYES? (OH DEAR.)
(3) SHE DOESN'T HAVE MUCH CLEAVAGE TO PROTECT.
CHAPTER 30 CONTAINS A NEW CHARACTER (?), AND THIS DOG-LOVING AUTHOR'S HAVING A TOUGH TIME OF THINGS.

ACTUALLY, I THINK KYUTARO IS MORE THE BLACK CAT OR CHIHUAHUA TYPE (ALTHOUGH NEITHER WOULD FIT FUMI'S CLEAVAGE). SEEMS TO ME THEY'D ALWAYS BE WARY OF PEOPLE. ATARU'S MORE THE FERRET TYPE.

I WONDER WHAT FUMI WOULD BE? SHE'S NOT ALWAYS THE MOST STABLE, SO...MAYBE A BROWN BEAR.

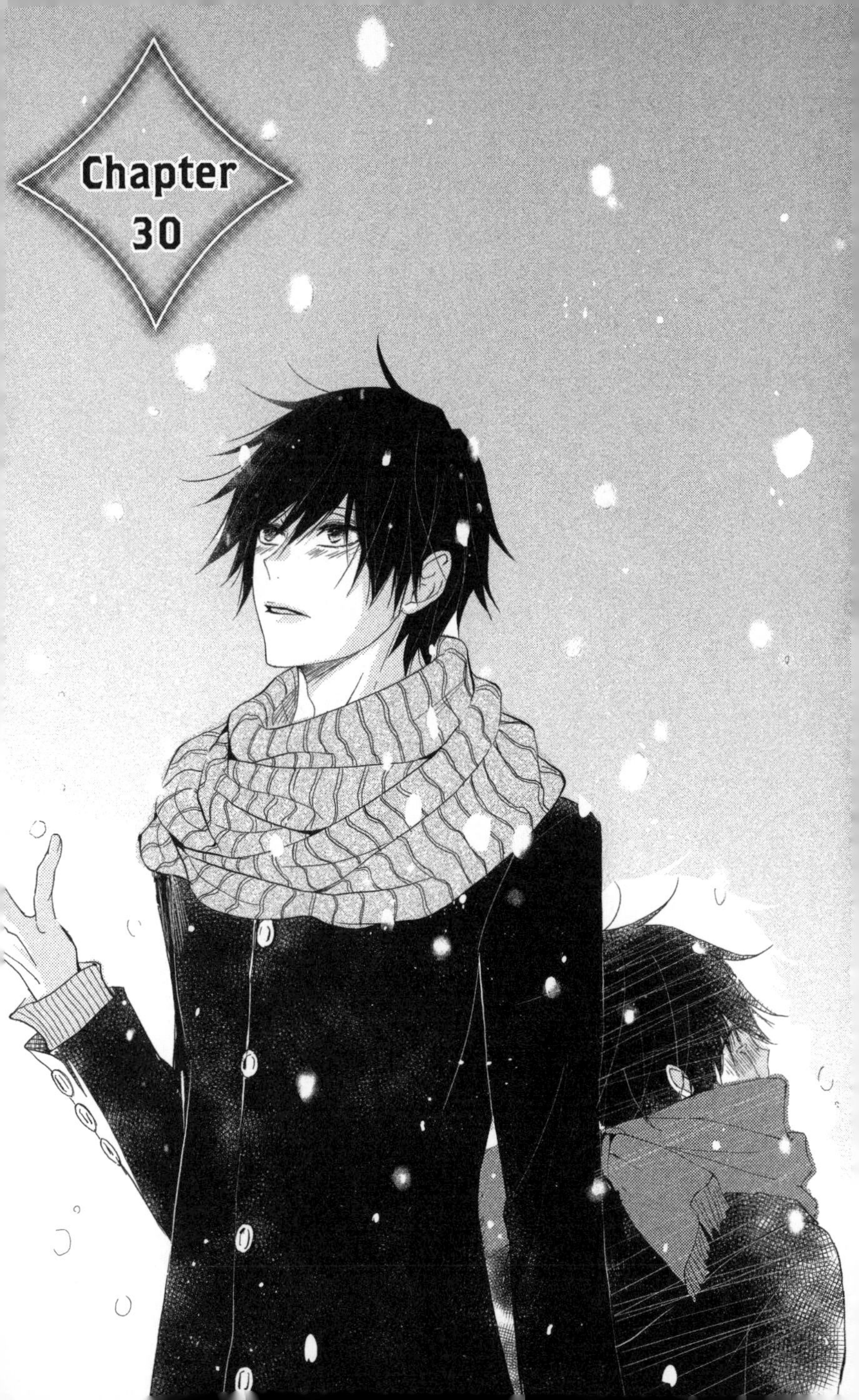
Chapter
30

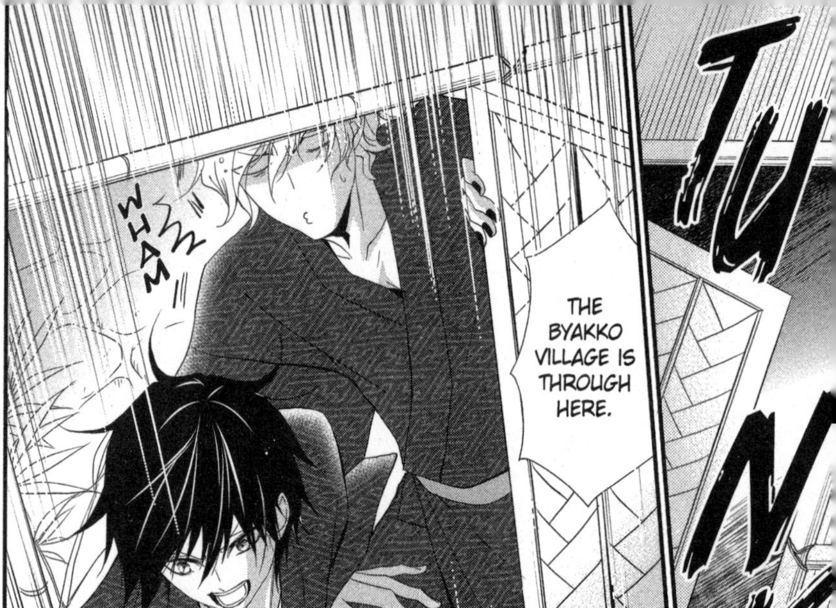
TUNK
THE BYAKKO VILLAGE IS THROUGH HERE.
WHAM
LET'S GO. WE HAVE TO GET FUMI BACK.

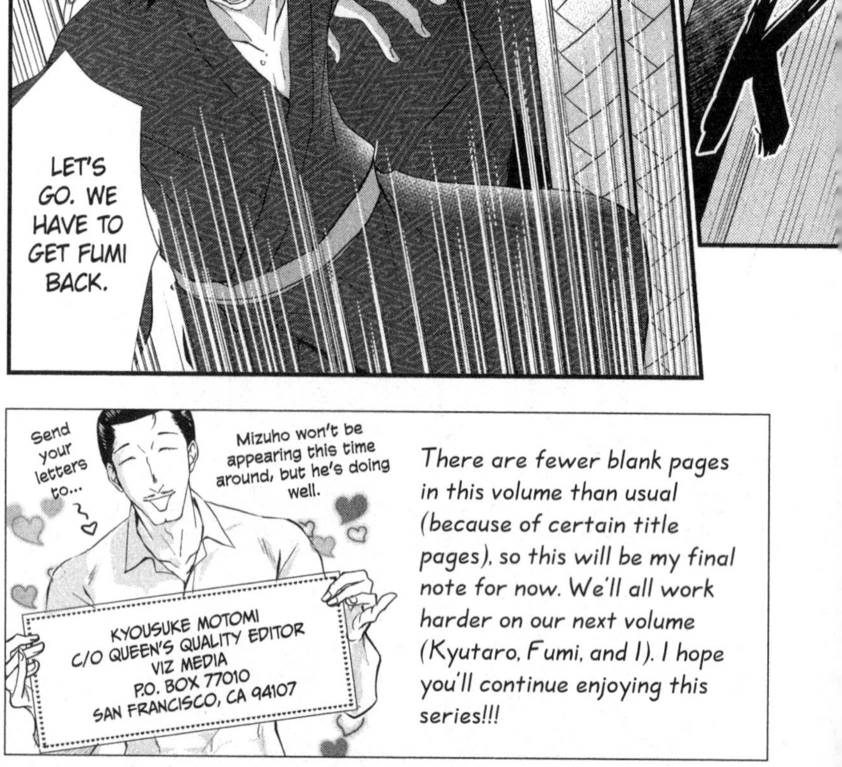
Mizuho won't be appearing this time around, but he's doing well.
Send your letters to...
KYOUSUKE MOTOMI
C/O QUEEN'S QUALITY EDITOR
VIZ MEDIA
P.O. BOX 77010
SAN FRANCISCO, CA 94107

There are fewer blank pages in this volume than usual (because of certain title pages), so this will be my final note for now. We'll all work harder on our next volume (Kyutaro, Fumi, and I). I hope you'll continue enjoying this series!!!

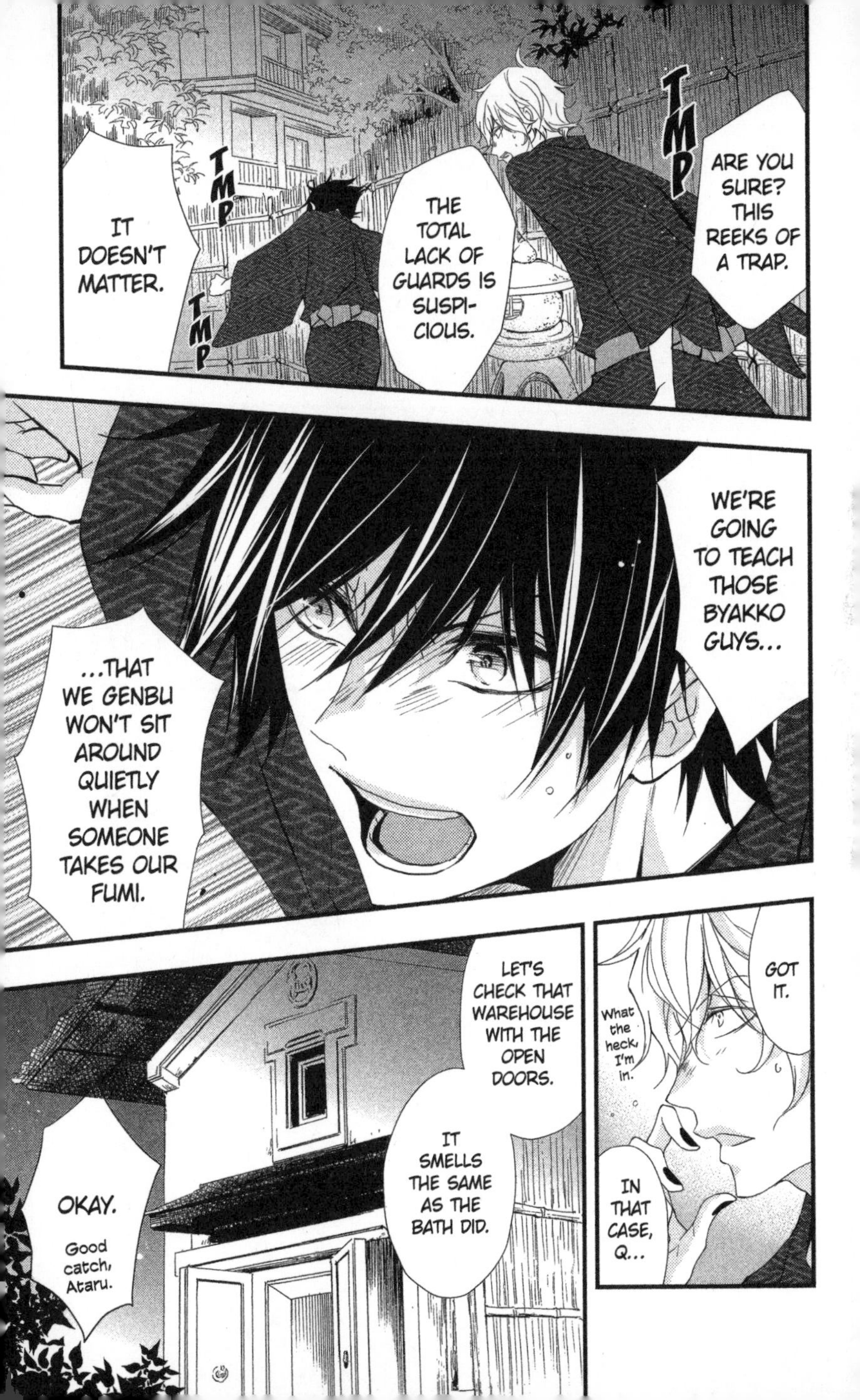
TMP
ARE YOU SURE? THIS REEKS OF A TRAP.
THE TOTAL LACK OF GUARDS IS SUSPICIOUS.
TMP
IT DOESN'T MATTER.
TMP
WE'RE GOING TO TEACH THOSE BYAKKO GUYS...
...THAT WE GENBU WON'T SIT AROUND QUIETLY WHEN SOMEONE TAKES OUR FUMI.
GOT IT.
What the heck, I'm in.
IN THAT CASE, Q...
LET'S CHECK THAT WAREHOUSE WITH THE OPEN DOORS.
IT SMELLS THE SAME AS THE BATH DID.
OKAY.
Good catch, Ataru.

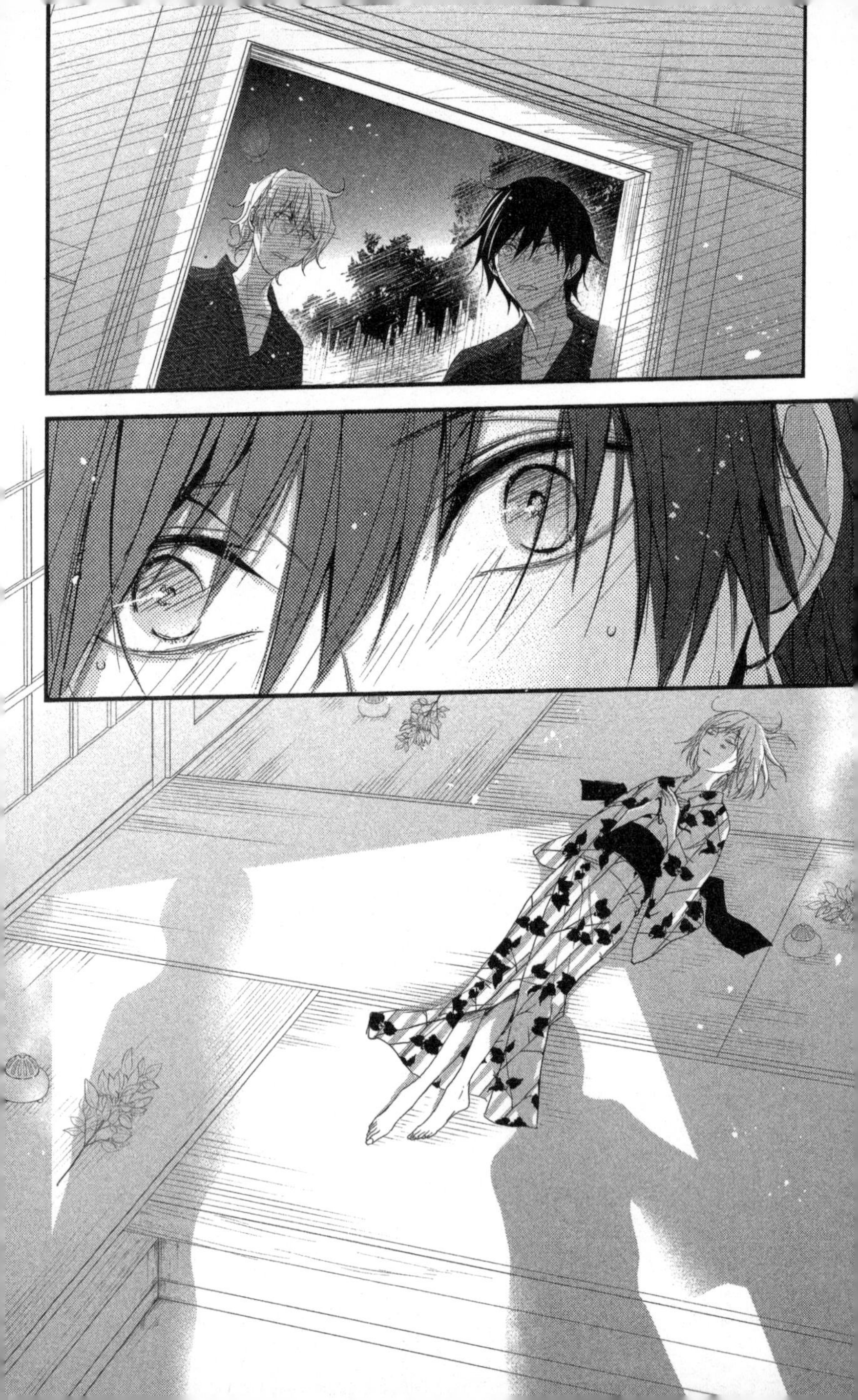

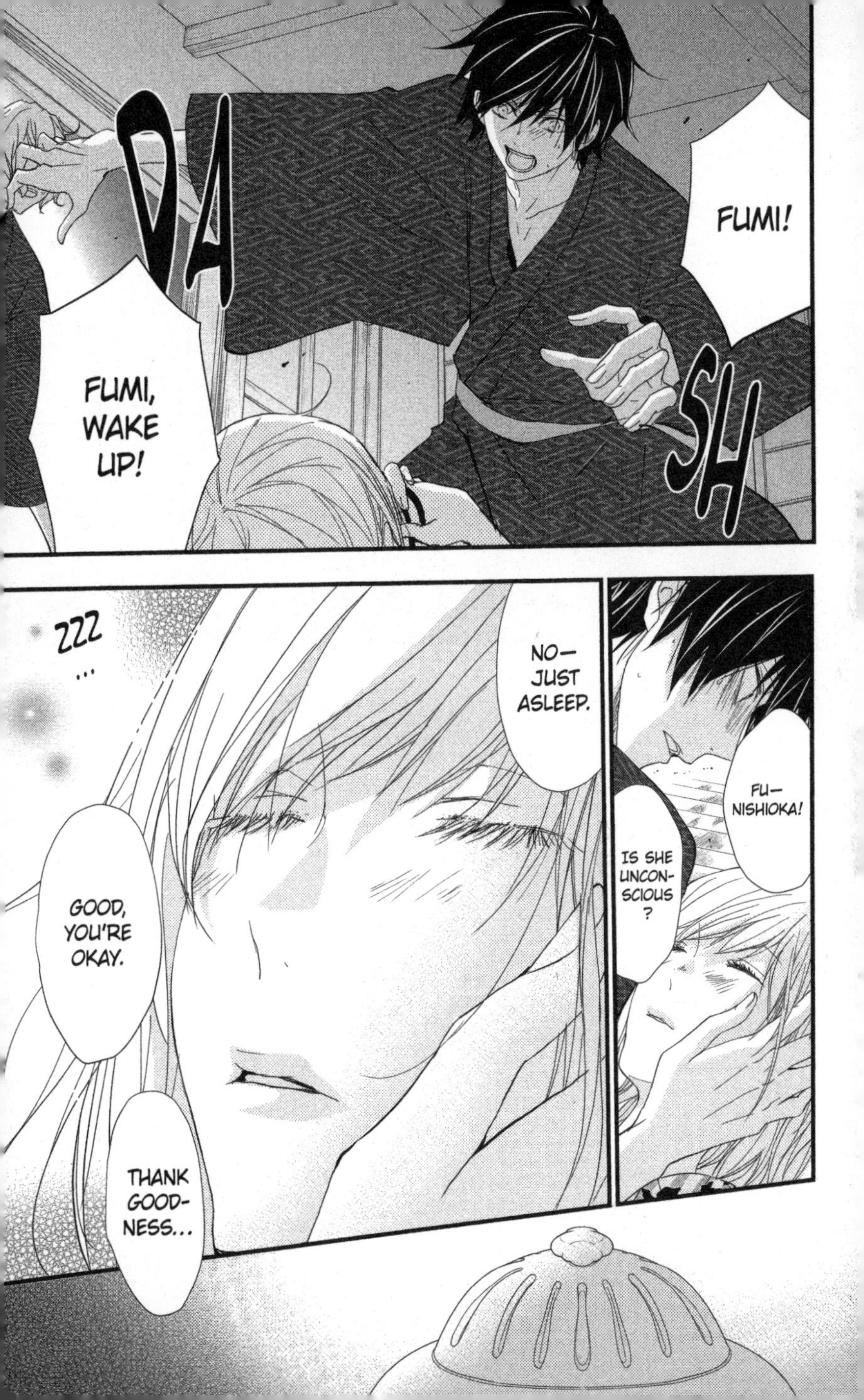
FUMI!
DA
SH
FUMI, WAKE UP!
FU— NISHIOKA!
IS SHE UNCONSCIOUS?
NO— JUST ASLEEP.
ZZZ ...
GOOD, YOU'RE OKAY.
THANK GOODNESS...

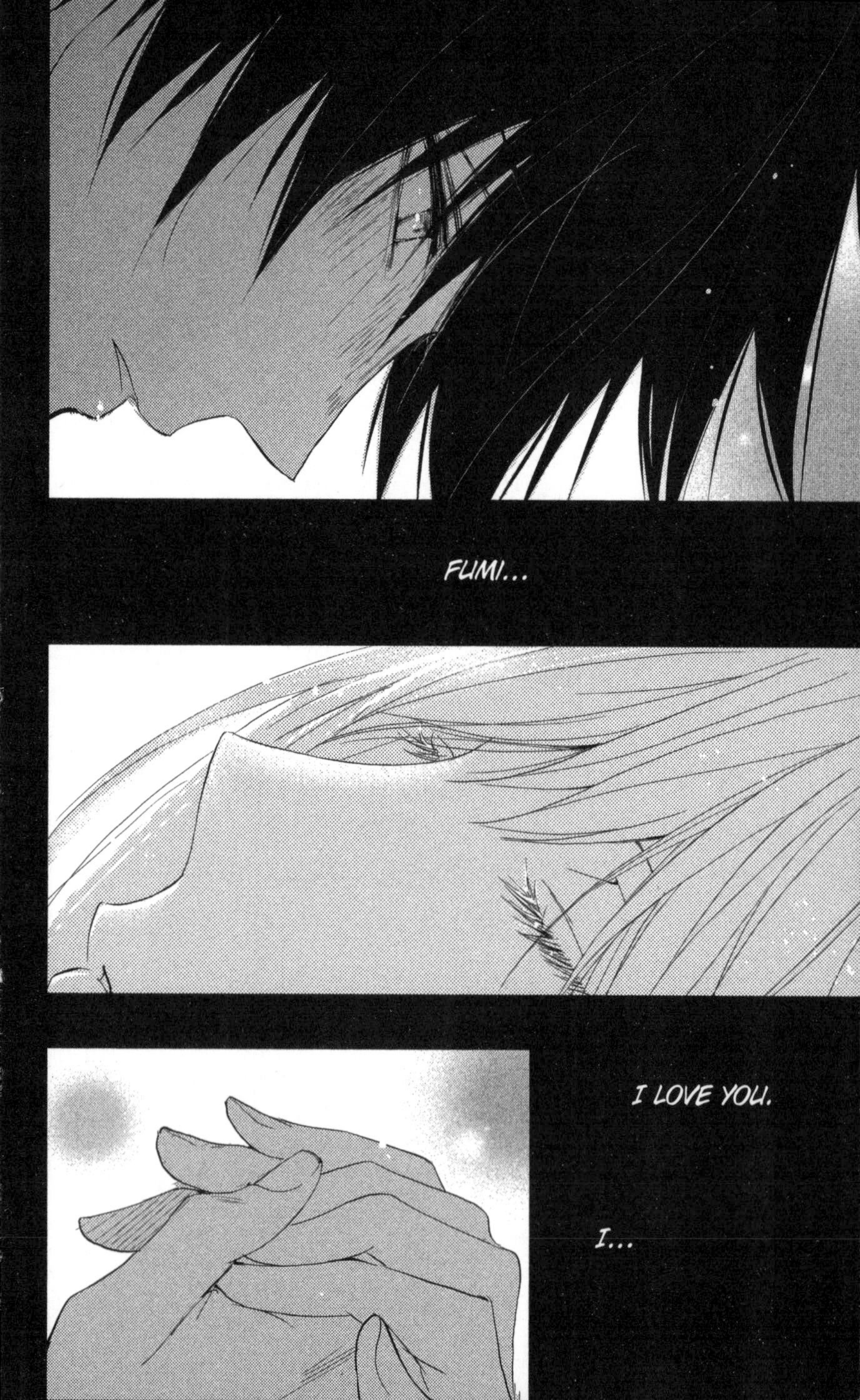
FUMI...
I LOVE YOU.
I...

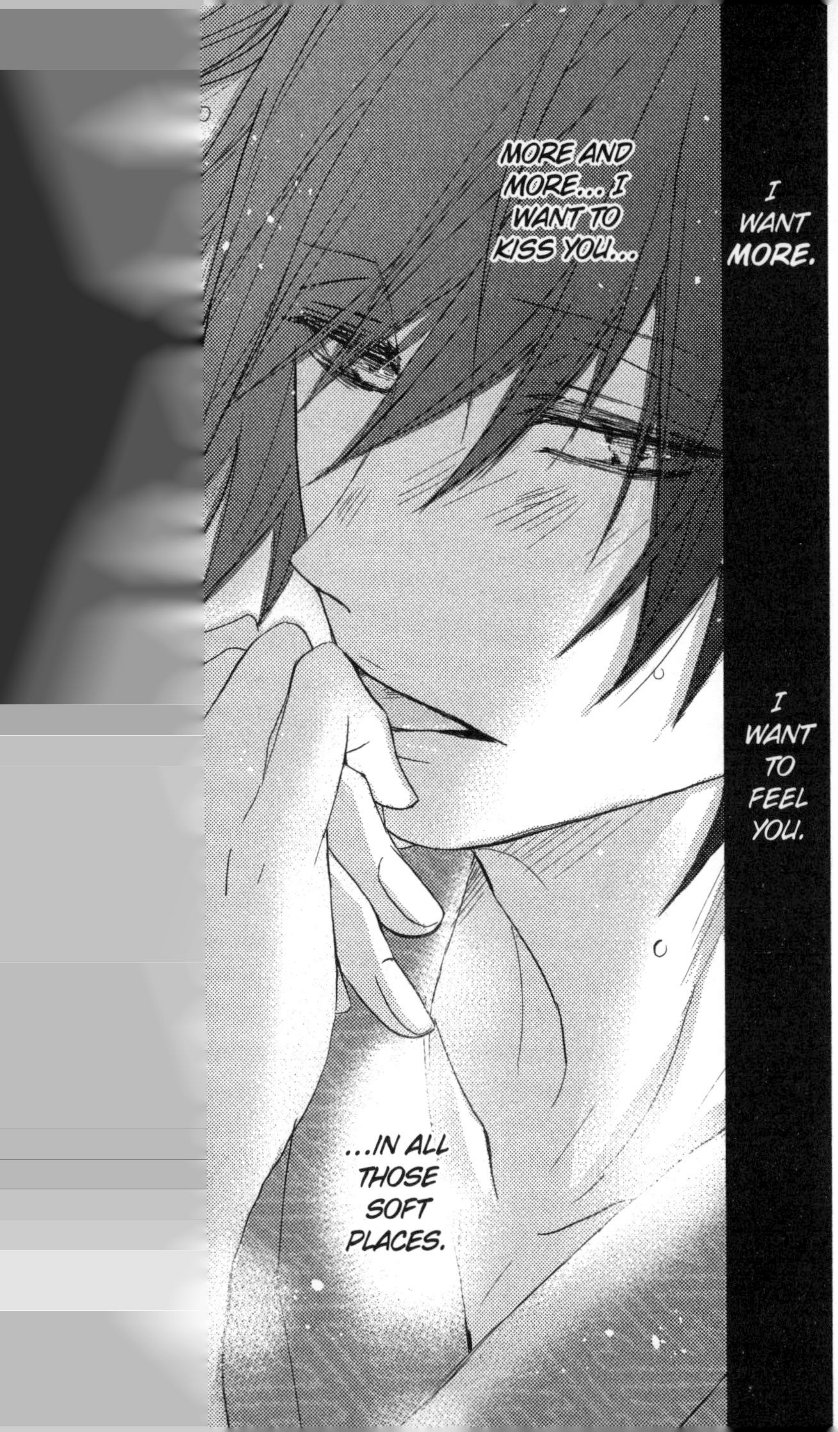
I WANT MORE.
MORE AND MORE... I WANT TO KISS YOU...
I WANT TO FEEL YOU.
...IN ALL THOSE SOFT PLACES.

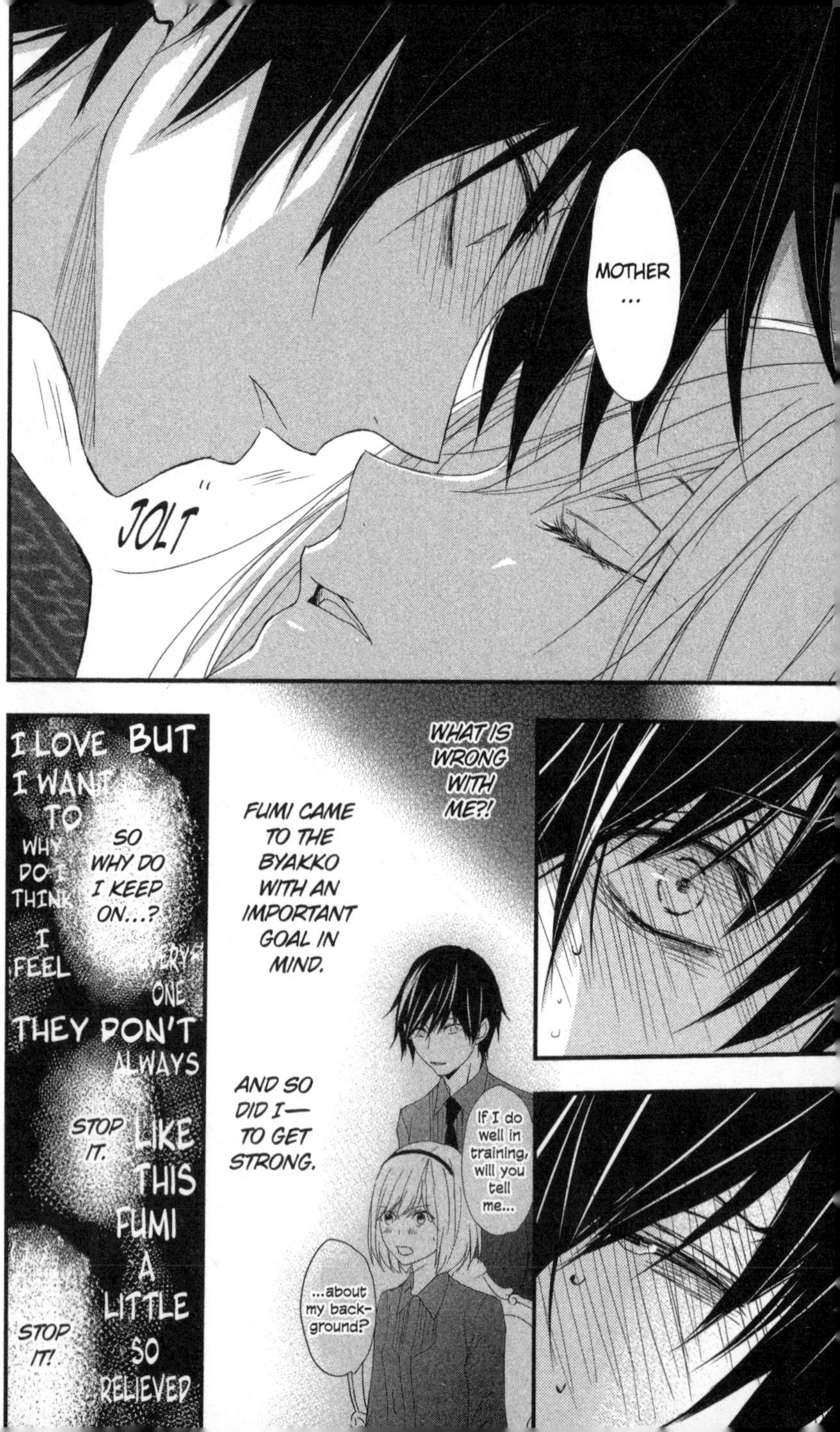
MOTHER ...
JOLT
WHAT IS WRONG WITH ME?!
FUMI CAME TO THE BYAKKO WITH AN IMPORTANT GOAL IN MIND.
AND SO DID I— TO GET STRONG.
If I do well in training, will you tell me...
...about my back-ground?
BUT
I LOVE
I WANT TO
SO WHY DO I KEEP ON...?
WHY DO I THINK
I FEEL
EVERY-ONE
THEY DON'T
ALWAYS
STOP IT.
LIKE THIS
FUMI
A LITTLE
SO RELIEVED
STOP IT!

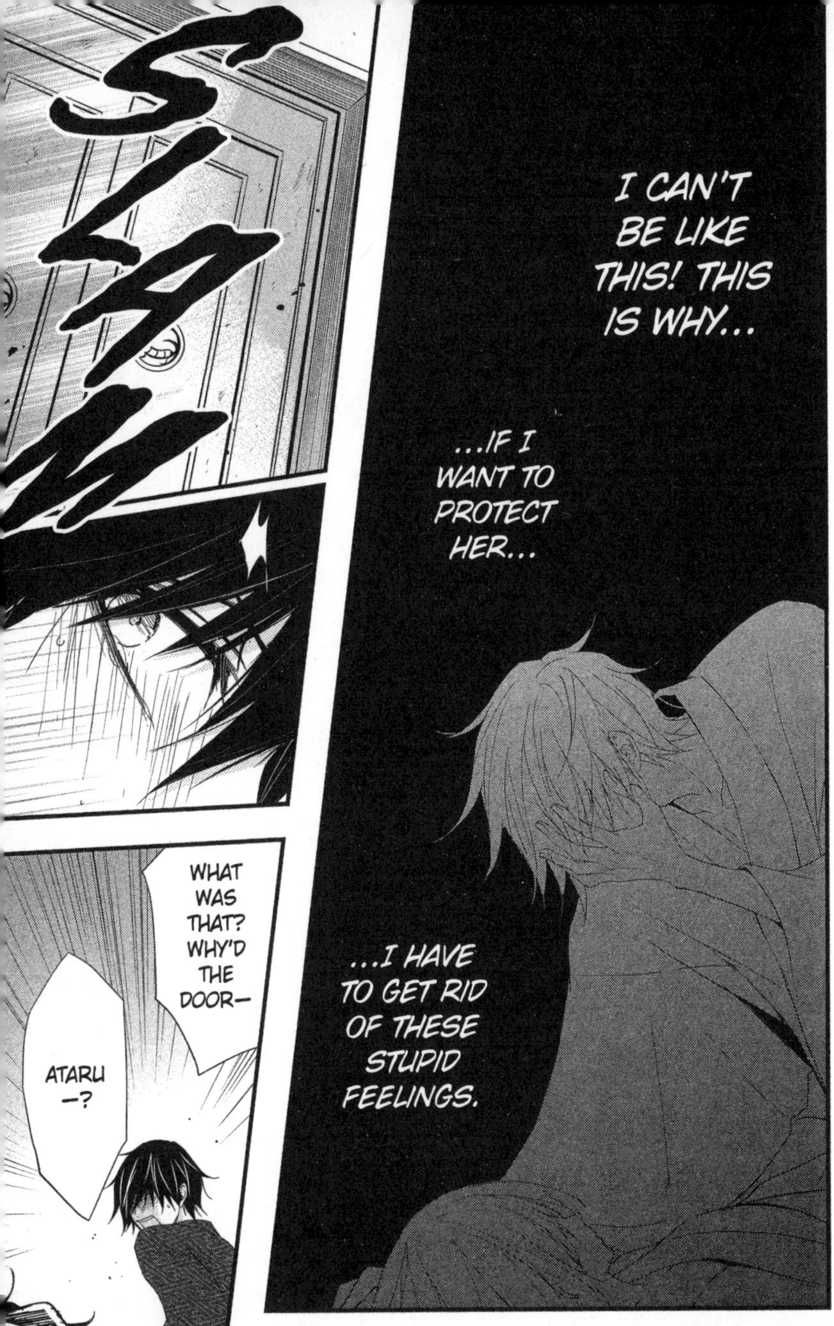
I CAN'T BE LIKE THIS! THIS IS WHY...
...IF I WANT TO PROTECT HER...
...I HAVE TO GET RID OF THESE STUPID FEELINGS.
SLAM
WHAT WAS THAT? WHY'D THE DOOR—
ATARU—?

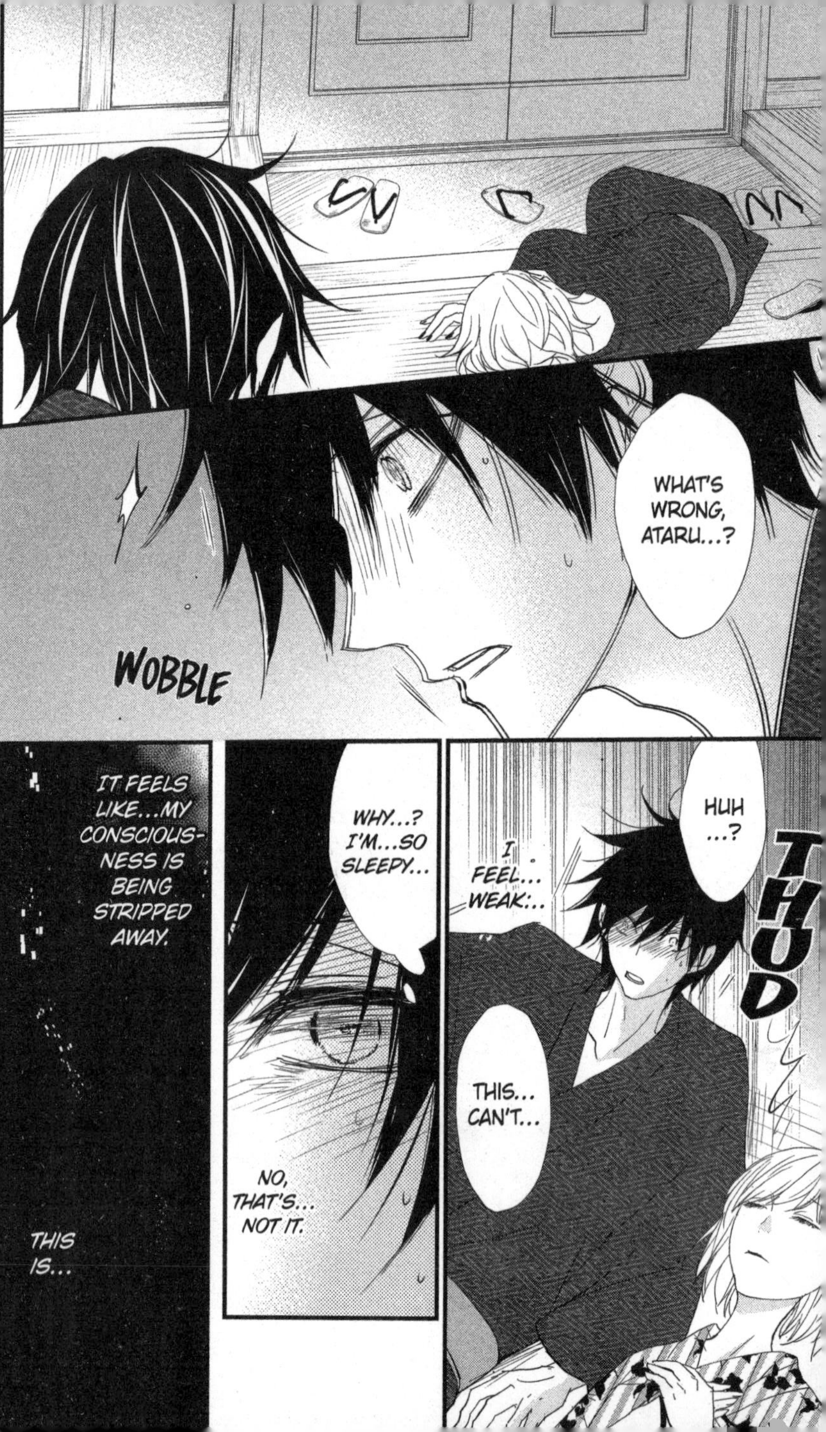
WHAT'S WRONG, ATARU...?
WOBBLE
HUH ...?
THUD
I FEEL... WEAK...
THIS... CAN'T...
WHY...? I'M...SO SLEEPY...
NO, THAT'S... NOT IT.
IT FEELS LIKE...MY CONSCIOUSNESS IS BEING STRIPPED AWAY.
THIS IS...

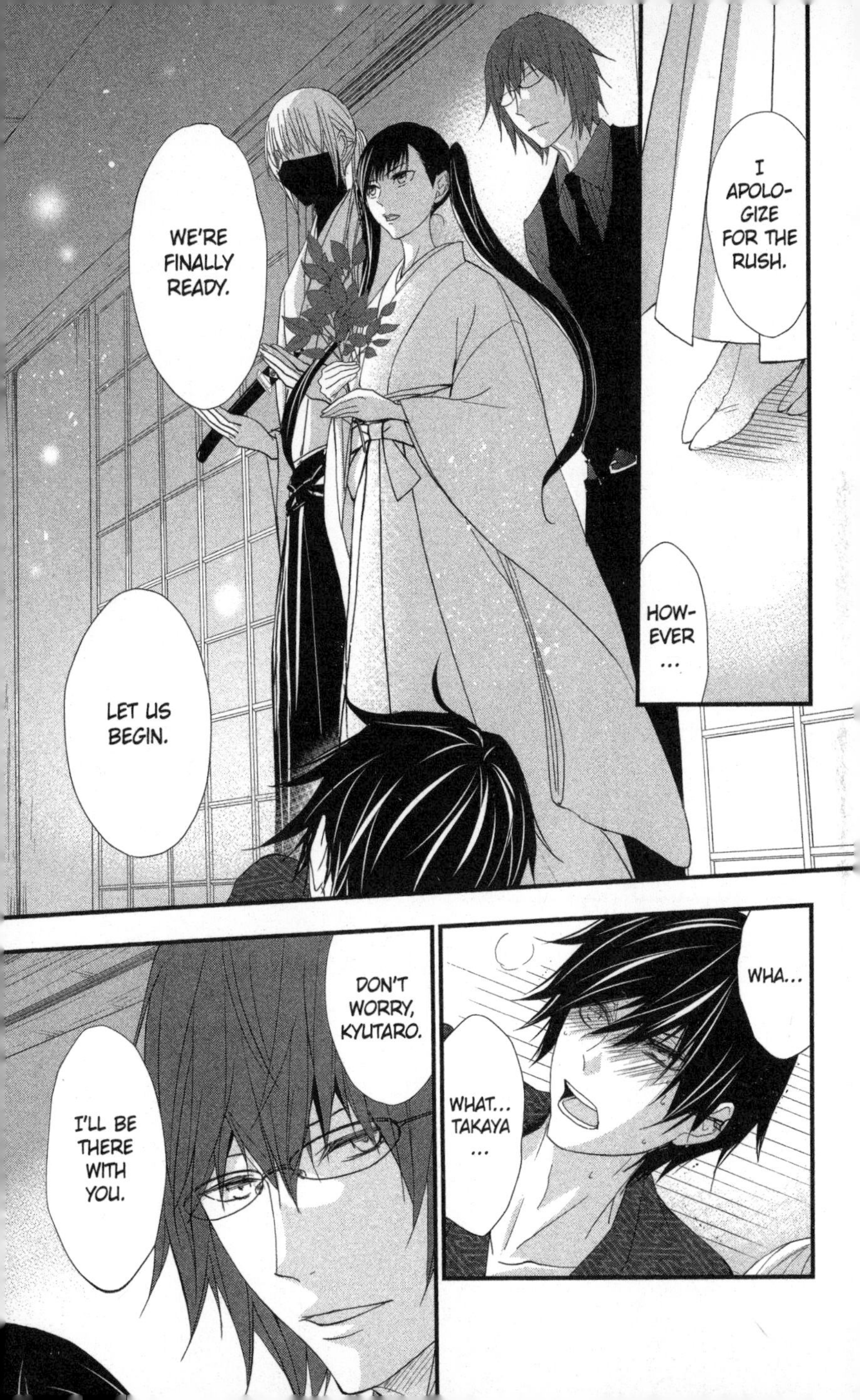
I APOLOGIZE FOR THE RUSH.
HOWEVER...
WE'RE FINALLY READY.
LET US BEGIN.
WHA...
WHAT... TAKAYA...
DON'T WORRY, KYUTARO.
I'LL BE THERE WITH YOU.

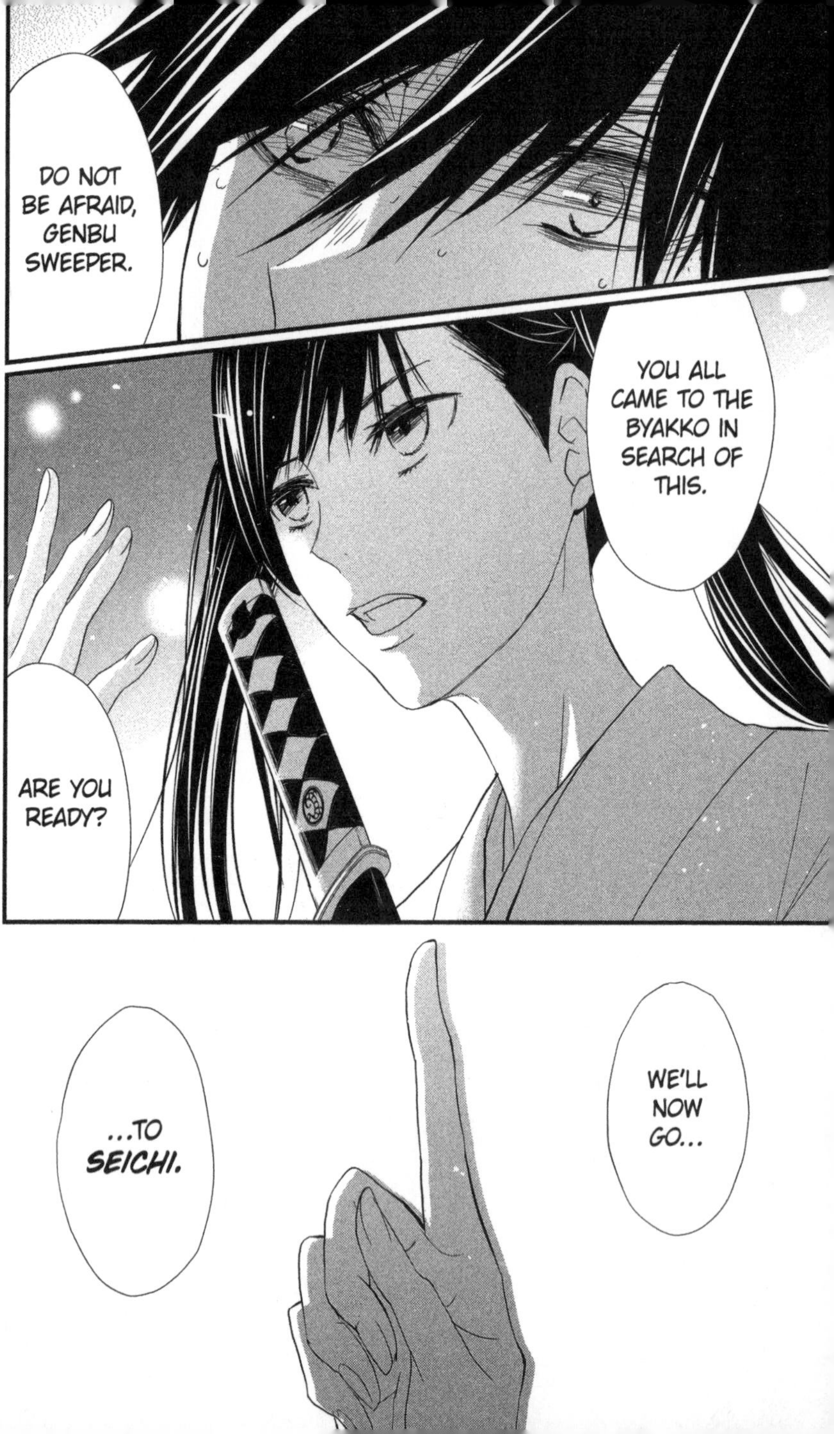
DO NOT BE AFRAID, GENBU SWEEPER.
YOU ALL CAME TO THE BYAKKO IN SEARCH OF THIS.
ARE YOU READY?
WE'LL NOW GO...
...TO SEICHI.

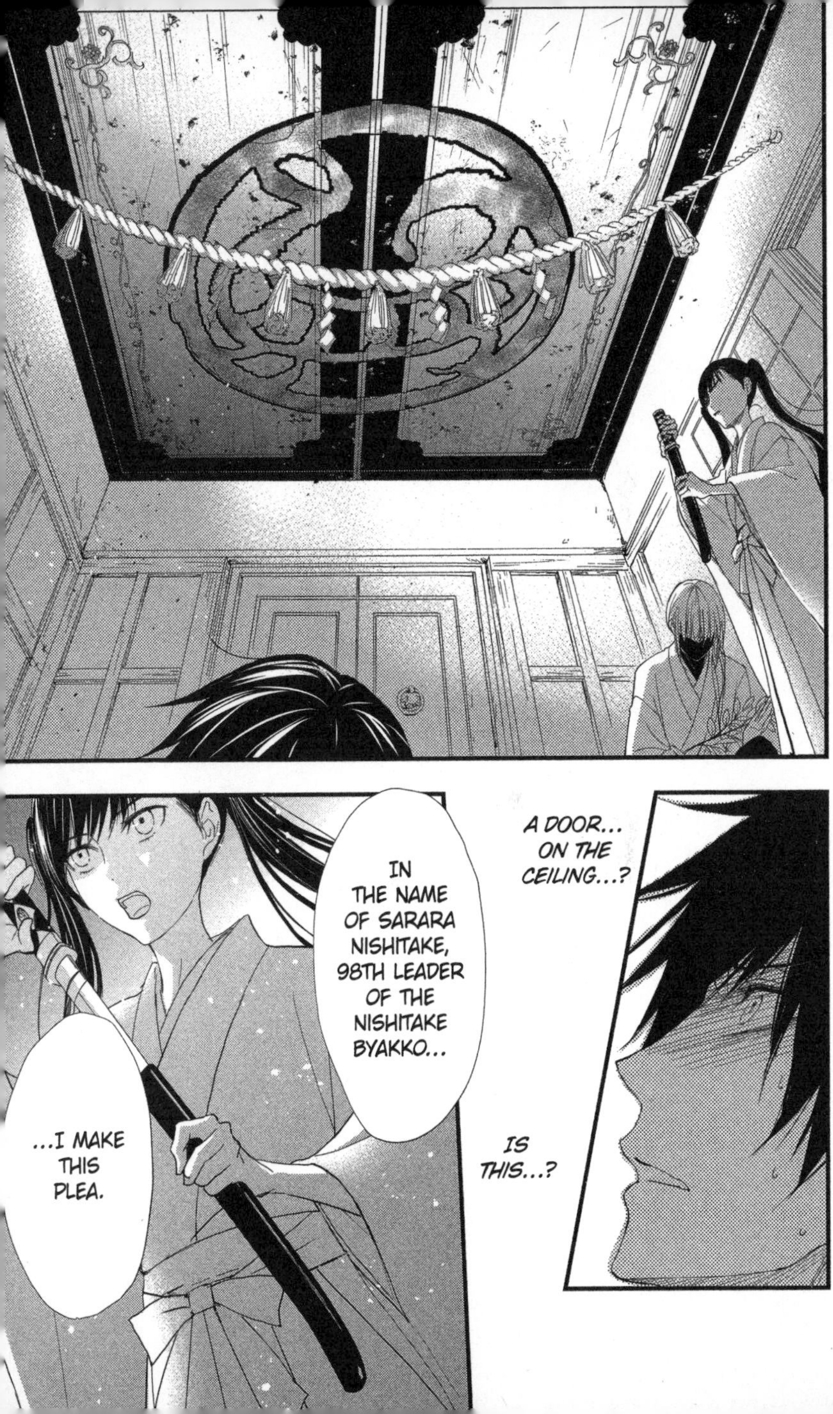
A DOOR... ON THE CEILING...?
IS THIS...?
IN THE NAME OF SARARA NISHITAKE, 98TH LEADER OF THE NISHITAKE BYAKKO...
...I MAKE THIS PLEA.

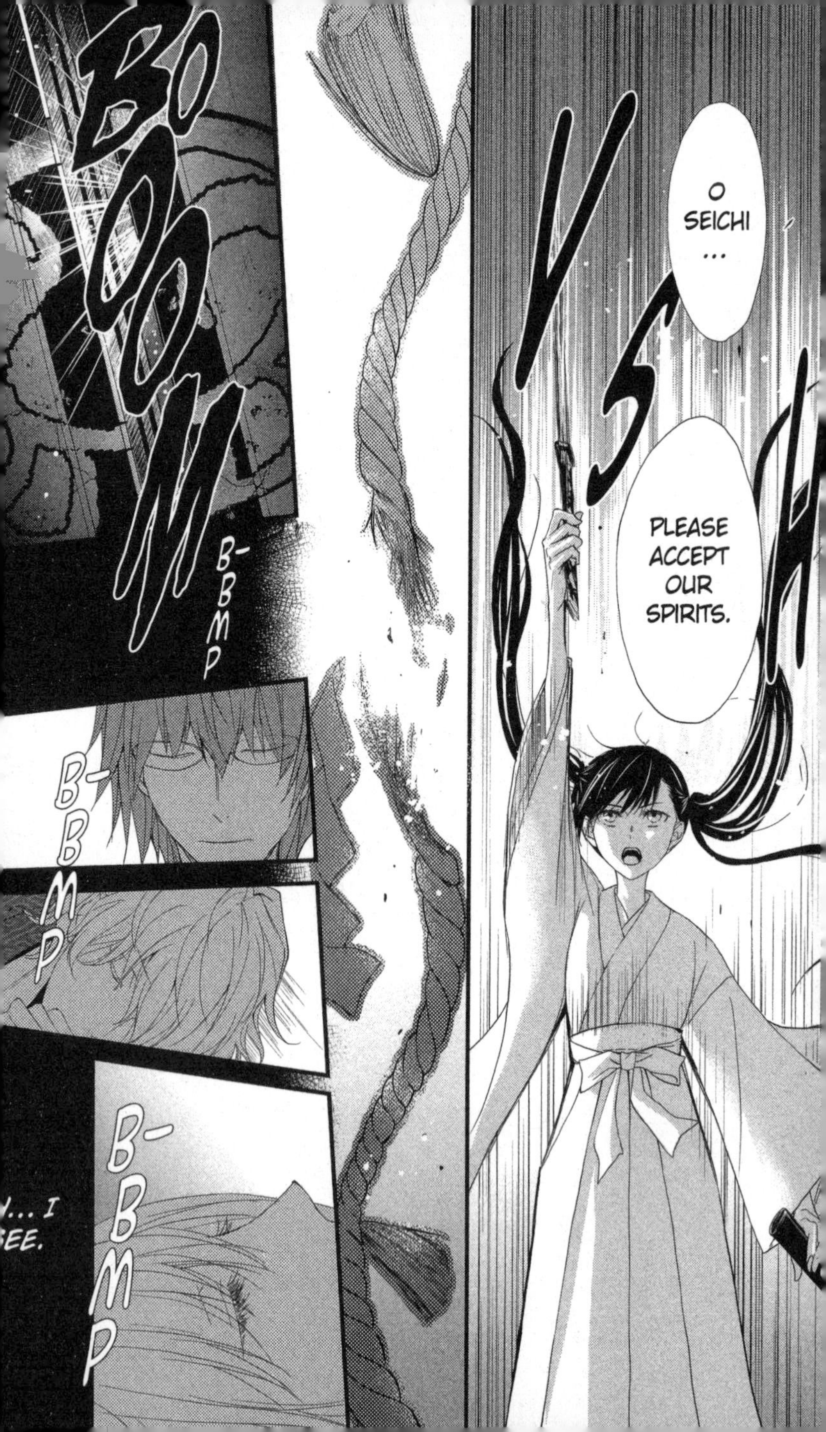

VSH
O SEICHI ...
PLEASE ACCEPT OUR SPIRITS.
BOOOM
B-BBMP
B-BBMP
B-BBMP

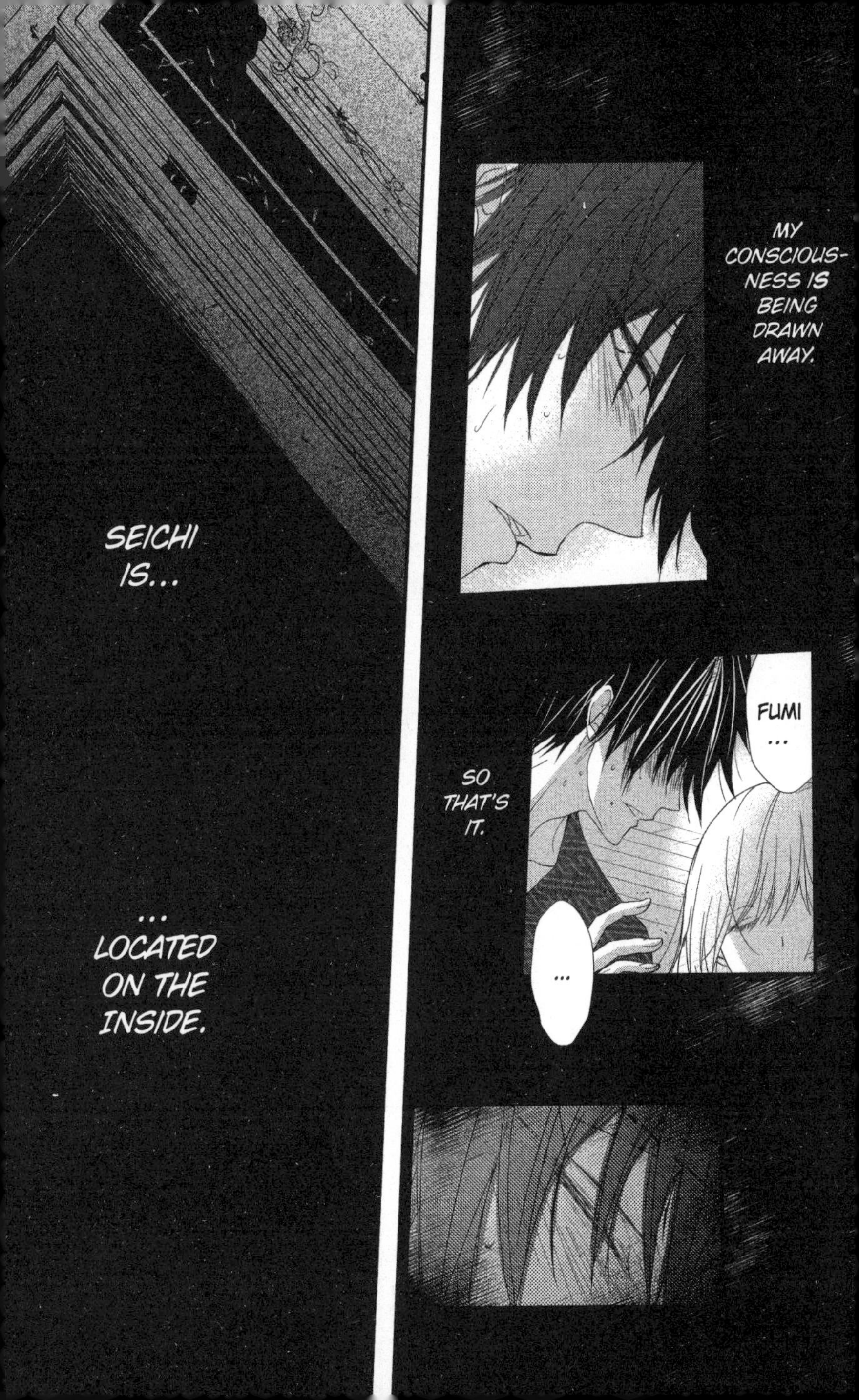
MY CONSCIOUS-NESS IS BEING DRAWN AWAY.
FUMI ...
SO THAT'S IT.
...
SEICHI IS...
... LOCATED ON THE INSIDE.

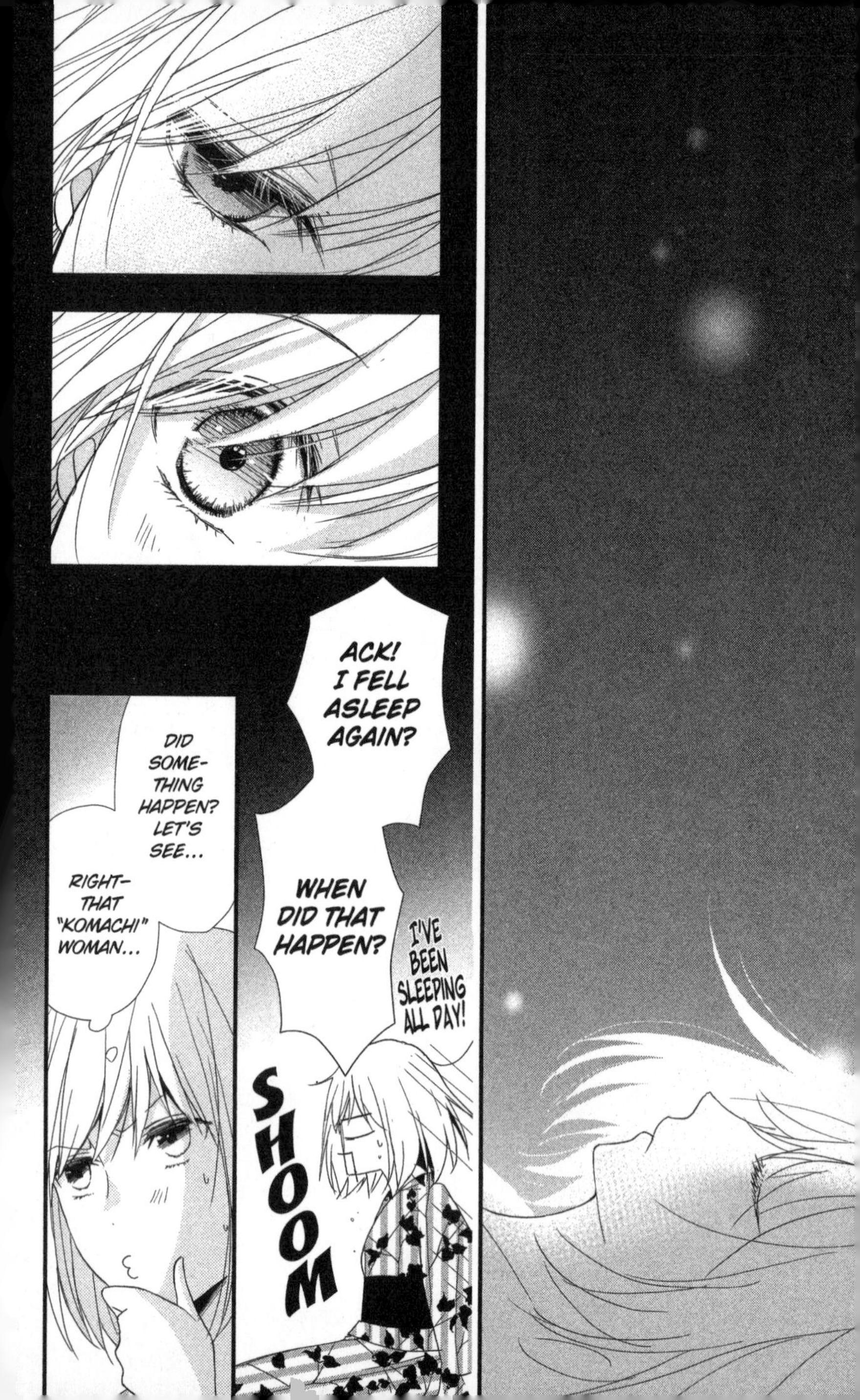
ACK! I FELL ASLEEP AGAIN?
WHEN DID THAT HAPPEN?
I'VE BEEN SLEEPING ALL DAY!
SHOOM
DID SOME-THING HAPPEN? LET'S SEE...
RIGHT—THAT "KOMACHI" WOMAN...

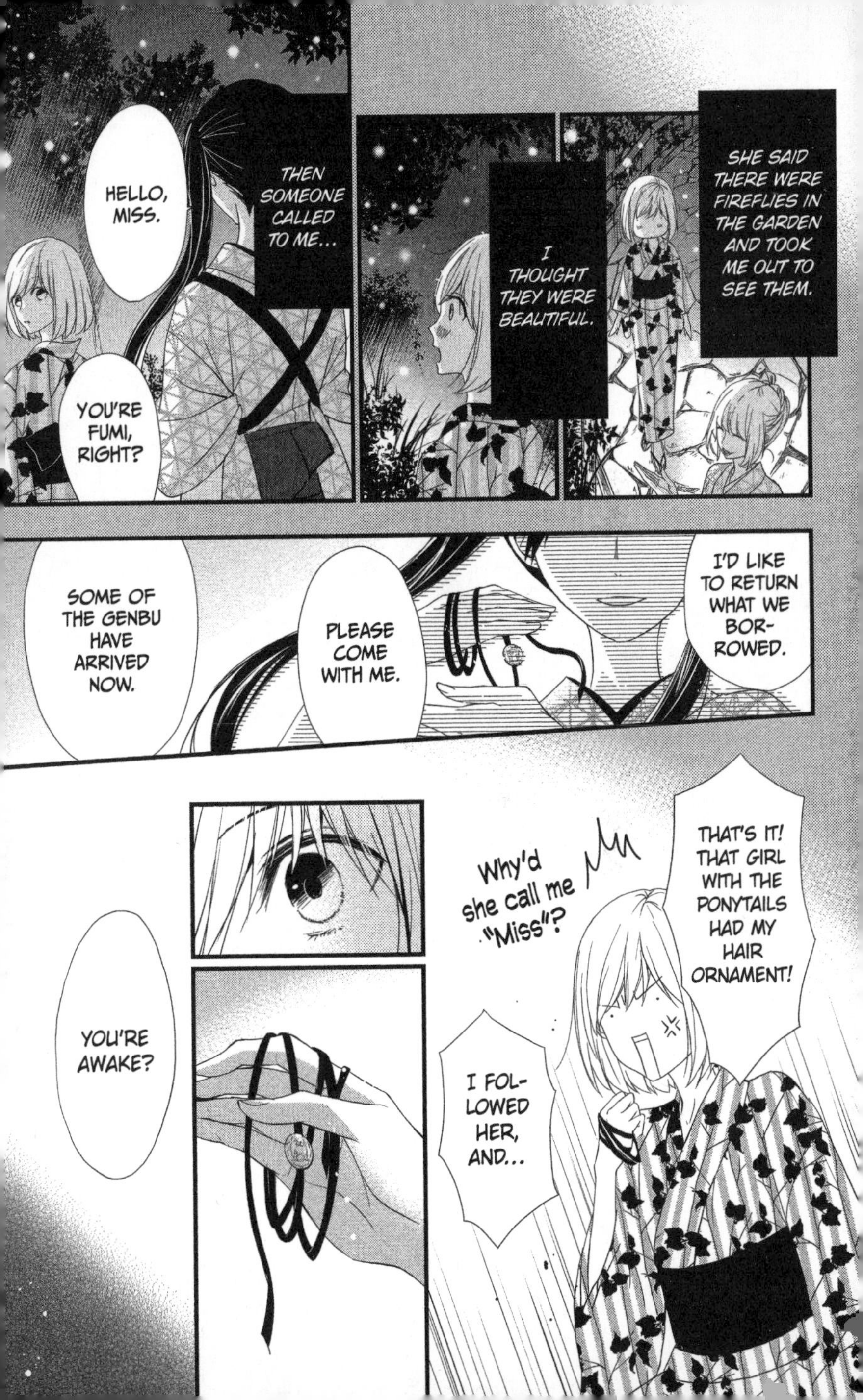
SHE SAID THERE WERE FIREFLIES IN THE GARDEN AND TOOK ME OUT TO SEE THEM.
I THOUGHT THEY WERE BEAUTIFUL.
THEN SOMEONE CALLED TO ME...
HELLO, MISS.
YOU'RE FUMI, RIGHT?
I'D LIKE TO RETURN WHAT WE BOR-ROWED.
PLEASE COME WITH ME.
SOME OF THE GENBU HAVE ARRIVED NOW.
THAT'S IT! THAT GIRL WITH THE PONYTAILS HAD MY HAIR ORNAMENT!
Why'd she call me "Miss"?
I FOL-LOWED HER, AND...
YOU'RE AWAKE?

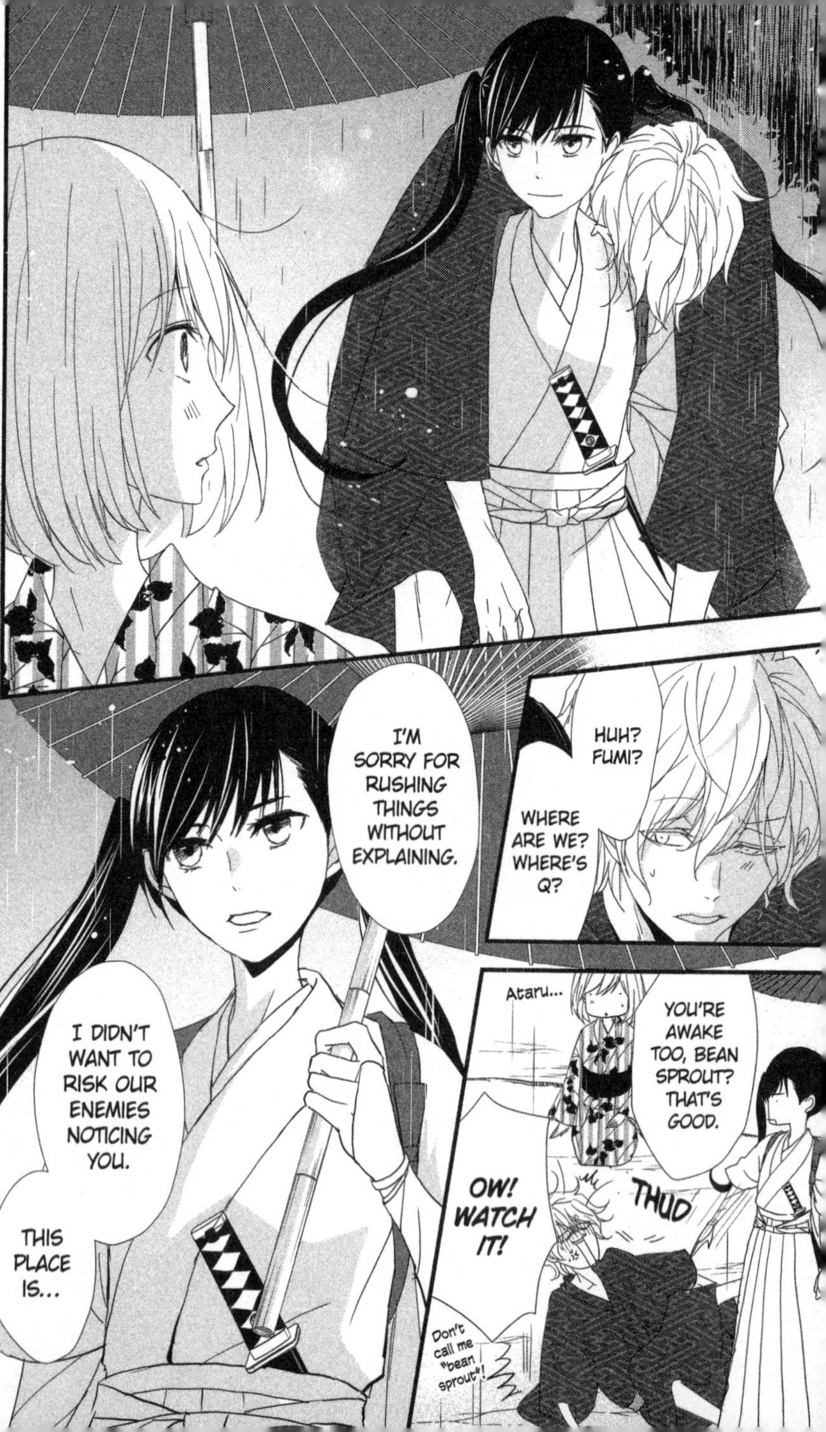
HUH? FUMI?
WHERE ARE WE? WHERE'S Q?
YOU'RE AWAKE TOO, BEAN SPROUT? THAT'S GOOD.
Ataru...
THUD
OW! WATCH IT!
Don't call me "bean sprout"!
I'M SORRY FOR RUSHING THINGS WITHOUT EXPLAINING.
I DIDN'T WANT TO RISK OUR ENEMIES NOTICING YOU.
THIS PLACE IS...

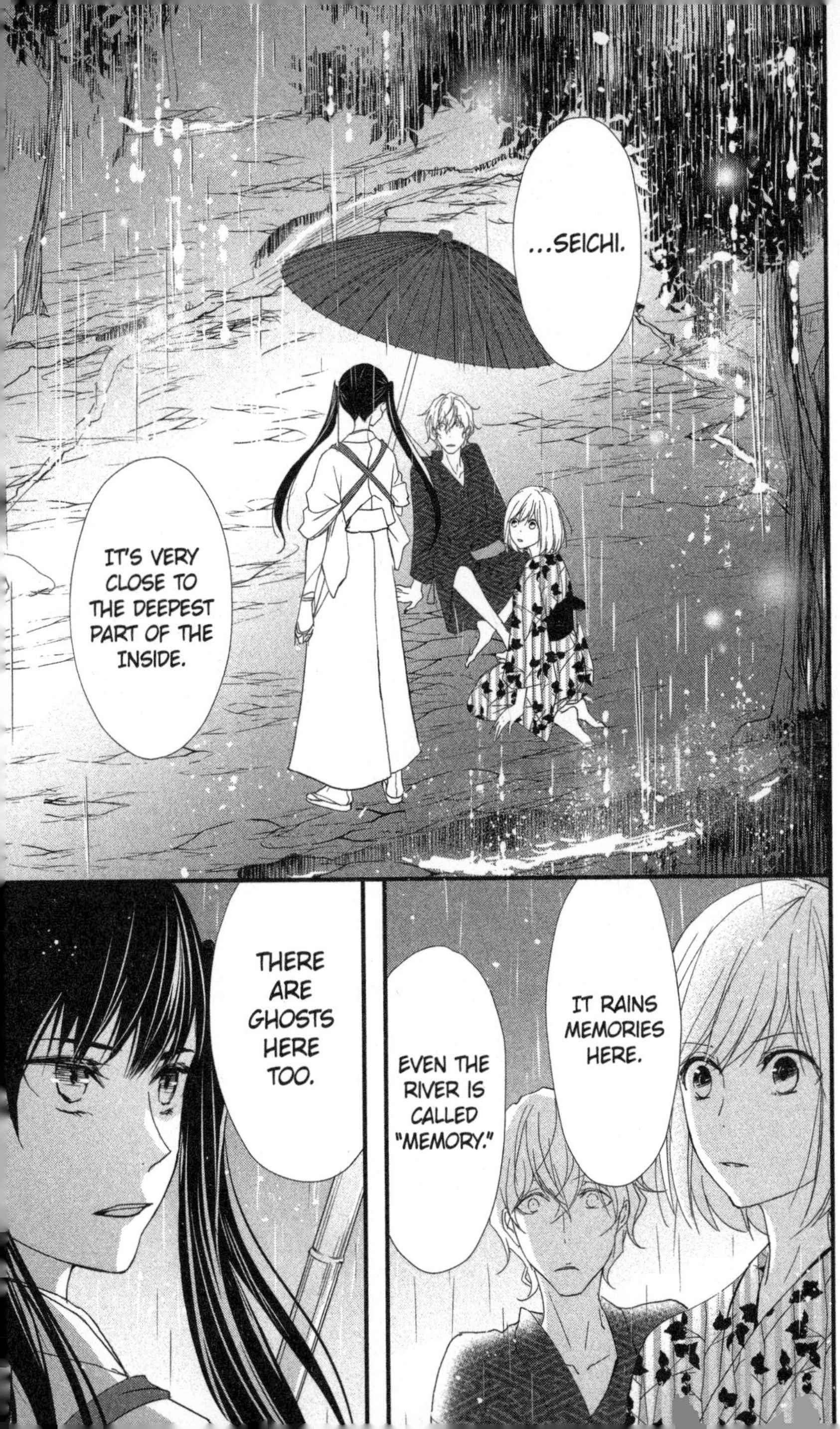
...SEICHI.
IT'S VERY CLOSE TO THE DEEPEST PART OF THE INSIDE.
IT RAINS MEMORIES HERE.
EVEN THE RIVER IS CALLED "MEMORY."
THERE ARE GHOSTS HERE TOO.

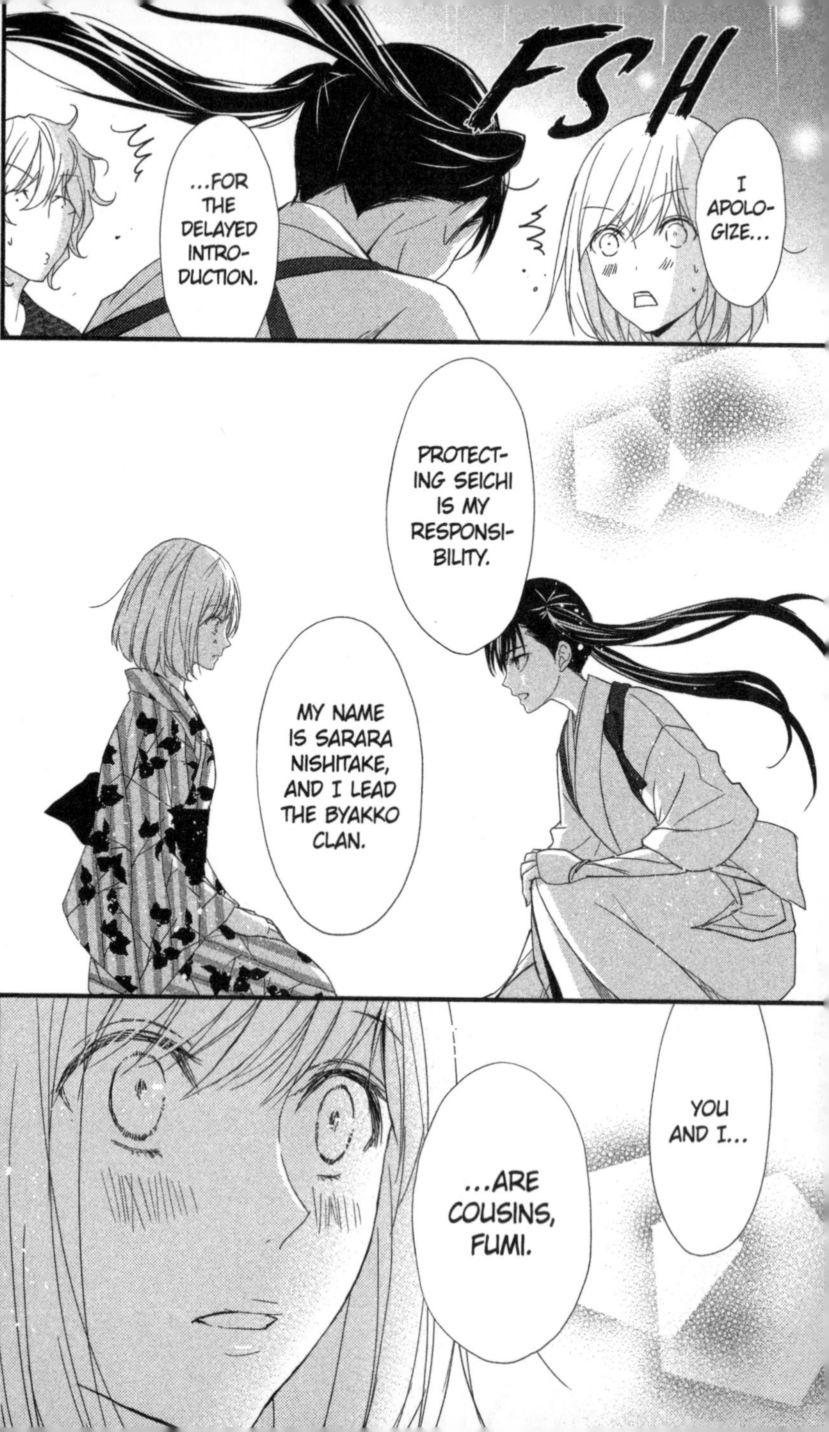
FSH
I APOLOGIZE...
...FOR THE DELAYED INTRODUCTION.
PROTECTING SEICHI IS MY RESPONSIBILITY.
MY NAME IS SARARA NISHITAKE, AND I LEAD THE BYAKKO CLAN.
YOU AND I...
...ARE COUSINS, FUMI.

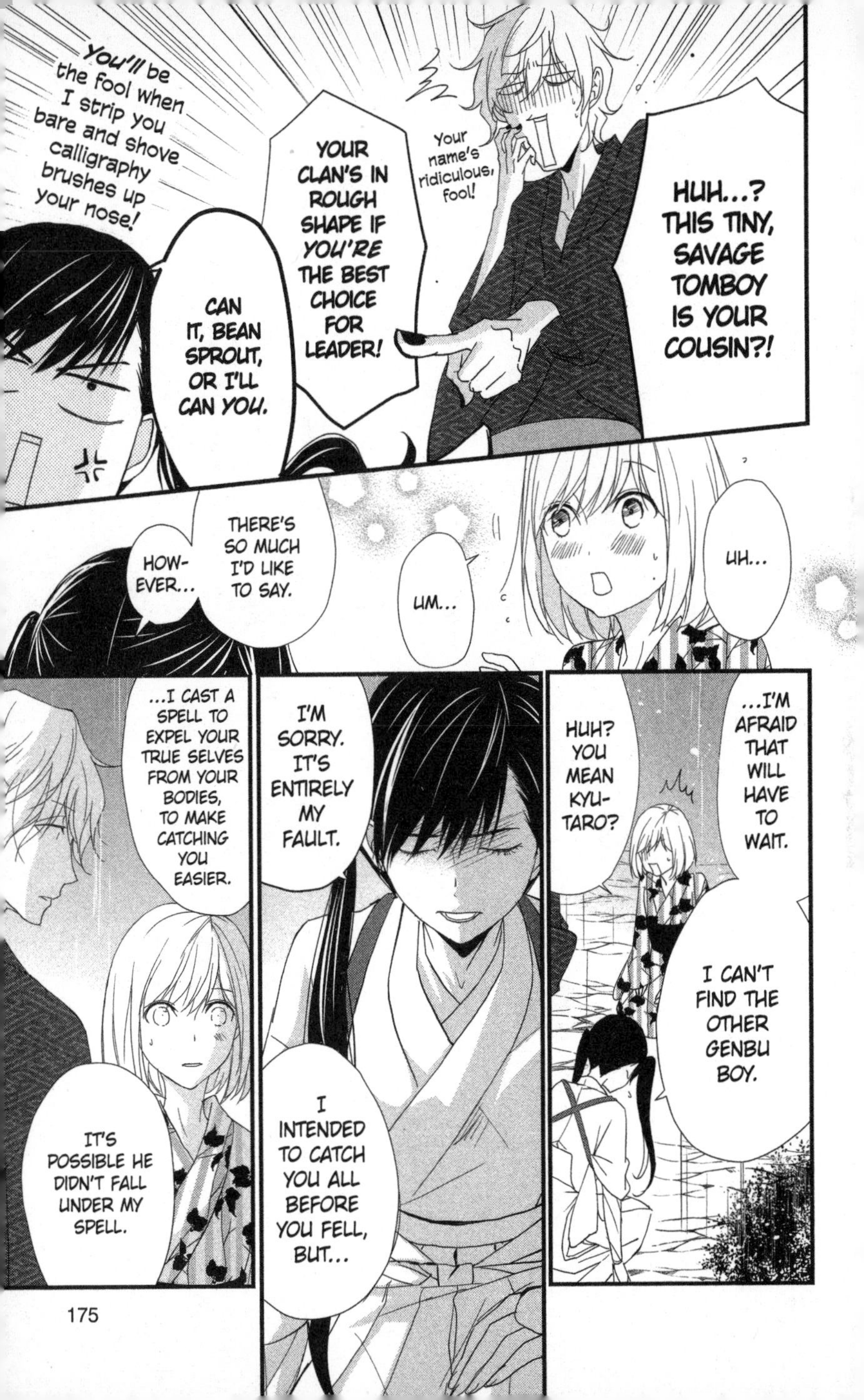
HUH...? THIS TINY, SAVAGE TOMBOY IS YOUR COUSIN?!
Your name's ridiculous, fool!
YOUR CLAN'S IN ROUGH SHAPE IF *YOU'RE* THE BEST CHOICE FOR LEADER!
You'll be the fool when I strip you bare and shove calligraphy brushes up your nose!
CAN IT, BEAN SPROUT, OR I'LL CAN *YOU*.
UH...
UM...
THERE'S SO MUCH I'D LIKE TO SAY.
HOW-EVER...
...I'M AFRAID THAT WILL HAVE TO WAIT.
HUH? YOU MEAN KYU-TARO?
I CAN'T FIND THE OTHER GENBU BOY.
I'M SORRY. IT'S ENTIRELY MY FAULT.
I INTENDED TO CATCH YOU ALL BEFORE YOU FELL, BUT...
...I CAST A SPELL TO EXPEL YOUR TRUE SELVES FROM YOUR BODIES, TO MAKE CATCHING YOU EASIER.
IT'S POSSIBLE HE DIDN'T FALL UNDER MY SPELL.

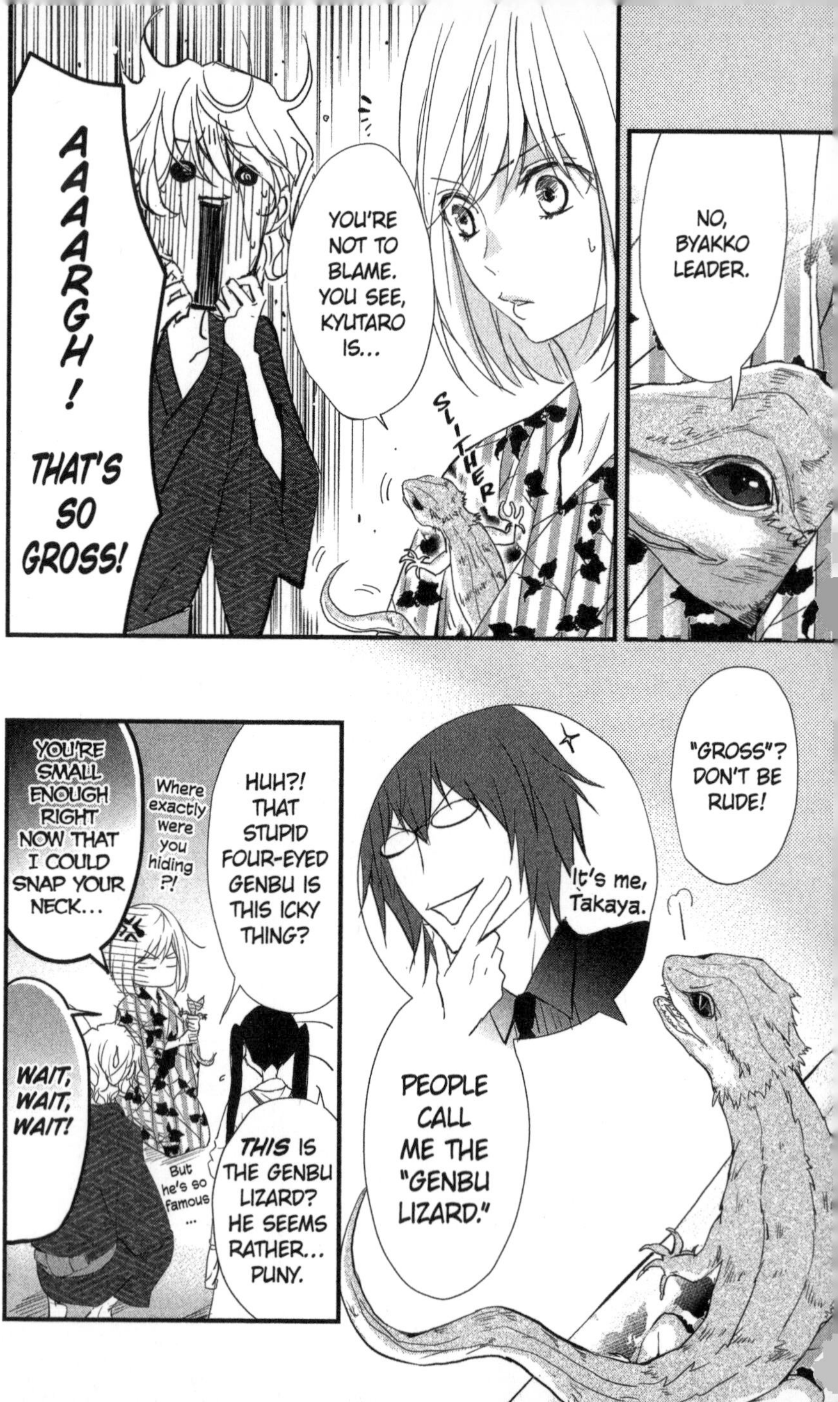
NO, BYAKKO LEADER.
YOU'RE NOT TO BLAME. YOU SEE, KYUTARO IS...
SLITHER
AAAAARGH! THAT'S SO GROSS!
"GROSS"? DON'T BE RUDE!
It's me, Takaya.
PEOPLE CALL ME THE "GENBU LIZARD."
HUH?! THAT STUPID FOUR-EYED GENBU IS THIS ICKY THING?
Where exactly were you hiding?!
YOU'RE SMALL ENOUGH RIGHT NOW THAT I COULD SNAP YOUR NECK...
THIS IS THE GENBU LIZARD? HE SEEMS RATHER... PUNY.
But he's so famous...
WAIT, WAIT, WAIT!

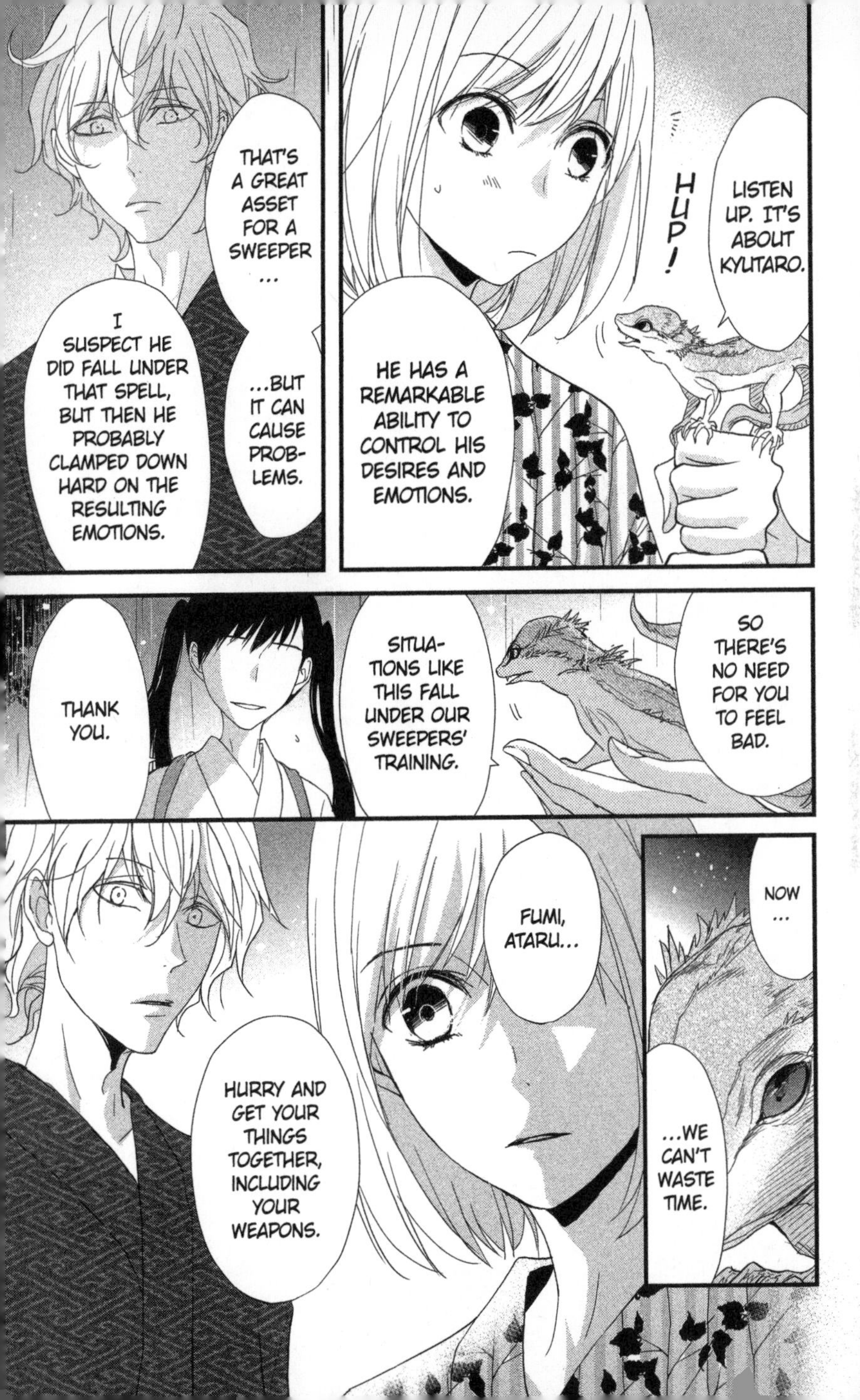
HUP!
LISTEN UP. IT'S ABOUT KYUTARO.
HE HAS A REMARKABLE ABILITY TO CONTROL HIS DESIRES AND EMOTIONS.
THAT'S A GREAT ASSET FOR A SWEEPER ...
...BUT IT CAN CAUSE PROB-LEMS.
I SUSPECT HE DID FALL UNDER THAT SPELL, BUT THEN HE PROBABLY CLAMPED DOWN HARD ON THE RESULTING EMOTIONS.
SO THERE'S NO NEED FOR YOU TO FEEL BAD.
SITUA-TIONS LIKE THIS FALL UNDER OUR SWEEPERS' TRAINING.
THANK YOU.
NOW ...
...WE CAN'T WASTE TIME.
FUMI, ATARU...
HURRY AND GET YOUR THINGS TOGETHER, INCLUDING YOUR WEAPONS.

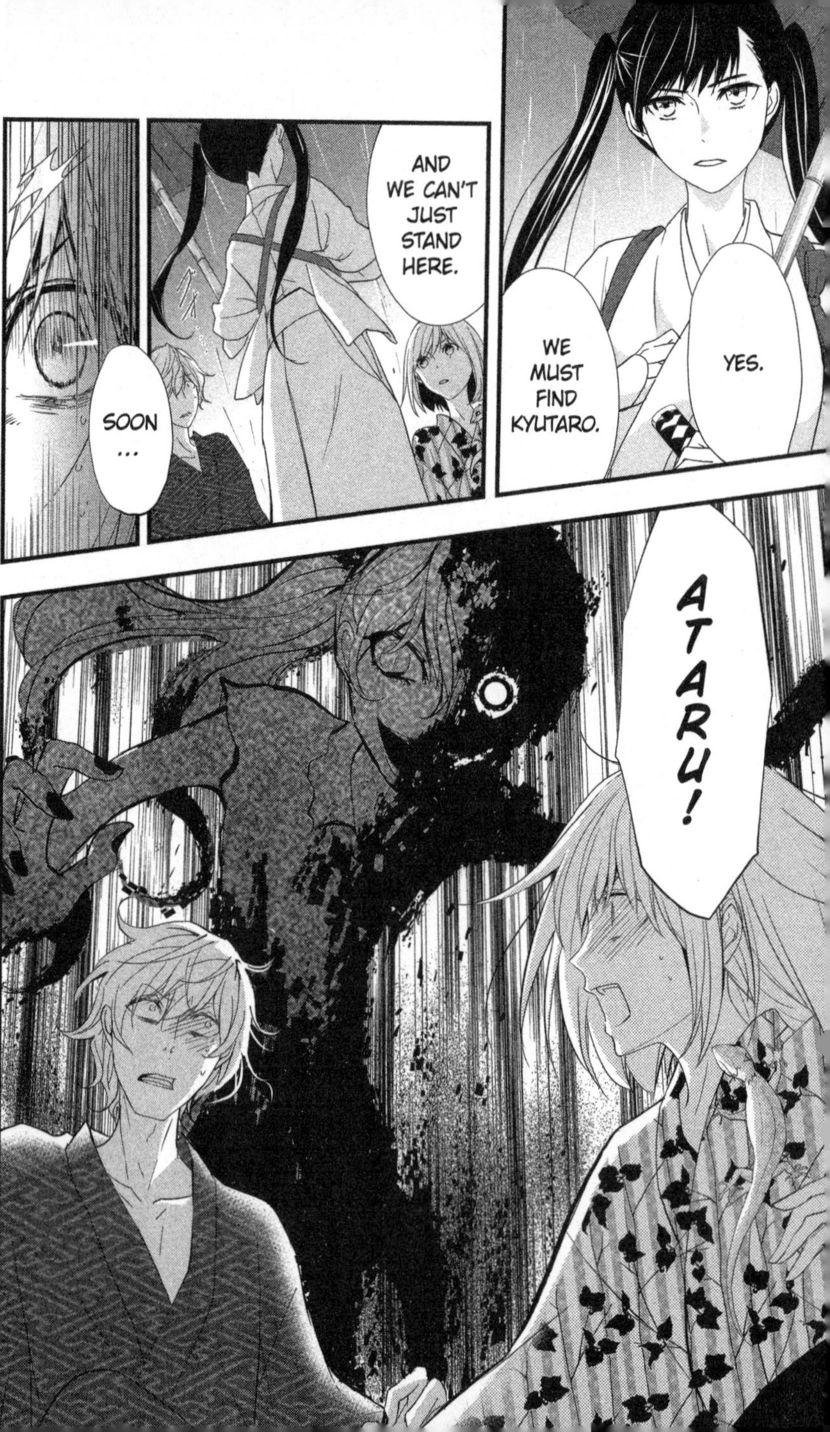
YES.
WE MUST FIND KYUTARO.
AND WE CAN'T JUST STAND HERE.
SOON ...
ATARU!

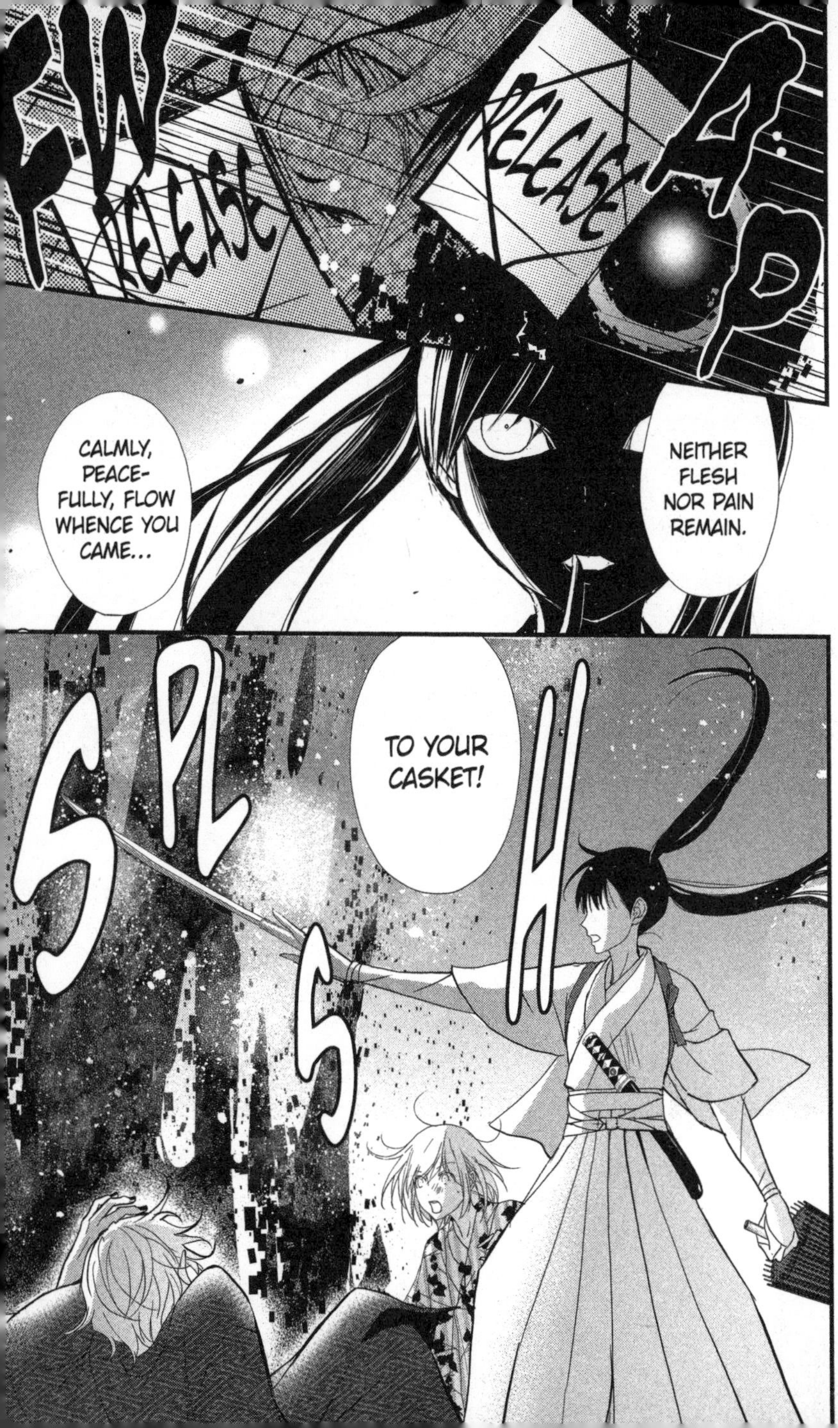
FWAP
RELEASE
RELEASE
NEITHER FLESH NOR PAIN REMAIN.
CALMLY, PEACE-FULLY, FLOW WHENCE YOU CAME...
TO YOUR CASKET!
SPLSH

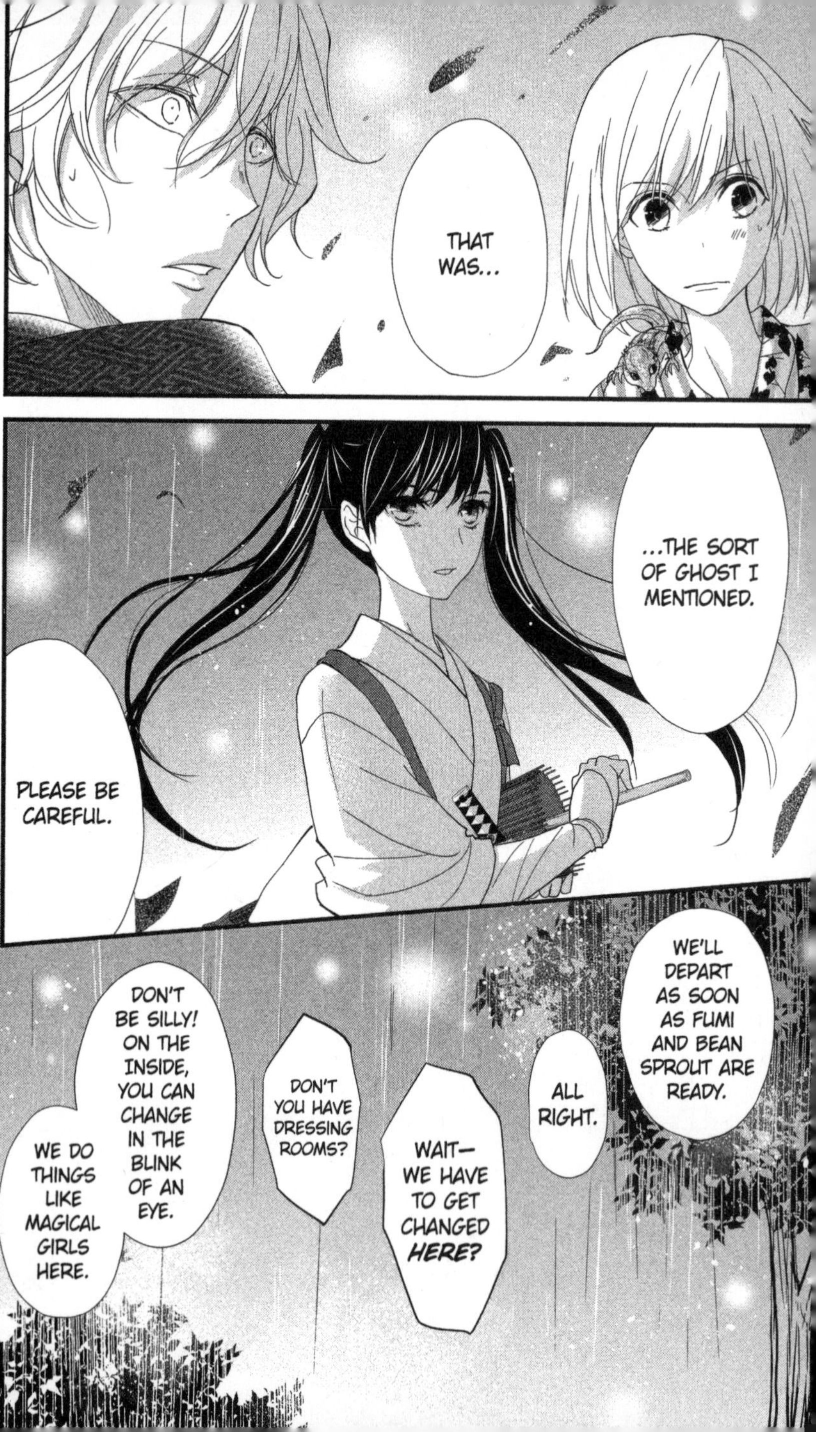
THAT WAS...
...THE SORT OF GHOST I MENTIONED.
PLEASE BE CAREFUL.
WE'LL DEPART AS SOON AS FUMI AND BEAN SPROUT ARE READY.
ALL RIGHT.
WAIT— WE HAVE TO GET CHANGED *HERE?*
DON'T YOU HAVE DRESSING ROOMS?
DON'T BE SILLY! ON THE INSIDE, YOU CAN CHANGE IN THE BLINK OF AN EYE.
WE DO THINGS LIKE MAGICAL GIRLS HERE.

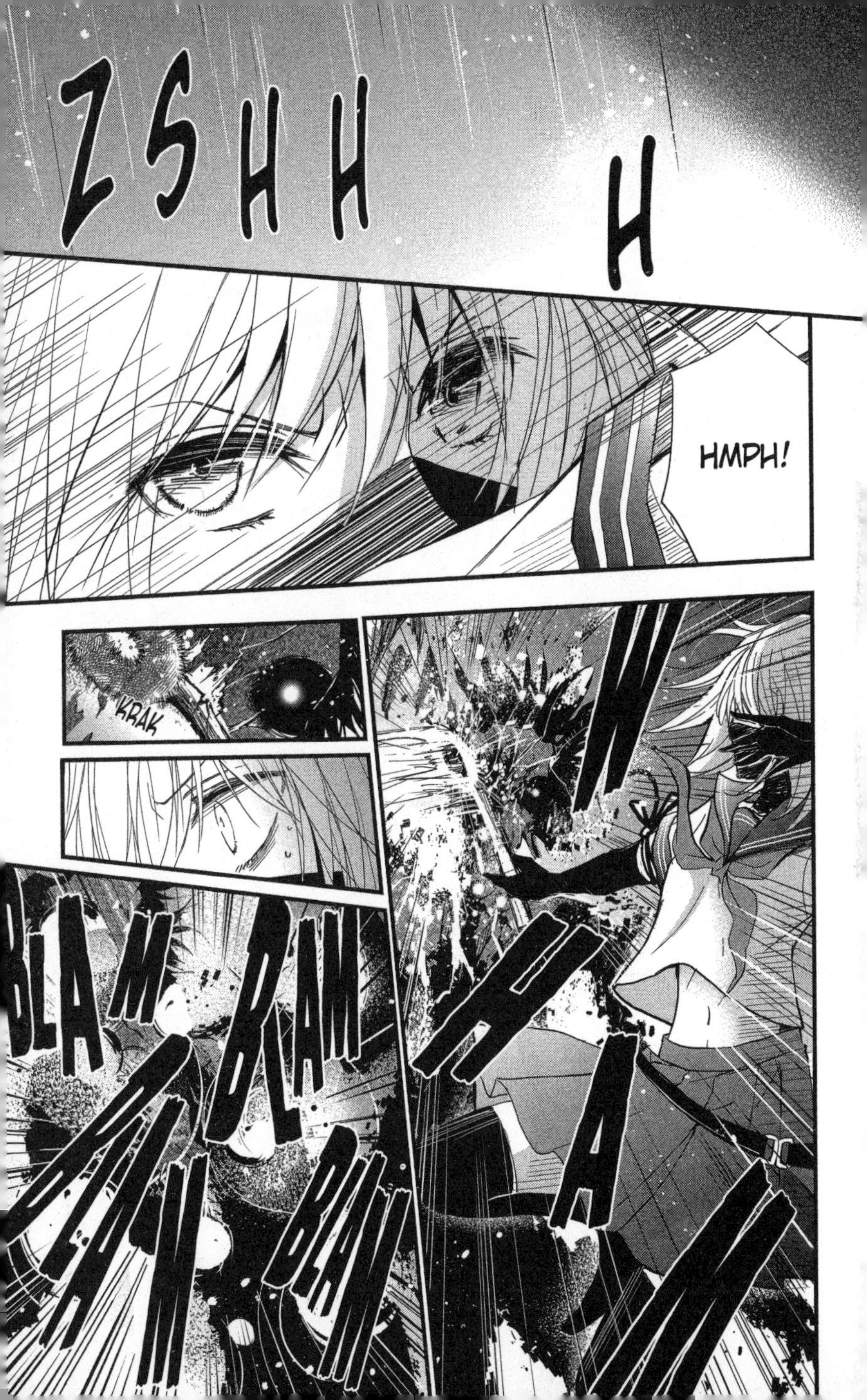
ZSHHHH
HMPH!
KRAK
BLAM BLAM
BLAM BLAM

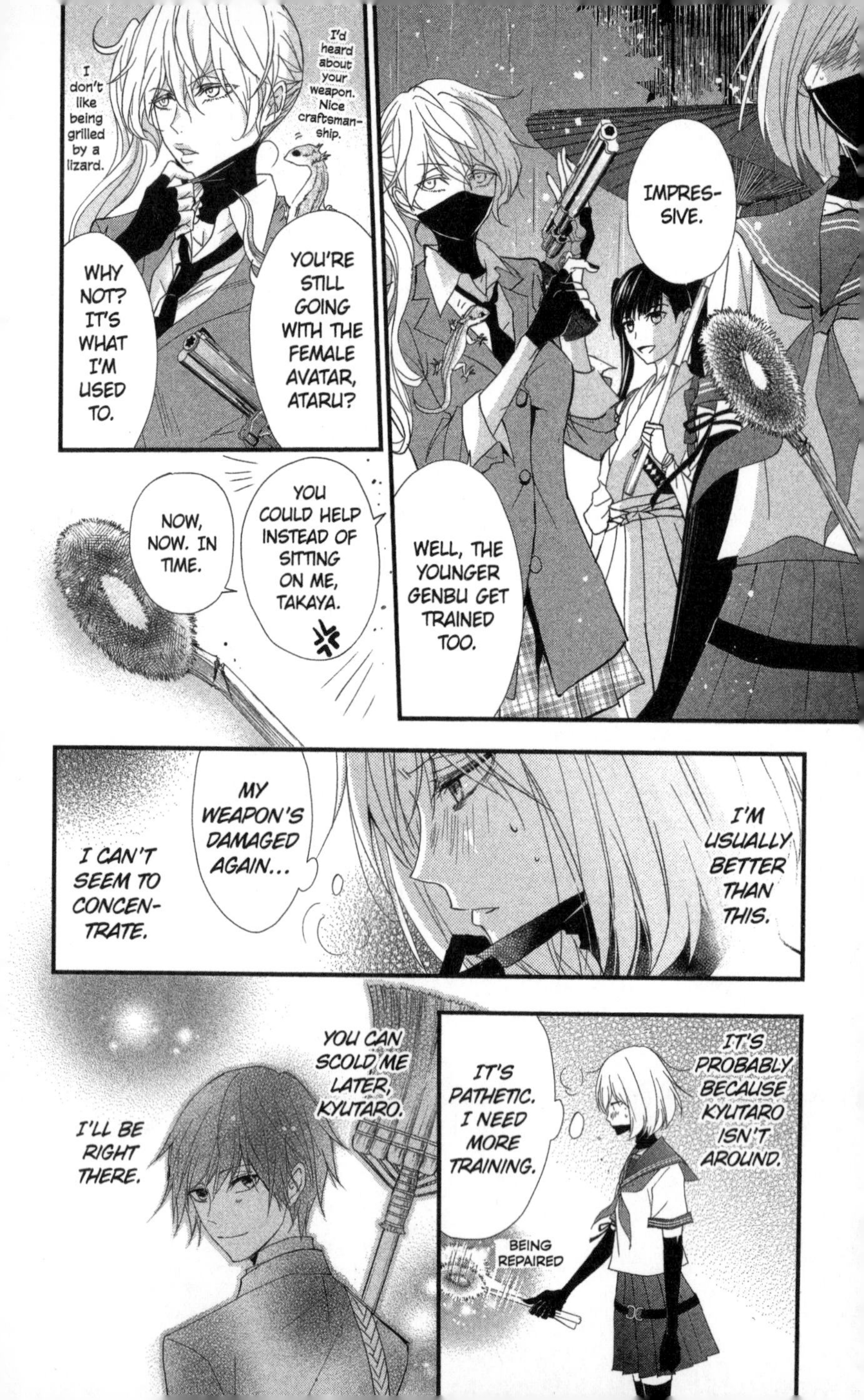
IMPRESSIVE.
WELL, THE YOUNGER GENBU GET TRAINED TOO.
I'd heard about your weapon. Nice craftsmanship.
I don't like being grilled by a lizard.
YOU'RE STILL GOING WITH THE FEMALE AVATAR, ATARU?
WHY NOT? IT'S WHAT I'M USED TO.
YOU COULD HELP INSTEAD OF SITTING ON ME, TAKAYA.
NOW, NOW. IN TIME.
I'M USUALLY BETTER THAN THIS.
MY WEAPON'S DAMAGED AGAIN...
I CAN'T SEEM TO CONCENTRATE.
IT'S PROBABLY BECAUSE KYUTARO ISN'T AROUND.
IT'S PATHETIC. I NEED MORE TRAINING.
BEING REPAIRED
YOU CAN SCOLD ME LATER, KYUTARO.
I'LL BE RIGHT THERE.

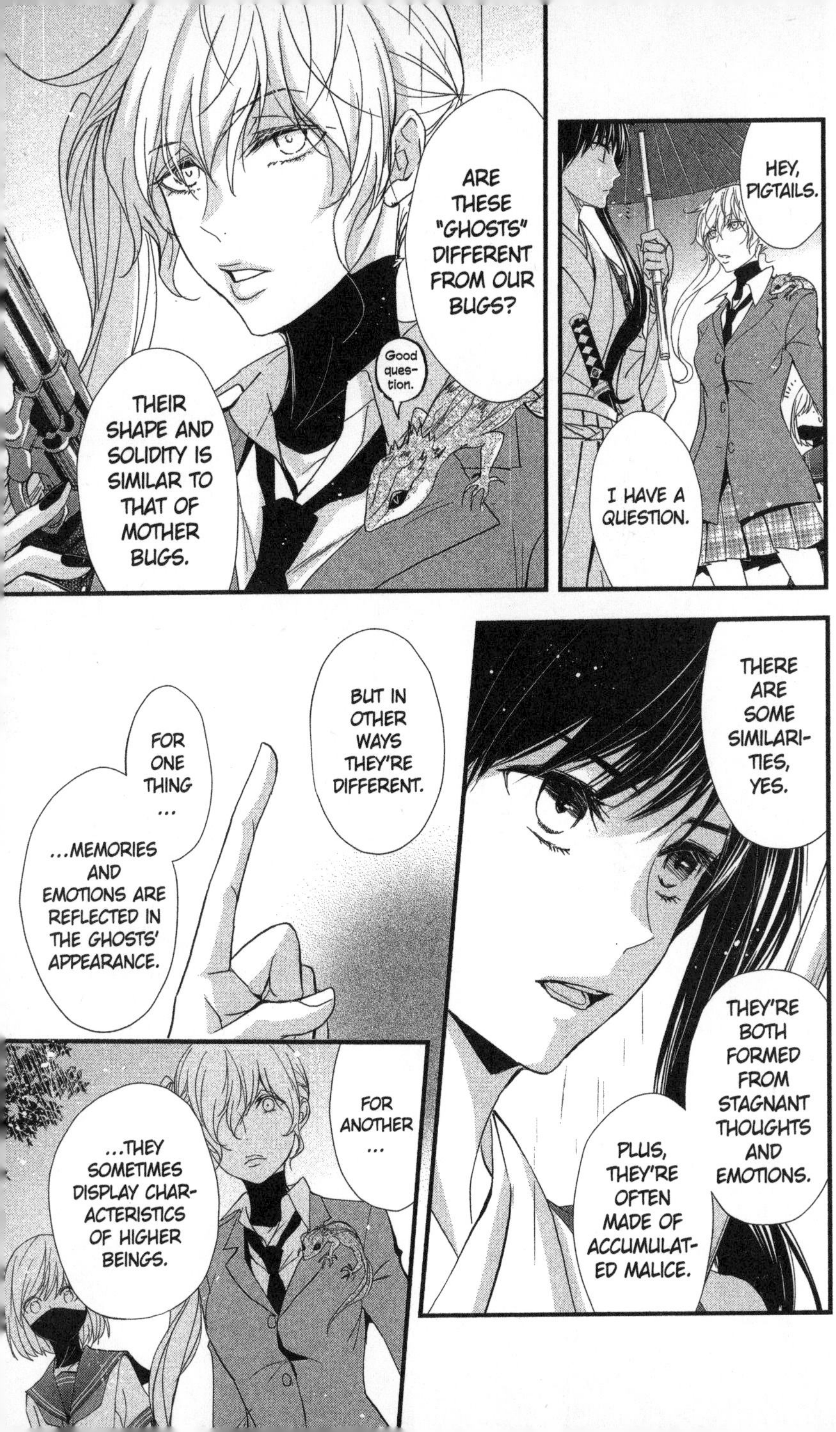
HEY, PIGTAILS.
I HAVE A QUESTION.
ARE THESE "GHOSTS" DIFFERENT FROM OUR BUGS?
Good ques-tion.
THEIR SHAPE AND SOLIDITY IS SIMILAR TO THAT OF MOTHER BUGS.
THERE ARE SOME SIMILARI-TIES, YES.
THEY'RE BOTH FORMED FROM STAGNANT THOUGHTS AND EMOTIONS.
PLUS, THEY'RE OFTEN MADE OF ACCUMULAT-ED MALICE.
BUT IN OTHER WAYS THEY'RE DIFFERENT.
FOR ONE THING ...
...MEMORIES AND EMOTIONS ARE REFLECTED IN THE GHOSTS' APPEARANCE.
FOR ANOTHER ...
...THEY SOMETIMES DISPLAY CHAR-ACTERISTICS OF HIGHER BEINGS.

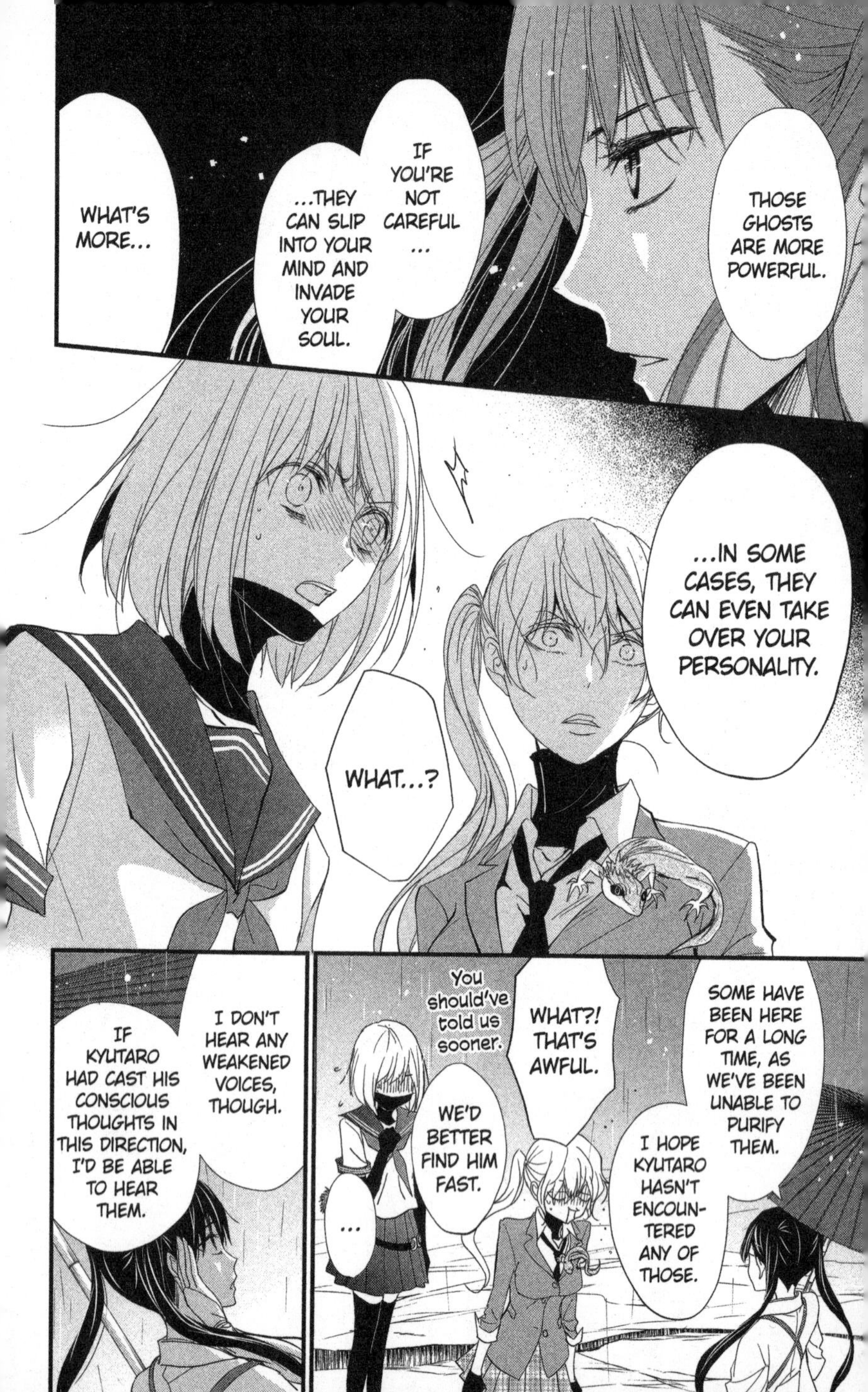
THOSE GHOSTS ARE MORE POWERFUL.
IF YOU'RE NOT CAREFUL...
...THEY CAN SLIP INTO YOUR MIND AND INVADE YOUR SOUL.
WHAT'S MORE...
...IN SOME CASES, THEY CAN EVEN TAKE OVER YOUR PERSONALITY.
WHAT...?
SOME HAVE BEEN HERE FOR A LONG TIME, AS WE'VE BEEN UNABLE TO PURIFY THEM.
I HOPE KYUTARO HASN'T ENCOUNTERED ANY OF THOSE.
WHAT?! THAT'S AWFUL.
You should've told us sooner.
WE'D BETTER FIND HIM FAST.
...
I DON'T HEAR ANY WEAKENED VOICES, THOUGH.
IF KYUTARO HAD CAST HIS CONSCIOUS THOUGHTS IN THIS DIRECTION, I'D BE ABLE TO HEAR THEM.

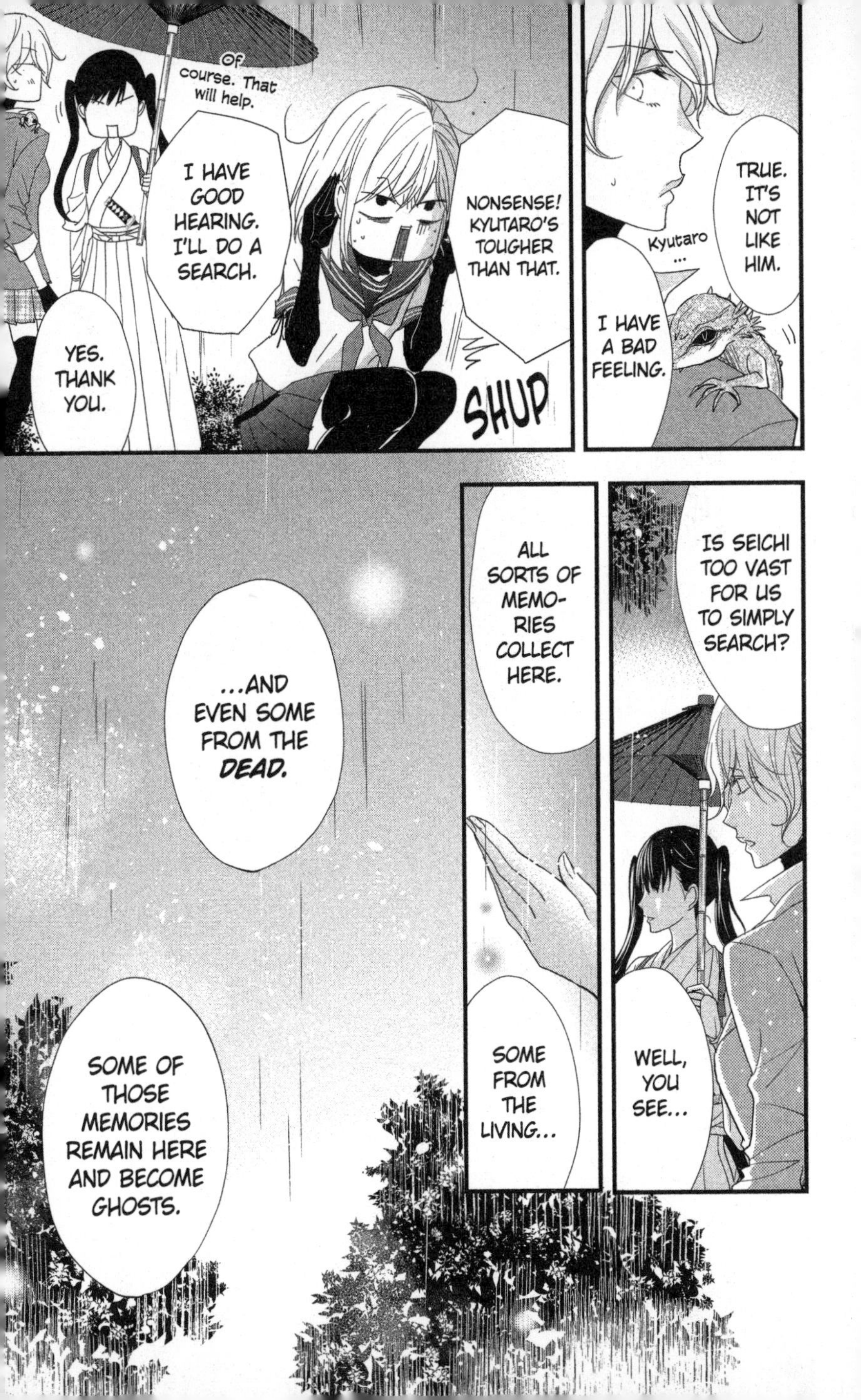
TRUE. IT'S NOT LIKE HIM.
Kyutaro ...
I HAVE A BAD FEELING.
NONSENSE! KYUTARO'S TOUGHER THAN THAT.
SHUP
Of course. That will help.
I HAVE GOOD HEARING. I'LL DO A SEARCH.
YES. THANK YOU.
IS SEICHI TOO VAST FOR US TO SIMPLY SEARCH?
WELL, YOU SEE...
ALL SORTS OF MEMORIES COLLECT HERE.
SOME FROM THE LIVING...
...AND EVEN SOME FROM THE *DEAD.*
SOME OF THOSE MEMORIES REMAIN HERE AND BECOME GHOSTS.

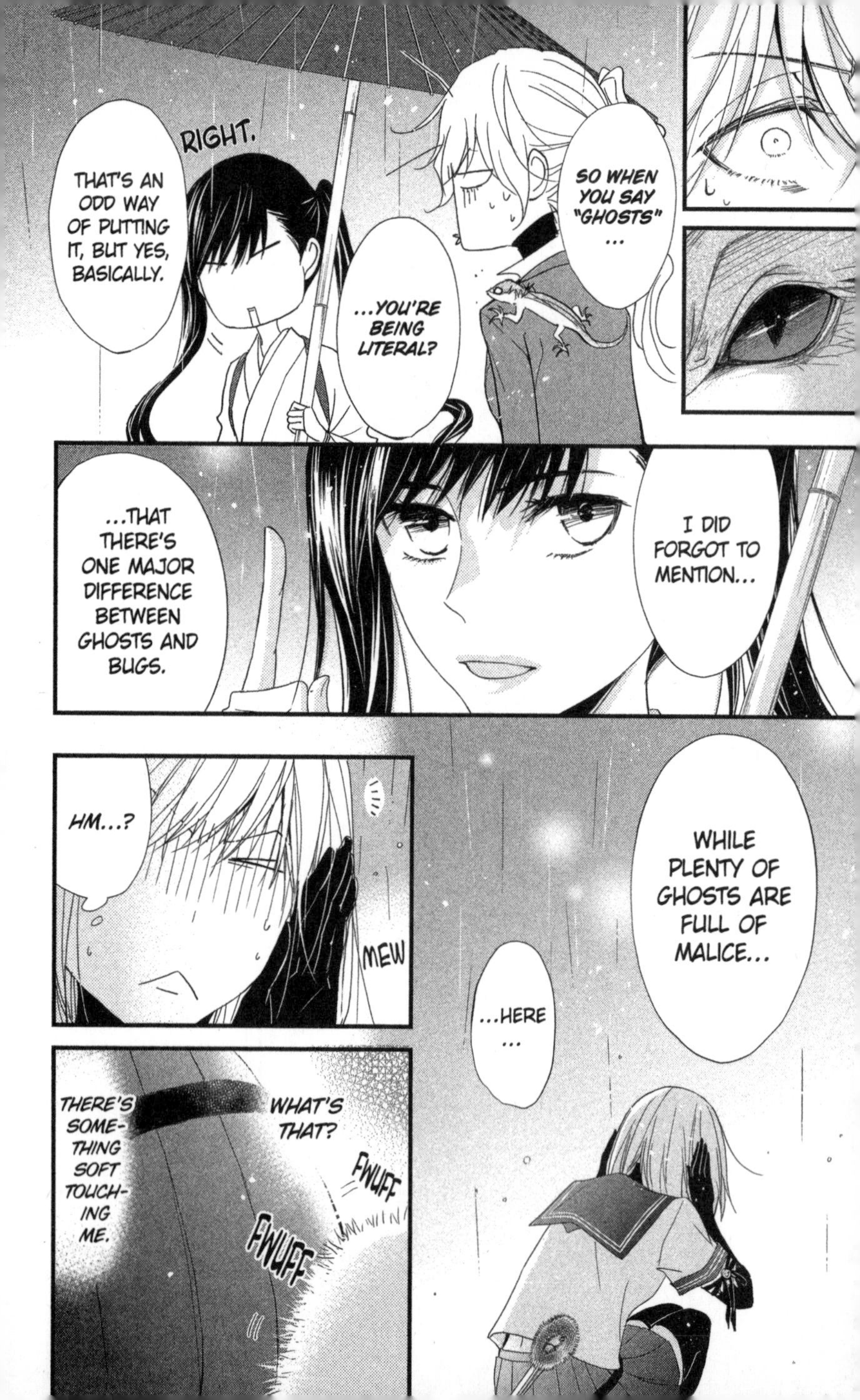
SO WHEN YOU SAY "GHOSTS" ...
...YOU'RE BEING LITERAL?
RIGHT.
THAT'S AN ODD WAY OF PUTTING IT, BUT YES, BASICALLY.
I DID FORGOT TO MENTION...
...THAT THERE'S ONE MAJOR DIFFERENCE BETWEEN GHOSTS AND BUGS.
WHILE PLENTY OF GHOSTS ARE FULL OF MALICE...
...HERE ...
HM...?
MEW
WHAT'S THAT?
THERE'S SOME-THING SOFT TOUCHING-ING ME.
FWUFF
FWUFF

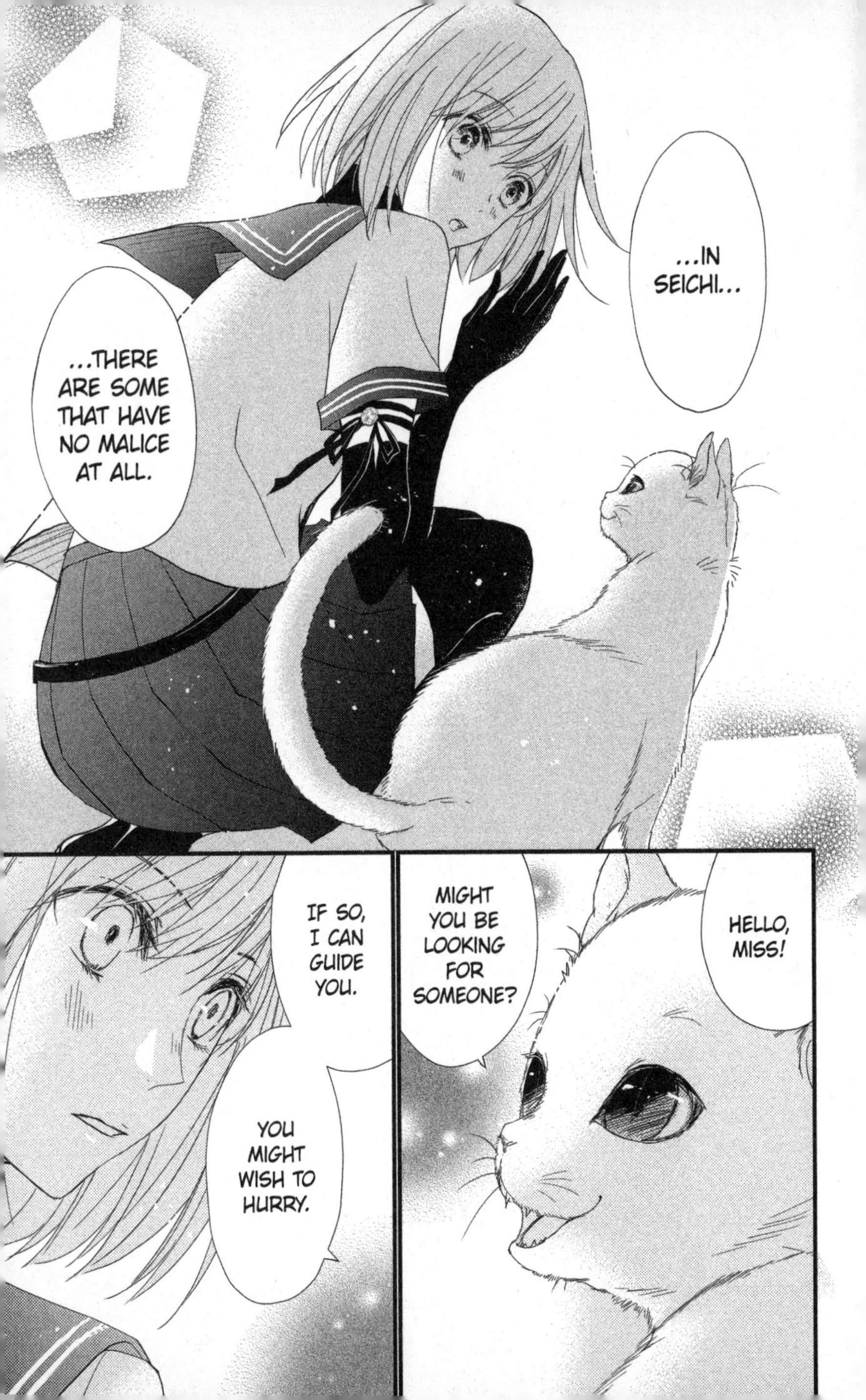
...IN SEICHI...
...THERE ARE SOME THAT HAVE NO MALICE AT ALL.
HELLO, MISS!
MIGHT YOU BE LOOKING FOR SOMEONE?
IF SO, I CAN GUIDE YOU.
YOU MIGHT WISH TO HURRY.

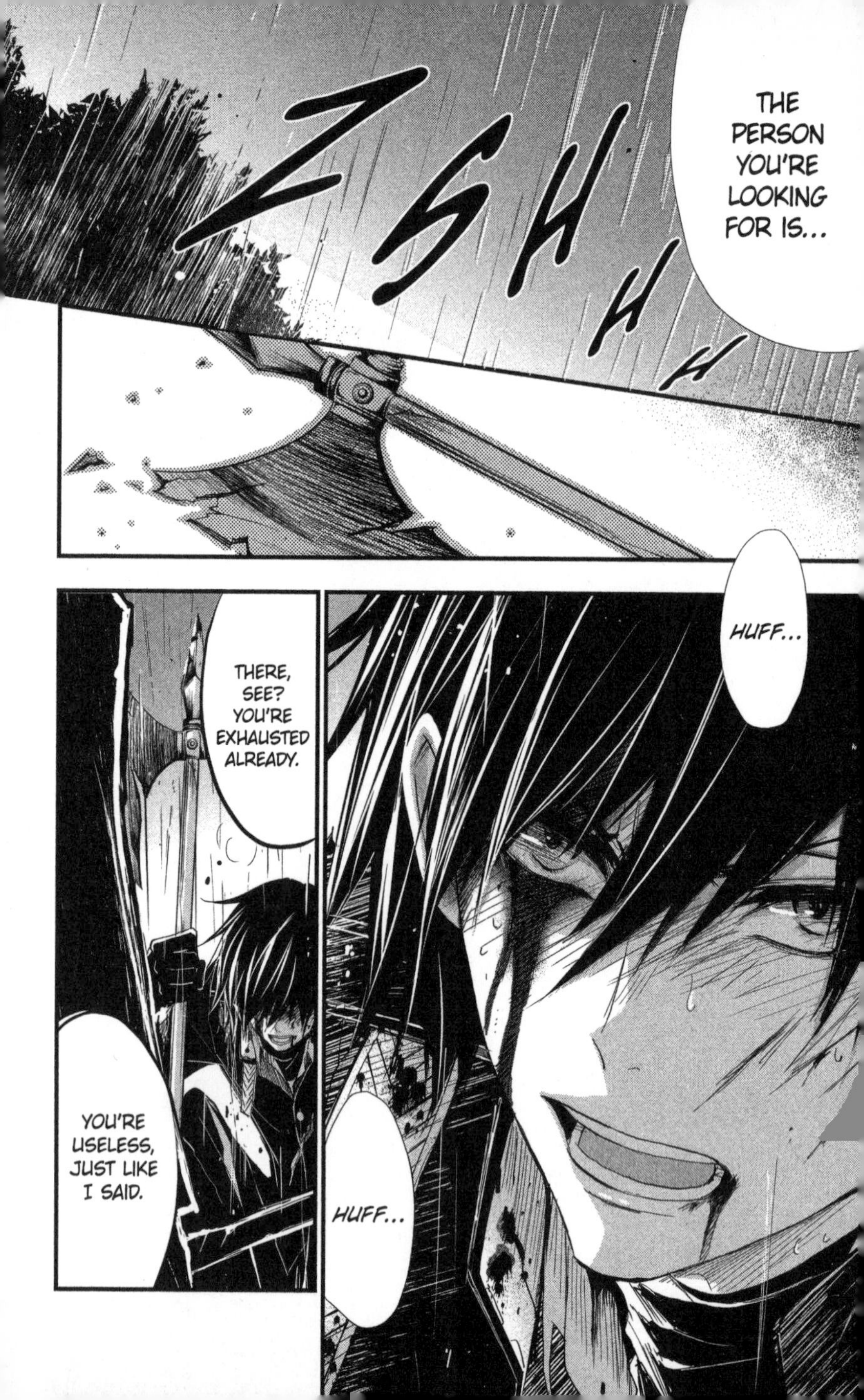
THE PERSON YOU'RE LOOKING FOR IS...
ZSHHHH
HUFF...
HUFF...
THERE, SEE? YOU'RE EXHAUSTED ALREADY.
YOU'RE USELESS, JUST LIKE I SAID.